LENI

THE LIFE AND WORK OF
LENI RIEFENSTAHL

STEVEN BACH

ABACUS

First published in the United States in 2007 by Alfred A. Knopf
First published in Great Britain in 2007 by Little, Brown
This paperback edition published in 2008 by Abacus

A CIP catalogue record for this book is available
from the British Library.

ISBN 978-0-349-11553-5

Typeset in Fournier by M Rules
Printed and bound in Great Britain by
Clays Ltd, St Ives plc

Abacus
An imprint of
Little, Brown Book Group
100 Victoria Embankment
London EC4Y 0DY

An Hachette Livre UK Company
www.hachettelivre.co.uk

www.littlebrown.co.uk

For David Thomson and Peggy Wallace

Art is moral in that it awakens.

—Thomas Mann

CONTENTS

Part Three AFTERMATH

LENI

BERLIN 1925

IF THERE WAS AN IDEAL PLACE for a pretty, emancipated, ferociously ambitious young woman to be in Berlin in 1925, it was on the gaudy, sprawling stages of Ufa film studio, and, at twenty-three, Leni Riefenstahl was there. She would later deny the fact (she would deny many), which was curious, for Ufa—the great Berlin dream factory known by its acronym (for Universum-Film-Aktiengesellschaft)—was then as close to a mecca for actors, filmmakers, designers, and visionaries as anyplace in Europe; it was the world's only meaningful rival to Hollywood itself.

By 1925 Ufa was releasing a major feature film each week from a gilt-edged roster of directors that included not only the legendary Ernst Lubitsch (already snapped up by Hollywood) but also F. W. Murnau, E. A. Dupont, and Fritz Lang, men (they were all men then) responsible for the creative brilliance of such films as *Nosferatu, Variety,* and *Metropolis.* All of them—when things got bad in Berlin—would follow Lubitsch west.

Europe's greatest stars worked on Ufa's stages—Emil Jannings, Henny Porten ("the Mary Pickford of Germany"), Lya de Putti, Asta Nielsen, Pola Negri, Yvette Guilbert, Conrad Veidt—and those who aspired to great stardom hoped to. Young Marlene Dietrich was there, frantic to be noticed in bit parts in silent costume dramas like *Manon Lescaut,* telegraphing her stage player's frustration at having—before talkies—no voice to deploy as part of her seductive arsenal. Her neighbor in Berlin and almost exact contemporary, sporty and vivacious Leni Riefenstahl, had a saucier kind of appeal, catching eyes in something called *Ways to Strength and Beauty* (*Wege zu Kraft und*

Schönheit), a full-length "culture" feature devoted to physical fitness and exercise, mostly in the out-of-doors and mostly in the altogether.

Leni Riefenstahl was bold and ready for anything in her early twenties. She would later wrap herself in a star's dignity and deny ever having been an unbilled day player even at Ufa, deny being in *Ways to Strength and Beauty*, deny ever having seen it or even having heard of it, though it became one of the great box-office sensations of the day. One might attribute her denials to latter-day remorse at having appeared on screen bare-breasted as Eve, wielding a comb or a fan as handmaiden to a Greek or Roman noblewoman in intimate bathing tableaux that glorified the physical fitness of antiquity by undraping enough modern-day pulchritude to propel the film to notoriety and huge Continental box office.

But the onetime bit player's subsequent denials had nothing to do with modesty, for she exhibits her charms on-screen with evident aplomb. The denials served, rather, the construction of a romantic image of instant stardom and spontaneous self-generation that she would refine and advance until she died in 2003 at the age of 101. Having once been just another anonymous wannabe seeking attention however she could get it, even in the freewheeling decadence of the ill-fated Weimar Republic, didn't suit the story line.

In truth, the bare-breasted five-minute bit was something of a comedown. She had earlier attracted attention as an expressionist dancer, a brief but addictive episode of celebrity interrupted by a knee injury. She already knew that facts—then as now—were irrelevant or even inimical to fashioning a public image. She knew how to selectively edit reviews to compensate for the shortsightedness of critics, how to attract sponsors with beauty and tears, and—judging from her sunny self-assurance on the silent screen—how to make the most of opportunity when it knocked even when wearing little more than a smile. One can easily forgive her disowning a few minutes of old film that the regime supplanting Weimar would denounce as un-German and an offense to German womanhood. There would be much to win or to lose from that successor regime and—later—much more to deny.

Her self-invention accelerated after luck and talent transformed ambition into success. Fate smiled on her in the person of Adolf Hitler, and she smiled back. Her eye for dynamic composition on the screen was equal to her eye for the main chance in life, and they combined to create a fateful myth whose troubling power has not faded. She became the most celebrated woman in Germany, the most famous female filmmaker in the world, and achieved more power and independence than any director before or since until catastrophe ran its course and left her standing in the ruins, protesting her fate and her innocence.

In such an unlikely and singular career, *Ways to Strength and Beauty* was just a footnote disintegrating in the vaults. For years, blurred stills circulated with claims that her image lurked here or there or somewhere. Recent writers (evidently without seeing the film) confide that she's there as a dancer or as an outdoor extra or that she isn't there at all.

By the end of her turbulent century, when she had become the oldest working filmmaker in history—and the most controversial—she waved away such rumors like the practiced diva she had become. She had spent more of her life sparring with interviewers and dueling with interrogators than she had spent actually making films. To every question that hinted at a challenge—about a film, a person, a party, a motive—there was a single, defiant question in lieu of an answer: "Of what am I guilty?" And if angry denials didn't silence skepticism, litigation did.

Journalists complained that she sounded like a "broken record" and wondered if her sense of truth had atrophied, or if decades of denial had usurped remembrance or corrupted recall. But even at one hundred, she could remember every f-stop, film emulsion, exposure, and splice in every movie she ever made. Still, as her astonishing energy ebbed away at last, she must have known that someday someone would rummage through the vaults and find her on celluloid in the film she never had heard of, just as she was in 1925 at Ufa, young and beautiful and guilty of nothing graver than vanity and ambition.

And there she is on-screen: vital and vivid and beguiling, challenging fame and confident of bigger things to come. Bigger than Ufa and Lubitsch and Lang, as it turned out; bigger than she could have dreamed. Bigger than almost anything, except the cost to her and others, which is, in part, the subject of the narrative that follows.

BERLIN

---

*Berlin was the place for the ambitious, the energetic, the
talented. Wherever they started, it was in Berlin that
they became, and Berlin that made them, famous.*
—Peter Gay

*Surely no city in the world—not Rome, not Pompeii—
suffuses such an appalling sense of history.*
—Michael Ratcliffe

ONE

METROPOLIS

I want to become something quite great.
—Leni Riefenstahl

LENI RIEFENSTAHL CREATED IMAGES from light and shadow, from movement, rhythm, passion, prodigious energy, physical courage, and driving, epic ambition. She had, she said, one subject—beauty—and searched for it in the natural world, mountain high and underwater deep; in the flags and torches of massed multitudes; in the struggle and transcendence of athletic competition; in the physical and erotic perfection of primitive warriors; and—from the beginning—in herself.

She was born Helene Amalie Bertha Riefenstahl on August 22, 1902, in Wedding, a sooty workers' district on the industrial edges of Berlin. The population of the city was then two million going on four, with growth so rapid that street maps were obsolete before printers could produce them. Disgruntled civic planners disparaged Berlin as a "nowhere city," a city "always becoming" that "never is," but advocates of change hailed "progress" and thrilled to restless urban rhythms as full of expectancy as its air—the fabled *Berliner Luft*—and just as vital and intoxicating.

The onetime river trading post and its mushrooming suburbs would incorporate as Greater Berlin in 1920, by which time the boundaries of "Athens on the Spree" were vast enough to embrace Frankfurt, Stuttgart, and Munich put together. It was a parvenu metropolis compared to Paris, London, or Vienna with their Roman roots and ruins, but it was also— quite suddenly—the third largest metropolitan area in the world: loud, aggressive, and going places.

"The fastest city in the world!" they called Berlin when Leni was born there. It had been the capital of Germany, of what was grandly styled the Second Reich, for only thirty years, but empire builders in a hurry boasted of its modernity, unperturbed that horses still pulled trolleys through gaslit streets, that running water (hot or cold) was seldom encountered above the ground floor, and that the Berlin telephone directory was a twenty-six-page pamphlet. Crime and vice were no more rampant and no less colorful than in London, Paris, Buenos Aires, or New York. News of the day—or the minute—rolled off the presses in every political persuasion from the hundred dailies and weeklies that were published there in a babel of languages, making Berlin the liveliest, most densely concentrated center of journalism in all Europe.

Berlin's boosters were too focused on the future to give more than a backward glance to such slums and laborers' districts as Wedding or to the workers' children, like Leni, growing up in them. Civic do-gooders nodded dutifully as Kaiser Wilhelm II reminded them of "the duty to offer to the toiling classes the possibility of elevating themselves to the beautiful." One had only to point inferiors in the direction of the Hohenzollern Palace, the Tiergarten, the Victory Column, the broad canals and their 957 bridges (more than in Venice), the Pergamon Museum with its antiquities, the Reichstag with its "To the German People" promise carved in stone beneath its sheltering dome of steel and glass; or to the glittering theaters, operas, and hotels, the promenade streets such as tree-canopied Unter den Linden or the racier Kurfürstendamm (Bismarck's answer to the Champs-Élysées) lined with shops and sidewalk cafés. If the toiling class infrequently abandoned the factory floors for tours of the more elegant venues of imperial Berlin, the kaiser graciously imparted his notions of art and the beautiful to them. "An art which transgresses the laws and barriers outlined by Me," he explained, "ceases to be an art." This rang with reassuring certainty to the aesthetically insecure and was a viewpoint that a later leader—a onetime painter of picture postcards and aspiring architect—would echo and that millions would accept with awed docility.

No city in Europe made such a cult of modernity. Berlin was rushing at the turn of the century to make up in future what it lacked in past, while custodians of nostalgia mourned "a vanished Arcadia" that had never truly been. Velocity, anonymity, and the cheek-by-jowl juxtaposition of promise and peril inspired songs, paintings, novels, plays, and—already flickering silently when Leni was born—films. Most of these works inspired awe and alienation, too, as ordinary Berliners wondered uneasily where all this urban energy would lead. Ambivalence would find disturbing graphic expression in the 1920s, but prophetic, ominous visions of city life that were dubbed "degenerate" from the start began appearing in the teens from such painters as Ernst Ludwig Kirchner, Emil Nolde, and Ludwig Meidner, who labeled his urban paintings "apocalyptic landscapes."

Berlin-Wedding had scant time for art or musings on modernity. It was a dense warren of factories, foundries, and labor. It was blocks of tenements—called *Mietskaserne*, rent barracks—crowding blue-collar families into one- or two-room flats stacked five or six stories high around sunless courtyards where life was harsh and suicide a daily occurrence. "Tenement sickness" was shorthand for tuberculosis and rickets in Berlin, where the infant mortality rate was almost 20 percent when the nineteenth century ended and more than double that in Wedding, where it reached a high of 42 percent just after Leni was delivered there.

Wedding was poor but not without altruism and aspiration. Its mean streets offered shelter to the homeless in a spartan doss-house, and there was a small pond for ice-skating. Someone in 1905 rented out part of a courtyard shed as a photographer's studio, and it wasn't long before one-reel movies were being shot there. In 1912, Wedding established Berlin's first crematorium to compensate for the scarcity and cost of open burial ground. Children played in courtyards; geraniums grew on windowsills;

music and love got made; and by 1918, nearly 40 percent of all Berliners lived in tenement districts like it. We see their faces in the etchings and prints of Käthe Kollwitz; their bawdy, earthy pleasures titillate still in the sketches of Heinrich Zille, the poetic folk satirist and painter who knew them best and once observed that you can kill a man with his lodgings as well as you can with an ax.

"I hated the class system," Leni Riefenstahl confided to a friend. She was turning ninety then, living in a sheltered lakeside villa in Bavaria, distant enough in every way from Wedding to give perspective on her birthplace, a basic tenement flat in the two-block-long Prinz-Eugen-Strasse. The rooms were first lodgings for first-time parents who were almost newlyweds, married in a civil ceremony on April 5, 1902, nearly five months before their daughter saw first light in August.

Leni's father, Alfred Theodor Paul Riefenstahl, was not yet twenty-four when she was born. He was one of three boys and a girl born to Gustav and Amalie (née Lehmann) Riefenstahl in 1878 in the rural Brandenburg district surrounding Berlin. His father had been a black-smith like his father before him, but Alfred—blond and burly and wearing an upturned Kaiser Wilhelm mustache—had been drawn to Berlin by economic opportunity. He styled himself "salesman" on documents, but in fact he was a plumber. He would in time build his own sanitation and ventilation business as domestic plumbing became standard: niceties turned into necessities, and a plumber into an entrepreneur.

Leni's mother, Bertha Ida Scherlach Riefenstahl, was almost twenty-two when her daughter was born. Bertha was a willowy beauty with dark eyes, curly dark hair, and a determined jawline, all of which she passed on to her only daughter, who was born cross-eyed. Bertha herself was the eighteenth child of a mother who died giving birth to her in Wloclawek (now in Poland) on October 9, 1880. Shortly after Bertha's mother died, her father—Leni's carpenter grandfather—married his children's nanny and fathered three more children, for a total of twenty-one.

There is a mystery here, one that might amount only to a niggling biographical puzzle were it not a hint of the shifting images of the past that Leni would manipulate as times changed and perspectives with them. Her background unavoidably aroused curiosity in the 1930s among powerful figures of the Third Reich as she rose to prominence among them. Rumors that she was Jewish—or partly so—gained currency in this period and traced an alleged line of Jewish descent through Bertha. Once aired, the rumors gained wide circulation in the European and American press during the early years of the Third Reich, though the allegations were never proved and were officially repudiated by the ultimate Third Reich authority, the Führer himself. Leni brushed the subject aside then and later as the poisoned residue of a malicious campaign orchestrated against her by Nazi propaganda minister Dr. Joseph Goebbels.

While some of the rumors were almost certainly inspired by Goebbels or others jealous of her position and privileges in the 1930s, not all of them were. Some of Leni's closest friends and colleagues, including Dr. Arnold Fanck, the film director credited with Leni's discovery, believed that Bertha was Jewish. As Leni's onetime mentor and lover—and later a Nazi Party member—Fanck's objectivity and veracity are not beyond challenge. Less equivocal is the testimony of art director Isabella Ploberger, who worked and lived with Leni and Bertha during World War II and took for granted that Bertha—"a lovely person, a fine person"—was Jewish. Ploberger believed that Goebbels knew this, which accounted for his animosity.

There are documents, to be sure. Chief among them is Leni's "Proof of Descent" ("Abstammungs-Nachweis"), the genealogical record of ancestry she prepared and submitted to the Reich's film office in 1933 to validate Aryan descent, necessary to work in the German film industry. This document has long been available but never fully scrutinized, not even by the Nazis for whom it was prepared. Bertha is inscribed there as the child of the carpenter Karl Ludwig Friedrich Scherlach (born 1842) and Ottilie Auguste Scherlach (née Boia), born out of wedlock on January 24, 1863, to Friederika Boia and an unknown father. Though Ottilie Boia and Karl Scherlach are said to have married in the Silesian town of Woldenburg (Dobiegniew in modern Poland), no record of the marriage is known to exist, and their union may have been by common law. But what has gone unnoticed and unremarked is that Ottilie Boia could not possibly have been Bertha's mother. Born in 1863, she could not have given birth to seventeen children before delivering Bertha in 1880. Ottilie was almost certainly the nanny that Leni's carpenter grandfather married after his first wife died in delivering Bertha, the birth mother who became a nonperson in the genealogy Leni tendered to the Third Reich. As for Ottilie, she lived out her days as Bertha's stepmother and Leni's stepgrandmother in a modest flat in Charlottenburg, the comfortable Berlin suburb where the adolescent Leni ran to her for strudel and sympathy when Alfred Riefenstahl's strict discipline became intolerable.

Third Reich genealogies required declaration of religion as well as race, and Leni's states that her forebears were Protestant. They appear not to have been devout. Since 1850, every birth, including Leni's, was recorded at a registry office rather than at a church after a christening (though Leni was confirmed as Protestant in a Berlin church at fifteen).

The city and culture in which Leni grew up were famously cosmopolitan; Jewish conversion to Christianity and cultural assimilation were commonplace, though racial identity, rather than religious, would be the Nazis' standard when theirs became the only one that mattered. No known documents fill the gap in Leni's ancestry, but the substitution of Bertha's stepmother for her birth mother on a Third Reich genealogical document is hard to fathom without considering a motive touching on race, since defining race was the point of the exercise. What is not speculative is Leni's ability to define and redefine her past as circumstance or occasion required. As for Bertha, Leni "loved her to distraction" until she died in 1965 at the age of eighty-four.

Alfred Riefenstahl inspired different emotions. He was a striver: rigid, efficient, conservative, and Leni's rival for Bertha's attention. His business depended on Berlin, though he felt ill at ease there with his provincial background and views of family life, especially after Leni's only sibling, a brother named Heinz, was born on March 5, 1906. Alfred's burgeoning business allowed him to move the family to a larger flat in Berlin-Neukölln just before Heinz was born and Leni began school. The old neighborhood and the new were similar (both would be centers of Communist agitation after 1918), so it came as a relief when the family could afford weekend excursions to a lakeside village about an hour southwest of Berlin by suburban rail.

Zeuthen was idyllic, green, and distanced Leni and little Heinz from the city's dangers. It was tranquil enough for hiking, swimming, and languidly watching clouds roll by. The cottage the family rented—and would eventually acquire—was a short walk through the woods to the railway line to Berlin and just across the lake from the *Gasthaus* run by Bertha's older sister Olga, who had alerted them to the area in the first place.

As a child, Leni was contentedly solitary except for her brother, perhaps a trait acquired because the family moved so often. After the apartments in Wedding and Neukölln and the weekend cottage at Zeuthen, there would be other flats in Berlin in the Goltzstrasse and in the Yorckstrasse, nearer the center of the city and her father's business. But she may have been solitary by choice because she saw herself as special and precocious and needed no supporting cast but Heinz and no audience but the indulgent Bertha, "always my best friend."

She began reading at an early age, she tells us, and started writing poetry and plays at the age of five after an excursion to the theater to see a performance of *Snow White*. Though Alfred preferred bowling or hunting with friends, he now and then treated his family to a show, stoutly impervious to the stage magic that would become a "driving force" for his impressionable daughter and remained one for his wife.

Bertha had dreamed as a girl of going on the stage and may actually have done so. A photograph taken before her marriage shows her dressed in the kind of dashing finery a Floradora girl might have worn: a short-sleeved, knee-length dress trimmed in garlands of flowers repeated in her hat and on the open fan in her right hand, cocked saucily on her hip. She told Leni that she had prayed while carrying her, "Dear God, give me a beautiful daughter who will become a famous actress." Once planted, the seed grew. What young girl could resist thinking herself the answer to a prayer?

"I dreamed my dreams," Leni said, creating meadowland theatrics in which she played the leading role and the obliging Heinz became her willing prop. Like her poems and daily life, her plays excluded companionship and outsiders. "I allowed no people into my verses, only trees, birds and even insects."

As she entered adolescence, she fantasized becoming a nun, but the cloister sounded confining and self-denial dreary. News reports of aviation exploits during the Great War excited images of adventure and daring. They also inspired her to imagine an entire airline industry on paper, scheduling flights between European cities and even calculating the price of tickets, as if emulating Alfred's administration of his plumbing business. "There was in me some organizational talent struggling to emerge," she remembered later, an aptitude that would prove indispensable when competing in the real world as a woman in a man's universe.

The only man of consequence in her teens was her father—busy, bourgeois, and authoritarian. After she completed elementary school, he enrolled her in a *Gymnasium,* as any upward-striving father of the day would have done. But mastery of Latin and Greek for a classical German education was too arduous or tedious, and she rebelled until she was allowed to enter a *Lyzeum,* where prestige and academic standards were less elevated and intellectual pursuits less demanding. Even so, her grades were unremarkable in mathematics and painting, and she did poorly in history. Her distinction as a student was athletic. She did well at gymnastics; she ice-skated, roller-skated, ran, swam, and tried (and failed at) diving. Her energy and endurance were as remarkable as her physical daring and tolerance for pain, double-edged attributes that would accompany her through a lifetime of mishaps and broken bones.

By her own account, nothing in or out of school so preoccupied her as fairy tales. Germany was the home of the Brothers Grimm, of course, but subscribing to a fantasy journal called *Once upon a Time* at fifteen, as

Leni did, suggests fixation rather than pastime, and the predilection for fairy tales and myths would survive and flourish.

Immersion in fantasy suggests retreat from reality. Though she would describe her childhood as sunny, burnished with a turn-of-the-century graciousness, the realities of daily life were drab and straitened, and her childhood photographs reveal a tense and wary child. When a sharp-eyed acquaintance pointed this out to her in 1992, Leni admitted, "It was not a happy childhood, but good. Not happy, because my father was a despot, towards all of us—my mother, me and Heinz. I don't doubt he loved and wished to protect us, but it was an incredibly repressive love, taking away from us almost any semblance of freedom. . . . It created an incredible resistance in me, a *screaming* resistance."

She meant *screaming* literally and could simulate ear-piercing rage well into her eighties. Outbursts of emotional vehemence, real or simulated, could abruptly segue to tears shed at will, and both techniques were invaluable when she felt threats to her independence from a man whose inflexibility had frustrated the youthful stage dreams of her mother.

Bertha and Leni joined grievances to become coconspirators in outwitting Alfred in his need for control. They visited the forbidden *Kino* picture shows together when "the despot" was hunting or away on business, or they crashed fancy dress balls to mingle among the privileged classes and learn how such people dressed. Freedom was both independence from control and heady self-assertion, fostered and encouraged by a willful, adoring mother who was companion, seamstress, and abettor all in one. These were "the good times when we all felt completely free."

As a teenager, Leni was strikingly pretty, with dark eyes (slightly close together) and cascading dark hair. Her body was well formed, graceful, and eye-catching, as admiring glances on city streets made thrillingly clear. But as her *Lyzeum* days neared an end, she felt as if she were drifting inside "a cloud of unknowing" and saw herself as "a dreamer, still vaguely searching for something more meaningful in my life." Berlin—the constantly changing, fastest city in the world—was happy to oblige.

She had fastened at sixteen on an advertisement soliciting movie extras. The film was titled *Opium,* one of many "enlightenment" films (*Aufklärungsfilme*) that used photogenic displays of depravity and flesh to warn audiences of the dangers of drug addiction and white slavery. *Opium*'s stars were a distinguished man of the theater, Eduard von Winterstein, and young film player Conrad Veidt, soon to be famous around the world as the somnambulist in *The Cabinet of Dr. Caligari.*

It is hard to imagine a title or theme more likely to alarm the restrictive Alfred Riefenstahl than *Opium,* but Leni had no plans to burden him with her intentions. For all her "clouds of unknowing" and independence crushed by paternal control, she was considerably less sheltered than Alfred guessed. She had already been approached while sauntering along the Kurfürstendamm by casting agents and directors eager to put her teenage charms on film. She had, in fact, already yielded to such flattering entreaties and made her (now lost) motion picture debut in a makeshift one-room studio, playing a chargirl among the cinders in a film whose title and director slipped from her memory, though the director's prophecy of "a great future" for her did not.

That future would not arrive with *Opium.* She was called back to the dance studio in which auditions were held for a second, then a third time, but the role she hoped to land—a young, bare-breasted opium addict whose search for pleasure leads to ruin—went to someone else. As Leni was leaving the studio in dejection, she caught a glimpse through an open door of dance students reflected in a mirror as they stretched at the bar. This scene reminiscent of Degas so intrigued her that "the desire to rush inside and join in was almost uncontrollable." But how? All she could count on was her mother's likely willingness to finance lessons while shielding Alfred from the news. This was, in fact, a moment in Western history that any father might have viewed as inopportune for ambitions that sounded dilettantish or self-indulgent, especially in Berlin.

Though she maintained ever after that she was oblivious of life around her, Leni's leaving the Kollmorgenschen Lyzeum in 1918 coincided with the dreadful climax of a world war that had begun with parades, songs, and flowers—"I stood on the curb as the soldiers marched off," she recalled—and was ending after four years of unprecedented carnage in mutinies, starvation, epidemics, and torrents of recrimination and resentment. November 1918 brought chaos and revolution following the kaiser's forced abdication and exile to Holland. The fastest city in the world had become the bloodiest, with Communists, Republicans, and right-wing loyalists to the monarchy exchanging gunfire in the streets.

The conviction that Germany had been "stabbed in the back" by politicians and diplomats became an article of faith for many in a city that had remained physically untouched during the long and ruinous war and could not, in consequence, conceive of the German military as anything but invincible. Especially despicable, even treasonous, were the men in top hats and morning coats who had placed their signatures on papers conceding defeat in a railroad car in France while the generals who had lost the war remained aloof and irreproachable. The Versailles Treaty would decree Germany guilty of warmongering and would vindictively impose reparations, payments that would cripple economic recovery, humiliate national pride, and create resentments of the sort that smolder until they ignite.

The assassinations in January 1919 of Karl Liebknecht and Rosa Luxemburg initiated violence and terror campaigns by right-wing extremists that brutally hastened the removal from public office of leftists and liberals. The murder tally reached five hundred by 1922 with no corresponding level of judicial censure from courts loyal to the ancien régime and openly hostile to the victims. All this and the establishment of the Weimar Republic—a democratic experiment viewed with suspicion by the left *and* the right—were major historical upheavals that failed to penetrate Leni's self-absorption, allowing her to drift through the civil strife convulsing around her without, as she put it, "the faintest notion why this was happening or what it meant."

It is a credible claim. Count Harry Kessler, the urbane aristocrat known as "the Red Count" for his radical political views, a man seismographically attuned to nuances of social and cultural change, noted a willful numbness to violence in Berlin. He wrote in his diary for January

17, 1919: "In the evening I went to a cabaret in the Bellevuestrasse. The sound of a shot cracked through the performance of a fiery Spanish dancer. Nobody took any notice. It underlined the slight impression that the revolution has made on metropolitan life. . . . This historic, colossal event has caused no more than local ripples. . . . An elephant stabbed with a penknife shakes itself and strides on as if nothing has happened."

The ripples grew larger with the daily struggle for survival. Postwar food shortages and influenza hastened a breakdown in prewar morality. The pervasive mood was one of perpetual emergency in which opportunism of every kind flourished until, as one observer put it, "a kind of insanity took hold." In this volatile atmosphere, Alfred Riefenstahl— still unaware of his daughter's new obsession with dance—decided to sequester her, to ensure her security and future as a German wife and mother by enrolling her in a domestic science school, where she might learn dedication to the safe conventions of *Kinder, Kirche, und Küche*.

No scheme could have been better calculated to provoke resistance in Leni, who thought of domesticity as drudgery if she thought of it at all. Dance, on the other hand, was freedom. It was physical movement and spiritual self-expression; it was daring and exhilarating and took place in the limelight. Movies such as *Opium* had attracted her but were primitive or sensational, with little of the aura of high art that enveloped dance. This was a moment at which such figures as Diaghilev, Nijinsky, and Fokine were mounting new dances to new music by Stravinsky, Debussy, and Satie. If Leni knew nothing of these artists—and it is unlikely that she did—revolution was in the air as well as in the streets, and the posters of celebrated dancers she saw on kiosks on every corner heralded something new and exciting to feed her dreams.

She could hardly have been better placed. Berlin bowed to none in its enthusiasm for dance. America's Isadora Duncan—barefoot in flowing robes that alluded to ancient Greece—had founded a dance school there in the teens. That had paved the way for such innovators as Mary Wigman, Germany's most celebrated expressionist dancer, her name a household word when Leni was still writing poems about insects. Scantily clad and barefoot, the earthy Wigman challenged the fastidious repertoire of pirouettes and *tour jetés* that had gone before. The drama and sweep of dance attracted the athlete in Leni; the solo stage for expressing inner beauty drew the self-absorbed aficionado of fairy tales.

The Grimm-Reiter School of the Dance, just off the barricaded Kurfürstendamm, had been the site of the *Opium* auditions, and it was there she began her coveted dance lessons, paid for by her mother. The rehearsal piano's rhythms were punctuated by gunfire in the streets, but Leni hardly noticed. She threw herself into her lessons like an athlete in training, punishing herself to compensate for her late start and displaying her gift for physical endurance as she graduated from beginners' classes to ballet. "No pain or strain was too great for me," she boasted. Bertha ran interference with Alfred, the subterfuge intensifying the bond between mother and daughter and making deception seem a justified means to an artistic or self-realizing end. "We had few scruples of conscience," Leni admitted.

Her dance school occasionally presented recitals headlined by former students who had made professional names for themselves. Easily the best known was Anita Berber, a beautiful and uninhibited Leipzig girl only three years older than Leni, who modeled for high-fashion magazines and had been in films since 1918. But Berber's fame—her notoriety, in fact—came from dramatic dances with such titles as "Morphium," "Suicide," and "Cocaine" that she performed nude. She would be dead at twenty-eight, ravaged by drugs and tuberculosis, but achieved a disturbing immortality in a famous portrait by Otto Dix: Looking depraved in red against a red background, she remains an emblem of Berlin decadence in the 1920s.

An appearance by Berber at a school recital was canceled due to illness, and Leni replaced her, mimicking dance routines (clothed) that she had seen Berber rehearse. This was not the kind of substitution to go unremarked. When Alfred heard of it, he was dumbfounded to learn that his daughter was dancing at all, much less in public with her name linked to that of the scandalous Berber. He erupted, threatening Bertha with divorce and Leni with boarding school, the stricter and remoter the better. Things once merely dubious to Alfred now seemed perilously out of control. It is not impossible to sympathize with the family man, laboring to sanitize and ventilate Berlin while his wife and daughter were defying convention behind his back. The dance school betrayal confirmed his sense that a kind of moral anarchy had seized Berlin since the end of the war. The city had become what people were calling it: no longer "Athens on the Spree" but the "new Babylon," "the national sewer."

Leni shrugged. She was used to his "roaring like a rogue elephant" and noted evenly that "whenever he smashed china in his temper tantrums, it was touching to see how he tried to glue it together again." But gluing together shards of betrayed trust was something else again. To calm threats of divorce and prevent her own banishment from Berlin, Leni affected compliance and suggested a compromise. She would give up dance and enroll in Berlin's State School of Arts and Crafts to study painting. It was not the domestic science program Alfred had hoped for, but "applied arts" had a solid sound, and he uneasily agreed. Leni made a brief show of contrition and reform but went about her studies with such an air of adolescent martyrdom and self-sacrifice that Alfred, sniffing fresh rebellion in the air, packed her off to boarding school once and for all.

He had made certain that dance played no part in the curriculum of the Lohmann School in Thale, in the Harz Mountains, but it may not have occurred to him that dramatic presentations did and that Leni would leap at them as a lifeline to her thwarted ambitions. She had packed her ballet slippers, to be sure, and found herself rooming with a girl named Hela Gruel, whose passion to become an actress had led to parental exile from the temptations of the city. The girls became allies, rising before dawn to practice the exercises demanded by their futures with "a kind of fanaticism," as Hela wrote after Leni had become someone to write about. "I want to become something quite great," Leni confided grandly but vaguely, leaving her options open. Greatness would probably have something to do with performing, she guessed, and temporarily adopted the stage name Hela invented for her: "Helene van Riefen."

Dance practice before dawn and evening performances of plays by Goethe and Schiller in the town's pine-scented outdoor theater only emphasized remoteness from the pace and opportunities of Berlin. Leni suffered through "Siberia," as she called boarding school, and may have realized that, for all their conflicts, she and Alfred were so often at loggerheads partly because they had so much in common. She had learned tenacity, obstinacy, and willfulness from him. She, too, could rage, but she could feign feminine submission when softness seemed tactically called for, could smile or weep or cling at will. Her mother's example had been no less instructive. She had learned from Bertha the practical uses of deception and the advantage of having a champion, a sponsor.

She resolved during her exile that "as long as I lived, I would never allow myself to become dependent on another human being. My decisions would always be my own." And because the only thing that mattered was "my own will," she did not hesitate to negotiate again with her father, wheedling, shedding tears, and overcoming his resistance with a smile and another "clever idea." She would return from "Siberia" to Berlin, she proposed, to serve as his secretary and personal confidante, working right in his office in the Kurfürstenstrasse, where he could keep an eye on her. It sounded so reasonable that he acquiesced.

At nineteen, she was back in Berlin.

TWO

DEBUTS

Personally, I am convinced that you have little talent,
and will never be more than mediocre.

—Alfred Riefenstahl

"HOW I WISH I WERE A MAN," Leni wrote a friend, explaining that "it would be so much easier to carry out all my plans." Her father, apprehensive about what those plans might be, echoed her theme in a complaint that sounded warily resigned, if not already defeated: "Too bad you were not the boy, and your brother the girl."

The point was Leni's independence, not broader issues of woman suffrage or emancipation. She was never to be a joiner or sister-in-arms for the rights or causes of others, though latter-day feminists, focusing on her gender instead of her sympathies, would try to claim her. Nor was there any hint of ambiguous sexuality. Leni's masculine aggressiveness in romantic arenas would become famous and the subject of common gossip, but not just yet and with no one but men.

Like most pretty girls, she had known she was alluring since the first head turned her way on the Kurfürstendamm. At nineteen, with hair piled high and loose, with her classically aquiline nose and her eyes shining enticingly from beneath lowered lashes, she had a look that was fresh without being immature. She moved with the graceful self-confidence of the athlete she was and the dancer she hoped to become. She spoke in a bright, high-pitched voice that hinted at good-time spontaneity and, fashionably slender, had a habit of overdressing in items Bertha ran up on the sewing machine—a black velvet wrap trimmed in false ermine was a special favorite—that suggested jazz-baby sophistication. She delighted in attracting attention, but her girl-about-town worldliness was mostly pretense at a time when, in novelist Stefan Zweig's formulation, "to be suspected of virginity at sixteen would have been considered a disgrace in every school in Berlin."

"I was a very late developer," Leni later confided to a friend. "No breasts, you know, and my cycle only began when I was twenty-one. Of course, I was always in love, from heaven knows when. The first one was a boy I saw in a street near our home—for a whole year I walked along it at the same time every day, just to see him, but it was ten years until I actually met him—and by then, of course, I was quite uninterested in him."

Which did not mean she was without suitors. She had a penchant for encouraging admirers of social or artistic pedigree until she was sure enough of their devotion to reject them with showy indifference. An early casualty was Paul Walden, the eighteen-year-old son of the free-living poet Else Lasker-Schüler (a possible role model for Leni, though Count Harry Kessler thought her "beastly"), who was involved with Franz Marc and the Blue Rider school of painters before she emigrated to Jerusalem in 1933. Young Paul's eager yielding to the temptations of Leni's lips earned him an elbow to the ribs, a mild enough fate compared to the one suffered by another Jewish boy named Walter Lubovski, whom Leni met at an ice-skating rink and turned into something of a love slave. She and her girlfriends made him cross-dress in their own garments and otherwise humiliated him until he slashed his wrists at the Riefenstahl cottage in Zeuthen, causing Leni to shove him—still bleeding—under a sofa to prevent discovery by Alfred. Young Lubovski survived long enough to enter a mental hospital and relocate to America, where Leni later learned he had gone blind. She reacted to his fate by noting, "He never forgot me as long as he lived."

In Berlin, she entered a beauty contest with Bertha's help and needle—wearing a "silvery green silk gown trimmed with a border of swan feathers"—and won second place, having billed herself as a dancer. Her victory attracted the interest of Berlin's preeminent fashion magazine, *Die Dame,* whose editor ordered, "Show me your legs, my lovely," and offered to sponsor a dance debut at La Scala, Berlin's hugely popular variety theater. Leni protested that she "never had any intention of appearing at a vaudeville house, even one as famous as La Scala. I am going to dance only in concert halls and on theater platforms." Such venues seemed within her grasp when dramatist Karl Vollmoeller invited her to his opulent Pariser Platz hideaway. Vollmoeller was the author of a famous play about nuns called *The Miracle,* which Max Reinhardt staged all over the world, often in real cathedrals. Leni rejected the playwright's offer to become her protector and "rich friend" on the grounds that "I am very self-willed and I often don't do what other people demand of me."

Taste, not virtue, was the theme. She was not defending her virginity, nor was she averse to sponsorship. But she wanted to do the choosing, and athletes, not sickly boys like Walter Lubovski or aging roués like Karl Vollmoeller, quickened her blood. When her father took her to the race-track, she studied the riders while he studied the odds. She found herself soon after dining with a celebrated jockey in the scarlet-draped *chambre séparée* of a fashionable restaurant, until the jockey's wife arrived brandishing a large umbrella. Interest in the races yielded to the lure of tennis.

At a Berlin sports club, Leni signed up for lessons from a tennis pro named Günther Rahn, who had been adjutant to the rakish German crown prince. Rahn claimed to have fallen hopelessly in love with his new pupil, but he interested Leni mainly because he was thick with tennis star Otto Froitzheim, who had won a silver medal in men's singles at the 1908 Olympics. Leni had been attracted to the thirty-nine-year-old Froitzheim since exchanging glances with him in a skating club locker room the year before. She doted on his reputation as an athlete and Lothario. His many conquests off the court included Pola Negri. Now that Leni was nearing twenty-one and Negri was forsaking Froitzheim and Berlin for

Hollywood, Leni decided that Froitzheim—whom she had never met and who was only four years younger than her father—should deflower her. She deflated Günther Rahn's passion by asking him to make the necessary introduction and arrangements. Rahn, a compliant sort, did as he was told and would remain compliant and useful for decades to come.

The arrangements involved a tryst at Froitzheim's Berlin flat, where Leni would give up her virginity after tea and a tango to phonograph records. Following the precoital ritual and a painful grapple on the living room sofa, the playboy tennis star retrieved his pants and dug into a pocket. "If you get pregnant, you can use this to get rid of it," he said, nonchalantly tossing her an American twenty-dollar bill.

The experience was "traumatic," Leni insisted, tantamount to a "rape," though it was also the beginning of a two-year affair. "In some mysterious way I was a slave to him," she reflected in later life, forgetting that she had initiated her despoiling, tango and all. "I could think only of escape from this bondage," she insisted, but, as escape proved impossible, got engaged to Froitzheim instead.

Leni's sexual initiation was calculated and sordid but bolstered her confidence, enabling her to convey self-assurance that could open doors or close them, depending on her mood. She could fall in romantic love, but female sexuality, pleasurably and athletically expressed, armed her in a man's world. She could be predatory or demure, but erotic interchanges fulfilled her narcissism and, however enjoyable, were sometimes utilitarian, too. Sexual adventuring was the order of the day. Journalist Sebastian Haffner was sowing oats in Berlin at the same time and noted that, after the armistice, "unromantic love was the fashion: carefree, restless, light-hearted promiscuity. Typically, love affairs followed an extremely rapid course, without detours. The young who learned to love in those years eschewed romance and embraced cynicism."

Leni eschewed romance and embraced the dance. She had earned the trust of her father (who knew nothing of her relationship with Froitzheim) since her return from "Siberia" by working efficiently in his office; had earned his sympathy by falling ill and having her gallbladder removed; had earned his grudging support by mounting a full-scale assault with a phalanx of allies in defense of her ambition.

She had not, in fact, been as meekly submissive as Alfred believed. When he discovered by chance that she was trying to get a chorus job on the stage, he bellowed outrage at her duplicity, and Leni fled to Ottilie's flat in Charlottenburg. Three generations of women—wife, daughter, and stepmother-in-law—closed ranks. Helpless before their determination, Alfred conceded defeat. "You are as stubborn as I am," he raged perceptively, agreeing that Leni could study ballet with Madame Eugenie Eduardova, a once-great ballerina from St. Petersburg. "Personally, I am convinced that you have little talent, and will never be more than mediocre," he complained, "but you will have no cause to say later on that I destroyed your life, or ruined your chances of a career."

Training with Madame Eduardova cast a new light on the secret relationship with Froitzheim. Leni suddenly decided she felt nothing but "repugnance" for him and told him in writing that she never wanted to see him again. She then persuaded Alfred to send her to Dresden to study in the prestigious dance school Mary Wigman had established there. Once in Dresden, she grew disgruntled. The training and technique were "too abstract, too rigorous, and too ascetic, where my own urge was to surrender completely to the rhythms of the music." She was saved from excessive rigor—and the anonymity of dancing in an ensemble—by Froitzheim, who arrived in Dresden, assuming correctly that Leni's haughty resolve never to see him again would not withstand exposure to his person.

Leni returned to Berlin and Madame Eduardova, enrolling simultaneously at the Jutta Klamt School to study modern and expressionistic dance. The affair with Froitzheim continued between his tours to exhibition matches and Cologne, where his celebrity had gotten him elected deputy police commissioner. Leni poured her conflicted emotions and energies into inventing choreography for the solo career she had now decided was her destiny.

In July, she traveled to Lake Constance with a fellow dance student named Hertha Hellway-Bibo to take advantage of a summer course run by the Klamt School. En route to Switzerland, they discovered the summer session had been canceled due to postwar inflation, which had been soaring since January. It had now spun out of control, with disastrous consequences for their pocketbooks. The German mark had so fallen in value that it took 160,000 of them to equal one American dollar.

With her parents on vacation, there was no point in returning to Berlin. Leni and Hertha spent a few days in Lindau, where Leni modeled for a young artist's illustrated edition of the Bible (she thought his sketches of her "dreadful"). She earned pocket money by coloring in picture postcards and hawking them to tourists at outdoor cafés. Finally they moved on—begging, borrowing, and relying on the kindness of train conductors—north to the Baltic Sea and the sunny beaches of Travemünde.

Leni was only days shy of her twenty-first birthday and resolved to celebrate it soon afterward with a dance recital in Berlin that would make her famous and prove to Alfred how shortsighted he had been about her talent. She pondered solutions to the inflation crisis that threatened her goal while practicing calisthenics on the beach in view of a darkly handsome young man observing her from a lounge chair in the dunes.

He was a young Jewish banker from Innsbruck named Heinrich Richard Sokal. At twenty-five, "Harry" Sokal had a slender, aristocratic face and was himself a phenomenon of the inflation. A clever young man born in Romania in 1898, he manipulated exchange rates so nimbly that he had become the youngest bank director in Austria. He was also an obsessive gambler, now passing a few August days at the shore and some solitary evenings in the local casino. "And after ten seconds," he later reported of the view from his lounge chair in the dunes, "I said to myself, 'This girl I must marry.' I was *hit*. She had so much charm in her movements, so much grace and humor and she was very, very beautiful."

Sokal plunged into pursuit. He sought Leni out in the hotel bar or dining room and was not dissuaded by the sporty young man she and Hertha had acquired as a third wheel somewhere between Lindau and the

Baltic. He invited her to local restaurants, and if Hertha and his potential rival had to come along, he was generous enough to invite them, too. He and Leni played tennis and swam over the next few days as he made his intentions obvious. "I realized he was crazy about me," Leni later wrote, "but I couldn't return his interest, alas. I liked him—and that was all." Sokal didn't think that was all, for he proposed to her after they began sleeping together. He expected the refusal he got, but proposing seemed a small enough gesture if he wanted to keep their affair going after Travemünde, and he did.

At twenty-one Leni was healthy, daring, self-dramatizing, energetic, headstrong, and intensely ambitious. If she had previously disregarded political events or social conditions in dreamy fantasy, the runaway inflation forced her to emerge from her schoolgirl's cocoon. The twenty-dollar bill Otto Froitzheim had casually tossed her for an abortion a few months earlier was worth 20 million marks by her birthday on August 22. A month later, it was worth 100 million, and the government took to overstamping existing paper bills with zeros until denominations reached the billions and, finally, *trillions* when the crisis peaked in November at an incredible 4.2 trillion marks to the dollar and paper money was selling by the pound, like salvage.

"The collapse of the currency not only meant the end of trade, bankrupt businesses, food shortages in the big cities and unemployment," historian Alan Bullock notes. "It had the effect, which is the unique quality of economic catastrophe, of reaching down to and touching every single member of the community in a way which no political event can. The savings of the middle classes and the working classes were wiped out at a single blow with a ruthlessness which no revolution could ever equal. . . . The result of the inflation was to undermine the foundations of German society in a way which neither the war, nor the revolution of November 1918, nor the Treaty of Versailles had ever done. The real revolution in Germany was the inflation."

That summer sixty-five people were killed in a Communist uprising in Hamburg; a failed putsch from the right in Munich would soon hurl a onetime Austrian drifter and corporal in the Bavarian Army into the world spotlight for the first time. Conspiracy theories about the economic crisis mushroomed: It was the despised Versailles Treaty; it was the Weimar Republic's constitution; it was the Jews and their banks. Or, as one observer reported, it was the government itself "deliberately let[ting] the mark tumble in order to free the state of its public debts, to escape from paying reparations." Meanwhile, the government responded to the emergency by issuing more paper money to meet the demand, which had the effect of pouring gasoline on a bonfire.

"Speculators and profiteers thrived," Ian Kershaw writes. Anyone with access to foreign currencies—especially American dollars—could live like Croesus. A rumor was taken seriously that Douglas Fairbanks and Mary Pickford were going to buy Austria. American literary critic Malcolm Crowley went to Berlin, where his friends Matthew Josephson and Harold Loeb were publishing their little magazine, *Broom*. Crowley was astonished to discover that "for a salary of a hundred dollars a month in American currency, Josephson lived in a duplex apartment with two maids, riding lessons for his wife, dinners only in the most expensive restaurants, tips to the orchestra, pictures collected, charities to struggling German writers—it was an insane life for foreigners in Berlin."

Leni knew a foreigner, not in Berlin but in Innsbruck. Harry Sokal had access to American capital. He also had influence at Innsbruck's Stadttheater, where the much-admired Viennese actress Elisabeth Bergner had recently appeared, as he informed Leni on a visit to Berlin. He then learned to his chagrin that Leni's traveling companion Hertha was enamored with him, but Leni merely laughed. "Don't worry about it," she said. "When I love something, she loves it, too." Sokal needed no more pointed encouragement. "I'm a gambler at heart," he told her, and offered to finance her dance debut in Innsbruck.

Leni was adamant that Berlin was the place for her first professional outing. She had even selected the venue, the distinguished Blüthner-Saal, where she had stepped in for Anita Berber while still a student. She had somehow persuaded Alfred to reserve the hall for an evening in late

October, and neither inflation nor Harry Sokal's connections in Innsbruck could dissuade her from a debut in the capital. Sokal, interested in dance only because Leni was, remained a businessman with a sense of the market. He insisted that a tryout evening—a dress rehearsal with an audience—was essential before exposing an unknown twenty-one-year-old to the Olympian critics of Berlin. He offered to finance a tryout closer to Innsbruck, in, say, Munich. What with inflation careening out of control, it cost him one American dollar.

Leni made her debut—her tryout—on October 23, 1923, in the esteemed Tonhalle in the center of Munich. It was an auspicious site, and, though the hall was only a third full and most of the spectators were there on "paper" (free tickets to fill the house), this was still a remarkable venue for an unknown dancer's first public appearance. (No one there could have known that, two weeks later, a short walk from the concert hall, Adolf Hitler's ill-fated putsch would falter in confusion and gunfire, a misbegotten debut on the world stage that looked like a fiasco.)

She shared her solo debut with absent composers—Chopin, Tchaikovsky, Schubert, Brahms, Grieg, and Gluck. A trio of house musicians accompanied her from the shadows offstage. The dances were her own, their titles signaling passionate emotions: "Three Dances of Eros"— "Fire," "Surrender," and "Release"; "Oriental Fairy Tale"; "Dream Blossoms." The costumes were of her design, too: brief, close-fitting tunics of flowing panels in earth-toned fabric calculated to reveal. No scenic design but a black backcloth competed with the view of the lithe twenty-one-year-old bending and swaying to the music in a spotlight now purple, now blue, now gold.

Others had contributed anonymously to that performance—her mother had sewn the costumes; Sokal had paid for the hall, the advertising, and the musicians—but the notion of Leni Riefenstahl as a solo, self-generated artist began that night. Harry Sokal had done a superior job of promoting the evening at the height of the inflation. He arranged for newspaper critics to review Leni's debut in Munich's morning editions, whose newsstand prices demonstrated the economic crisis: The

Münchner Zeitung, which reviewed her performance three days later, sold for 300 million marks per copy, which leaped to 500 million the following day. The day after that—when Leni was dancing and reading her reviews in Berlin—a copy was priced at 1.5 billion marks.

The reviews were remarkably positive for an unknown dancer with no better credentials than a desire to be noticed and to please. None failed to comment on her youth and beauty or appreciate the audacity of her self-presentation. The critic in the *Münchner Neuesten Nachrichten* called her "a young dancer graced by nature with beauty and form," and the one from the *Münchner Zeitung* remarked on "beautiful looks and an obviously unorthodox temperament [that] enables her to hold the attention of her audience to the end." The first quibbled about "sentimentality," and the second sighed that she risked "no particular daring."

Her Berlin debut took place at the Blüthner-Saal on October 27, four nights after Munich. This time the auditorium was full, thanks to friends and family, and she viewed her success as "a triumph beyond my wildest dreams," perhaps because her father admitted to her after the concert, "Now, I believe in you."

Her timing was opportune, not least in occurring at the end of an economic emergency that had affected German theater no less than any other area of life. Theater had never come to a standstill because it never does in crisis, though the financing of new productions had been crippled, which made the hiring of halls by such nonprofessionals as Harry Sokal in Munich or Alfred Riefenstahl in Berlin practical. Novelist Alfred Döblin recalled visiting a theater in Berlin the same week Leni appeared onstage in Munich. He noted that, although it was raining fiercely in the streets, no one in the audience had brought a raincoat: True theater lovers could still pay millions for a ticket, but not for a ticket *and* the cloakroom.

Two weeks after Leni's first appearance in Berlin and a week after the Nazis' failed putsch in Munich, the Weimar government stabilized German currency by simply lopping off all the zeros. The exchange rate went overnight from 4.2 trillion to 4.2 to the dollar. Theater managers eager to attract audiences that had abandoned them during the worst of the crisis scrambled to book attractions, and Leni found herself one of them, dancing in Berlin at Max Reinhardt's Deutsches Theater and in his more intimate Kammerspiele. The bookings came about through Karl Vollmoeller, whose offer to be her "rich friend" she had once rejected, though she sent him two tickets to her concert—as a nose-thumbing gesture, she said. Vollmoeller told her he brought Reinhardt along as his guest and took credit for the limited bookings that ensued. Other engagements followed in quick succession, almost all of them arranged by Leni herself, though Harry Sokal was not inactive on her behalf, as she would discover.

None of this might have happened without the currency reform. It meant that Leni could now earn 500 to 1,000 marks per engagement, or about $125 to $250, very respectable sums in 1923 and 1924, which allowed her to leave Bertha's sewing machine behind and buy pretty new clothes at the better shops. Film offers came her way, including a screen test for Germany's foremost producer Erich Pommer and expatriate American director Arthur Robison. A picture titled *Pietro the Corsair* called for a female dancer, and Pommer offered her what she remembered as 30,000 marks for the role, or around $7,500, a handsome sum she turned down, ostensibly to continue dancing, though a likelier factor was conflicting schedules. She was overbooked.

All told, she gave seventy concerts from October 1923 to May 1924, roughly one appearance every three days, including those she gave at hotels to defray the cost of lodgings. She traveled overnight by train from Berlin to Frankfurt, Leipzig, Düsseldorf, Cologne, Dresden, Kiel, Chemnitz, and Stettin, appearing with what she called "indescribable success from press and public." There were engagements outside Germany as well. Harry Sokal arranged one (finally) in Innsbruck; she danced in Prague and then, in February 1924, in Zurich, where she and Sokal suffered the first of many stormy collisions of ego and agenda.

Leni arrived in Zurich to discover that Sokal, without her knowledge, had arranged bookings in London and Paris that she had assumed were spontaneous tributes to her new renown. Deflated and angry, she inter-preted the meddling as another ploy in Sokal's ongoing matrimonial pursuit, an Alfred-like attempt to control her and stifle her independ-ence. She slammed the door to their adjoining hotel rooms and rejected him, the bookings, and the four fur coats—two mink, one ermine, and one leopard trimmed in leather—he had given her. "I had the feeling of being bought!" she lamented, jettisoning Sokal from her life and art, in spite of his beating on the hotel's walls and doors and threatening suicide, threats that proved as hollow as her resolve to banish him forever.

Leni's life as a dancer came to an effective end four months later in Prague, when she injured her left knee onstage. After limping painfully through a few remaining engagements, she consulted orthopedic spe-cialists in Germany, Holland, and Switzerland. They advised rest, and more rest. Her entire career on the dance stage had lasted eight months—from October 1923 to June 1924—but remained in her memory the most fulfilling part of her life. As a centenarian, she declared, "I wish with body and soul that I had stayed a dancer. Of all the things I have done in my life as an artist, it was dancing that most fascinated me and made me happy."

The claim is easy enough to credit. Dancing was her youth, the begin-ning of fame, and the end of dependency. Never again would she have to endure the humiliation of being dismissed as mediocre or the impotence of being anonymous or, paradoxically, have the freedom to strive and fail that anonymity affords, heedless of costs or consequences. And when she danced, she danced alone, in splendid isolation.

Even Sokal later allowed that he deserved no credit beyond facilitating the initial engagement in Munich. He was frank about that gesture as a lover's stratagem and admired Leni's brash self-confidence and resource-fulness. She kept a scrapbook of her reviews and edited them into a press book that she printed up and circulated to managers and booking agents. She excerpted her reviews as any performer would, selectively and with the box office in mind. The critic in Berlin who had written that she was merely "an attraction for the vaudeville stage" was not included, nor was the one who called her—meaning well, perhaps—a "charming wonder girl." If a review called her dancing "marvelously gifted" but "problematic," she could still quote the line that referred to "all the grace of a swaying poppy, a bending cornflower." If she misdated a review, making it seem that the critic was reviewing one performance instead of another, no manager was likely to notice or object.

In retrospect, one might conclude that the richest yield of her dance career was the schooling it furnished in publicity and image building. She grew most creative with the reviews in Berlin, written by the career-makers or -breakers that Sokal had cautioned her about. The most widely read was Fred Hildebrandt's in the liberal *Berliner Tageblatt,* so authoritative that it would be reprinted in hardcover for posterity. He wrote discerningly about her concert, comparing her to the divas of modern dance she was clearly hoping to challenge. As Leni quoted what she called his "hymn of praise":

> When one sees this perfectly shaped creation stand in the music, it fleetingly crosses one's mind that there might indeed be splendors of dance that none of the [others] has achieved . . . the glory of the dancer who appears once every thousand years with consummate grace and singular beauty.

This was praise, indeed, and Leni would quote it for the rest of her life, never mentioning—perhaps even forgetting—that Hildebrandt had gone on to write:

> But then this girl begins to unfold her body and the notion wilts: the glory fades, the tone grows flat, a wonderful dummy moves, undoubt-edly taking pleasure in the space around her, filled with thirst for rhythm and longing for music. . . . [But] finally, the sight inspires . . . a quiet sadness that such superficial perfection is not blessed with the grace of an inner gift, with the grandeur of genius, or with the flame of the demonic.

After manipulating others' images of herself, Leni insisted that reality conform to her version. Carefully trimmed press releases became "history," making eight months of dance loom larger and more brilliantly than they had in life, deflecting attention from what came later. Notices for a debutante that were respectably enthusiastic became hosannas announcing the arrival of a genius, the kind "who appears once every thousand years." And this transformation of the ordinary to the heroic would, in time, become her trademark and superlative skill.

It is possible today to see her dance briefly on film, but that is a poor substitute for a live theater full of music, movement, and colored lights. Mostly there are some still photographs and yellowed newspaper clippings. One of them—a review from Berlin's most discerning dance critic, John Schikowski, writing in *Vorwärts*—characterizes the young dancer thus: "All in all, a very strong artistic nature, that within its own territory is perfectly adequate. But that territory is severely limited and lacks the highest, most important quality: that of the soul."

She read that review and quoted from its more enthusiastic passages, but she would never publicly acknowledge the part of the judgment so at odds with her own self-estimation and so far from her aspirations. It is the kind of critique that damns with faint praise, and it may have left a bitter taste, for about the time it appeared, after just eight months on the dance stage, Leni was already moving on.

THREE

CLIMBING

A picture is going to be made. Do you want to collaborate with us?

—Leni Riefenstahl to Harry Sokal, 1925

MOVIES WERE INEVITABLE. Leni shared her crib with them—or nearly so—for the first exhibition of motion pictures before an audience had taken place, in Paris, in 1895, only seven years before she was born. The images that Bertha and Leni treated themselves to at the *Kino* when seeking refuge from Alfred's domestic control had been primitive, mere shadows of things to come from picture pioneers in Berlin and elsewhere who were inventing a grammar of film, making it up as they went along.

Leni's adolescent film foray as a chargirl in that unnamed, forgotten picture was an early signal that she was not immune to the camera's lure, and her tryouts for *Opium* suggested she was undaunted by rejection. After her "unexpected, incomprehensible, unbelievable success" as a dancer, she had not hesitated to detour and test her photogenic potential for Erich Pommer at Berlin's prestigious Ufa film studio. Finally, at some point after she injured her knee, she ignored her doctors' injunctions to rest and secured an unbilled bit part at Ufa in *Ways to Strength and Beauty,* the studio's full-length "culture" documentary that promoted physical fitness and calisthenics as the path to what the filmmakers ambitiously called "regeneration of the human race."

The film was a sensation on its release in 1925, crowded as it was with male and female athletes exercising as their Maker had made them. Censors were mollified by the many scenes alluding to classical antiquity—in several of which Leni appeared nude to the waist, dutifully tending to the needs of a well-upholstered noblewoman of Athens or Rome at her undraped *toilette*. Exposed skin raised eyebrows but little alarm in German films, not when vaudeville and stage shows in Berlin regularly featured fully nude showgirls: A hit of the day at the Komische Oper was a musical revue titled *A Thousand Naked Ladies* (*Tausend nackte Frauen*), which delivered more or less what it promised. If guardians of public morality frowned at displays of flesh, they cheered at what a film historian calls the film's barely concealed "advocacy for restoring Germany's military capability," stripped away in 1919 by the Versailles Treaty. *Die Weltbühne*, a liberal publication, voiced concern that such an uninhibited promotion of health and fitness was a not-very-veiled appeal to "the reestablishment of conscription and compulsory military service."

Ways to Strength and Beauty alluringly promoted athletics in service to the fatherland. Pulchritude and power were not only healthy; they were patriotic. To ensure that the message was clear, director Wilhelm Prager charged Ufa's music director, Dr. Giuseppe Becce, with preparing a score for the film made up entirely of martial music that could be played by pit orchestras and piano players wherever the film appeared.

Leni's unblushing appearance in what was a more or less straightforward propaganda film escaped reviewer attention for all its decorative appeal, though a single publicity still identified her by name in a popular illustrated magazine. She later denied being in the film or even having seen it or heard of it, possibly because she received no billing, unlike her onetime dance teacher Mary Wigman, whose ensemble dancers were also in the film and received credit.

There is another likely explanation. Seen today, *Strength and Beauty* is most notable for its sports footage. Swimming, diving, dancing, group calisthenics, rows upon rows of flawless bodies swaying in coordinated rhythms and geometric patterns flow by, all of them near prototypes for imagery Leni would later perfect as a director (there are even naked African dancers like those she would photograph in middle and old age). It is not unreasonable to imagine that when she reprised such visual motifs a dozen years later in *Olympia*—including generous allusions to antiquity—it seemed prudent to soft-pedal a by then mostly forgotten precedent.

Leni's knee injury healed. Surgery and reconditioning made a return to the dance stage possible in late 1925, with a return engagement in Berlin in January 1926. She had acquired her first apartment away from her parents in the Fasanenstrasse and was still involved with the mostly absent Froitzheim, who continued to suggest marriage by long distance, a limit on independence she continued to resist. Her "comeback" to dance felt like a replay and in the end lasted only a few weeks. "I sensed that I had made no progress," she admitted. "The interruption had been too long," and, after her fleeting debut on film, she was restless again for "something more meaningful."

For the rest of her life, she related in exactly the same way how that something turned up. In June 1924, she was waiting on the elevated platform of Berlin's busy Nollendorfplatz station for a train to carry her to yet another medical probing of her knee. Her attention drifted, she said, to the poster of a nearby cinema announcing *Mountain of Destiny*, "a film about the Dolomites by Dr. Arnold Fanck." The illustration featured a mountaineer "swinging from one wall to the next" against a backdrop of clouds and jagged peaks. She stared "as if hypnotized" while her train arrived and departed without her. She went to the movies instead of to the doctor and saw the film that "changed my life completely."

Mountain of Destiny (*Der Berg des Schicksals*) was the most recent and most impressive example of what were called Alpine films, entertainments that offered spectacular mountain photography in which skiers and climbers communed with and battled nature. Popular with cult audiences, the Alpine genre had recently incorporated dramatic narratives, resulting in box-office success that caught mainstream exhibitors napping.

These outdoor films were the antithesis of the studio films that were the glory of the silent German industry. Those pioneers projecting primitive shadows on the walls in Berlin had found their grammar and their wings, their creative flights powered by the talented designers, architects, and cameramen working on confined studio stages on which they achieved a polish and virtuosity that made Berlin Hollywood's only meaningful international competitor—many would claim its superior—until the coming of sound. Such great classic films as Robert Wiene's *The Cabinet of Dr. Caligari,* Ernst Lubitsch's *Madame DuBarry,* Fritz Lang's *Die Nibelungen,* and—even then being assembled by special-effects artists— Lang's *Metropolis* and F. W. Murnau's *Faust* were all studio-made films, their magic conjured on silent stages from light, shadow, and papier-mâché. They inspired international admiration, nowhere more than in Hollywood, which hired German talent as quickly as passports could be issued.

Alpine films, by contrast, were shot on location and in nature, in sunshine and snow. They glowed with health and appealed to the nationalistic sentiments of German audiences as an indigenous, homegrown counterpart to Hollywood's idealized American West. They seemed as pure as their pristine settings, as removed from the uncertainties of postwar civilization as their cloud banks billowing in silent majesty above the peaks. Their solitary heroes were played not by actors but by climbers and skiers, and their dramas felt like spiritual journeys hinted at in lofty titles like *Mountain of Destiny.*

Alpine narratives were primitive and melodramatic but resonated with ideals of the German Romantic movement and its heroic striving for the unattainable. They pictorialized a relationship of man to nature like that of the poet Novalis, who "listened to the plants conversing with each other," as Heine put it. Critics routinely alluded to the Romantic school when reviewing these films, and every schoolchild recognized the influence of the paintings of Caspar David Friedrich, whose "sweeping unpeopled mountainscapes" (Eric Rentschler's nice phrase) could have served as prototypes for their virtuoso camera work.

Because of the hardships for those making them, the films were the product of a small circle of dedicated specialists who endured months on isolated locations under often-brutal weather conditions. There were no camera tricks to their vertiginous stunts, and if audiences doubted that, titles on-screen assured them that what they saw was as real and as dangerous as it looked. Even the awkward acting of crew members, who often worked before as well as behind the cameras, contributed a feeling of verisimilitude that authenticated the action and stirred audiences weary of the polish and artifice of studio films.

What Leni saw that June day in *Mountain of Destiny*—and on subsequent visits to view it again—was crude and uninflected melodrama. But as a glimpse into a world far from the noisy elbowing of postwar Berlin, it came as a revelation. "The very first images of mountains, clouds, alpine slopes and towering rock fascinated me," she remembered. "I was experiencing a world that I did not know, for I had never seen such mountains. I knew them only from postcards, on which they looked rigid and lifeless. But here, on the screen, they were alive, mysterious, and more entrancingly beautiful than I had ever dreamed mountains could be."

Critic and film theorist Siegfried Kracauer saw *Mountain of Destiny*, too, and thought such films "incomparable achievements" as documents of nature. Dramatically he dismissed them as "sparkling ice-axes and inflated sentiments," but he read subtexts in them that he famously elaborated in *From Caligari to Hitler,* his post–World War II study of German films and their audiences from 1918 to 1933, a work that remains indispensable and controversial. It is commonplace to discount his perceptions as twenty-twenty hindsight, but he was a daily film critic in Germany when the Alpine films were new and wrote about them then with clear-eyed prescience. He detected "a kind of heroic idealism" that was "kindred to Nazi spirit," already struggling for power and intoxicating itself with mystical slogans while rabble-rousing in streets and beer halls. "Immaturity and mountain enthusiasm were one," he later wrote, "symptomatic of an antirationalism on which the Nazis could capitalize." As a Jew and working journalist, he knew that most of these films were shot in "the Holy Tyrol," an intensely Catholic region in which the Austrian

Ski Association, an amalgam of ninety-six ski clubs boasting ten thousand members, voted an Aryans-only policy excluding Jews as early as 1923.

Master of the Alpine film—commonly called its "father"—was Dr. Arnold Fanck, the man who made *Mountain of Destiny*. Fanck was a geological engineer who claimed never to have seen a professional film before he made his first in 1913, editing it in his mother's kitchen on equipment he learned to use by trial and error. Fanck had been sent as an asthmatic child to Davos, where he fell in love with the Alps and became a renowned high-altitude skier. After working as a newsreel cameraman during the war, he began making his own films in 1920 with a documentary called *Wonders of the Snow Shoe,* followed by other ice-and-snow epics he produced through his own small company in his native Freiburg.

He was a gifted innovator who experimented with lenses, camera speeds, and film stocks. He admired avant-garde still photography and adapted its high-contrast images, backlighting, and other art techniques to pictures that moved. He trained a cadre of young cameramen who, as "the Freiburg school," would become some of the most accomplished cinematographers in film history. Cameras were hand-cranked then (at no standard speed) and without viewfinders. A cameraman could only judge exposure, focus, and framing by trial, error, or intuition. The only way to be sure of what he was getting on film was to drape a black cloth over the camera body and look directly through the film itself to see the image *as he was photographing it*. Most often he was blindly judging exposure, focus, and framing while cranking the camera without gloves in subzero weather, as often as not on skis or clinging to the side of a mountain or glacier.

As Fanck's filmmaking grew more confident, he attached cameras to skis for dizzying downhill-racer views or supplied skiers with magnesium torches for nighttime runs that created dramatic chains of fire on film. He experimented with exposures and filters to capture cloud- and mountainscapes that anticipated the images Ansel Adams would later make in Yosemite. He used low angles and backlighting to surround his players with luminous halos that imbued them with the same aura of spiritual grandeur as the mountains they climbed. His sense of drama was crude, his pictorial sense unparalleled. A contemporary writer notes his "diagonal division of the screen, traces, curves and signs in the snow, *Jugendstil* ornaments, circular cut-outs of images, little points emerging on the horizon, which rush up to the camera and then disappear out of the picture in giant close-up." Such images filled *Mountain of Destiny*, and would fill virtually all of the films Leni would make in years to come.

The unpredictability inherent in producing Fanck's films made them difficult to budget and impossible to schedule. In their infancy, they had no established market, and Fanck was forced to distribute them himself, renting theaters to show them in. His turn to story films broadened his audience. Word of mouth and a growing German obsession with outdoor sports attracted viewers—the same ones flocking to *Ways to Strength and Beauty*—in numbers that distributors couldn't help but notice. *Mountain of Destiny* opened in May 1924 in Berlin's Theater am Nollendorfplatz, a legitimate theater Fanck had rented and refitted as a cinema. Even so, it was only after the film's popular success that a distribution company acquired it for general release, around the time Leni bought a ticket and saw it for herself.

She was "spellbound." In her early twenties now, she had a lover who bored her, a dance career interrupted by injury, and a bare smattering of film experience. She no longer needed her mother's complicity or her father's consent. All she needed, she decided, was some way to get from Berlin to the Dolomites, where *Mountain of Destiny* had been filmed, so she could introduce herself to a new destiny of her own.

Harry Sokal hadn't felt banished forever when he and Leni parted four months earlier in Zurich. He had abandoned any notion of a love match, but their affair had been spirited and satisfying, and he was prepared for mutual interest to draw them together again. He was unsurprised, therefore, to hear from Leni shortly after she saw *Mountain of Destiny*. He was sorry about her knee and generously agreed to her suggestion that the Dolomites in July at, say, Lake Caro (the Karer See in

German, or Lago di Carezza in Italian), not far from Innsbruck, sounded like an ideal place for a reunion. He even agreed to Leni's bringing Heinz along, for Sokal liked her younger brother, thought him "a lovely boy," and sympathized with his being forced to study engineering so he could work for Alfred's firm instead of pursuing his dreams of architecture and interior design.

Financed by Sokal, the trio lodged at the luxurious Hotel Karersee. Leni described the scene as "a magic world" that "brought back to mind all the long-forgotten fairy tales of my childhood." She exulted in "red cliffs looming upward from green meadows to the blue heavens; the shimmering colors of tiny mountain lakes, nestled like butterflies among secret, dark-green fir trees." Her detailed recall makes it all the more odd that in none of her accounts of this trip does she mention Sokal's presence or the crucial role he would play in what happened next.

Nor, according to Sokal, had she been candid about *Mountain of Destiny*. She not only never mentioned Fanck's film—let alone that it was her principal motivation for their reunion—but she elaborately affected disinterest in films in general. Sokal thought her beautiful enough to be a film star and had inquired repeatedly if she had any interest in becoming one, a question that was neither idle nor lacking in self-interest. Bored with banking and Innsbruck, he was already dabbling in film finance through Albert Pommer, the older brother of Ufa's Erich Pommer, but whenever he brought the subject up, Leni shrugged. That changed when there was a screening at the Hotel Karersee for film financiers from Rome and Milan to which hotel guests were invited. The film—chosen to encourage interest in local production—was *Mountain of Destiny*. When the screening ended and the lights came up, Leni turned to Sokal and announced loudly enough for everyone to hear, "*That's* the kind of picture I would like to make."

Sokal had no idea she had already seen the film but was uncomfortably aware that she had been attracted to the picture's bronzed leading man, Luis Trenker, who had been discovered by Fanck in nearby Bolzano, where he worked as a mountain guide and architect. As Leni was expressing her enthusiasm, Sokal remembered, "suddenly there was Luis Trenker, standing there with the projector. *He* had shown the film." Leni at once declared, "I'm going to be in your next picture." Trenker, glowing with star aura and never deficient in ego, thought her manner "a trifle exalted" and asked if she knew the first thing about mountain climbing, an activity he took so seriously he composed his own "Mountaineer's Ten Commandments." Leni assured him, "I'll learn how."

"So we talked with Trenker," Sokal said, "and found out that the director, Dr. Arnold Fanck, was staying in Berlin. The *next* day—and that was typical of Leni—she went to Berlin. Which reminds me of one phrase that I heard again and again over the many years that I knew her: 'I *must* meet that man.' Whenever there was an interesting person on the horizon, whether it was an artist or a great sportsman, a great tennis player or a great skier, a great actor or a 'statesman' like Hitler . . . 'I *must* meet that man.' And she always did."

Leni had, by chance and calculation, brought together elements that would change her life, though she could not orchestrate them alone. Her setting out for Berlin with nothing more than a telephone number for Dr. Fanck (supplied by Trenker) would have seemed foolhardy to anyone not familiar with the beginnings of her dance career the previous October. But Sokal had been there and was not surprised to learn that, once in Berlin, Leni called on Günther Rahn, the tennis pro who had arranged her seduction by Otto Froitzheim, and asked him if he could arrange a meeting with Dr. Fanck. He could.

They met at Rumpelmeier's pastry and coffee shop on the Kurfürstendamm. She introduced herself, she said, showed Fanck her photographs and the press book of her dance reviews, told him she intended to be his new star, and left. Then, according to her account, she went directly to a telephone booth and called a young surgeon she knew named Dr. Pribram, who had earlier proposed a never-performed surgical technique that would either restore her injured knee or paralyze it permanently. Insisting that he operate immediately, she checked into the hospital that same evening and was wheeled into surgery the next morning, visions of the Alps swimming through the anesthesia. Though no one knew she was in the hospital or why, she said, an unshaven Dr. Fanck materialized at her bedside three days later with the fully finished screenplay he had feverishly prepared after she left him at Rumpelmeier's. Scrawled across the title page were the words "*The Holy Mountain*, written for the dancer, Leni Riefenstahl."

If we discount the leaps this scenario makes in terms of credibility, we are left with the same sort of impetuous calculation that characterized the start of Leni's dance career and would be repeated at every major turning point in her life. Hers is the only published version of meeting Fanck, but he would later relate privately that he had known who she was from the start and had even seen her dance. Trenker added that, after meeting her in Berlin, Fanck announced by post that Leni was "the most beautiful woman in Europe" and that, with his help as her Pygmalion, she would "soon be the most famous woman in Germany."

Sokal offers an intriguing variant to these accounts. He recalled that three days after Leni left Lake Caro for Berlin, she sent him a telegram saying she had met Fanck, who was already writing a script for her. "A picture is going to be made," she wrote. "Do you want to collaborate with us?"

Sokal did. He wrapped up his affairs in Innsbruck and left for Berlin and Ufa. Sokal joined Fanck as producing partner in *The Holy Mountain* and made a personal cofinancing agreement with Ufa for its production and distribution. It was the first time a Fanck picture had ever had a distributor and outside financing before production began.

In his own way, Sokal was as impetuous and calculating as Leni, for his deal-making with Ufa went beyond *The Holy Mountain*. He discovered through banking contacts that Fanck's firm, the Freiburg Mountain and Sport Film Company, which included elaborate developing and printing facilities, was near bankruptcy as the result of Fanck's filmmaking. Sokal persuaded Ufa to join him in buying out Fanck's company, while acquiring personal options on future Fanck productions. Leni's starring in *The Holy Mountain* was accomplished without so much as an audition, and, though her casting may not have been a condition of Sokal's cofinancing the film, a partner's recommendation cannot have hurt.

Sokal later said that he recognized as soon as he arrived in Berlin that Fanck was "very much in love with Leni and, well, I must say this: when the shooting of the picture started, my personal relationship with Leni was at an end." Looking back, he insisted, "I don't think she started her love affair with Fanck because she thought that he was going to direct a picture with her. Maybe it influenced her a little bit, but not much. When she had sexual relations with a man, it was *not* for purely sexual reasons. It was always the personality of the man that interested her, that made the man attractive. It was never purely sexual."

Leni maintained that she had no sexual relationship with Fanck, though he "grew more deeply in love with me day by day." Fortunately, her convalescence from the knee operation gave Fanck time to prepare the film and to cast Luis Trenker as her leading man. Leni, meanwhile, learned that Otto Froitzheim was dallying with a woman he met on an exhibition tennis tour of Italy and seized on his philandering as the excuse to break their engagement. Looking back, she called it, without elaboration, "the most painful decision I had ever made."

Free of Froitzheim and with a January start date for *The Holy Mountain*, Leni was relieved to find that her knee operation had been successful. She could embark on her film career and resume dancing later in the year, the comeback that would quickly begin and quickly end. "That was a very schizophrenic time for me," she acknowledged. "I loved this and I loved *that*, and it was an internal struggle for many months. But I decided on film."

The Holy Mountain was a love-triangle melodrama with pretensions to tragedy that may have been conceived before Fanck ever met Leni and that he retailored to her talents by making the female character a dancer. She was "Diotima," a beautiful young woman from the city with an affinity for the sea, at whose edge she dances in the film's prologue. The sea, a title reads, "is her love, but her life is her dance, the expression of her stormy soul." Diotima is dancing professionally at a luxurious Alpine resort much like the Hotel Karersee. She meets two uncomplicated villagers who are best friends; each falls in love with her without suspecting the other's interest. Trenker was the mountain climber called "The Friend," while "Vigo" was played by Fanck's nephew, Ernst Petersen, a competitive skier like the character he played. The rivals find themselves at the picture's climax high in the mountains, bound to each other by a rope as Vigo dangles over an icy mountain crag and cannot be pulled to safety. There is no escape unless The Friend cuts Vigo loose to fall to his death. The mountaineers' code triumphs. The Friend leaps into the abyss, still tied to his comrade and choosing death over betrayal. Diotima is left to mourn them both and descends from the mountains back to the sea where she expresses her grief in dance.

The picture explicitly contrasts the purity of the mountains with the corrupted flatland, a high-low thematic opposition that would mark almost all of Leni's creative work. Characters do not confront each other with emotions but with worldviews. Early on, Diotima encounters the Trenker character as he is about to go climbing. "It must be beautiful up there," she muses in the intertitles. "Beautiful, hard, and dangerous," he confirms. "And what do you seek up there?" she asks. "Myself," he answers. "And nothing else?" she queries. "What do *you* seek up here—in nature?" he challenges. "Beauty!" she says, to which he replies, "And nothing else?"

The Holy Mountain offered the conspicuous photographic beauties of all Fanck's films but added a new dimension in showcasing Leni and her dancing. The picture began with full-screen close-ups of her face with her eyes closed ("a death mask," remarks one film historian), serving notice that Fanck had discovered a new female star, an unexpected element in a film about masculine heroics. Fanck had featured women in perfunctory sweetheart roles before, but Leni's presence marked the first time a woman provided a central focus and dramatic fulcrum. Romantic rivalry transformed man versus nature into man versus man *in* nature, though comradeship remained the sacred virtue. "A love story between two men," one scholar describes it, "brought to a head over the body of a woman."

Leni performed dances she had done onstage and adapted them herself for the screen, a signal that she readily grasped the nature of film composition as opposed to the three-dimensional world of the stage or concert hall. Ufa agreed to supply her with a pianist during rehearsals, both for the film (though it was silent) and to prepare for the dance comeback that lay still ahead. For the actual shooting, Fanck hired a violinist who played while suspended by rope from a cliff overhanging the seashore where Leni danced to the rhythm of waves whose crashing made the violin inaudible. A pit orchestra would play a score in theaters, its rhythms cued to Leni's movements on-screen.

Fanck's films always sacrificed character to the elements, and *The Holy Mountain* was no exception. The love triangle set the narrative in motion but was abandoned except for an elaborate hallucination fantasy once the mountain ascent began that led to the film's climax. Diotima's dancing is dramatically irrelevant. She is merely the decorative pretext for getting the two rivals on the icy crag, where they can die not for love of her but, as the titles announce, for "the great word that stands over mankind—*Fidelity* [*Die Treue*]." Death is nobler than survival; comradeship trumps romantic love. The woman remains an outsider, picturesquely suffering the tragedy her presence has set in motion, both figure of Fate and its victim, the paradigm Leni would later apply to her own life.

By all accounts, she was genuinely inspired by the purity of the mountains. Isolation felt like freedom and solitude; altitude was exalting; extremes of weather were bracing; even the absence of creature comforts seemed to confer virtue. She was eager to endure hardship, if only because Trenker had openly derided her ability to do so. But she learned to ski; to climb; and to endure cold, wind, and the physical ailments that went with them. She could thrive as the only female among a dozen or more men, living for months in tents and cabins in bitterly cold weather and still smile for the cameras. Physical courage was the one personal quality she possessed that colleagues and even enemies could later praise without reservation.

She was too finely attuned to upward mobility not to appreciate that

Fanck offered her unique entrée into a notoriously risky profession. His film world was not for the faint of heart or the conventionally ambitious; its hazards were too real for that. But Leni could also see that she had broadened the appeal of a heretofor limited genre and had secured with one film a niche in the film world that no other actress was willing or able to fill. Which did not preclude conflict.

To prepare for *The Holy Mountain*, she had gone with Fanck to Freiburg shortly before Christmas. At his private studio, she submitted to two screen tests, one tense and labored that made her look "ugly and strange," and a second, more relaxed, that gave her the confidence to trust Fanck's cameras and lights and that revealed to her from the outset "that film without technique is nothing."

Trenker came to Freiburg, too. Leni's interest in him ensured tension with Fanck, whom she tended to take for granted, "because he loved me." Trenker was another matter. Sleeping with him represented "the first time that I ever lay in a man's arms under the spell of a happiness I had never known before." When Fanck discovered his stars enjoying spells of happiness in his own home, he reacted. As in almost all Leni's portraits of lovers she rejected, Fanck "looked thunderstruck" and threatened suicide. He ran from the house in the middle of the night, she said, to throw himself into the river from an ice-covered bridge. Leni rescued him with the help of passersby and checked him into the hospital. She then asked herself, with no apparent sense of chagrin, "What would happen now? What was I to do? The film couldn't possibly be made."

Fanck was released the next day "raving like a madman," as Leni remembered it. His own recollection of events was somewhat different. "As I walked through the library into my living room after dinner," he recalled, "Leni was sitting on the corner of my sofa—and in front of her on his knees was Luis Trenker. That's the First Act, I thought, and withdrew discreetly." The scene would, in fact, turn up in the film almost as Fanck described it, though it would be Trenker observing his rival's head in Diotima's lap, the crisis of (mis)comprehension that would send the hero on his fatal climb.

In spite of his "sexual obsession" for Leni and her unsettling effect on his personal life, Fanck appreciated her value to his films. In an unpublished interview three years before his death in 1974, he confirmed that he had seen Leni dance before writing his script and thought her "like a child. And the public liked that very much. She still had this naïveté." That childlike quality and careless audacity he encountered in real life inspired his script. "What if a dancer like this meets a man from the mountains?" he asked. "They would fly towards each other, but then it would probably end in catastrophe." He accepted the irony that he had supplied the catastrophe with his casting. "Then Trenker came. He had the right profile, the right face. He fell in love with her and vice-versa, and by the close of the film, the unhappiness was already there."

There, too, was Leni's skill at dominating the exclusively male society in which she found herself now and for almost all the rest of her professional life. Her father had accustomed her to confrontations with men, and she had learned early to stand her ground. She knew how to charm or burst into tears, and then there were what she called the "love things."

"All of them were in love with me," she said, "the director and Trenker and all of them and I couldn't leave [the location]. Oh, it was a drama always!" The conflicts and tension that began in Freiburg with Fanck and Trenker continued in the Tyrol with an augmented cast of characters.

Fanck's script called for Leni to ski and do some climbing through the snow, skills she didn't yet have. She went to Cortina d'Ampezzo with Trenker, where cameraman Hans Schneeberger joined them. Schneeberger was Trenker's best friend, an experienced downhill racer nicknamed "Snow-flea" because of his effortless leaps and jumps on skis. Leni took skiing lessons from him that encouraged familiarity. A predicament was averted when she almost at once broke bones in her foot, the first in a series of injuries and mishaps to plague production: Schneeberger injured his spine in a ski race; Ernst Petersen, as Vigo, broke his foot; Hannes Schneider, a famous Austrian ski champion who taught Diotima to ski in the film, broke his thigh in four places and almost died. Weather added its delays, and January's shooting was pushed back until April, by which time the major set constructed for the film, an enormous cavern cum ice palace that was Trenker's hallucination at the end of the film—"the holy mountain" in which he and Diotima wander in a dream/fantasy sequence—melted as the *Föhn*, the warm wind peculiar to the Alps, thawed ice that had been painstakingly shaped for months on an armature of metal pipes.

By April, the film's principals were bivouacked in a remote mountain cabin overnight. Leni said that she was forced to sleep between her lover and his best friend on a single bunk and that Trenker misinterpreted the position of her head on Schneeberger's arm. Fanck, also present, maintained that he heard arguing during the night and chose to consider it "none of my business." The next morning, however, "I go out in front of the hut and discover one of the two on the very top of those mountains which are difficult to climb; then I see the other one on a different mountain peak. For me this is *The Holy Mountain*, Third Act. Oh, well," he added fatalistically. "I was a dramatist."

Sokal had still another version and thought it affected the picture. "Leni always confided in me after our intimate relationship had ended," he said. "I know *everything* about her up to a certain time, including that Trenker was the one man she couldn't conquer. She slept with Trenker [but couldn't win him] and tried to find consolation sleeping with Schneeberger—the same night! Crying her heart out because she just couldn't conquer Trenker. When I saw what was happening, I was worried to death, because that couldn't go well with the production. So I tried to get out of the contract and got Ufa to take the whole picture."

With Sokal's withdrawal, Ufa, unaccustomed to location shooting that was beyond studio control, grew impatient with delays and summoned Fanck to Berlin, threatening to shut down the picture. Fanck took footage with him, leaving the others behind. Leni offered to sell some jewelry to buy film stock so they might continue shooting in his absence, with Leni directing her own performance. She and Schneeberger filmed some scenes of Diotima that they sent to Berlin for Fanck's approval, and Leni later claimed that he wired back: "Congratulations! Ufa wild about rushes. Film to be completed." Fanck's private assessment of the footage, he said late in life, was "very nice pictures of Leni with a little crown of flowers in her hair, picking flowers, shots of romping sheep, and so on. A little bit too sweet, but photographically very beautiful." Leni's footage stayed in the picture.

Ufa was sufficiently impressed by Fanck's own footage to allow him to continue, not anticipating injuries and weather conditions that would extend production for the better part of two years. *The Holy Mountain* had officially begun production in January 1925 and finally premièred on December 17, 1926, at Ufa's Palast am Zoo, the company's flagship theater in Berlin. Leni danced onstage before the film began to a pit orchestra playing Schubert's *Unfinished* Symphony. She continued her performances during a then-phenomenal five-week run. The picture was a popular breakthrough in Germany and, when it opened in England, France, and America, became the first international success of Fanck's career.

The Holy Mountain launched Leni at home and abroad. Her reviews were mostly gratifying, and one, in the *Neueste Nachrichten* in Vienna, hailed her as "one of the greatest actresses in film." Cooler heads prevailed in Berlin, where the *Morgenpost* wrote that "as an actress Leni Riefenstahl gives nothing. Nor does she photograph to much advantage. Her hopping around is here and there hardly bearable." But critics had negligible effect at the box office and little if any on audiences, who found her "hopping around" artistic and provocative. So did the reviewer who had earlier written that her performing onstage lacked "soul." He reversed his opinion in finding her dancing on film "a complete work of art" that was "at least as effective as the original dance on stage." When the picture opened in New York in 1927 as *Peaks of Destiny*, the reviewer for the *New York Times* noted: "Leni Riefenstahl, who impersonates the dancer, is an actress with no little charm. Her overacting is to be blamed on Dr. Fanck."

She was a new kind of star and, for Fanck, a new kind of muse. She had suffered frozen eyelashes and frostbitten fingers and toes; had survived entanglements with Sokal, Fanck, Trenker, and Schneeberger; and was now poised on some high-altitude pinnacle of movie fame where the obvious question was clear as the Alpine air: How high is up?

FOUR

HIGHER

. . . so near the clouds and the stars . . .
—Leni Riefenstahl

Thou shalt undertake no ascent without being ready. . . . Thou shalt take thy time to reach thy maximum strengths, and not race the second hand of the stopwatch. Thou shalt not devour the peaks.
—Luis Trenker

"THE FILM IS A MASTERPIECE," Siegfried Kracauer wrote of *The Holy Mountain* when the picture was first released, but only, he elaborated, for "small youth groups that attempt to counter everything that they call mechanization by means of an overrun nature worship [and] a panic-stricken flight into the foggy brew of vague sentimentality." His critique was blistering but is most notable for being a contemporary view and not the product of conventional hindsight.

Other voices on the right and on the left were raised with equal vigor to point out themes that may have been unintended in an adventure film but reflected cultural and political issues that were pervasive in the Weimar Republic even when it came to the livelier arts. A Berlin reviewer wrote of the film that "there is an outpouring of more unbearable braggadocio here, more bloated bamboozlement and deceit than in a score of

Hitler rallies." The critic for *Die Weltbühne* deplored master race aesthetics in "the obtrusive propaganda for noble-blond, high-altitude humanity." The right-wing press was more favorably impressed. "The holy mountain rises like a symbol," one conservative paper wrote. "The path German film must follow leads upwards, steep and rocky"—and then, in caps—"THIS WAY, GERMAN FILM, TO THE HOLY MOUNTAIN OF YOUR REBIRTH AND THAT OF THE GERMAN PEOPLE!"

The Holy Mountain is a rarity and an oddity now. It has fallen into that gulf of oblivion where most silent films reside and is exhumed from time to time mainly because of its pairing of Leni and Trenker, both of whom became major film figures in the Third Reich and personal antagonists until Trenker died in 1992. Leni's Diotima, seen today, is the performance of a newcomer, one who labors under dated conventions of film acting already abandoned by the subtlest and most advanced practitioners of the silent era. She is pretty without being a superlative beauty, and her eagerness to please has charm, but the future belonged to the cooler underplaying of Garbo and Dietrich—both of them in Berlin at the time, working less hard and to greater effect. Her dancing, in one of the two filmed records we have of it, is energetic, forceful but strenuous, and lacking in fluidity, grace, and—surprisingly—sex appeal.

Her shortcomings were partly those of her director, whose powers as an innovator were offset by limitations that made *The Holy Mountain* little more than beautiful pictures about sentimental heroics. But for all his weaknesses—more apparent now than then—Fanck was Leni's professor as well as her patron. He gave her a foundation in filmmaking that would prove indispensable for everything that followed. She would later be cruelly disparaging of him in private, but in public, she acknowledged what is surely true. "He taught me that everything has to be equally well photographed: people, animals, clouds, water, ice. Every single shot, said Fanck, had to be above mere mediocrity; the most important thing was to avoid routine and to see everything with absolutely fresh eyes."

Sold-out performances of *The Holy Mountain* at Berlin's premier movie palace altered Fanck's reputation from pioneer eccentric to main-stream success. Leni's presence had given his film a romantic dimension that expanded his audience, but her habit of referring publicly to *The Holy Mountain* as *her* film and ceaselessly reminding the press that it was "already dedicated to me when in manuscript" nettled him. Particularly galling was her boast to *Film-Kurier,* the widely read Berlin counterpart of *Variety:* "I have every reason to call it my own. It is not just that I play the main part in it [*sic*]. I was also involved in the direction, working together a great deal with my director, Dr. Fanck."

Industry insiders may have smiled at the boasting of a tyro, but Fanck did not. Leni was not just another new star grabbing credit. She was a woman who had toyed with his emotions by encouraging and then frus-trating his sexual attraction to her, betraying him serially with his colleagues in the close-knit world he introduced her into, not just Trenker and Schneeberger, but cameraman Sepp Allgeier and Hannes Schneider, too, the Austrian ski champion who taught Leni's Diotima to ski and—after the Nazis imprisoned him and then allowed him to emigrate to America—voiced bitter regret that he had ever been involved with her, on-screen or off.

Fanck found it particularly difficult to adjust to Trenker as a rival. Their relationship was further strained when Trenker derided Leni to the press as an "oily goat," blaming her for a decline in Fanck's artistic powers, a gratuitous suggestion that was as debatable as it was painful. The airing of insults hinted at a newsworthy romantic rivalry to the press, which was useful to Leni's image (and to Trenker's) but damaging to Fanck's marriage. He would soon leave his wife and Freiburg for Berlin, but rumors in the tabloid press attracted the attention of Ufa, on which he was dependent for financing after Sokal's withdrawal in the wake of Leni's casual affairs and the commotion they caused.

Fanck had already written a new script for Leni and Trenker called *A Winter's Tale (Ein Wintermärchen)*, full of fantasy scenes like the hallu-cinatory dream sequence of *The Holy Mountain,* a scenic tour de force, which, for all its icy splendor, had had almost no dramatic impact and suggested to Ufa an inclination toward grandiosity whenever Fanck strayed from skiing and mountaineering.

A Winter's Tale had been made to measure for actors who were now openly feuding. It was set in what Leni called "a dream world of snow, ice, and light" that featured dual roles for both stars (one of Leni's was a dancer). She thought the script prefigured the films of Walt Disney, though the existing pages suggest a darker version of Oz, with scenes set in a sunless Berlin tenement like the one Leni grew up in and featuring another bizarre ice castle, complete with ice king and queen. The time and cost overruns of *The Holy Mountain* had unsettled Ufa executives. This new venture looked dubious, particularly for a company staggering under the burden of Fritz Lang's *Metropolis,* the most expensive film in Ufa's history, which proved, in spite of its influence and reputation, a box-office disaster. It plunged the studio into the most serious of its recurrent financial crises, precipitating a change of ownership that had ominous overtones.

The new master of Ufa was right-wing publisher Alfred Hugenberg, future chairman of the right-wing German National People's Party and Hitler's finance minister in the early days of the Third Reich. When Hugenberg took control of Ufa in March 1927, shortly after the release of *The Holy Mountain,* he stated publicly that he had done so to further the "national cause," an open challenge to the already shaky Weimar Republic.

Hugenberg's critics said his power derived from his knowledge of people and "their taste for the mediocre, their lack of civic courage, their intellectual dullness, and their gullibility." An early media mogul of vast influence, he brought desperately needed funding to Ufa, which had, in fact, been born as a political entity and had never been, like its French and American rivals, a product of laissez-faire capitalism. The company had been created secretly by Gen. Erich Ludendorff and the German high command in 1917 as a propaganda tool in the final days of the Great War. With Hugenberg now at the helm, it could express political views that pleased right-wing industrialists, nationalists, and Ufa's creditor banks, who were mostly in overlapping camps. Still, Hugenberg was a businessman, eager above all to make money and avoid risk.

Hugenberg's Ufa rejected *A Winter's Tale*, and Fanck abruptly substituted an innocuous ski picture that could begin shooting in May. *The Great Leap* (*Der grosse Sprung*) was a comedy, another attempt by Fanck to extend his range, but one that seemed perversely inspired by Trenker's notorious "oily goat" remark. Leni was cast as "Gita the goat girl," a simpleminded goatherd in bizarre peasant costumes that submerged the physical charms she had displayed in *The Holy Mountain*. Trenker agreed to turn in another of his trademarked hero-of-bronze performances, but not as Leni's love interest. That role went to cameraman Schneeberger, the only member of Fanck's team who could perform acrobatic skiing stunts, including pratfalls in an inflated rubber suit that made him resemble the Michelin Man and cushioned his comic somersaults, including the one that landed him on the back of a startled cow. Fanck justified casting Leni as the goat girl by saying he "felt sorry for her" after Trenker's remarks to the press, but it looked as much like revenge as sympathy. Leni, thumbing her nose at both men, accepted the challenge of slapstick in the snow for which she had neither the training nor the comedic talent.

She may have endured the indignities for the sake of her new lover. She had moved from her small flat in the Fasanenstrasse into a penthouse apartment at Hindenburgstrasse 97 in Berlin-Wilmersdorf together with Schneeberger, now officially her companion as well as her cameraman and costar. Coincidentally or not, the other penthouse on the sixth floor belonged to Sokal and the actress he would marry, Agnes Esterhazy.

Schneeberger—"Snowflea"—was seven years older than Leni, "but he was a child," as Sokal remembered him, who "liked to be protected by a woman." Even Leni admitted, "He liked being led. He was the passive partner, I the active one." Slight and dark, with an imposing nose beneath gentle, mournful eyes, Schneeberger was from the Austrian Tyrol and, like Trenker, had studied architecture. During the war, he had been decorated for bravery in a famous military incident in Italy. Though he and Leni had already been intimate, their love affair began in earnest when

Fanck ordered Schneeberger to teach her the fundamentals of climbing for *The Great Leap,* insisting she learn to scale the razor-sharp Dolomites as a goatherd would—barefoot. If any undertaking illustrated Leni's courage and determination to achieve authenticity on-screen, this was it. Her dance training had strengthened her feet sufficiently to prevent missteps even on near-vertical walls that she clung to without dizziness, exhilarated by the altitude. It was "a terrible grind," she said, but "a marvelous feeling to be so free, so remote from the world, and so near the clouds and the stars."

The Great Leap shot from May to November, with supplemental studio shooting in Berlin. It opened at the Ufa Palast am Zoo on December 20, 1927, a year and three days after *The Holy Mountain* had opened there, but slapstick did nothing to advance Leni's reputation as an actress, and even the barefoot climbing scenes, which had drawn blood on location, were written off by reviewers as having been faked in the studio.

Depressed by the film's reception, Leni fled Berlin for St. Moritz and the 1928 Winter Olympics, which Fanck was filming with multiple cameras and cameramen, including Schneeberger. No official Olympics film had previously been made, and, though Fanck was the obvious candidate, his film was a perfunctory record of events, not enlivened by the triumphs of Norway's teenage ice-skating star, Sonja Henie.

Leni had obtained a commission from *Film-Kurier* to report on the event. Her article appeared on February 17, 1928, and notes the colorful entrance of the competitors, flags flying as they marched into the stadium, colors brilliant "as Persian carpets" against the snow. Her written impressions suggest events she would later film with famous results: "Prelude to the Olympics," she wrote, "the strongest right at the beginning! Twenty-five nations march into the ice stadium in a snowstorm. It is bitter cold, but so what? This is the moment that gives the Olympics meaning: twenty-five nations united. The crowd cheers and hurrahs and shouts with joy." She was proud of her journalistic debut and would recycle it in her first autobiographical book in 1933, the year Hitler came to power, describing the "brotherhood" among the participants: "There are the fighters, the sports heroes—proudly they carry their flag, proud to be the chosen of their land." Her eye for beauty and atmosphere quickened at the sight of "so many beautiful people . . . men with bronzed faces, girls sweet as they are in films. Everybody meets at Sunny-Corner, at Bob's, or at Hanselmann's for cocktails. Everything so cheerful, gay, and competitive under the famous Engadine sun in a blue winter sky."

After St. Moritz, Leni resigned herself to the "gray hell" of Berlin. She found that, after the volatile relationships with Sokal, Fanck, and Trenker, living and working with Schneeberger made the ordeal of *The Great Leap* endurable, but the picture had aimed at Buster Keaton's art without Keaton's genius. Fanck's humor was forced and crude. Once again he was the master of cliffs and clouds, out of his element with actors.

Leni already found Fanck wanting as an artist and a colleague, though she did nothing to discourage his writing love letters to her even after she began living with Schneeberger. She registered no qualms about accepting a grand piano from him, above which she hung an oil portrait of herself by Eugen Spiro. Fanck's value as a teacher was simply too great to forgo in the absence of any other mentor bearing other offers.

And then, surprisingly, there was an assignment that had nothing to do with mountains, skis, or Fanck. Her first picture away from him came after *The Great Leap* opened and was filmed quickly in Vienna without attracting any attention whatever. *The Fate of the House of Hapsburg—Tragedy of an Empire* (*Das Schicksal derer von Habsburg—die Tragödie eines Kaiserreiches*) dramatized the story of Mayerling and the double suicide of Crown Prince Rudolf and his mistress Baroness Marie Vetsera. Leni was cast as the unlucky Vetsera but came down with diphtheria after arriving in Vienna with Bertha, now her most devoted fan. She got through the role and the picture, but the film is lost except for a few sequences in which she does not appear. It created so little stir that even close associates such as Sokal were unaware she had made it. She admitted the film's existence and her part in it only reluctantly (claiming she had never seen it), after researchers unearthed fragments in the 1980s, almost six decades after it was made.

Having Sokal as a next-door neighbor on the penthouse floor in the Hindenburgstrasse proved fortuitous. Since his initiation into the film business with *The Holy Mountain*, he had established himself as a producer with two conspicuous pictures: *The Golem*, with Paul Wegener, and *The Student of Prague*, with Conrad Veidt. Both were remakes, but prestigious and successful ones. He released them under his own Sokal Film banner, a going concern that gave him credibility with bankers that Fanck lacked.

Socially, the onetime lovers remained compatible and used their adjoining penthouse space to entertain. Sokal knew Leni's career was languishing after *The Great Leap*, and he was willing to cohost soirées that might result in projects for either or both of them. Bella Fromm, the social and diplomatic reporter for Berlin's liberal *Vossische Zeitung*, wrote that they "entertained lavishly" for such guests as heavyweight champion Max Schmeling, World War I aviation ace Ernst Udet, and—on a return visit from Hollywood—film director Ernst Lubitsch. When not entertaining with Sokal or when Schneeberger was shooting a film, Leni looked in on the salon of Betty Stern, a vibrant Jewish hostess who loved intrigue and being a friend of the famous. Stern introduced her favorites to one another (Elisabeth Bergner and Dietrich among them) for romance or jobs, a social skill she converted to a career as an agent in Paris after the Third Reich diminished the cachet of Jewish hostesses in Berlin.

Leni was a small fish in a large pond and—however gray her hell—immersed herself in it. She saw Josephine Baker dance in bananas and marveled at Anna Pavlova in tulle. She met the young editor of an automobile magazine named Erich Maria Remarque, who was struggling with a fondness for cognac, a faithless wife, and a manuscript he would title *All Quiet on the Western Front*. She saw and was electrified by Sergei Eisenstein's *Battleship Potemkin*, a huge popular success in Berlin. She made friends with Walter Ruttmann, whose dawn-to-dusk documentary *Berlin: Symphony of a Great City* blazed still-fresh trails for future filmmakers, including herself. She tried her hand at screenplays, such as *Maria*, "a love story with a tragic ending," that she tailored to herself and that never got made.

Berliners still call this period "the Golden Twenties." Darkness would soon fall, but our contemporary images of the city as decadent and doomed come largely from images created later (*Cabaret* is only the most obvious example) that retroactively overlay awareness of tragedies yet to come. The reality of the city was more various. It was a bubbling stew of entertainments of all kinds—sentimental or raucous amusements, avant-garde experiments, and calculated provocations, all of them shadowed by a war that they had survived but that none had escaped, as Remarque's dedication in *All Quiet* famously noted. Leni moved among the revelers and the rebels but was not suited by schooling or temperament to endorse or challenge the pieties of convention. She considered herself an artist, but an intuitive one searching for a cause, a mission, or an aesthetic that would inspire and fire her imagination.

She was impulsive, not intellectual, and there were curious gaps in her cultural background. She admitted to being twenty-three before she ever heard of *Penthesilea*, Heinrich von Kleist's drama in verse about the last Amazon queen and Achilles. A major work of dramatic literature, Kleist's play (Leni called it a "story") was regularly performed on Berlin stages of the 1920s. Not knowing then who Penthesilea was might be compared to a present-day aspiring actor in the English-speaking world never having heard of Mary Tyrone or Major Barbara. Kleist's warrior-queen would eventually obsess Leni, but as a young actress, her sketchy education put her at a disadvantage, and her tastes remained naïve in an age of sophisticated experiments. The jazzy dissonance of Brecht and Weill's prostitutes and petty gangsters did not sing to her sensibilities: She wanted to distance herself from their lowlife world, not hum along with it. She remained culturally a tourist in the city of her birth, a sightseer sampling other people's art while trying to find ways, means, and creative motivation for her own.

The one thing she could do that no other actress could was sell tickets while climbing mountains. In spite of *The Jazz Singer's* opening in America in late 1927 and the interest in (and threat of) talkies, there remained an audience faithful to the mute grandeur of Alpine films.

Their aura of remote, heroic isolation was enhanced, not diminished, by silence, and, though sound would finally change everything, live music from the orchestra pit was enough for now and could not drown out the eloquence of the silent moving image.

Fanck, meanwhile, was scrambling for new projects. He sat down and "in a single night" wrote a treatment for another mountain film focused again on a woman and two men. He tried to sell the new project to Universal, then actively engaged in film production in Germany, but the company's American office found the story thin. Fanck showed it to Harry Sokal over lunch and a glass of wine in Berlin. "It was six or eight pages," Sokal recalled, "and I wrote a contract during lunch, buying the treatment, the shooting script, engaging him as director, and committing to a contract for Leni to play the lead. Everything on a paper napkin." Sokal, hoping his involvement as producer, after *The Golem* and *The Student of Prague,* might cause Ufa to reconsider working with Fanck, took the project to them, and "they *laughed* at me. They said, 'That's an expensive picture and it's quite out of the ordinary and there is no star in it—Leni Riefenstahl doesn't mean a thing.' "

Sokal was convinced enough of the commercial appeal of Fanck's story to undertake interim financing on his own. Negotiating with Leni, he cited Ufa's verdict on her star appeal as grounds for a reduced fee, which triggered her indignant claim that he "tried to take financial advantage of me by offering a fee amounting to only ten per cent of what I had received for any previous role." She attributed his parsimony not to Ufa's lukewarm reaction or to business conditions but to a desire to inflict humiliation. Sokal countered her solipsism by explaining that his money was so tight he didn't have funds to insure the actors, much less pay their normal fees. Eventually Leni's money was doubled from two thousand to four thousand marks, with Fanck contributing half that sum from his own fee, still netting her only a fifth of what she was used to.

She was in no financial position to turn down work, but she was also determined to broaden her range and image and saw a way to break free of Fanck's limitations. She badgered Sokal that Fanck could not direct the dramatic sequences of the picture, now titled *The White Hell of Piz Palü* (*Die weisse Hölle vom Piz Palü*). Sokal was taken aback, but, in the end, her suggestion smacked less of betrayal or disloyalty than it seemed a shrewd aesthetic judgment. He respected Fanck as "a man who knew the mountains and everything that could happen in the mountains—comedy or drama or tragedy. But he knew *nothing* about *people*." Fanck knew enough, however, to resist sharing responsibility on what was his own story and project. "But he agreed to it finally," Sokal said, "not thinking [the other director] necessary, of course, and that's what made it a great picture."

The other director was G. W. Pabst, one of the most prestigious talents in Europe. He had directed Garbo in *The Joyless Street*, the picture that took the Swedish actress to Hollywood and screen immortality. He would soon direct a talking and singing version of Brecht and Weill's *The Threepenny Opera* with Lotte Lenya. He is perhaps best known today for directing American actress Louise Brooks as Wedekind's notorious Lulu in *Pandora's Box*, the picture he had just finished shooting when he accepted Sokal's bid to join Fanck in codirecting *The White Hell of Piz Palü*.

Pabst was a peculiar choice for an Alpine film but a tantalizing one for a young actress hoping to make the indelible impression Garbo had made under his guidance, a feat even Louise Brooks could duplicate. He was regarded as a psychological realist with penetrating insights into the darker areas of human behavior, exactly the kind of human terrain that eluded Fanck. Pabst brought with him from *Pandora's Box* Gustav Diessl, who had played Jack the Ripper to Louise Brooks's Lulu, and screenwriter Ladislaus Vajda to add psychological depth to Fanck's one-dimensional adventure script.

The story resembled his earlier triangular melodramas: A doctor, enigmatic and melancholy, returns to the mountain of Piz Palü, where his bride died in an avalanche for which he blames himself. On the mountain, he meets a honeymooning couple, played by Leni and Ernst Petersen (Vigo in *The Holy Mountain*). The honeymooners insist on joining the doctor on his dangerous climb to the site of his wife's disappearance. There the trio are trapped—as the wife had been—by an avalanche and almost freeze to death. Their salvation comes in a daredevil airplane rescue by real-life aviator Ernst Udet, but the mournful doctor stays behind—cocooned in ice—sacrificing himself for the young couple as expiation for his wife's death.

Shooting in Berlin and the extremely high altitudes of Switzerland's Bernina Alps took place from January to June 1929, a concentrated production period that reflected the efficiency of Pabst's studio training as much as it did Sokal's desire for economy. Leni protested having to work with Gustav Diessl as the doctor ("The picture will be ruined," she predicted in a striking error of judgment) and charged that Fanck, pursuing authenticity, treated her sadistically in the climbing sequences, notably when staged avalanche scenes unexpectedly turned real and almost suffocated her while Fanck's cameras kept turning. An assistant director on the film agreed that "Pabst and Fanck both had a secret sadistic drive. We really froze. . . . And I must say Riefenstahl was wonderful, never mind what she did later during the Third Reich. In this picture she was driving herself as hard as anybody and more." So hard, in fact, that extended periods of subzero temperatures brought on severe frostbite and a permanent bladder infection.

The more interesting result was that Leni never gave a performance— even under her own direction—that was so unmannered and convincing. For the first time on-screen, she seemed to inhabit her role as comfortably as her parka. She conveyed compassion for the enigmatic doctor and an ambivalent fascination for his strange obsession with an artlessness she would never again achieve on-screen, even when portraying herself. The picture was silent, the range of emotions narrow, but if any film suggests the actress she might have become under the guidance of a talented director, this is the one.

The conventional view of Leni as an actress is that, in her early films with Fanck, she was uncomfortable before the camera, but it is truer to say that she openly courts it and is too self-aware to share the screen. She doesn't act with her fellow players; she acts at them, the camera always in the corner of her eye. Her lack of dramatic training—which would have taught her to listen to her fellow actors, to modulate and shade her responses to theirs, to *re*act with subtlety and spontaneity—shows. None of this was anything Fanck could identify or alter, but Pabst, with his extensive directing experience in the theater as well as films, could and did. He persuaded her to play to the other actors rather than to the camera, gave her a sense of the psychology of situation and character, and made her part of a unit. Such an opportunity would not come again.

The White Hell of Piz Palü was to be Fanck's most successful picture and Leni's best as an actress, their one collaboration seen with any frequency today even though it is silent (a version with added sound was released in the mid-1930s). It opened at Berlin's Ufa Palast am Zoo on November 15, 1929, after earlier openings in Vienna and Hamburg, where it played the largest cinema in Europe and became the second biggest box-office hit of the year in Germany. "I passed the theater at ten o'clock in the morning and saw a line standing at the box-office," Sokal remembered. "I couldn't believe my eyes. It was absolutely unheard of at ten in the morning and only then did I know the picture would be a success."

Universal reversed its earlier negative opinion and distributed the picture in America, where it premièred at New York's mammoth Roxy Theater. In the *New York Times,* Mordaunt Hall wrote, "Leni Riefenstahl is convincing," and remarked on "a swift undercurrent of tenseness and anticipation that carries one along through the avalanches, up the precipitous and threatening mountainside and finally to the climax of the rescue." *Variety* noticed Leni and thought her "a typical German sporting type but too buxom for the average American taste." At Universal, the only taste that mattered was that of studio chief Carl Laemmle, who wanted more of the same.

Fanck set about providing more of the same in a new script. If working with Pabst had whetted Leni's appetite to be a dramatic actress, the experience had sharpened Fanck's to prove that he, too, could direct actors. He may also have had some lingering need or hope to win Leni back romantically, for she was abruptly available. During the making of *Piz Palü*, Schneeberger had become friendly with the aviator Udet, who introduced him to the high life in nearby St. Moritz. The little cameraman found the uncomplicated girls there more appealing or less demanding than Leni, though he waited until Ufa sent him to Hungary on assignment to tell her so. He wrote saying he had fallen in love with someone new and didn't want to see her again.

Leni was dumbfounded. Her first assumption was that "black magic" was to blame, that "someone had put a spell on him." Her second was to mutilate herself with a penknife on "arms, legs and hips" to distract her from "mental anguish [that] burned like the fires of hell. . . . I swore to myself, never again would I love a man so deeply."

Self-mutilation suggests a serious psychological crisis, but it was not one to induce self-doubt for long. And she had admirers, however unwelcome she found them. She complained that during shooting on *Piz Palü*, "Every night I found poems and love letters [from Fanck] under my pillow and it was extremely annoying." Schneeberger may have thought so, too, but Pabst was again directing Louise Brooks, and—annoying or not—Fanck was the one director who wanted her without reservation.

His new script was titled *The Black Cat* and was based on campfire tales and some notes he had made about the military exploit for which Schneeberger had been decorated during the war. He and sixty other combatants had taken an Austrian mountain stronghold subsequently detonated from within by the enemy. Only a handful survived the explosion to hold their position under Schneeberger's command. Fanck combined these events with an unrelated incident involving a mountain guide's daughter—"the black cat"—who acts as a spy and warns the trapped soldiers about the impending catastrophe, in which she is killed. "At last," Leni exulted, "I had a chance to play a dramatic part."

No studio proved eager to finance a war film featuring Leni Riefenstahl as a patriotic spy. *The Black Cat* sputtered briefly to life when Sokal, who still had options on Fanck's services and films, decided he could raise financing for it. Just as funds seemed about to materialize, Luis

Trenker announced that he was making a film called *Mountain in Flames* (*Berge in Flammen*), the story line of which was plainly based on Schneeberger's wartime exploits minus the romantic spy overlay. Trenker's film was thus more historically accurate as well as more dramatically direct. When it was released in 1931, *Mountain in Flames* was a huge success, glorifying nationalism in combat and confirming critical dismay about the blurring of Alpine derring-do and military heroism. It secured Trenker's major stardom, making of him an iconic folk hero as unique in German-language films as John Wayne would become in American English. It also intensified the bitterness Leni felt toward him, equaled only by the scorn Trenker felt for her, which would have noisy public consequences.

Leni and Trenker were never an ideal fit. She was romantically striving to become something "great" but ill defined, while he was what he was from the beginning, a man's man who could rise at dawn and exult without self-consciousness that the earth looked so pure "it was as if angels had carried it down overnight, fresh from Heaven."

He had been sexually attracted to her at their first meeting but skeptical about audacity that looked reckless and egocentric. He and Fanck and Schneeberger and the rest of that exclusively male world she excited and disturbed had been skiing and climbing since boyhood and had limited tolerance for outsiders, no matter how alluring or available. They had paid their dues and earned their stripes, and had reverence for the mountains they knew they could climb but never subdue. Leni was a woman, a latecomer, an arriviste, and a catalyst for rivalry. Like the city she came from, she was too ambitious, too noisy, and in too much of a hurry.

The first of Trenker's "Mountaineer's Ten Commandments" cautioned, "You shall undertake no ascent you are unequal to," but "Thou shalt devote thyself to a goal suitable to thy abilities." If his ego was as large as the Matterhorn, so was his sense of proportion, something he believed Leni lacked. His commandment continued, "Thou shalt not devour the peaks," and while Trenker respected her courage, he recoiled from her ravenous appetites.

As producer of *The Black Cat*, Sokal sued Trenker and his backers for plagiarism, but Trenker "would go through wars to achieve his ends," Sokal realized, and the actor won the case on appeal, leaving the producer empty-handed and ruefully philosophical. When Sokal saw Trenker's completed film, he bowed to the inevitable. "Let's forget about it," he said, "because the Trenker version is better for very simple, classical reasons: unity of time, place, and action. And because in the Trenker version 'the black cat' no longer existed."

Nor did any immediate opportunity exist for Leni to become the dramatic actress and star she wanted to be. She had perhaps outsmarted herself. She had made herself indispensable to a cultish genre and now—thoroughly identified with it—felt trapped. She was stalled and, like the country she lived in, on the precipice of something, facing an uncertain future with more restless anxiety than patience or foresight.

FIVE

ABOVE THE CLOUDS

Dr. Fanck directs using glaciers and avalanches and storms. . . . Natural elements become dramatic elements. . . . And there the art begins.

—Béla Balázs

FROM THE BEGINNING, Leni had been dutiful about the donkey-work of becoming a star. She lent her face to advertisements for skin creams and her name to endorsements for footwear; she dressed down in schoolgirl middies for magazines promoting wholesomeness out of doors and dressed up in satins for soirées that pulsed with jazz and joie de vivre in urban tabloids. Producers noticed her as fans did. She was pretty and could pantomime passably on skis or while climbing cliffs, but no one thought of her for the plum roles, the ones that made you a legend or took you to Hollywood. Pola Negri was in Hollywood; Lya de Putti was, too; Camilla Horn—who'd won the virginal Gretchen role in *Faust* that Leni tried out for wearing an ill-fitting blond wig—was sailing to America and trysts with leading man John Barrymore. Leni was mostly on the sidelines in photographs snapped at film society shindigs or out of sight and mind on a glacier somewhere.

She couldn't know it then, but she would never be part of the studio-based film industry she pursued with such dogged intensity. She never worked more than a week or two at a time in any of the studios of Berlin,

and then only for the quick interior or pickup shot for one of her mountain movies. Except for *The Holy Mountain,* which Ufa distributed, her
films were released by minor companies that lacked Ufa's prestige and its
ties to MGM and Paramount in America. No one shunned her—and
Universal liked her—but luck plays a role in all careers, and her luck had
made it hard to imagine her anywhere that didn't require ski poles or a
rope.

Never being a film industry insider would, in fact, turn out to be a
stroke of good fortune, though it didn't look that way as the 1920s
careened to an uncertain end. The paradoxical advantage was that never
having been part of the day-to-day industry, she was unaware of its conventions and certainties. She would be free to innovate and invent to her
purposes once the reins of moviemaking were placed in her hands.

For now, she had little choice but to try swimming in the mainstream.
She complained to a sympathetic journalist, "I do not like civilization. I
like nature, pure and unspoiled," reflecting the impact Fanck's ethos had
had on her. But opportunity was in Berlin, pregnant with novelties
spawned by the rubbing of creative elbows in a kind of hedonistic cultural
promiscuity. Every cabaret, theater, cinema, opera house, art gallery,
publishing house, and sidewalk café was teeming with artists—from
cynics to visionaries—crossing genres or inventing new ones. Classical
composers wrote jazz for organ-grinders; painters designed ballets; actors
swung from trapezes; cathedrals became theaters; theaters became cir-
cuses; a film star might become anything.

After *The White Hell of Piz Palü,* she cultivated Pabst in Berlin like an
acolyte. "Suddenly she started coming on the set every day," Louise
Brooks complained, "trying to wheedle him to get him to use her in a picture." Brooks was then starring in her second Pabst film, *Diary of a Lost
Girl,* and remembered Leni as "a strange-looking girl [with] rather an
oval face, mildly pretty [though] the profile was sharp and intelligent, a
hook nose, a strong, strong face. But she came on the set to make love to
Mr. Pabst," Brooks fumed to film historian Kevin Brownlow, "and that
made me mad."

Leni's pursuit of Pabst netted no new roles and maybe wasn't meant to. When Leni was "gabbing and laughing off in a corner with Pabst," as Brooks described her behavior, she was picking the director's brain to learn what she couldn't learn from Fanck. She later claimed that Pabst was actively encouraging her to become a director, but he may have found it easier to flatter such an unlikely ambition than to explain why he wasn't casting her. And it was unlikely that a pretty young woman should aspire to such a role in a male-dominated industry. After three decades, apart from actresses and the occasional writer or editor, a mere handful of women had emerged as creative forces in motion pictures. Female directors were not unknown in Berlin or Hollywood, but they were anomalies on both sides of the Atlantic.

A decisive incident strengthened Leni's still-forming aspirations when Harry Sokal sent her to Paris to oversee the deletion of ten minutes from *Piz Palü* for its French release. In Leni's late-life version, she did the editing herself, to Pabst's praise and enthusiasm for her future as a director. Fanck, jealous of his reputation as a master editor (though finesse in editing was Pabst's specialty, not his), dismissed Leni's claim that she cut so much as a frame. An assistant of his named Fredersdorf had done it, Fanck said, and, because of Leni's distracting presence, had done it so clumsily that the picture failed to attract an audience in France.

Relations between mentor and pupil were increasingly strained, though not yet to the breaking point. "Fanck never forgave me," she said about the Paris editing, but she said something similar about most of their personal crises, and the frustrating truth was they needed each other. She needed parts, and Fanck needed Leni—or a Leni counterpart—to obtain financing and maintain the loyalty of audiences who had made *The Holy Mountain* successful and *Piz Palü* resoundingly so.

It was characteristic of Leni to keep her private agenda in balance with her practical needs. As with Sokal, her disputes with Fanck resulted in tension without rupture. Her manipulative skills had been evident since adolescence and were by now shrewdly honed. Sokal was impressed that, "however short the relationship with a particular man had been, she always stayed friends." There were exceptions, such as Trenker and eventually Sokal himself, but in general, she was adept at enlisting her admirers' support for her ambitions even after the affairs ended.

Her romantic exploits were well known, but no one looked askance at high spirits or disdain for convention. She was an actress in a milieu that flaunted originality in romantic behavior as in other areas of life, but there are no known accounts of her as perverse heartbreaker or vamp. Her screen image was demurely modest and rather too full of pluck. If sexual attraction was at issue, she suffered as the innocent and inadvertent victim of her beauty. Off the screen, her string of partners testifies to her resolve to remain independent and to a healthy sexual energy she projected that would—incredibly enough to those who experienced it—retain its power well into her nineties, when her dress, manner, movements, and flirtatiousness suggested a woman half a century younger.

As she neared thirty and *Piz Palü* failed to open new doors, she resigned herself to two more Alpine films for Fanck and Sokal. The first was originally titled *Above the Clouds* but soon became *Storm over Mont Blanc* (*Stürme über dem Montblanc*). Here again, the story climaxed with aerial stunts from daredevil aviator Ernst Udet, again playing himself. This time Udet flew in *Moth*, his famous single-engine plane, through a spectacular electrical storm to rescue a meteorologist slowly freezing to death in a mountaintop weather station. Udet landed his plane directly on Mont Blanc for Fanck's cameras, a first in aviation and in films. Leni, as usual, played the only female role, an astronomer's daughter in the valley below. She leaves her telescope behind to organize Udet's airlift when other rescue attempts fail as avalanches crash and glaciers split open, barring climbers' ascents. Her character engages in some high-altitude flirtation with the meteorologist and some lowland fending off of his smitten best friend's attentions in the triangular dynamic that was now de rigueur in Fanck's formulaic storytelling.

Leni's role offered no new challenges beyond a few lines of dialogue. *Mont Blanc* was the first sound film for everyone involved, complicated for Leni by a somewhat shrill voice that recorded with a strong Berlin accent she softened with the help of a voice coach. Her main contribution to the production was "discovering" the nonactor who played her love interest. Sepp Rist was a Nuremberg police radio operator and skier of the Trenker type who looked, someone said, like a "Dürer woodcut." Leni insisted she had forced Fanck to hire him, though cameraman Sepp Allgeier, who knew her tastes, had called Rist to her attention.

Allgeier was a Fanck veteran and had worked as a cameraman on all Leni's pictures except the one in Vienna. His contributions to *Storm over Mont Blanc* went beyond suggesting new faces. *Mont Blanc* vied with *Piz Palü* as the most spectacularly photographed of the Fanck films, especially admired for Allgeier's billowing cloudscapes: the camera soaring through banks of cumulus formations so awesome and majestic that Leni would later appropriate them—and Allgeier—to lend awe and majesty to a film project of her own.

Mont Blanc seems more narratively consistent than many Fanck projects because, as on *Piz Palü*, he had a cowriter—a "dramaturgical collaborator," Fanck called him, who would not receive credit on-screen. He was Carl Mayer, Germany's most eminent scenarist. *The Cabinet of Dr. Caligari* and Murnau's *The Last Laugh* (*Der letzte Mann*) were only the best known of his many credits. Exactly what he did on *Mont Blanc* isn't known. His contribution may have been structural or limited to the few lines of dialogue the actors required for the postdubbing microphones.

Mayer had become involved by chance. A book was in preparation about the making of the picture that would include hundreds of still photographs from the film and an introductory essay by Mayer's friend, critic, and film theorist Béla Balázs, who thought Fanck "the greatest film portrayer of nature." Balázs was Hungarian, Jewish, and a Communist who, virtually alone among heavyweight critics of the day, took Fanck seriously. He would write in his introduction, "Dr. Fanck directs using glaciers and avalanches and storms. . . . Natural elements become dramatic elements. . . . And there the art begins." He spent time on the Bernina locations of *Mont Blanc* together with Mayer, and there they met Leni, in whose future both men would soon play pivotal roles.

Storm over Mont Blanc was shot from March to August 1930 and opened in Berlin in early 1931 after a Christmas première in Dresden. More than a year after the Wall Street crash and the beginning of the worldwide depression, it outgrossed even *Piz Palü* at the box office. Of all Fanck's story films, this one struck the purest notes with climbers, who were always quick to protest anything artificial or tawdry. An influential Alpine publication wrote that "whoever has seen and understood this film knows why we climbers feel an inner compulsion to climb ever higher until we are above the clouds." The commentator saw in Sepp Rist's meteorologist a man who "would prefer to struggle with Nature—would *ten times* prefer to struggle with the violence of the storm or the dangers of the avalanche, to struggle against hunger and cold than to have to battle human weakness and the disillusionments of the wide world below."

It was praise of the sort to alarm Siegfried Kracauer, who saw in the same film character only "the perpetual adolescent" familiar from the many "half-monumental, half-sentimental concoctions of which [Fanck] was the master." But to Leni, the crushing disappointment was that her performance attracted little attention ("mountain-possessed as ever," Kracauer called her). When the picture opened in New York as *Avalanche*, the reviewer from the *Times* failed to mention her at all.

Adding insult to injury, Fanck and Sokal proposed another ski comedy called *The White Frenzy* (*Der weisse Rausch*), which was made without incident—or imagination—from December 1930 to May 1931 and opened at the Ufa Palast am Zoo in December, almost five years after Leni's debut on the same screen. Half a decade of film work had led to another routine Sokal production of a mediocre Fanck comedy with crudely postdubbed sound, in which Leni's dialogue amounted to outbursts of "Oh, marvelous!" when nothing was. She played a flighty urban interloper learning to ski in costumes ostentatiously monogrammed "LR." The picture found its audience but, apart from some impressive ski-racing footage, was a throwback to the strained pratfalls of *The Great Leap*. The idealistic dancer of *The Holy Mountain* had become the butt of the joke in a trivial film that was all skiing and only partly talking.

Sound came more slowly to Berlin than to Hollywood, though sound films had been publicly exhibited there off and on since the early 1920s. Amplification and projection difficulties had discouraged public acceptance, though the technique of sound-on-film that would eventually triumph in America and the rest of the world had been perfected—and on public view—in Berlin as early as 1922. Sound was an inevitability but brought with it the financial burden of converting not only production facilities but also thousands of theaters worldwide. It disrupted long-established methods of production, paralyzing camera movement and style, making films less purely visual than they had become over three decades of visual storytelling only now reaching its zenith, and nowhere as stunningly as on celluloid made in Berlin.

Alpine films such as *Mont Blanc* and *Piz Palü* remained largely immune to the frantic changes taking place in the studios because of their limited dependence on character and language. Among the easiest to dub, they were free of the tyranny of the microphone and the need for precise synchronization. They could experiment in postproduction with sound effects, as *Mont Blanc* did in manufacturing the ear-splitting crack of a glacier breaking apart or the roar of a descending avalanche. These were essentially silent pictures with sound added as enhancement or afterthought, often very creatively, and many who worked in them—Leni included—would remain makers of silent films, adding manipulated sound as a separate, sometimes abstract element.

Alpine films continued to please their loyalists but were subject to the depressed economic conditions of the industry and the larger society. Everywhere in Berlin, one could see or read about signs of mounting unemployment, of destitution in which whole families chose suicide over the humiliations of cold, hunger, and homelessness. Bank failures and violence in the streets from marauding gangs of brownshirts accompanied austerity programs that seemed to administer misery rather than alleviate it, or so the bitter joke went.

The Golden Twenties were over, and resentments and frustrations festering since 1919 were boiling to the troubled surface. As Ian Kershaw notes, "The depth of anger towards those held responsible was one side of the response. The desire for social harmony and unity—to be imposed by the elimination of those seen to threaten it—was the other." The death of the unloved Weimar Republic was only a matter of time, though anxiety at what might replace it kept pace with the growing economic crisis. If that were not enough, an industry dependent on international markets for its survival was suddenly confronted by what had formerly been the most irrelevant of questions: language.

At first, pictures with international appeal were simply made in multiple languages. Erich Pommer, back in Berlin after a sojourn in Hollywood, produced sophisticated musicals at Ufa that capitalized on London-born Lilian Harvey's ability to speak and sing in her native English as well as in fluent French and German. Her musical *Liebeswalzer* was shot in all three languages and released as *Valse d'Amour* in France and *Love Waltz* in England. In America, films based on *Moby Dick* and *Kismet* were made in both English and German in 1931, and when MGM trumpeted to the world that "Garbo talks!" the world discovered that she talked English or German, depending on which version of Eugene O'Neill's *Anna Christie* you saw.

German stars had found ready acceptance in Hollywood in the late silent period, no one more than Emil Jannings, who had sailed grandly to America in 1926. Everywhere regarded as "the greatest actor in the world," Jannings won the first Academy Award ever presented to an actor. But the portly Teutonic star, like many transplanted Europeans, had never learned to speak English well enough to make a smooth transition to the demands of Hollywood talkies, and he returned to Berlin in 1929 for a highly touted sound debut to be produced by Pommer at Ufa.

Ernst Lubitsch, who had directed Jannings in Berlin as Louis XV and Henry VIII, was now the most prestigious of Hollywood directors and was courted homeward to guide Jannings's talkie debut. Lubitsch's financial demands equaled his prestige, and Pommer contracted instead with the slightly cheaper Josef von Sternberg, the Austrian-born American who had guided Jannings to his Oscar-winning performance in *The Last*

Command. Sternberg, a brilliant pictorialist, had already completed a talkie at Paramount and, though he had lived in the United States since early childhood, still spoke German fluently.

The plan was for Jannings to act in a film about Rasputin, the sinister Russian monk who had already been the stuff of several recent films. Sternberg insisted instead on adapting a 1905 novel by Heinrich Mann titled *Professor Unrat*, which Pabst had once tried to make with Jannings. The book was a biting satire on bourgeois morality about a professor who falls in with a slatternly cabaret singer, but Sternberg had something else in mind: a tale of passion and pathos with a femme fatale to take the professor and the world by storm. He briefly considered trying to interest Gloria Swanson in the role, but the picture was to be made simultaneously in German and English, which eliminated Swanson and opened the project—now titled *The Blue Angel* (*Der blaue Engel*)—to a well-publicized talent search in Berlin that was of obsessive interest to actresses who saw themselves playing a part that might take them to Hollywood.

Sternberg arrived in Berlin in late 1929, just as *The White Hell of Piz Palü* was being readied for release, and Leni convinced herself that she was in the running for the role of the femme fatale cabaret singer. She wangled an introduction to Sternberg through Karl Vollmoeller, the playwright roué who was now lending his prestige to Sternberg's project as a screenwriter. Leni went so far as to confide to Hans Feld, editor of *Film-Kurier*, that she expected to win the part after a series of private lunches and dinners she said she had orchestrated with Sternberg. That she spoke English haltingly and could not sing a note in any language at all was no deterrent to her ambitious fantasies.

Leni may have been seductive and tenacious, but her intuition was fallible. Her peripheral status in the film industry left her self-absorbed and oblivious to common gossip about Sternberg's sexual fixation on Marlene Dietrich, who could speak English *and* sing and was then doing both on a Berlin musical comedy stage. Leni believed that Sternberg was in love with *her* in what she called "an unfortunately one-sided romance" in which Sternberg sent her lilies of the valley, called her "Du-Du," and offered to take her to Hollywood, where he would make her as big a star as he correctly predicted he was going to make of Dietrich.

Sternberg may well have welcomed Leni's company as respite from the demands of *The Blue Angel* and its leading lady, who was at least as ambitious as Leni and a good deal more emotionally demanding. Leni and Dietrich knew each other only slightly, though they lived on the same block in Berlin, but it is difficult to imagine them as competitors for any role either actress ever played, except—perhaps—as Trilby to Sternberg's Svengali. Dietrich famously played that role and would remain a lifelong irritant to Leni, though the only meaningful comparison between them was as onetime compatriots who achieved international fame and had diametrically opposed relationships to the future even then stalking Germany.

Still, being "discovered" by a powerful male figure and propelled by him to fame and independence had been a strategy of Leni's at least since Fanck. It was hardly an original tactic but satisfied her lifelong need to feel chosen and destined, even if her prodding and plotting left destiny little room to maneuver on her behalf. She had engineered Fanck's discovery of her and was attempting to do the same with Sternberg, foreshadowing a campaign yet to come that would prove more successful and significant.

There is no evidence whatever apart from Leni's reminiscences that Sternberg ever considered her for the role of Lola Lola in *The Blue Angel*. Her assertion that "Sternberg visited me on Hindenburgstrasse almost every evening" is difficult to credit, given Dietrich's demands on his romantic and professional attention, not to mention the presence of his wife in Berlin, who posed problems all her own. The claim that he took Leni "along with him to Babelsberg to show me his rushes [because he] was interested in my opinion, and wanted to hear it before Pommer got to see the footage" is surely fantasy. Sternberg was the prototypical auteur, jealous of every prerogative of independence he had been able to wrest from an industry notorious for creative interference. He had struggled his way up from Jewish immigrant poverty in America and, having achieved prominence, provocatively—in the end ruinously—styled himself as arrogant, unapproachable, and inscrutable. While it is possible he dallied with Leni and allowed her to believe whatever she wanted, his soliciting opinions about a work in progress from anyone at all—let alone an eager actress—is too out of character to be credible. Always taciturn, Sternberg's most voluble comment about Leni came long after her work as Hitler's filmmaker had irredeemably defined her in his judgment. Shortly before his death in 1969, a film student working with him in America asked about her. Sternberg tugged at his pipe and—inscrutable as ever—replied, "She was a talented admirer of my work."

Leni's losing the prize role to Dietrich did not end her campaign for Sternberg's attention: Hollywood was on her mind and would remain there, especially now that Berlin seemed on the verge of economic or social collapse. She continued visiting Sternberg on the Ufa sets, though she had another motive in dropping by than flattering the American director. One of Sternberg's cameramen on *The Blue Angel* was Hans Schneeberger, the former lover whose utility to Leni was vibrant with potential no matter how painful their parting had been. Leni had made up her mind that if G. W. Pabst and Josef von Sternberg were not going to "discover" her and cast her in a star-making film, she would do so herself.

SIX

THE BLUE LIGHT

*I used everything I had to get what I wanted. There
was never anything impossible to get.*
— Leni Riefenstahl

SHE WAS NOT DIFFIDENT in announcing her goal, though she
would later maintain that "it hadn't even occurred to me that I could
direct." Such modesty was a late-life, postwar disclaimer of ambition
and drive, when she was hoping to convey not force but a demure help-
lessness in the face of power. Nor did relentless determination jibe with
being a dreamer, a mere medium or conduit for creative energy—a persona that somehow absolved her of responsibility for what that energy
produced.

At the time, however, she was enviably clear-sighted about the path
she intended to follow. "I see everything with the eyes of a filmmaker,"
she wrote shortly after finishing *Mont Blanc*. "I want to make pictures
myself. I see mountains, trees, men's faces quite differently in their particular moods and movements and have an ever stronger yearning to
create films myself."

She had learned much about technique and exercising control from
observing Fanck—and Pabst and Sternberg—but she needed a vehicle
and financing. The first she attempted to create herself but finally conceded, "I am not gifted as a writer." Nevertheless, she sketched out a

story she would title *The Blue Light* (*Das blaue Licht*) while on location for *Mont Blanc* in 1930 and expanded it to an eighteen-page outline during the shooting of *The White Frenzy* a year later. She felt confident enough to expose her effort to friends, who were encouraging, and to producers, who were not. One of the least enamored of the idea was Fanck, for whom her desire for autonomy came as an affront. He had artistic and stylistic reservations, too. The gauzy romantic narrative that Leni said she had based on a mountain legend clashed with his patented brand of heightened realism that exalted endurance and the elements. Leni's treatment was a soft-focus fable to play out against mountains that, however majestic, were mere backdrop. That was, of course, Leni's point: Fanck's films were *about* the mountains in the end, the ordeals and reverence they inspired, while *The Blue Light* was designed to shift attention to the foreground, onto the character she had invented for herself.

The Blue Light—"a legend of the Dolomites," she would label it—tells the story of Junta, a beautiful, half-wild mountain girl, and the Alpine village of Santa Maria, where a mysterious blue light emanates from the summit of nearby Monte Cristallo during the full moon. Local youths have repeatedly plunged to their deaths while struggling to scale the mountain in search of the source of the enigmatic blue aura. Only the beautiful and solitary Junta knows its secret and can negotiate her way up the forbidding mountain, causing local peasants to view her as a witch. Ostracized and stoned by the superstitious villagers, Junta lives in an isolated mountain hut with her young shepherd brother, where a painter visiting from Vienna (Vigo) finds her and—though she speaks only Italian and he only German—falls in love with her. At the next full moon, he secretly follows her arduous path up Monte Cristallo to a hidden grotto of exquisite natural crystals whose refractions of moonlight produce the beautiful blue light. When another village youth dies attempting the dangerous climb, Vigo sketches a map of Junta's route for the villagers in order to prevent more deaths and dispel the myth that she is a witch. They use his map to discover and plunder the crystals. Junta finds her grotto looted, its light extinguished forever, and tumbles to her death.

Until now, Leni had played mostly young women she resembled—athletic, vivacious, and independent. But in designing a vehicle for herself, she reverted to a fairy-tale world she had never wholly abandoned, setting her story in an imagined past (1866), further distanced by a contemporary framing device. The film would begin in the present with a stylish couple arriving in Santa Maria in their sporty touring car. Noting images of Junta everywhere and the villagers' brisk sale of them as if they were religious tokens, the couple becomes intrigued by her portrait on the cover of a volume provided by their innkeeper. Junta's story unfolds in an unbroken flashback, ending with a return to the modern couple, moved and chastened by her tragedy.

Leni was never to acknowledge that she borrowed the "legend" she claimed she heard in the Dolomites from a novel titled *Rock Crystal* (*Bergkristall*), published by the Swiss author Gustav Renker in 1930 as she was finishing *Mont Blanc*. Fanck knew the novel, however, and said that her refusal to credit it stiffened his opposition to the project. In Renker's story, a visiting painter sets out to solve the mystery of a blue light emanating from a mountain grotto "at midnight when the moon is full." Other, less direct sources and influences crept in as well, including the poet Novalis's "blue flower," symbol of the quest for the unattainable, which Leni had already adapted a decade earlier as a title and theme for one of her solo dances.

Leni insisted instead that "everything that happened came from my head." Describing her creative process, she focused exclusively on Junta, the one element of *The Blue Light* that *was* hers. "I began to dream, and my dreams turned into images of a young girl who lived in the mountains, a creature of nature. I saw her climbing, saw her in the moonlight, I watched her being chased and pelted with stones, and finally I dreamed of this girl as she fell away from a wall of rock and slowly plunged into the depths."

The dream became Junta—the only screen role Leni would ever invent for herself and the one with which she would permanently identify, insisting that Junta's story prefigured her own as metaphor: the misjudged innocent, victimized by the greed and envy of enemies unable to comprehend her idealism and love of beauty.

She had put together a scene outline that excited her as an actress and would-be director, but needed a fully structured script. She turned to Béla Balázs, the Hungarian critic and film theorist who had written so glowingly about Fanck. She was friendly with Balázs from his visits to Carl Mayer while he was working on *Mont Blanc,* and when he called on Fanck in the Arlberg Mountains during the filming of *The White Frenzy,* she seized the opportunity to show him her treatment and invite him to write the screenplay. He was intrigued. He considered himself a "ladies' man" and, though a dedicated Marxist, did not shun the fruits of capitalism. He regularly took work in the film industry, most recently coauthoring the script for Pabst's sound film of *The Threepenny Opera.* Leni admitted she could not pay Balázs his fee and suggested he defer it until the film was released and earning profits, the same proposition she would make to Schneeberger when persuading him to sign on to her project as cameraman.

"Balázs was not immune to feminine charm and beauty," his biographer writes, "which Riefenstahl never hesitated to use to achieve her goals." She told Balázs that, after selling her jewelry and mortgaging her apartment in Berlin, she still lacked money for a director and would therefore be forced to direct *The Blue Light* herself. Would he consider directing the scenes in which she was on-camera as Junta? He would.

"I find in Béla Balázs, apart from Schneeberger, my best collaborator," Leni told the press about her distinguished writing colleague, because he "transforms my outline into poetic scenes." That transformation was complete by June 1931, when the two finished their script with the aid of Carl Mayer, who would forgo credit as he had on *Mont Blanc.*

Leni, Balázs, and Schneeberger styled themselves a filmmaking cooperative, three musketeers with a camera, agreeing to share creative honors equally for *The Blue Light,* a communal touch that may reflect Balázs's Marxist philosophy. The opening credits would read: "A mountain legend from the Dolomites, rendered in images by Leni Riefenstahl, Béla Balacz [*sic*], Hans Schneeberger."

Supplementing their labor force were Fanck veterans who, despite their master's derision of the project, felt no conflict of loyalties in working for his apprentice. Young Heinz von Jaworsky, who had been Leni's secretary since completion of *Mont Blanc*, graduated to camera assistant; Walter (Waldi) Traut, a former extra in Fanck pictures, signed on as bookkeeper-accountant; Walter Riml, the string bean–thin cameraman who performed stunts on skis as half of a slapstick comedy team (with skier Guzzi Lantschner) in *The White Frenzy*, agreed to work as still cameraman; and Karl Buchholz, production manager on *Mont Blanc*, joined the group in charge of organization and management.

Financing was less easy to come by. *The Blue Light* looked like little more than a vanity project to the studios, which rejected it as "too boring" when Leni knocked on doors trying to secure the money. "I showed my *Blue Light* to the whole industry, to every person," she admitted later. "A hundred times I went to every company, from Ufa to the smallest. Everyone said, 'No. It is nothing.' " Faced with blanket rejection, she spun failure as a virtue. "I wanted to make a film without the film industry, without a producer, and without a director," she announced, as if she hadn't exhausted every opportunity for conventional backing and actually preferred working without studio support, an impression of valiant, solitary creativity she elevated to a credo once the film was finished. By 1933, in spite of collaborators sharing on-screen credit with her, she was calling it "entirely my own."

There was, she knew, a personal source of finance who had always been forthcoming, always available, though it nettled her to call on him again hat in hand. Before she did, she incorporated herself as Leni-Riefenstahl-Studio-Film GmbH to ensure copyright and creative control. Only then did she invite Harry Sokal and his H. R. Sokal–Film Company to join in partnership with her, to supply or secure the money and distribution she needed in order to begin shooting *The Blue Light* in July 1931.

Creative control and artistic autonomy are not synonymous, though

Leni would blur the distinction and make it official. By 1938, half a dozen years after its first release, *The Blue Light* was reissued in a radically different Germany from the one in which it had been made. Leni recut it slightly and gave it—or allowed it to acquire—presentation credits reflecting her stature as an artist in and for the Third Reich. The new credits read: "a mountain legend told and shaped into images by Leni Riefenstahl." Hans Schneeberger was relegated to a standard camera card among the technical credits, and the names of Jewish participants, including Balázs and Sokal, vanished altogether.

But before everything changed, Leni had been a brilliantly effective catalyst. On her first film—virtually without funds or leverage—she had motivated the collaboration of Béla Balázs and Carl Mayer, men Billy Wilder, then working in Berlin, called "the shining lights of motion picture writing." In spite of their past relationship, she persuaded Schneeberger—the man who had photographed Dietrich to international stardom—to shoot the film as her equal creative partner. She had enlisted a small but expert staff of technicians, all trained by a master of no-frills location shooting, and, perhaps most crucially, had convinced Sokal to overlook the past and abandon his studio-oriented production activities to join her as financer and nominal coproducer.

She was what no one then called the auteur, the prime mover and creative force behind a production that may have been independent by default but whose outsider status established a pattern of working free of interference. Even Sokal stayed in Berlin, deliberately distant from the locations, working with laboratories and the distributor, unwittingly encouraging her to think of him not as a partner but as a benefactor. As director, cowriter, editor, and star, she was permitted by circumstance to work in an atmosphere of freedom that every director hopes for but that few in film history have enjoyed so completely or with such an eager sense of entitlement.

It was her eye—Schneeberger notwithstanding—controlling the vision. Her innocence of studio practice drove her to invent and improvise; her stubbornness led her to create and solve problems no one around her was presumptuous or foolhardy enough to suggest might be avoided or couldn't be solved. Her fascination with photographic values led her to rely on Schneeberger's experience with lenses, film stocks, and filters or to challenge his expertise and force him to experiment. It was her insistence that green and red filters together—which should have canceled each other—would create a "magical effect," and they did. It was his decision to use a new infrared stock from Agfa that resulted in iridescent light effects in black and white that look extraordinary even today. The low blue sensitivity of the film turned daytime skies dark, creating a day-for-night effect indispensable for nocturnal climbing scenes that could only be performed and shot in daylight; the sun—against a morning or an evening sky—photographed as if it were a moon on a midnight ground. In some accounts, the idea to use infrared film came from Balázs, who had seen it used on an earlier picture of his called *The Lioness* (*Die Löwin*). In any case, Leni's aggressiveness pushed Schneeberger to striking effects that neither might have accomplished alone, resulting in a photographic style that captured waterfalls, fields of flowers, the village, the crystal grotto, and—crucially—the leading lady in a painterly, luminous glow.

Shooting *The Blue Light* from July to September avoided extremes of weather, but the director and her crew of six lived without amenities, often sleeping in the open or in hay stalls offered by local peasants. Treks to barely accessible shooting sites were accomplished on foot, as were daily deliveries of exposed film to remote village postmasters for forwarding to Berlin for processing. As a result, Leni later overstressed the arduous nature of her style of film production, acting as if physical difficulties did not occur in the making of virtually every film—including those made under sophisticated studio conditions—because she didn't know they did. Her difficulties were real and their solutions frequently ingenious, but her emphasis on them underscores how obsessively she focused on technical mastery— "Film without technique is nothing"—and how "beauty" at the expense of narrative was always her weakness. Later, annotated accounts of the hardships of filmmaking would also deflect attention from *what* she put on film.

Intimations of this are already present in *The Blue Light*. One of her genuine triumphs was casting the villagers with authentic mountain and farm people from the Sarn Valley whom she met while scouting locations, acting on a tip from Willy Jaeckel, the artist who had sketched her for his illustrated Bible in Lake Constance just before she met Sokal. Her photographer's eye for faces here is superb. She saw—and Schneeberger captured—a Dürer-like quality, both worn and dignified, in the landscapes of their faces. Most of them were peasants who had never seen a film, let alone been in one. She courted them and gained their trust and permission to film them as part of the village mural. It seems not to have occurred to her—and it occurs to few observers today—that she used the biblical dignity their faces suggest as mere decoration. Her images of them purport to honor their venerable beauty, but the narrative function they fulfill is as agents of ignorance and greed. They look good, but they destroy.

The film's supposed origin in legend encourages one to view it as a primitive or naïve work in spite of its virtuoso photographic effects. But the original version—before the contemporary frame was removed during the Nazi period—juxtaposes modernity (the worldly vacationing couple) and a past permeated with nostalgia for the primitive and unattainable, the sort of thing to cause Kracauer-like critics to read prefascist, antirational tendencies into the film. But Leni articulated something very like this at the time, describing her intention as "the redemption of realism—modernity's technical frenzy and unrest—through romanticism."

A significant part of the film's romanticism flows from the director's fascination with the beauty of the leading actress. She looks strikingly like the American film star Paulette Goddard, whom Chaplin is said to have modeled in *Modern Times* on Leni's tattered Junta. In no other film was Leni so lovingly or beautifully photographed, and lingering over that beauty nearly crippled her initial edit. In one version, she took her cut to Fanck for his approval and advice. He made changes. Fanck's gesture was acknowledged at the time, and Leni spoke graciously about it in public, but privately she recoiled in horror, calling his work "a mutilation."

Fanck's memory of events was, unsurprisingly, different. He was not above malice when his headstrong pupil sought his help on a project he had counseled against, but he had been involved—"remote control directing," he called it—during production, as Leni relied on him (and Sokal) to inspect her rushes for quality as they were developed at the labs in Berlin. After Fanck saw her first cut, he claimed that "of about six hundred splices, none were done right. Each time she cut out the motion and left the static parts. She didn't understand that film was movement."

According to an unpublished interview Fanck gave near the end of his life, it was not Leni who asked him to recut the film but an executive named Levi at Aafa, the distributor Sokal had secured, who insisted after a screening Sokal and Fanck attended that Fanck "save the film." Leni had no choice but to agree, Fanck said. "I worked from nine in the evening to three or four in the morning re-editing" in the cutting room in his villa in Berlin-Wannsee. "On one wall there was a long light-box with eight hundred clips at the top, in three sections. In the middle I put the film she had done. I took apart what she had spliced together, asked the girl who worked as my assistant to find and clip together the trims, the beginnings and ends of these shots, and I reassembled the footage. When Riefenstahl came she saw what I was doing and said, 'God, what are you doing! You are taking my whole wonderful creation apart.' And I said, 'What do you mean by "creation"? There is no *form* here at all.' She got hysterical. She was very, very excited. The room next to the cutting room was the dining room and she went in there and rolled on the carpet, completely hysterical. I went into the kitchen, got a bucket of water and poured it over her. That quieted her down. I said, 'Go into my bedroom, put on one of my nightshirts and my robe and come back again.' Then she sat down and didn't say another word. She watched. I explained every splice I made and why I did it, showing her the principles behind each cut. When we were through the first reel, we went into the projection room and viewed the film. She looked at it in astonishment. 'Suddenly everything is moving!' And I said, 'Yes, and now you understand the first principle of making films.' "

Leni told a more dramatic tale. "I showed [Fanck] the film," she said, "and he told me, 'Oh, that is not good. This must be changed.' I said, 'I would be very happy if you would help me, *very* happy. Can I come tomorrow?' And when I came the next day, I nearly *died* because he had taken apart my film. Everything was changed. I went into shock; I fell down crying.

"That same night I phoned Guzzi Lantschner, who was not a cameraman yet, only a friend of mine. He came from Innsbruck because I thought I was going to die. I took a big washtub to put all my material in that Fanck had clipped to the glass walls in his cutting room. He didn't say to me, 'Leni, you must do this so or so or this.' He just did it and in my eyes it was *kaput*. It was cut like a ski picture, with a lot of short shots. So I put it all in the washtub and I took it home. For five days I was sick and then I started the work anew. I had to put together a new film, and later sometimes Fanck would say to me, '*I* cut your film, I *saved* it.' Why? Because he made it *kaput*? After that I had nothing more to do with him. Dr. Fanck was my slave because he loved me. But after that, he went against me in hate."

Having nothing more to do with Fanck was not a practical solution, though in years to come she would refuse to talk to interviewers who had spoken with him first. But in February 1932, the experience of showing her rough cut—not just to Fanck but to Sokal and Aafa as well—had been "shattering," Leni admitted in a letter to Balázs, then in Moscow. She confessed that the film had seemed "boring and unintelligible." It was "incredibly stiff, exaggerated and unnatural" in spite of its luminous images. "In short, dear Béla," she wrote, "you can have no idea of the struggles and difficulties that you—thank God—have escaped." She admitted that Fanck's reel-by-reel intervention was turning a "picture book" into a movie and much later acknowledged, "I learned cutting from him. I saw how he did it." What Fanck taught her was editing on and for movement, skills that served her superbly on assignments yet to come.

The première of *The Blue Light* at the Ufa Palast am Zoo on March 24, 1932, was, she wrote, "an undreamt-of-success, a triumph beyond my wildest dreams—a sensation." Most of the reviews were positive, one or two of them glowing, though to say that "Berlin critics outdid one another with their accolades" was an exaggeration born of elation.

As Sokal remembered it, "*The Blue Light* got bad critical reviews in Berlin, and especially from the so-called 'democratic' papers, which were considered Jewish, like the *Berliner Tageblatt*. The essence of the reviews was that the picture was phony romanticism—not real, but phony. And when the picture was distributed more widely in Germany, the more to the right the papers were politically, the better the reviews were. It was very strange because it was the first Alpine picture that wasn't a box-office success. When the first bad reviews appeared, I was as mad about it as Leni because I loved the picture. I *still* love it. Leni came to me extremely upset, of course, and said, 'What do these Jewish critics understand about our mentality? They have no right to criticize our work.'

"She had forgotten entirely that she was not the only one who made that picture; that there were Jewish people involved like the great Béla Balázs, who directed *all* the scenes she was in and Carl Mayer [on the script]. But the fact that *The Blue Light* got bad reviews from Jewish critics influenced her so much that she went entirely over into the Nazi camp, even though she had Jewish collaborators."

The *Berliner Tageblatt* review that Sokal referred to must have stung, for it appeared in the paper Leni's parents read and called the picture "inwardly sick," an exceptionally harsh judgment. Many reviews were favorable, and the important *Film-Kurier* found it "unforgettable" and "transporting," and concluded that "Leni Riefenstahl has achieved what she was striving for: a unique film-poem."

Leni later disputed Sokal's assertions of anti-Semitic vindictiveness though he was not alone in recalling such outbursts. On November 3, 1932, Leni was the subject of a radio interview conducted by Rudolf Arnheim, the psychologist and art theorist. Arnheim would become part of the Jewish flight from the Nazis and reported late in his life that Leni told him during the broadcast, "As long as the Jews are film critics, I'll never have a success. But watch out, when Hitler takes the rudder everything will change."

If Arnheim remembered correctly, Leni was prescient. Once the rudder was in Hitler's grasp, the official explanation for the box-office failure of *The Blue Light* became Jewish critical sabotage. When it was rereleased in 1938, cleansed of credit to Leni's Jewish collaborators Balázs and Sokal, press releases charged that "the Jewish press" had been "calculatedly malicious" in 1932. This notion had been introduced by film critic Paul Ickes in his foreword to Leni's autobiographical book *Struggle in Snow and Ice* (*Kampf in Schnee und Eis*), published just after the Nazis seized power in 1933. Ickes's repudiation of the "liberal" and "unscrupulous" bosses of "the so-called German film" was an unmistakable reference to Jewish executives, quite as clear to readers as his elation that a new and better day had dawned for Germany and Leni. "The same press," he wrote, "that was so under the spell of the money-making economy that it trespassed against the spiritual revival of the people, withheld its allegiance from Leni Riefenstahl, for allegiance depends on understanding, and no understanding was possible."

With or without Jewish critics, the picture was not the commercial or popular success Leni (and Sokal) had hoped for. Audiences drawn by Leni's name were perplexed by the tragedy-fantasy so unlike the adventure films of avalanches and narrow escapes they were used to. The film did no better on Swiss or Austrian screens, but was well received in Paris and London, where Alpine films were a novelty and thus unburdened by expectations that *The Blue Light* couldn't meet. Leni traveled to London for the Rialto Theatre première on October 30, 1932, and returned the following year to lecture admiring undergraduate members of the Oxford German Club. The film was entered in the first Venice Biennale in Mussolini's Italy and won a Silver Medallion before there was a "best picture" Gold Medallion. When it opened in New York in May 1934, the *New York Sun* called it "one of the most pictorially beautiful films of the year. Leni Riefenstahl—author, director and star—is an expert climber as

well as a handsome woman." The *Herald Tribune* praised its "sheer pictorial beauty" and remarked on "how flawlessly this girl, who plays the
lead and also wrote and directed, accomplished her task," suggesting that
credits for the filmmakers' cooperative had already been jettisoned for the
international release. The *Times* found Leni "attractive" and added that
"a summary of the story gives no adequate idea of the beauty of the
action and the remarkable camera work, especially in connection with the
light effects."

In the end, *The Blue Light* gave Leni a new and unique identity as a
filmmaker but did not catapult her into a new orbit among actresses. Nor
did it secure for her any immediate work as a director. She had no new
ideas of her own and had, as she told Balázs, "only one wish: to be free of
this work and able to forget everything and get healthy again." The
financial hopes she had for *The Blue Light* went unrealized, and she told
Sokal, when he was forced to leave Germany to survive, that he could sell
rights to the film abroad, but it had no real market beyond its first release,
and its financial fate has gone undocumented.

Sokal's flight from Nazi Germany ended a decade-long relationship. He had been central to her emergence as dancer, actress, and film
director and, in enforced exile, may have felt entitled to do whatever he
could to finance his freedom. What is certain is that he took the negative of *The Blue Light* with him as a form of insurance and maintained
thereafter that he acted honorably in a series of murky transactions. It
is likely that rights to the film netted so little that nothing was left to
distribute to Leni or anybody else, including the still-unpaid Béla
Balázs.

Shortly after completion of *The Blue Light*, Balázs had accepted an
invitation to make films in the Soviet Union and left Berlin for Moscow,
where Leni had written him in February 1932. After repeated inquiries
by mail and a personal entreaty delivered during a visit to Berlin in
January 1933, just days before Hitler seized power, he finally threatened
to sue.

He may have actually done so. A year later, just after Leni made her first film for the Third Reich, she decisively disposed of Balázs and his fee. She wrote a letter on stationery from Berlin's Hotel Kaiserhof to the Gauleiter (district administrator) of Franconia (which included Nuremberg), one Julius Streicher, who was also publisher of the vehemently anti-Semitic *Der Stürmer,* a distinction that would place his shaved head in a noose at the end of World War II.

The Hotel Kaiserhof was located across the Wilhelmstrasse from the Chancellery; Hitler had lived there before becoming chancellor, and it remained home away from home for upper-echelon Nazis and their guests. Leni was there on December 11, 1933, ten days after the Berlin première of her first film made directly for the Nazis, *Victory of Faith* (*Sieg des Glaubens*). The letter she wrote out by hand that night read:

> I grant to Herr Gauleiter Julius Streicher of Nuremberg—publisher of *Der Stürmer*—power of attorney in matters of the claims of the Jew Béla Balacs [*sic*] on me.
>
> [signed] Leni Riefenstahl.

Though Leni was later to cite Balázs as one of her lifelong Jewish friends and as evidence of her lack of anti-Semitism, she never referred to this letter in any way. Nor was Balázs ever compensated for work from which his name and credit had been expunged.

A hint of the accounting for *The Blue Light* survives in the testimony of stock film footage collector and merchant George Rony in Los Angeles, who confirmed that he purchased limited distribution rights to the film as well as its negative "through an agent" after Sokal's arrival in America in 1941. Rony was a Russian who had worked as an assistant to Eisenstein before making his way to Berlin. He fled the Nazis in 1933 after being forbidden to work because of his politics. In America, he earned his living recycling stock footage of actual events, principally the Bolshevik Revolution and the rise of Hitler, though he admitted dealing occasionally in feature film material if it had a documentary look. Rony said that Leni tried to sue him after the war when she learned that he had acquired rights to *The Blue Light*. She was especially distraught that he had the original negative, which she had not been able to use for revisions she made to the film in 1938 and again in 1952, when she had been forced to utilize dupe negative material, though the postwar revision may have been made only to secure new copyright in her name.

Rony felt himself a victim of the Third Reich, which Leni personified in his mind. He had a prudish streak that was repelled by her associations with such Nazi leaders as Hitler and Goebbels and by what he called her "alley cat" and "nymphomaniac" lifestyle, and he scorned her as "absolutely unscrupulous and a congenital liar."

Leni claimed that she tried to buy her negative back from Rony but that he set an unrealistically high price of six thousand dollars on it, which she was unable then to pay. Rony grew tired of her threats to sue and countered that if she continued harassing him, he would "burn the negative" to spite her and would do so without a moment's regret. "I'd lose a couple of thousand dollars, but it doesn't matter to me," he shrugged, hinting perhaps at the low price the negative may have commanded when Sokal was forced to market it in exile.

During filming of *The Blue Light*, Leni had been diverted by nothing not related to the film. But two witnesses recalled that shortly thereafter, she found time to do some reading. Sokal was one, and the other was Heinz von Jaworsky, who worked as Schneeberger's assistant on the picture. The young Heinz ("Henry" in America) was amused when he saw her reading on the train back to Berlin after a brief holiday in Switzerland. He was familiar with the book she found so absorbing. It was *Mein Kampf*, by Adolf Hitler, and she "was fascinated by it," he recalled. "During this train ride she tried to convince me that it was a beautiful book. I laughed and we got into an argument. Then she said, 'You'll see. You'll see. They are right.' "

When Leni arrived back in Berlin to begin editing *The Blue Light*, Sokal remembered her thrusting *Mein Kampf* at him, saying, "Harry, you must read this book. This is the coming man." There was a breath-taking insensitivity in recommending a virulently anti-Semitic text to a

Jew, but Sokal was unsurprised to hear her add something he'd heard her say so often that he all but discounted it: "I *must* meet that man." He might have paid closer attention had he heard her tell Heinz von Jaworsky on the train—with uncanny prescience—"I'll work for them."

Two

ASCENT

By the clever and continuous use of propaganda, a
people can even be made to mistake heaven for hell,
and vice versa.

—Adolf Hitler

Go laughing down the way of your great calling. Here
you have found your heaven and in it you will be
eternal.

—Julius Streicher to Leni Riefenstahl

SEVEN

LIGHTNING

Once we come to power, you must make my films.
—Adolf Hitler, 1932

All I thought about was my small circle, my own life. I was terribly busy.

—Leni Riefenstahl

LENI CLUNG TO THE ASSERTION that she first heard the name of Adolf Hitler while on a publicity tour for *The Blue Light* in 1932, advancing the notion that a shrewd and alert young woman was oblivious of the most controversial and talked-about figure in postwar Germany. Hitler had been spectacularly adept at inflaming public opinion and generating headlines since his failed Munich putsch in 1923 and had led his National Socialist Party from a meager 2.6 percent of the popular vote in 1928 to an imposing 37.4 percent in July 1932, about the time Leni claimed she first heard of him. While short of a majority, the July vote gave the National Socialists the largest percentage of any national party in an election that drew almost 85 percent of eligible voters, putting Hitler on the threshold of power, if not yet in the Chancellery.

"I was terribly busy," Leni said to explain her insularity. "All I thought about was my small circle, my own life." Work kept her on the move, she said, distant from centers of news and information, though she tended to exaggerate her isolation. She was once adamant that she had never heard radio until 1938, though she'd spoken on it herself—with Rudolf Arnheim—as early as 1932. Her detachment from daily events did not prevent her assembling scrapbooks she was still perusing with pride at age one hundred containing every article or review that mentioned her name, some of which, such as dissenting reviews for *The Holy Mountain,* had actually mentioned Hitler and his party.

It is a matter of curious fact that she was indeed physically absent from Germany at pivotal moments to come, but her claims of unawareness had less to do with reality than with a desire to emphasize an artist's indifference to the mundane. And when she did become aware, it was the *man* who interested her, not his ideology, about which she affected the same naïveté as millions of other Germans who, as Rebecca West put it while observing the aftermath in a Nuremberg courtroom, "did not know enough to come in out of the rain, even when it turned to blood." Hitler intrigued Leni as he intrigued many, but her curiosity, despite later denials, was stimulated by *Mein Kampf,* his unambiguous political testament, which she read in full or in part before meeting the man himself, as von Jaworsky and Sokal remembered and as she confirmed in 1938 to an English journalist: "I read it on the train, on the set, by the mountain streams and forest. It made a tremendous impression on me."

Anyone who has glanced at even a page of *Mein Kampf* experiences what a German historian calls its "maniac egocentricity and utter lack of humanity." Its racist agenda is apparent on the first page of its preface, where the author declares his intention "to destroy the foul legends about my person dished up in the Jewish press," a remark that may have struck a chord with Leni when she stewed over unfavorable reviews. If she was as naïve as she later claimed—"I was so ignorant that I wasn't even quite sure what concepts like 'right' and 'left' meant"—then whatever she saw "on the train, on the set, by the mountain streams and forest" focused her sympathies.

As 1932 got under way, she was in debt, had no job offers, no ideas for future work, and no mentor as a result of the editing battles with Fanck on *The Blue Light*. Fanck was then at Universal Studios in Hollywood, discussing an American-German-Danish coproduction to be shot in Greenland, and was adamantly opposed to the studio's desire that Leni play the female lead. The part was that of a daredevil lady pilot, and Fanck was proposing the German flier and nonactress Elly Beinhorn for the role. Universal executives, however, wanted to repeat the success of *The White Hell of Piz Palü* by reuniting Fanck, Leni, Gustav Diessl, and Ernst Udet for *S.O.S. Iceberg* (*S.O.S. Eisberg*), about the airborne rescue of an expedition stranded on icebergs breaking up in the North Atlantic.

There was nothing in the role to advance Leni's standing as an actress and it was less prominent than almost anything she'd played thus far, but the picture needed a woman and she needed work. Her memoirs record that she rejected the part but that "Universal wanted to have me at any price." Any price proved to be ten thousand dollars, or about forty thousand marks, a healthy enough sum in 1932, though hardly record-breaking. With Fanck in Hollywood still refusing to cast her, she traveled to Dresden to call on Universal's man in Germany and the producer of *Iceberg*, Paul Kohner, later an important agent in Hollywood. Kohner would discover at *Iceberg*'s Berlin première on August 30, 1933, eight months into the Third Reich, that his name had been removed from posters and the credits because he was Jewish. His consternation changed to outrage as Leni walked onto the stage of the Ufa Palast am Zoo and, instead of taking a bow, raised her arm to the crowd in an exultant Hitler salute.

When Leni sought him out in Dresden in the spring of 1932, he was trying to lose weight at a resort spa in anticipation of his forthcoming wedding. He later confessed to director and editor Andrew Marton that during a sudden cloudburst, he had yielded to Leni's seductive charms in an abandoned summerhouse on the spa grounds, a quick carnal romp that resulted in remorse and his guilty endorsement of the notion that Fanck should cast her. Fanck still wavered on his return to Germany. He recalled, not without bitterness, that "Leni came to me crying in Berlin, begging me not to take away the $10,000 salary she would get. She softened me up, recalling all the hardships she went through in all my other films. I agreed, thereby damaging the film, for her performance was not realistic."

It was not salary alone that attracted her. Filming in the virgin territory of Greenland in a project that featured Danish explorer Knud Rasmussen was appealing, as was the idea of working again with familiar colleagues including Udet, Diessl, and Sepp Rist as costars; as well as Schneeberger (who would photograph) with his camera assistants Waldi Traut, Heinz von Jaworsky, Guzzi Lantschner (her friend from Innsbruck), and others. Many had worked on *The Blue Light* or her earlier pictures, and a few nursed bruises acquired in pursuit of her fleeting affections, among them Walter Riml.

After acting in *The White Frenzy* and shooting stills on *The Blue Light*, Riml noted Leni's interest in a newcomer to the *Iceberg* crew, a green-eyed stuntman and mountain guide named Hans Ertl—"without a doubt, the most attractive male member of the expedition," Leni admitted. Riml cautioned Ertl, "Don't let that little tramp bamboozle you with her wiles. She can't keep her hands off young studs like us. But we are only bonbons to her . . . snacks to be nibbled as long as she has fun!" Ertl, six years younger than Leni and as handsome as a leading man, was more intrigued than put off by Riml's warning and soon found himself a willing Leni conquest.

An additional incentive was that before leaving for Greenland, Leni negotiated with Manfred George, editor of *Tempo,* Berlin's evening newspaper, to write a series of articles about the filming that she could then publish in book form. George would flee Nazi Germany (he was Jewish) before the book he indirectly commissioned saw print under the title *Struggle in Snow and Ice* (*Kampf in Schnee und Eis*). But the most powerful enticement the picture offered Leni was that the American-financed production would be made in German and English versions and "might help to establish my reputation in the United States."

S.O.S. Iceberg would, in the end, be shot with different directors for the different versions, with Leni playing opposite different leading men, though that had not been the original plan. The change came about after months of filming in Greenland, when it seemed clear to Universal that Fanck was amassing miles of footage of icebergs, polar bears, and Eskimos paddling kayaks but very little story. The footage of icebergs heaving up from beneath still waters like frozen cities and then violently breaking apart was stunning, and Fanck planned to use his outtakes in documentary short subjects once the picture was released. But Universal was alarmed by an already weak dramatic narrative now smothered under what looked like a deluge of travelogue footage.

American director Tay Garnett was sent by Universal to Berlin to review the footage. There, screenwriter Edwin Knopf (brother of publisher Alfred A. Knopf) provided dialogue for the English-language version as well as script revisions to accommodate footage already shot. Hollywood's Rod La Rocque was already in Europe with his wife, Vilma Bánky (then playing opposite Luis Trenker in his latest film), and would act opposite Leni in the English-language *Iceberg*, though Garnett would dub both of them with the voices of others in London.

Fanck resented Garnett's interloping, as he had resented Pabst's, but Garnett would film scenes with Leni and La Rocque far from Fanck's disapproval on man-made iceberg sets built on the high ground of the Swiss-Italian border south of Davos and its ski resorts. All of that lay ahead when Leni signed her contract.

To launch the picture, Universal's publicity department organized an international press conference to publicize the departures of Fanck, Leni, Udet, and the scientific members of the expedition when they left Berlin in May by private railway car for Hamburg, where they would board the *Borodino* and sail for Greenland. Topical interest was great because the plot of *S.O.S. Iceberg* alluded to the disappearance and death in Greenland of explorer Alfred Wegener, a scientific tragedy that had become a sensational news story two years earlier. A Hollywood-orchestrated press campaign featuring the sole female cast member of an international production would have been an irresistible opportunity for an actress of even routine ambition. Which makes it all the more remarkable that Leni chose at the last moment to miss the press conference and the much-ballyhooed departure from Berlin altogether. A more enticing offer had come her way.

Between finishing *The Blue Light* and its release in March 1932, Leni had had time on her hands. She overcame her indifference to politics by joining twenty-five thousand others at a Hitler rally in Berlin's giant Sportpalast. She later said that Ernst Jäger, editor of *Film-Kurier* (who had written so glowingly about *The Blue Light*), had somewhat cryptically urged her to attend. Jäger, a Gentile whose wife was Jewish, offered no explanation but may have assumed that the vulgarity of a Nazi rally would be obvious to her and discredit the policies advanced in *Mein Kampf*. If so, he was wrong. Leni took his suggestion and elbowed her way into the Sportpalast on February 27 for her first glimpse of the Austrian-born orator and politician, who had only the day before become a German citizen, thus making himself eligible for elective office in the country he would soon dominate.

"It was like being struck by lightning," Leni said. Hitler's presence and performance inspired in her the kind of hyperbole one associates with the born-again true believer. "I had an almost apocalyptic vision that I was never able to forget. It seemed as if the earth's surface were spreading out in front of me," she recalled decades later, "like a hemisphere that suddenly splits apart in the middle, spewing out an enormous jet of water, so powerful that it touched the sky and shook the earth. I felt quite paralyzed." The imagery is ecstatic and erotic, baptismal and orgasmic. Joachim Fest, in his commentary on Hitler's oratory, might have been glossing Leni's description in referring to "the peculiarly obscene, copulatory character of [Hitler's] mass meetings: the silence at the beginning . . . finally the frenzy, more climaxes, and then the ecstasies released by the finally unblocked oratorical orgasms."

Spellbound accounts of first exposure to Hitler the orator are not rare, and many felt compelled to adopt the language of religion; Nietzsche's sister told Count Harry Kessler that she considered Hitler "a religious rather than a political leader." An American journalist, on hearing him speak in Munich, styled him "an evangelist speaking to a camp meeting, the Billy Sunday of German politics. His converts moved with him, laughed with him, felt with him . . . [they became] an instrument on which Hitler played a symphony of national passion."

An earlier portrait in musical terms was painted by Ernst "Putzi" Hanfstaengl, the Harvard-educated, piano-playing scion of a wealthy Munich family who used his dollar earnings to finance Hitler and his party in the early 1920s. "He had a command of voice, phrase and effect which has never been equaled," Hanfstaengl recalled with the ear of the occasional composer he was. "Sometimes he reminded me of a skilled violinist, who, never coming to the end of his bow, always left just the faint anticipation of a tone—a thought spared the indelicacy of utterance."

Journalist Sebastian Haffner recorded an entirely different reaction shortly after Leni attended her first rally, shuddering at "those speeches: the delight in threats and in cruelty, the bloodthirsty execution fantasies." Haffner, Berlin-born and Gentile, would seek escape in London from those "unable to see that it was hell personified that challenged them."

The present-day view of Hitler as a mesmerizing orator is, to a significant degree, a legacy of Leni's rendering of him in films yet to come. The legend of the orator-as-hypnotist would serve as a mass alibi, a morally evasive justification used by millions who claimed, not entirely untruthfully, that the panoply of banners, uniforms, and trumpets diverted them from what was being said. The message was never obscure, though, as William Shirer observed, "it did not matter so much what he said but how he said it."

The speech Leni heard in late February survives. It focused on unemployment, on terrorist threats to public order from the far left, and on the failures of the Weimar Republic and the aging president Paul von Hindenburg to contain the economic crisis. Leni was so "deeply affected" by what she heard that she found herself "unable to hail a cab."

Though she claimed that she "unreservedly rejected his racist ideas," that failed to inhibit her desire to experience the lightning bolt in person.

With departure for Greenland and *S.O.S. Iceberg* imminent, she wrote him in care of Nazi Party headquarters in Munich, the splendid Barlow-Palais newly streamlined for power as the "Brown House." She posted her letter on May 18, 1932, dangerously close to her scheduled departure date for Hamburg from Berlin, where photographers and reporters would be waiting with publicists and a cast and crew of thirty-eight—plus three stunt planes, two motorboats, forty tents, two tons of luggage, cameras, film stock, lighting equipment, miscellaneous provisions, and two polar bears borrowed from the Hamburg zoo.

Three days later and one day before the press event, she received a call from Hitler's adjutant, Wilhelm Brückner, inviting her to a personal meeting with Hitler at the North Sea fishing village of Horumersiel, near Wilhelmshaven, the following day. Aware that she might well be risking her career, "my curiosity and the exciting prospect of meeting Hitler were stronger." As the Universal entourage waited for her at Berlin's Lehrter Station, she boarded another train at another station for Wilhelmshaven, arriving at four o'clock in the afternoon on May 22.

She was driven to Horumersiel in an official Mercedes with adjutant Brückner and upper-echelon Nazi escorts, including Hitler's SS body-guard Sepp Dietrich and press chief Otto Dietrich. Brückner explained that just before her letter arrived, Hitler had been musing about films and declared, "The most beautiful thing I have ever seen in a film was Riefenstahl's dance on the sea in *The Holy Mountain*." The arrival of her letter prompted the invitation, inspiring Leni to wonder, "Was this chance or fate?" as if she had done nothing to set the wheels in motion.

She found Hitler, she later wrote, "unexpectedly modest" and "natural and uninhibited, like a completely normal person." Strolling on the beach, the politician and the actress talked about her films, all of which Hitler said he had seen, adding that he had been most impressed by the just-released *Blue Light*. At some point in the conversation, he abruptly announced, "Once we come to power, you must make my films."

If Leni's version is accurate (there is no other known account), it was a significant moment in film history and an extraordinary one in her own, notwithstanding her reported protest that she could never make "prescribed films" because "I have to have a very personal relationship with my subject matter. Otherwise I can't be creative." And she could never join the Nazi Party because "you have racial prejudices . . . so how can I work for someone who makes such distinctions among people?"

This, if true, was bold in the extreme and suggests that a young woman of thirty who didn't know the difference between the right and the left was aware of the racial policies of a man she had traveled miles to see, putting in jeopardy a film role she had fought—and seduced—to get. But Leni wrote only that her reply pleased Hitler for its show of independence and inspired a physical advance. Putting his arms around her in an awkward, though unmistakably romantic embrace, he noted the coolness of her response, withdrew, and "beseechingly" pleaded, "How can I love a woman until I have completed my task?"

The impetuous moment has been questioned by students of Hitler's psychology, if only because his sexuality remains something of a mystery. Leni's own reluctance to be the object of romantic attentions is surprising in view of later testimony from witnesses who reported that her conduct around him seemed calculated to produce exactly the response she says she recoiled from in Horumersiel. "Putzi" Hanfstaengl observed them together in Leni's Berlin apartment late one night in the early thirties after Hitler had become chancellor. She was "giving him the works" in "a real summer sale of feminine charms," thought Hanfstaengl, who believed Hitler was impotent and possibly homosexual. He concluded that if Leni "can't manage this no one can" and was unsurprised that her behavior threw the Führer "into a panic."

Such incidents hint at Leni's adroit use of the idea of their relationship to enhance her image then and later. Considerable glamour—not alone in Germany—clings to Third Reich personalities whose proximity to the Führer, physical or psychological, allowed them to claim intimacy and distinction within the vast impersonality of the regime. For Leni, there was nothing subtle about this. One of her most trusted collaborators, cinematographer Walter Frentz, who became Hitler's personal newsreel cameraman during World War II, noted, "She was not a mistress or sweetheart of Hitler, but was cunning enough to let people believe she might be. She acted as if it were true because it got her everything she needed for her films." No one was sure how far her influence with Hitler extended, though it seemed prudent to assume, in the paranoid atmosphere of the dictatorship to come, that she might not hesitate to go directly to him in matters of her goals or complaints, and, as will be seen, she often did.

It is almost certain, most observers agree, that Leni couldn't or didn't seduce Hitler or allow herself to be (physically) seduced by him. If her personality didn't argue against it, his did, with his compulsion for privacy and what Fest calls "the advantages of living in semi divine remoteness." The closest we come to a definitive answer may be an offhand remark Leni made when reminiscing in her eighties. "I suppose had he wanted to," she told a friend, "I would have become his mistress; had he asked, it would have been inevitable. I'm so glad he didn't."

If securing Hitler as a sponsor was not the point of her journey to Horumersiel, Leni surely realized from her meeting with him that he could be a powerful ally. It is probable she had no idea how to maximize the opportunity, though there was nothing perfunctory in Hitler's treatment of her. The day after their get-acquainted stroll along the beach, he ordered an official private plane to fly her to Hamburg, where she joined the *Iceberg* film crew as it set sail for Greenland.

Leni remembered being the soul of discretion following her visit with Hitler. "I told no one my secret," she wrote, though her fellow passengers on the *Borodino* thought her arrival in a "private airplane of the Nazi party" with "a tremendous bouquet of flowers" could not have been more revealing—or ostentatious. She arrived clutching her copy of *Mein Kampf* and "large photographs of Hitler, some of them eight by tens, some two feet by three feet, and spent all her time—when she wasn't shooting—re-photographing these images of Hitler against the icebergs, the fjords, surrounded by Greenland natives, even a whale that came in and was dissected in the background," recalled one observer. "We didn't know what she did with these photographs, but she guarded the negatives and took them back [to Berlin]. They were very important to her."

She shot in Greenland from June to September, sometimes exploring fjords and icebergs with mountaineer-stuntman Hans Ertl, the two of them scrambling over the ice, as Ertl gleefully recalled, dressed only in climbing boots. Sometimes she worked on her location reports for *Tempo*, which never alluded to Hitler. Mostly she suffered from a recurrence of the bladder infection (it may have been colitis) that had first afflicted her while making *Piz Palü*. As her health worsened, she was sent back to Berlin in late September with production on the film not yet completed.

She resumed shooting in early February 1933 with Tay Garnett and Rod La Rocque in Switzerland, but her medical hiatus allowed her to further her acquaintance with Hitler. The Nazi leader had spent the summer campaigning in a spectacular tour of Germany by air—"The Führer over Germany" was the double-edged slogan coined by Goebbels—the first election campaign anywhere to exploit aviation and the full range of new media. Air travel enabled Hitler to give twenty major speeches to a million voters in a single week; fifty thousand phonograph records of his speeches were distributed to those not on his flight path; short-subject talkies of his speeches were filmed and shown in sympathetic cinemas before the feature attraction. In the end, election gains again fell short of an absolute majority. Goebbels remarked in quiet desperation, "We must come to power in the foreseeable future [or] we'll win ourselves to death in elections." The official party newspaper, the *Völkischer Beobachter*, printed a less ironic and more determined view. "The basis of our struggle is hatred for everything that is opposed to us. Now no quarter will be given."

That summer had seen unprecedented political violence in Germany. Street clashes between Communists and Nazis left hundreds wounded and nearly as many dead. Nazi propaganda blamed the violence on Marxist provocations and renewed the call for *Ordnung*—order. Hitler tried in August to negotiate his way into the chancellor's office by pressuring President von Hindenburg. The old field marshal, enfeebled but unyielding at eighty-four, distrusted Hitler and his brownshirts and was fearful of the terror that might result from appointing him to office. Hitler rejected a compromise offer of a vice-chancellorship out of hand. "I did not form the party to haggle, to sell it, to barter it away!" His all-or-nothing demands left him furious and empty-handed. It looked—to everyone but Hitler—as if Nazi power had peaked. "The question," he told a reporter who remembered Mussolini's march on Rome in 1922, "is not whether I shall march on Berlin but rather who will have to march *out* of Berlin."

Leni was absent during these events but cannot have been oblivious of them on her return to Berlin on September 28. Nor did she need newspapers, for she could go directly to the source. She called on the man now universally known to his supporters as *der Führer* at the Hotel Kaiserhof with photographs she had taken in Greenland, perhaps those her shipmates wondered at that included his own image. She was his personal guest at a reception at the home of Dr. Joseph Goebbels and his wife, Magda, where she met other Nazi notables, including Hermann Göring, the second most prominent man in the party and a much-decorated flier in the war, a friend of her friend Udet, who had flown in the same squadron.

Hitler found time to visit Leni's flat in the Hindenburgstrasse accompanied by Goebbels, "Putzi" Hanfstaengl, and personal photographer Heinrich Hoffmann to admire stills from *The Blue Light*. She was the Führer's personal guest at the Sportpalast in Berlin on November 2, just before yet another election, when he told his ecstatic followers, "I've chosen my path and will follow it to its end."

Naïveté and boredom with politics had given way to being an outsider among insiders, watching, listening, and absorbing impressions she would later transform into still-powerful images on celluloid. She would never be a party member—only 5 percent of German women ever joined the Nazi Party, the only one in Germany never to elect a woman to the Reichstag—but she was establishing herself among the inner circle before Hitler came to power and while power was still in doubt.

She became ever more visible at social functions for the party elite. Magda Goebbels invited her to an intimate gathering on the evening of November 6, the date of the last fully free elections to be held in the Weimar Republic, though no one knew that then. The mood was sepulchral as the vote came in, exposing significant weakening at the polls. The party suffered a net loss of two million votes, and its percentage fell from the July high of 37.4 to 33.1, while the Communists increased their showing from 14.5 to almost 17 percent, a trend that suggested the beginning of the Nazi end to many relieved observers. Two days later, Leni managed to be in Munich—"Capital of the Movement" and Hitler's favorite German city—at a Bavarian restaurant called Sternecker, where Hitler kissed her hand and dismissed the ominous portents of the vote. "Only the weak have deserted us," he assured her, "and that is good!"

But 1932 was ending in darkness with few hints of dawn. The November election resulted in a loss of seats in the Reichstag; provincial elections on December 5 revealed a disastrous 40 percent erosion in the Nazi position; perpetual electioneering had depleted the party's coffers; morale was plunging and inner-party conflicts rising. Hitler seemed as far from the Chancellery as ever, just as the severest blow came on December 8, with the resignation from the party of Gregor Strasser, precipitating what looked like the final, fatal crisis.

Strasser had been a party member since 1920 and was widely esteemed as Hitler's right hand in party organization. Fully as racist and ruthless as Hitler, Strasser pressed a socialist agenda within the party, while Hitler seemed obsessed by nothing but acquiring power. Strasser rejected Hitler's all-or-nothing strategies and, following the setbacks of 1932, was offered a vice-chancellorship by General von Schleicher, "the fifty-seven-day chancellor," an undisguised attempt to circumvent Hitler, co-opt a chief lieutenant, and split the party. Strasser publicly resigned when Hitler accused him of treason, shaking to its foundations a political movement that had seen no greater crisis since Hitler's release from prison in 1925.

Leni had been to the theater on the evening of December 8 and dropped by the Hotel Kaiserhof on her way home. She was spotted in the lobby by Hitler's adjutant Brückner, who told her, "The Führer would like to see you." Brückner escorted her through hotel hallways to Hitler's private apartment. There she discovered her Führer raving, pacing, threatening suicide, and on the edge of a breakdown. "He obviously needed someone in whom he could confide," she told herself.

The anecdote—so improbable that Gitta Sereny calls it "grotesque"— is nonetheless revealing about its teller. The historical records show that Hitler spent the early evening of December 8 at the home of Goebbels and returned to the Kaiserhof at 2:00 a.m. for strategy meetings that lasted until six in the morning with Goebbels; Heinrich Himmler, leader of the SS; and Ernst Röhm, leader of the SA, or storm troopers. Goebbels later confirmed that suicide and depression had been themes of a dark and despairing night, but they signified only how "deeply wounded by [Strasser's] treachery" the Führer was, not his readiness to collapse in Leni's arms or plunge from a rooftop. As for Strasser, whose protégé he had been, Goebbels jotted in his diary that he was "a dead man," as he soon was.

It is possible that Leni's oddly fortuitous appearance at the Kaiserhof resulted in a fleeting moment with Hitler between crisis meetings with his top aides. But the melodramatic narrative she spins suggests not only her fascination with Hitler but also her need to appear central to the drama, at the heartbeat of history while—like Junta—remaining blamelessly apart from it, an involuntary casualty, fate's inadvertent victim. She ends her account of the scene with Hitler, one of the few in which she is completely alone with him, this way: "Without having uttered even a single word, I left the room."

Hitler reclaimed his self-confidence and control of the party. Leni left Berlin in late January for Switzerland and the resumption of shooting on *S.O.S. Iceberg* after fending off Béla Balázs's demands for his outstanding fee on *The Blue Light*. The *Iceberg* cast and crew began shooting in February under Garnett's direction on iceberg sets constructed of iron pipes and burlap, watered and iced over in the mountains of the Bernina Pass.

On January 30, 1933, Leni and Hans Ertl were partying with a few others in a hotel sauna in nearby Davos. According to Ertl, Leni was the sole woman among a group of high-spirited men that included a Swiss ski champion named Walter Prager, a former climbing partner of Ertl's. Prager was training Leni for the upcoming Parsenn Derby ski race, in which she would compete and place second among women skiers. Leni took note of "his special charm, his vivacity, his personal appeal," and made him her new lover. Ertl moved on, willing to share anything with a friend, he said, except the woman in his bed.

It was just as well. Ertl was unlikely to have remained an attraction for Leni because he was as competitive and ambitious as she was. He would soon be climbing the Himalayas and would work as a cameraman for Fanck and Trenker before returning to Leni's domain as one of her most indispensable collaborators and a frank enthusiast of the Third Reich. His friend Prager's ambitions were more modest, his charms those of the passive consort, like Schneeberger before him. Leni described their affair, which would last the better part of the next two years, as "not a tempestuous love, more a rather tender romance."

Late in life, she wondered that, "oddly enough, I have never fallen in love with men who were socially, politically or artistically prominent," but men with strong senses of identity and destiny were potential competitors and threats to her independence. Achieving control over powerful men was less an erotic satisfaction than a way of manipulating opportunity and neutralizing obstacles. Fame and power are never without allure, but she needed to achieve them for herself, not as by-products of proximity or reflected glory.

As Ertl remembered the evening of January 30, 1933, the party in the sauna was interrupted by a telephone call. Ertl left the heated cabin to answer and heard a voice on the other end ask for Leni: Hermann Göring was calling from Berlin. Ertl, assuming it was a practical joke, summoned Leni, who emerged from the sauna and took the call. It was, indeed, from Göring, president of the Reichstag, informing her that Hitler, after the setbacks and turmoil of the previous months, had succeeded at last in forcing Hindenburg to name him chancellor of Germany. Berlin was erupting in celebrations, and a torchlight parade of twenty-five thousand Hitler supporters in full Nazi regalia was at that very moment marching from the Chancellery through the Brandenburg Gate and into history.

Ertl remembered Leni's giddy delight at the call, the mere fact of which was an indication that somebody thought courtesies were due her, even if, as Ertl reported with cheerful malice, she absorbed the news that the Thousand Year Reich had begun when she was "stark naked."

Shooting resumed on *S.O.S. Iceberg* in February. By May, Leni was back in Berlin, where everything seemed new.

EIGHT

THE TURNING POINT

*There is an unsolved riddle in the history of the creation of
the Third Reich. I think it is much more interesting than the
question of who set fire to the Reichstag. It is the question:
"What became of the Germans?"*

—Sebastian Haffner

She is the only one of all the stars who understands us.

—Joseph Goebbels

HITLER'S ACCESSION TO THE OFFICE of chancellor in 1933 initiated what came to be called "the seizure of power" (*Machtergreifung*),
though it was not violent, illegal, or inevitable. It was achieved through
a drive to absolute political authority that was unremitting and without
scruple, sustained by shrewd exploitation of economic and civic crises,
both actual and self-created. But victory was not achieved by will alone,
relentless as it was. Equally vital were "chance, frivolity, and bad luck"
among Hitler's opponents, who deluded themselves that they could control him.

Apart from the Nazis' never securing a clear political majority, the most
intractable roadblock to the Nazi leader's becoming chancellor had been
President von Hindenburg, who distrusted Hitler and openly disparaged
him as "the Bohemian corporal." By 1933, the aged field marshal yielded to

pressure and personal exhaustion brought on by a chain of crises that seemed occasioned by the Weimar constitution he had sworn to uphold in 1925. In naming Hitler to the office of chancellor, he unwittingly assured that constitution's destruction. No critic lashed out more harshly or presciently than the belatedly clear-eyed general Erich Ludendorff, who had marched at Hitler's side in the Munich putsch of 1923. "You have delivered up our holy German Fatherland to one of the greatest demagogues of all time," Ludendorff wrote Hindenburg two days after the fateful decision. "I solemnly prophesy that this accursed man will cast our Reich into the abyss and bring our nation to inconceivable misery. Future generations will damn you in your grave for what you have done."

Other voices were raised in alarm even as the torchlight processions wove strings of fire across Germany that for millions seemed to cauterize unrest and apprehension in the camaraderie of mass ritual. Even nonsupporters welcomed the call to national regeneration and the end of a democratic process that had proved impotent to unify a fractured and humiliated nation.

"Hitler is Reich Chancellor. Just like a fairy tale," Goebbels told his diary on January 31. The faithful were jubilant, and Leni, as she acknowledged, was one of millions caught up in the surging euphoria. By the time she returned to Berlin in May from skiing in Switzerland, the groundwork for dictatorship had been laid, aided by what Joachim Fest terms a "mass desertion to the Nazi camp" in a "fog of nationalistic slogans."

It happened with speed so breathtaking that it astonishes more than seven decades later. On February 4, less than a week after his appointment to office, the new chancellor issued a decree—with the support of the president and the cabinet that had been confident they could tame him—granting himself the power to ban publications of rival parties and forbid them the right of assembly. The measure, he explained, was justified by newspaper criticism of his revered composer, Richard Wagner, and was meant "to preserve the present-day press from similar errors." Five days into the new regime, the arts had been enlisted in the name of patriotism as political tools subject to party control.

The burning of the Reichstag three weeks later, on February 27, became a galvanizing public event and pretext for further action. Whether setting the home of the German parliament ablaze was an act of arson by Marinus van der Lubbe (a twenty-four-year-old unemployed Dutch bricklayer and Communist sympathizer found in the building and subsequently beheaded for the crime) and part of a Bolshevik conspiracy, as the Nazis claimed, or was planned and executed by the regime itself, as many believed, remains a subject of debate. Not open to doubt was the benefit to the Nazis of what could unequivocally be labeled an act of terrorism. The Reichstag fire provided Hitler with what he called "a God-given signal" to suppress opposition by enacting, with Hindenburg's support, an emergency decree "for the protection of the People and the State" curtailing basic civil rights, including habeas corpus. It was not the first time the Weimar constitution had been suspended in reaction to a perceived emergency, but it would be the last.

The decree read, in part, "Curbs on personal liberty, on the right of free expression of opinion, including freedom of the press, of association, and of assembly, surveillance over letters, telegrams and telephone communications, searches of homes and confiscations of as well as restrictions on property, are hereby permissible beyond the limits hitherto established by law." Such measures have found echoes in more recent times as responses to acts of terrorism, though Hitler's dramatic expansion of executive power, restrictions of civil liberties, and surveillance of citizens were openly detailed in the Nazi press.

The decree was, in miniature, a blueprint for dictatorship and the Gestapo and legally cleared the way for "protective custody," for broadening the catalog of crimes subject to the death penalty, for confiscating private property, and for granting power over the states to the central government, effectively nullifying the federal system.

These emergency powers were made permanent a month later in the Enabling Act of March 23—"The Law for Removing the Distress of People and Reich"—which ended the Weimar Republic without any need to abrogate the constitution that had created it. The Enabling Act not only annulled civil rights, it also transferred the right to make laws from the Reichstag to the chancellor and the right to draft laws from the president to the chancellor, including the power to rewrite the constitution and conduct foreign policy without oversight. The legal basis for dictatorship was thus secured as the Reichstag—minus its Communist members, all of whom were now under arrest or in flight—passed the Enabling Act and, for all intents and purposes, voted itself out of existence.

The last fully free German election until after Hitler's death had taken place only a week after the Reichstag fire, on March 5, as a last pretense at gaining a legitimate majority. Even with the advantages of a state-controlled press and the financial backing of industrialists convinced that they had everything to gain and little to fear from a Hitler-led regime, the Nazis again failed to achieve a majority. In a Goebbels-orchestrated campaign whose violence claimed the lives of at least fifty-one of the Nazis' opponents and eighteen of their own, the party polled only 43.9 percent of the vote in spite of public anxiety exploited by Goebbels's fearmongering as the smoke still rose from the ashes of the Reichstag. Artificially amplified to 51.9 percent by including the votes cast for their conservative coalition partners, Hitler and Goebbels declared a "glorious triumph." The swastika banner was raised over public buildings for the first time in a show of triumphalism; the black, red, and gold of the Weimar flag was replaced by the old imperial colors of black, white, and red, an unmistakable homage to militarism and the ultimate visual symbol of power that was no longer in dispute or doubt. Hitler had been in office little more than a month.

Public announcement of the establishment of the first concentration camp, in a former gunpowder factory at Dachau, came two weeks later, on March 20, from Heinrich Himmler. The camp and others like it were designated to accommodate and "reeducate" more than four thousand political prisoners arrested the night of the Reichstag fire (many of them public figures), a number that would grow to twenty-five thousand by the end of June. There was nothing secret about it: Newspaper headlines in

Dachau, the sleepy town outside Munich known for its landscape and genre painters, welcomed the camp as a sign of "happier days" and "hope for the Dachau business world." Posted notices and members of the Dachau SS warned residents not to come within 150 meters of the triple barbed-wire perimeter of the camp or risk being shot on sight. Fifty such camps would be in operation by the end of 1933.

Dachau's ceremonial opening was April 1, the day of the Führer-decreed nationwide Jewish boycott. Placed in charge of the boycott targeting Jewish business owners, shopkeepers, doctors, lawyers, and other professionals was Julius Streicher, publisher since 1923 of the virulently anti-Semitic *Der Stürmer*. Hitler ordered the boycott as a safety valve to alleviate simmering violence among the ranks of the storm troopers (SA) and to demonstrate that a decade of racist harangues had not been mere rhetoric. International reports of Nazi violence against Jews—including murders—had already prompted protests in America and England. Threats of the Nazi boycott triggered the American Jewish Congress's rally at New York's Madison Square Garden on March 27 calling for a global counterboycott of German goods. The action in Germany was scaled back but not halted. Streicher's official proclamation noted negative foreign reaction, for which Germans, he said, should hold the victims responsible: "Show the Jews that they cannot besmirch Germany and disparage its honor without punishment." The one-day boycott—on the Jewish Sabbath—was the first officially, openly sanctioned public display of state-sponsored persecution that would lead to Auschwitz.

The boycott was less successful at coalescing universal support than expected, though Goebbels called it "an imposing spectacle." Ian Kershaw cites "almost a holiday mood" as shoppers created rushes on Jewish stores before the boycott began. Many regarded it as just another incident in centuries of racist bullying that wasn't—they eagerly pointed out—exclusively German. Still others viewed the random violence, crudely painted Stars of David, and exhortations to beware Jewish merchants as the moment to declare their support for the new regime.

Though Leni claimed ceaselessly that "my parents didn't belong to any party," her father, Alfred, formally joined the Nazi Party on April 1, 1933, the day of the Jewish boycott, receiving membership card number 1,670,383.

The book burnings in Berlin and other university towns in Germany burst into world headlines the night of May 10, blazing with volumes that right-wing student organizers had seized from local libraries and bookstores. The bonfires signaled zealous condemnation of un-German influence, homegrown or foreign. The works of Albert Einstein, Thomas Mann, Heinrich Mann, Karl Marx, Sigmund Freud, Kurt Tucholsky, Erich Maria Remarque, and scores of others—including Heinrich Heine, who once observed that a country that will burn books will burn people—were hurled onto hundreds of pyres fed by works of non-Germans and non-Jews such as André Gide, Upton Sinclair, and Helen Keller, creating front-page news around the world.

The flight of Jews and political dissidents to Prague, Vienna, Paris, Amsterdam, and the United States had begun, fully noted by the world press. Einstein's exile and renunciation of his German citizenship was news Goebbels's propaganda services could not control or bury, nor did they try. "We do not want to be the land of Goethe and Einstein," wrote Berlin's *Lokal-Anzeiger* on May 7 in a spirit of good riddance.

Though Hitler's political machinations had been mostly conducted out of public view, evidence of a new order launched by repression and terror—not limited to the establishment of the concentration camps—was available to the world press, not in spite of the Nazis but because they wanted their achievements broadcast as widely as possible. They were fulfilling promises Hitler had made in *Mein Kampf* and in countless speeches across Germany with results that were widely apparent, later claims of ignorance—inside and outside of Germany—notwithstanding. A culminating example was the publicizing of the imprisonment of Carl von Ossietzky, pacifist editor of *Die Weltbühne*, who had castigated the Nazis four weeks before Hitler became chancellor for their "loudmouthed brutality and brainlessness." He had been incarcerated since the night of the Reichstag fire, his "disciplining" deemed useful to the restoration of order. Ossietzky was awarded the Nobel Peace Prize in 1935 while imprisoned in Oranienburg, but not even the prestige of the Swedish Academy could cut through the barbed wire behind which he died in 1938. Hitler simply forbade German citizens thereafter to accept the Nobel Prize, and the Germans complied. In the words of Joachim Fest, "Hitler did not come as a thief in the night."

Leni returned to Berlin sometime in early or mid-May, having missed the main events and improbably claiming unawareness of them, though her future employment depended on her careful observance of their consequences. At almost thirty-one, she had a new lover in Walter Prager and a still-unsatisfied ambition to become a dramatic actress, one eye steadily trained on Hollywood.

She had made up her mind to star in an espionage film similar to the recent screen excursions of Garbo and Dietrich as seductive spies in *Mata Hari*, in which Garbo danced, and *Dishonored*, in which Dietrich straightened her silk stockings before a remorse-stricken firing squad. Leni's project, an idea suggested earlier by Fanck, was *Mademoiselle Docteur*, based on the exploits of a female German agent in France during the war. She took it to Ufa and came away having convinced herself they were "excited" and "willing to produce and finance it." Their interest, according to internal memos, was tepid because of the war theme and their skepticism that Leni could act the part, even under the competent direction of Frank Wisbar (later to find himself in Hollywood) from a script by Gerhard Henzel.

On May 16, a week after the book burnings in Berlin and a day after similar incendiary demonstrations in Hamburg, Leni donned an evening gown and posed for photographers at a performance of *Madame Butterfly*. She was the guest of Goebbels and his wife, Magda, with whom she had socialized in Berlin during her hiatus from *S.O.S. Iceberg* between late September and the New Year. She later reported that Goebbels spent much of the opera surreptitiously thrusting his hand under her dress. His groping incensed her, she wrote, though not enough to curtail their social or professional relationships.

Goebbels had been named Minister of National Enlightenment and Propaganda (a post created for him) following the recent and final parliamentary elections in March. The most intellectual of major Third Reich figures, fascinating to many and repellent to more, Goebbels had been—apart from Hitler himself—chiefly responsible for the creation of the Hitler cult and the myth of the New Germany Hitler embodied.

Goebbels was small, swarthy, and sleek, always impeccably well dressed and groomed. He limped due to a shortened leg and a clubfoot that were the results of a childhood bout of osteomyelitis, a bone marrow infection. The deformity embittered and goaded him, an ironic prank of fate for a fervent proselytizer for a master race of tall, blond athletes. He compensated for his lack of Aryan perfection with glinting intellect and compulsive sexual adventuring, especially with beautiful actresses. He was an orator second only to Hitler, possessed of a commanding speaking voice—sometimes strident, sometimes seductive—and projected a charm that some found reptilian, though his magnetism (or his power) made many women overlook his infirmity as they facilitated his reputation as the most notorious womanizer of the Third Reich.

Physically unfit for the military, he claimed to have been a wounded war veteran until the fiction was exposed. He tried his hand at writing a novel and some plays before discovering National Socialism in the early twenties. He attracted attention as the protégé of Gregor Strasser in Berlin and derided Bavarian party leaders as "Munich big shots" and Hitler himself as "petit bourgeois" until meeting and being embraced by the future Führer in 1926. He switched his allegiance from Strasser and transformed himself into the most passionate of disciples, recording in his diary, "Adolf Hitler, I love you." It was he who made "*Heil*, Hitler!" an official form of greeting. The Führer myth had found its Orpheus.

Cold, calculating, opportunistically rather than ideologically anti-Semitic, and visionary in his uses of propaganda, Goebbels had a passion for Hitler that was abject if not pathological. "He is a genius," he confided to his diary. "The natural, creative instrument of a fate determined by God. I am deeply moved. He is like a child: kind, good, merciful. Like a cat: cunning, clever, agile. Like a lion: roaring and gigantic."

Such fealty and a genius for agitation were soon rewarded. He was made Gauleiter of Berlin, where he founded the Nazi newspaper *Der Angriff* (*The Attack*) in 1927. He institutionalized the torchlight parades, the nighttime bonfires, the processions of Nazi banners, the massed formations of marchers, and other elements of Nazi iconography that would become spellbinding through Leni's manipulation of them on film. But visual style was the least of it. In his role as minister of propaganda, he would control, through ideological "coordination" or "alignment" (*Gleichschaltung*), the Nazification of not only press and radio but all of German culture, including music, theater, dance, painting, sculpture, and, most obsessively and passionately, film.

If he did not invent modern political propaganda, he will do as its Machiavelli. The arts of image making suited his cynicism and contempt for the masses. He understood, as the Russians and few others then did, the propaganda potential of the new technologies of film, radio, phonograph records, and even the infant television. The casting of a messianic aura around a charismatic leader, the sowing of confusion and exploiting of resentments, the cynical use of distortion and disinformation that are staples of modern media politics have their origins in techniques he developed or perfected.

Unlike his contemporary counterparts, he did not shrink from the term *propaganda* or frankly defining what it was. "Propaganda has absolutely nothing to do with truth!" he proclaimed. "That propaganda is good which leads to success, and that is bad which fails to achieve the desired result, however intelligent it is, for it is not propaganda's task to be intelligent." He may have merely been echoing Hitler's conviction that propaganda "is a means and must therefore be judged with regard to its end," but his pragmatic attitude toward propaganda would later be a major source of friction with Leni. What he viewed with matter-of-fact cynicism as expedient, she wanted seen as Art. The conflict would add to tensions created by his predatory sexual habits and his rapport with Hitler, which made them rivals for the Führer's affections and favor.

Goebbels's ministry opened its doors officially on the day of the Jewish boycott. The following morning, the *New York Times* reported on its front page that the new minister had written the six American film companies with offices in Berlin that they were to dismiss "all your representatives, rental agents and branch managers of Jewish extraction immediately." The directive continued, "I emphasize that it is not religion but race that is decisive. Christianized Jews are thus equally affected. In place of these gentlemen, only members of the National Socialist Party shall be employed." The American companies, all of them heavily Jewish, temporized in consideration of their market share. After a visit to Germany, MGM's Irving Thalberg announced, "A lot of Jews will lose their lives," but "Hitler and Hitlerism will pass; the Jews will still be there." By the time the Warner Bros. representative in Berlin, Joe Kauffmann, was hunted down and murdered by brownshirted thugs, it was evident that the Nazis threatened more than markets.

Goebbels's letter—widely reported—was the first unmistakable, unavoidable signpost to the future for anyone like Leni who hoped to work in the German film industry in any capacity whatever. As film historian David Stewart Hull points out, "In an effort to please the government, the film companies voluntarily began to ease Jewish actors and actresses out of their films, although this requirement had not yet become law." With *Mademoiselle Docteur* being written and opportunities certain to expand with exclusion of Jews from the industry, Leni ensured her employability by preparing her Proof of Descent as required by the Reich's film office, falsely entering her mother's stepmother, Ottilie, as her biological grandmother.

Contrary to a long-standing myth that show business and entertainment are immune from economic conditions, the worldwide film industry was suffering depression doldrums like every other business. In America, only MGM was operating in the black. Paramount, Warner Bros., Universal, United Artists, and Fox had all gone into receivership in 1932 as audiences and receipts dwindled. Germany remained the fourth most active film industry in the world after the United States, England, and France, releasing 127 feature films in 1932 to America's 547, England's 169, and France's 158. The language barrier had exacted its toll since the introduction of sound, but giant Ufa still took in ten million marks in net profits in 1932, a figure that plunged to a paltry forty thousand marks by the end of 1933. Of twenty-nine film stages in Berlin, twenty-eight were active when Hitler took office. By the end of the year, eighteen stood silent and empty.

Ufa's worldwide prestige was intact but waning. It had largely been the product of "the Friedrichstrasse crowd," the Nazis' sneering allusion to the business address favored by Jewish producers. The new minister of propaganda met with party members employed by Ufa and told them that under the influence of "profiteers," the industry had "performed disgraceful boot-blacking service" instead of fulfilling its highest objective as "a pioneer fighter for national culture."

Goebbels assembled prominent industry figures in the banquet hall of the Hotel Kaiserhof to elaborate on what films he would favor in the future. Present were executives, producers, directors, and such stars as Emil Jannings, Hans Albers, and Conrad Veidt along with lesser names and anonymous technicians, some of them Jewish and some wearing brown shirts and swastika armbands. Goebbels took a deceptively conciliatory tone. "Art is free and should remain free," he announced, adding dissonantly for Jewish ears in the audience, "We have arrived" and "We shall not leave."

He cited a quartet of films he admired that the German industry might emulate: Sergei Eisenstein's *Battleship Potemkin*, the sensational hit in Berlin of 1926; *Anna Karenina*, with Greta Garbo and John Gilbert (titled *Love* in America), of 1927; Fritz Lang's nationalistic saga *Die Nibelungen*, of 1924; and *The Rebel* (*Der Rebell*), of 1932, Luis Trenker's film about anti-Napoleonic loyalists in nineteenth century Tyrol. What was remarkable, even bizarre, about this list was not the films but the artists who made them. Eisenstein was a Marxist, a Jew, and a homosexual; *Anna Karenina* bore the fingerprints of Jewish Irving Thalberg for Jewish-dominated MGM; Fritz Lang was, as everyone in the banquet room knew (including Lang, who was there), half Jewish; and Luis Trenker's codirector on *The Rebel* had been Jewish Kurt Bernhardt (known as Curtis Bernhardt in Hollywood exile), and his producer was Jewish Paul Kohner of Universal and *S.O.S. Iceberg*. Not one of these films could have been made or distributed with its credits intact in Germany the very day Goebbels singled them out as exemplary.

No one missed the odd and twisted racial undertone, if only because other areas of German cultural life were already being "coordinated" on political and racial lines. The civil service law of April 7, a month before Goebbels spoke to the film industry, gave legal status to the racial concepts "Aryan" and "non-Aryan," which were derived from spurious theories of genetics and racial purity discredited everywhere but in the Reich. Persons "of non-Aryan descent" and others whose "former political activity" did not "offer a guarantee" of state interests were to be removed from civil service positions "even if the necessary conditions required by current law do not exist." As the German civil service included schools and universities, the law removed thousands of scientists, artists, scholars, administrators, and teachers from their positions and accelerated the Jewish exodus from Germany already in progress. The flood of exiles represented, in Peter Gay's estimation, "the greatest collection of transplanted intellect, talent, and scholarship the world has ever seen."

Coordination of the film industry began voluntarily immediately after Goebbels's speech at the Kaiserhof in anticipation of measures analogous to the civil service law that would govern the film world. The expected rules were announced on June 30, effective the following day, and decreed exclusion of Jews from the motion picture industry. Foreign companies or productions were to be managed by native-born, non-Jewish Germans or approved persons of German descent. The same day, Goebbels retaliated against the Actors and Directors Association—which had filed a brief on behalf of Jewish members whose "distinguished service at the front during the war" should exempt them from racial decrees—by disbanding the association. These were matters of common knowledge, as unambiguous as the swastika or the fact that racial exclusion spelled catastrophe or exile for some and opportunity for others.

All of Leni's accounts of this period claim that she remained in Switzerland working on *S.O.S. Iceberg* and skiing until June—in some versions, until July—and learned only later of the changes in Germany or missed them altogether, though in truth she was back in Berlin and attending the opera by mid-May, when literary bonfires were still smoldering. Even if she had lingered in Davos as she claimed, the ski resorts of German-speaking Switzerland were not sealed off from news of the outside world. Though her exact return date is uncertain, her visit to *Madame Butterfly* on May 16 followed a daytime meeting with Goebbels at the ministry. He had then suggested she might think of making "a Hitler film. She is over the moon [*begeistert*] about the idea," he noted in his diary. There followed more than a dozen meetings over the summer during which mention of current events presumably took place. Conversation about "her new film" continued in friendly fashion with the propaganda minister on the evening of June 11, and, though she claimed to be oblivious of political matters, Goebbels assured his diary that evening, "She is the only one of all the stars who understands us."

Two days later, he recorded that Leni reported she had "spoken with Hitler" and "is now starting her film." He noted a pleasant social evening at Hitler's residence on June 15 with Leni and others. "Very nice," he noted. "Late to bed." And so on.

Leni would later characterize Goebbels as her nemesis, but it is evident that in the early summer of 1933 she was cultivating and receiving his support for a film about Hitler that he had personally suggested to her. In spite of the groping incident at the opera, they were in frequent contact and on amiable terms socially and professionally.

What Goebbels meant by "a Hitler film" is not known, but Leni's enthusiasm appears to have been genuine. Goebbels's diary entries show signs of being unpremeditated, even though they were intended for eventual publication, and some of them turned up in edited form in the 1930s as propaganda for the movement, even in English translation. It has been suggested that, far from being tainted by intended publication, they may be all the more trustworthy for that. Once part of the public record, they would be open to challenge. In any case, there seems little reason to distrust the warmth with which Goebbels writes about Leni, from his earliest mention of her in December 1929 after a screening of *Piz Palü*, when he jotted admiringly, "Also in the film is the beautiful Leni Riefenstahl. A splendid child, full of grace!"

Diary entries clearly spell out Leni's eager preparation for the "Hitler film" she was about to make and argue against hostility on Goebbels's part. Her later charges are strident, unvaried, and self-righteous, as if the antagonism of a Goebbels—so repugnant and reprehensible—would validate her own political purity. But Goebbels's diaries, not fully revealed until after German reunification in 1989, compromise a past she had spent decades revising and improving, as she had once improved her dance reviews.

The summer of 1933 was a turning point and her "Hitler film" its fulcrum. Without it—or without the Führer and his propaganda minister—her rise to international fame might never have happened or might have happened with consequences less remarkable and, almost certainly, less controversial. She cannot, of course, have known that. Like many of her generation, she was to distance herself from history by protesting rhetorically, "I, I alone, I should have been able to foresee that one day things would change?" But if she was blind to what was to come, her eyes were open to what *was* because they had to be if she wanted to work at all, and she must have communicated that to Goebbels, whether sincerely or as opportunistic flattery. "She is the only one of all the stars who understands us" was not meaningless to him or to her fortunes in the new order. She saw with the clarity of self-interest the many advantages a reduced field of rivals within the film industry offered her as an actress or filmmaker or both. She had sought and found favor with Hitler before he became Führer, attracted as she was by his ideas and personality. If, as she claimed, he had said to her that "you must make my films," the time had come to uncoil the possibilities of that casual remark.

NINE

TOTAL DEVOTION

The laws of the Gestapo alone will not suffice. The masses need an idol.

—Adolf Hitler

It is certainly to be hoped that this film will be shown in all cinemas outside Germany, if one wishes to understand the intoxicating spirit which is moving Germany these days.

—*London Observer*, December 3, 1933

ROADS NOT TAKEN ARE SIGNPOSTED, if at all, for backward glances, and Leni was looking restlessly to the future. She could not know that her expressed enthusiasm for "a Hitler film" in 1933 would both place her on a path to unimagined success and divert her from her "most fervent wish," to win renown as a dramatic actress. *S.O.S. Iceberg* would do nothing to further such aspirations, but her hopes had been quickened just before Christmas 1932 with the arrival from Hollywood of Josef von Sternberg. He had come back to Berlin, he told her, because Ufa's Erich Pommer had invited him to make another film there after the huge international success of *The Blue Angel*. He sent Leni flowers, she recounted, called her "Du-Du" once again, and by candlelight they speculated about Hitler and his racial policies, which Sternberg, like many Jews, dismissed as "just campaign rhetoric."

When Leni screened *The Blue Light* for him, his praise for her directing segued to his appreciation for her acting. "There is no greater antithesis than that between you as Junta in *The Blue Light* and Marlene as Lola in *The Blue Angel*," he told her. "I made Marlene: she is my creature. Now she's an international star. And you—when are you coming?"

Leni's is the only account of these moments. Sternberg's visit to Berlin was real enough, and his encouragement may well have intensified dreams of Hollywood and worldwide stardom, but if she hoped that his plans at Ufa or farther west might include her, she was to be disappointed. Sternberg was not in Berlin at the behest of Erich Pommer, who was then packing his bags for New York and the Fox Film Corporation, where Jewish producers were more likely to remain active than in Berlin. The rub was that Sternberg's instincts for politics were as primitive as Pommer's were prescient. Sternberg had flamboyantly "retired" at the age of thirty-eight to protest contract disputes with Paramount in Hollywood, where he had made Dietrich the studio's most glittering asset. He had traveled to Berlin to persuade Pommer and Ufa to finance future Dietrich-Sternberg collaborations, but, with Pommer in virtual flight, he found himself dining instead with studio magnate Alfred Hugenberg, shortly to become finance minister for the Nazi regime, which would ban *The Blue Angel* as un-German and immoral. Sternberg's fantasies of creative sanctuary in Berlin went up in the smoke of torchlight parades on January 30, and he left shortly thereafter, noting from his taxi window on the way to the station a curious red glow in the clouds that he discovered only later had been the reflected fury of the conflagration at the Reichstag.

Leni was in Switzerland by then, but her return to Berlin in May inspired her to do for herself what Sternberg could not do. She proposed *Mademoiselle Docteur* to Ufa as a vehicle for herself as an actress, not a director. She did so, she claimed, because she was "penniless, with barely enough money to pay my back rent." If so, she was a charity case with an elegant apartment, a full-time maid, and friends in high places.

She had more than a dozen known encounters with Goebbels that summer, including official meetings, social occasions, a day alone with him at his home in Berlin, private screenings at Hitler's residence, and day trips out of Berlin to observe location shooting of films for Ufa, now effectively under his control. She attended the opera and theater with his entourage, including his sleek, blond adjutant Prince Friedrich Christian zu Schaumburg-Lippe and the amusing "Auwi," a fanatically dedicated SS officer more formally known as Prince August Wilhelm von Hohenzollern, fourth son of the exiled kaiser. She got acquainted with Prince Philip of Hesse, Hitler's emissary to Mussolini (and son-in-law of the king of Italy), and Marshal Italo Balbo, a Mussolini intimate who was a much-decorated flier and the Italian minister of aviation. The plumber's daughter who hated the class system was comfortably strolling paths of elite privilege within the new regime.

She spent time with Hitler as well. They enjoyed a picnic excursion to Heiligendamm on the Baltic Sea in late May with Goebbels and Magda. She was summoned to his Chancellery office on two occasions in June and was a guest at his private residence as well. There was another trip to the Baltic in July in a touring car party that included the Goebbelses with Hitler's adjutant, Wilhelm Brückner, and his personal photographer, Heinrich Hoffman. The outing was crowned by the hospitality of Frau Viktoria von Dirksen, wife of the ambassador to Tokyo and one of the ambitious Berlin hostesses who found Hitler charming enough to promote in society while concocting vain matrimonial intrigues.

Leni's summer was less self-absorbed and uninformed than usual, she admitted, for when she discussed her "Hitler film" with its subject at the Chancellery in mid-June, she confronted him with her distress at his racial policies and the emigration of so many Jewish artists and intellectuals. On her mind were not only the marquee names such as Einstein, Elisabeth Bergner, Thomas Mann, Bruno Walter, and virtually the entire creative ensemble of artists and architects of the Bauhaus, but friends such as Manfred George of *Tempo*, who had written her from Prague of his struggles to get a visa for America, and Béla Balázs, who had written from Moscow inquiring about his fees for

The Blue Light. "I wept as I held these letters in my hand," she wrote in her memoirs.

Hitler preferred not to discuss the Jewish question with her. He suggested instead that she take over "the artistic aspect" of filmmaking in Germany alongside Goebbels. She went pale with the memory of Goebbels's busy hands, she recalled, and declined "this honorable task" because she couldn't make films "that I don't have a feel for." Hitler, accomodating her willfulness, suggested she make a film about Horst Wessel, the Nazi pimp whose murder in a drunken brawl had been mythologized as political martyrdom (the "Horst Wessel song" had become a second national anthem) or perhaps, the Führer mused, "one about my movement."

"I can't, I can't," Leni replied. "Please don't forget I'm an actress—with all my heart and soul."

She quickly thought better of her refusal to make the Horst Wessel film, which would subsequently be made by others. Two days later, on June 22, she apologized for her abruptness by sending the Führer an eight-volume first edition—gold-embossed and bound in white leather—of the works of philosopher Johann Gottlieb Fichte (a gift to her from Fanck) with the inscription "To my dear Führer, with deepest devotion." Hitler was a Fichte enthusiast, as she knew, and he not only read her offering but also, as Timothy Ryback recently noted in 2002 after studying the volumes, marked a hundred pages with "a veritable blizzard of underlines, question marks, exclamation points, and marginal strikes."

Leni later insisted that her most decisive meeting with the Führer came in the last week of August, when Hitler—unperturbed by or forgetful about her devotion to acting—inquired into her progress on the rally film she was to begin shooting the following week in Nuremberg. "Didn't the Propaganda Ministry inform you?" he asked when she "stared at him in amazement."

He maintained he had given the order to Goebbels through his adjutant weeks earlier: Leni was to make a film of the 1933 Nazi Party Congress in Nuremberg, the first such rally since Hitler had become

8. Oktober 1926
3. Jahrgang / Nr. 41

Preis: 20 Pfennig
Erſcheint wöchentlich

Münchner
Illuſtrierte Preſſe

Verlag Knorr & Hirth, G. m. b. H., München

Das war ein ſonniger Herbſt ....
Die Berliner Filmſchauſpielerin Leni Riefenſtahl bei einem Ausflug

Ufa

A star is born: Leni welcomes early fame
as cover girl of Munich's *Illustrated Press*, 1926.

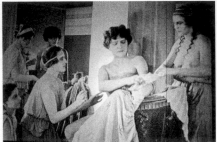

In 1925 Leni appeared unbilled—and largely uncostumed—in the box-office sensation *Ways to Strength and Beauty*. Though she later denied being in it or even having seen it, these never-before-published frame blow-ups confirm decades of unsubstantiated rumors.

Leni's career as a dancer lasted only eight months but . . .

. . . led to her role as the dancer Diotima in *The Holy Mountain*,
the picture that made her a star in German Alpine films.

Dr. Arnold Fanck, "father of the Alpine film,"
shares a meal with his hungry discovery circa 1927.
He was director, mentor, and lover.

Leni and Fanck (next to her) relax on location in a mountain cabin
with rescue dog and crew including (at far right) cameraman Hans Schneeberger,
who would supplant Fanck as her lover.

Leni's films for Fanck demanded daring and courage.
She performed her own stunts, whether on skis, climbing mountains,
or—as here in *Storm Over Mont Blanc*—traversing a
glacial crevasse without a net.

Fanck's Leni in *The Holy Mountain* (1926) . . .

. . . in *The Great Leap* (1927) . . .

. . . in *S.O.S. Iceberg* (1933) . . .

. . . and with Gustav Diessl in *The White Hell of Piz Palü* (1928)

Leni's first film as director—
The Blue Light (1932)—starred her
as Fanck would not: a fairytale
heroine for whom nature was
mere backdrop.

On location for *The Blue Light*, Leni waits in costume
for Schneeberger (arm extended) to set up a shot.

Leni's Leni: Junta from *The Blue Light*—beautiful, innocent,
and persecuted, as Leni saw herself.
This image hung on Leni's bedroom wall until she died.

chancellor. Leni protested that she had never heard of it. Hitler erupted, she said, ranting that the only conceivable explanation for Goebbels's not having told her of the commission was envy within the propaganda ministry that "such an honor" was being awarded to a woman who wasn't even a party member.

Leni's entreaties to be relieved of the assignment because of her "most passionate desire . . . to work as an actress" fell on deaf ears. Hitler insisted that only she had the artistry to make a film that would transcend the "ordinary newsreel footage" piled up by party functionaries. Leni returned home, she later said, to find a letter from Ufa canceling *Mademoiselle Docteur*, thus leaving her not only "penniless" but without the one project she had counted on. She was left with no alternative but to go to Nuremberg and film the rally, an undertaking that would change her life.

Contradictions bristle. Ufa didn't cancel *Mademoiselle Docteur*; it had never been scheduled. The company's reservations about her acting were not voiced—and then only internally—until September 5, two days *after* she finished shooting the rally film in Nuremberg. And if Goebbels had failed to tell her about the commission, what had they been talking about from May to August in their meetings about "a Hitler film"?

The customary assumption has been that Leni's postwar need to distance herself from the Third Reich led her to fictionalize the circumstances of the work she did in Nuremberg, none of which she would ever acknowledge as propaganda. But that was semantics: Goebbels was propaganda, she was not Goebbels, therefore and ergo. She knew the assignment was, if not propaganda, then carefully framed political persuasion, even if ambition or inspiration drove her to produce something that transcended Goebbels's utilitarian definition. Her contemporary interviews about "the tasks I have set myself," which centered on showing "the bond between the Führer and the people," defined the nature of her assignment, whatever label she attached to it or didn't.

What is undeniable is that with only *The Blue Light* to her credit, she was a surprising choice to film the 1933 rally, and Hitler's entrusting her with it presented Goebbels with practical problems having nothing specifically to do with her. On May 11, the day after the Berlin book burnings, he had announced that film activities for the party would be the sole responsibility of the newly formed film division of his propaganda ministry, headed by party officials Arnold Raether and Eberhard Fangauf, who had been responsible for party rally films since 1927. Goebbels had, in effect, granted a filmmaking monopoly to subordinates months before Hitler awarded the rally commission to Leni, which suggests that in proposing "a Hitler film" earlier in the summer, he had had something different in mind. This is almost certainly the case, for the new regime had been so preoccupied with "coordinating" German life since the seizure of power that a firm decision to proceed with the 1933 rally in Nuremberg instead of Stuttgart—or at all—was not reached until late July. This raises the possibility that Leni was telling the truth about her August interview with Hitler but that she accepted the rally commission as a substitute for a "forgotten" and now lost project that may never have been fully conceived.

As the first mass rally since the seizure of power, the party congress of 1933 importantly marked the transition of such gatherings from campaign revels to events of state. The more or less annual rallies had grown from loosely organized "Party Day" parades and speeches in Munich and Weimar to grandiose rituals that drew tens of thousands, then hundreds of thousands of the party faithful to lake-studded park grounds on the outskirts of Nuremberg, the medieval city Hitler styled the "symbol of the first Reich" and designated the Third Reich's rally site "for ever."

The 1933 congress, from August 30 to September 3, was designated the "Reich's Party Rally of Victory" (*Reichsparteitag des Sieges*), and Hitler himself would title Leni's film of it *Victory of Faith* (*Sieg des Glaubens*). What he had seen in *The Blue Light* to persuade him that she was the ideal filmmaker for the event is unknown, but heroic photographic effects and romantic mythmaking may have been enough. "The masses need an idol," he knew, and he had one in mind. Her not being a party member or political thinker was irrelevant. Thousands of brownshirts and hundreds of thousands, even millions of moviegoers needed adrenaline, not doctrine.

But Goebbels knew that Leni's presence among his men in a stadium swarming with flag-hoisting, beer-fueled roisterers could spark territorial disputes, and he was right. She would come to view such head-butting conflicts as conspiracies or vendettas and wield them as evidence of her independence from the party. More to the point, she was a woman with a reputation working in a man's world—and party—that was blatantly antifeminist. She was competing with men she had displaced through a relationship with the Führer that invited speculation she actively encouraged, one that gave rise to resentments and unsavory wisecracks. There was a well-known beer hall joke that had gone around ever since her early Alpine days and nights with Fanck and Trenker. She was derided then as "the nation's glacial crevasse" (*Landesgletscherspalte*). Her current visibility among Nazi bigwigs now fed rumors that elevated her to "crevasse of the Reich" (*Reichsgletscherspalte*), which did little to inspire respect from men disposed to view her presence behind a camera as illegitimate no matter how she got there.

While Goebbels's diary leaves little doubt that he enjoyed her company and the luster she added to his entourage, Leni's accounts of their relationship would become increasingly vitriolic. She referred to him as "the cripple" in private and was repelled by what she described as his unannounced visits to her apartment, where he fell to his knees, clutched at her ankles, and sobbed with desire, or his grabbing her breasts in his office, "his face completely distorted" with lust. Certainly Leni was tempting enough to inspire any number of sexual fantasies—"full of grace," Goebbels had called her—but his reported lunges furnished her with a rationale for their later conflicts, though they largely concerned money and logistics: He "hated me for repelling his sexual advances."

If there is evidence that Goebbels was guilty of not informing her of the Nuremberg assignment, it is that on receiving the commission to film the 1936 Olympics in Berlin, Leni insisted that Hitler formally extend it *through* Goebbels so he "could not later claim that he knew nothing" of

Hitler's orders. She never advanced this proof publicly, because to have done so would have conflicted with too many fictions about the Olympics yet to come, but at least one perceptive acquaintance suggests that Leni protested too much, that her animosity toward Goebbels stemmed not from his obstruction of her goals but from her "shame" that she had so calculatedly used him to realize them.

It is clear that Goebbels set in motion some sort of "Hitler film" in May. Leni and Goebbels discussed it; she and Hitler discussed it. But her campaigning for the Nuremberg commission, once plans for the rally were finalized on or about July 25, remains a possibility. She visited Goebbels's Berlin residence three weeks later, on August 13, a Sunday, the one day he returned alone to Berlin from a family holiday in Heiligendamm, leaving Magda and their children behind. His diary notes only that he was "at home" engaged in "conversation with L. Riefenstahl. Film topics."

He was back in Heiligendamm on Monday, and Leni drove herself there on Tuesday—"on her own from Berlin," as Goebbels noted. She stayed overnight and returned to Berlin the following day. The "film topics" they discussed are unspecified, but it is surely notable that "the last week of August," when Leni says Hitler amazed her with news of the rally film, was a week in which his calendar indicates he wasn't in Berlin at all, but in Munich, Berchtesgaden, Königsberg, Danzig, and on to Nuremberg for the rally itself.

In any event, public announcement of Leni's "artistic direction" of the rally film "at the special request of the Führer" was made on August 23, although press releases noted that overall supervision remained with Arnold Raether of the film division. Two days later, Leni told journalists she would drive herself to Nuremberg to begin preparations for filming, taking only one day off to attend the première of *S.O.S. Iceberg* in Berlin.

She arrived in Nuremberg on Sunday, August 27, three days before the rally was to begin, and, as Goebbels had feared, almost at once clashed with the film division over equipment, manpower, and camera place-ments, the last issue aggravated by independent cameramen granted

access to the rally stadium for newsreels, some of which she would incorporate into her own footage. The expected attendance at the rally, open to
anyone with thirty pfennigs to buy a ticket, was an impressive 350,000,
including regiments of Ernst Röhm's SA men in brown shirts and
Heinrich Himmler's SS men in black. Conflicting agendas and last-
minute preparations added to the general confusion, while Hitler and
Goebbels conferred in Munich and Berchtesgaden about the sequence
and contents of rally oratory only days before it was to begin.

Leni had the good fortune to make almost immediate contact with the
tall, handsome, twenty-eight-year-old Albert Speer. A party member
since 1931, Speer would become famous as Hitler's architect and wartime
minister of armaments, a post that would result in his standing trial for
war crimes in Nuremberg and serving a sentence of twenty years in
Spandau prison. In 1933, he was "chief designer" for the rally, though he
had met Hitler only once in person, when securing the Führer's approval
for the backdrop he had designed for the stadium speaker's platform: a
stylized wooden eagle about seventy-five feet across that even Speer
thought looked as if it were "nailed to a truss like a butterfly."

Speer's eagle was approved. The commission for the rally had come to
him as the result of his staging of a nighttime event on Berlin's
Tempelhof Field the previous May Day. Overnight he had converted
what he called "a stage set for a provincial shooting match" into a ceremonial landscape that revealed his gift for dramatic theatrical settings. He
placed "huge, marvelous flags" at the back wall of the parade ground,
two vertical swastika banners fifty feet high on either side of a black,
white, and red imperial banner. In front of them, he built a high speaker's
platform where Hitler could stand in the glow of klieg lights borrowed
from a nearby film studio. As one of Speer's biographers described the
effect, Hitler "stood high up and far removed from the waiting throng, his
figure bathed in glowing brightness, invoking the awakening of the
nation, unity at home and strength toward the outside world."

Speer's critics dismissed the design as "big, that's all," but it utilized
grandiose motifs that became fixed elements of Nazi iconography and

defined Nazi public display, especially the Nuremberg rallies. His design catapulted him from obscurity and—incorporating Goebbels's massed marchers and torch-lit parades—institutionalized a so-called fascist aesthetic largely misattributed to Leni because of her manipulation of it on film, including the photographing of the Führer from below, a crowd's-eye view that kept him "high up and far removed." This was, of course, as Speer had positioned him, but was also instantly recognizable as the way Fanck had photographed and ennobled his heroic strivers in one Alpine film after another.

Speer, a skier and climber since boyhood, knew these films. He had admired Leni on-screen and was gratified that "we got along from the first moment, worked together in a good way, did what we could to help each other." Leni reciprocated Speer's regard, finding him "extraordinarily attractive and impressive," and came to consider him "the most important—and certainly the most interesting—man in Germany after Hitler." She thought him a run-of-the-mill architect, in spite of the many contributions he made to her filmmaking, "but he was extraordinarily intelligent, burningly ambitious, and he had much more than a gift—a genius—for organization."

Their bond was cemented by what a Speer biographer who knew them both called their "total devotion to Hitler." But Speer's was not blind; his genius for organization owed much to his acute sensitivity to shifting power alignments within the party. When Leni complained to him of suffering "humiliation" at the hands of Goebbels's lieutenants, he explained to her that Goebbels was irrelevant to the rally, which was under the control of Robert Ley, chief of party organization. "Nobody understands, but that was a fact," Speer maintained in a late-life unpublished interview. "Goebbels hadn't anything to do with the party rally, because [it] was under the jurisdiction of Ley [who] was very proud that he was now responsible for the rally" and was preoccupied with several hundred thousand bellies to fill and bodies to bivouac.

While this was true in a bureaucratic sense, the film division was on the ground in Nuremberg, where it could make mischief by stirring up an investigation into rumors that Leni's mother was Jewish, based on gossip at Ufa that originated with a woman who was married to a studio screenwriter and claimed to be Leni's first cousin. The film division's Arnold Raether, who resented Leni's presence from the start, took the matter not to Goebbels, his direct superior, but to the Führer's deputy, Rudolf Hess. In the crush of preparations, Hess's investigation reached no conclusion until September 6, when the rally was already over. Then it merely cited the Proof of Descent Leni had earlier filed with the Reich's film office, in which her mother's mother was incorrectly entered, a detail that went unremarked. Until then, Hess's skepticism of Leni had been intense in Nuremberg, partly due to reports that she had been overheard speaking disparagingly about Hitler and other party members. Hess interrogated Speer in the matter, to whom Leni wept while declaring herself innocent. Speer supported her to Hess, though, in his seventies, he admitted that "I was present when Riefenstahl, in a restaurant with her staff, was a little bit frank and made some mocking remarks about the bellies [of the SA] not being so good for photographs or some such thing. . . . [Hess] asked me and, of course, I said it was nothing."

Speer could protect her from Hess, and his sensitivity to power shifts among what he called the "network of mutually warring bureaucracies" was indispensable in guiding her cameras through the politics of filming: when to focus on Röhm, when on Himmler or on Hess, how much prominence to give Julius Streicher or the Hitler Youth or the foreign dignitaries present to demonstrate their goodwill toward the new regime. He helped her select camera placements in space he had designed (and would rebuild on a grander scale the following year) and conspired with her to hide the SA potbellies she mocked behind thousands of swastika flags during nighttime ceremonies illuminated, as her Fanck films had been, by magnesium flares and torches. His familiarity with hall, field, meadow, and stadium aided her in choreographing the rows of drummers marching ten and twelve abreast in shot after shot and ensured that his trussed butterfly—the wooden eagle—loomed with appropriate symbolism behind the Führer whenever possible.

But it was Leni's eye making the film, and Speer was awed by how "totally involved" she was, "not in the manner of a genius" but as one dedicated to "hard work." He stated frankly that their task was "to glorify the party and to glorify the strength of Hitler's power and *mainly* to show to the common people a close-up of how this rally was, to impress emphatically with a picture that was as impressive as possible."

Leni had engaged Sepp Allgeier as cameraman, and a new recruit, Franz Weihmayr, joined them. Speer suggested a young man named Walter Frentz, who had recently done documentary filming of kayaks and Eskimos, and she added him to her camera team, a step that would lead to his becoming Hitler's personal cinematographer during World War II. As a special assistant, she wanted and got her brother, Heinz, on loan from Alfred's plumbing and heating business in Berlin. Alfred's largesse extended to loaning money for out-of-pocket expenses before financing began to flow from Berlin, which, as a party member since the April boycott, he could justify as doing something for the movement.

Leni's career genius lay partly in daring to do what others could not or would not, as she had done as a dancer and an actress. She knew that party cameramen would be photographing events with deference to rank and that the newsreel photographers would grab whatever they could. Only Leni and Allgeier sensed the intangible values of context and atmosphere, the very reasons Hitler had chosen Nuremberg as the rally site "for ever."

They rose early on the first day. While virtually every other camera team was preparing for the evening's opening ceremonies, they explored picturesque streets that Albrecht Dürer and Hans Sachs had walked in order to film half-timbered houses and bridges over the river Pegnitz as the city awoke. The fog lifted from the spires of Gothic cathedrals, fountains splashed in the medieval marketplace, street life stirred, flocks of pigeons rose, and a household cat cast drowsy, curious glances from a windowsill at the unfolding scene.

Ordinary Nurembergers—the *Volk*—assembled wooden bleachers in the square as swastika banners unfurled from windows in narrow cobbled streets. The Ur-German city (as the film would call it) was visibly quickening with anticipation. Leni and Allgeier exposed half an hour of footage capturing "the bond between the Führer and the people" before anyone else in Nuremberg had cranked a camera.

Leni's early start was essential. Hitler had placed a plane at her disposal to fly her from Nuremberg to Berlin and back again so she could attend the *S.O.S. Iceberg* première at the Ufa Palast am Zoo that evening and make a radio broadcast afterward. She arrived at the theater by motorcade to discover that the composer of the impressive score, Paul Dessau, a Jew, had already fled into Swiss exile. Paul Kohner was there to discover his name expunged from posters and to watch Leni stride onto the stage in a floor-length evening gown and greet the crowd with her arm raised high in the Hitler salute for which he never forgave her.

She was back in Nuremberg the next morning. The real making of the film would be in editing, for, even with three personal cameramen, she had too little footage to construct an hour-long film without contributions from "all of the German newsreels," as the opening credits would acknowledge. Though she was adamant about the purely documentary nature of her work, she staged scenes in a studio after the rally was finished, aided by Speer, who rebuilt sections of the Luitpold Hall for backdrops. Orators were relit and speeches rephotographed. Fresh-faced Hitler Youths and sculpture-ready SA and SS heads were positioned for close-ups and reaction shots in the manner of a fiction film. Smoothly gliding tracking shots—impossible outside of a studio in 1933—were made and cut into the finished film with barely detectable differences in lighting.

Leni disputed Speer's account of the refilming in *Inside the Third Reich*, his post-Spandau memoir that became an international bestseller. In it, he had misdated the occasion as 1935. On reflection—and after a tongue-lashing from Leni—Speer admitted he couldn't be certain of the year the studio staging had taken place and recanted, as Leni noted in her memoirs, where she devoted an entire chapter to what she called "a figment of Speer's imagination." Admitting that he rebuilt the speaker's podium after the rally, she allowed only that a camera error had required reshooting "a sentence a few seconds long" from Julius Streicher. But both their accounts are faulty. Speer gets the date wrong, and so does Leni in trying to explain away his recollection. Streicher makes no speech in her film of 1935. He does, however, in *Victory of Faith* in 1933 and in the film that was to follow in 1934, where he proclaims that "a people that does not protect its racial purity will perish!"

Leni never refers to this speech. It contradicts her assertion that no political or racial statements occur in any of her films, though it would be hard to find one more blatant. Nor was she aware when writing about Speer's "error" that he had elaborated in an unpublished interview about the reshoot that "she wanted to have one head that was listening carefully. And I did quite a piece of acting, listening. She cut it into the finished film and I was very proud to be there. If I were to see the film and *that's* in, then it's the film for which the speeches were specially made." Speer is easily identifiable, listening attentively in medium close-up in *Victory of Faith*. His confusion about dates is not remarkable because similar reshooting would be repeated in the future, as cameraman Walter Frentz and others confirm.

Leni's editing time was relatively brief, less than three months. *Victory of Faith* premièred on December 1, 1933, at the Ufa Palast am Zoo. She was there now, not as a star, but as moviemaker for the Reich, with Hitler, Goebbels, Röhm, and others seated in the Führer loge to honor her a bare ten years after she first set foot on a public stage. An orchestra played Richard Strauss's "Festival Prelude," and Hitler's bodyguard band played the "Badenweiler March" before the curtain went up. After it came down to thunderous applause on the image of a swastika flag unfurling against one of Allgeier's masterful cloudscapes, Hitler presented Leni with a diva-sized bouquet onstage. Some reports say she fainted.

Reviews in the party-controlled press were rapturous. *Victory of Faith* was "a filmic oratorio," a "triumphant symphony of images." Goebbels's *Der Angriff* cited its historical significance. "This film is a contemporary document of inestimable value," the paper editorialized the morning after the première. "It documents the transition of the Party into a State" and made it "a source of strength for the people as a whole."

Another view appeared in the *London Observer*. "The film is one long apotheosis of the Caesar spirit," the paper reported, "in which Herr Hitler plays the role of Caesar while the troops play the role of Roman slaves. It is certainly to be hoped that this film will be shown in all cinemas outside Germany, if one wishes to understand the intoxicating spirit which is moving Germany these days."

But *Victory of Faith*'s intended audience was internal, not external, and its public life would be short. Before it was withdrawn seven months later, for reasons to become apparent, one estimate held that twenty million Germans saw it in theaters, schools, and community halls. Commercial distribution benefited from the mood of resurgent nationalism, and its use as a propaganda tool was straightforward. One witness, then a schoolboy, recalled his entire *Gymnasium*'s required attendance at a screening at the Ufa Palast in his hometown of Heilbronn. James May was one of three Jewish boys in the class "forced to sit in the first row of the theater," he recalled, "and while all stood up and sang patriotic German songs, we three had to remain seated. After the performance, and in front of our professors, we were beaten up. One of the professors said, 'The world will learn from this!' " (*"Das macht Schule in Ausland!"*) When classmates climaxed the beating by urinating on the Jewish students, the professors refrained from registering disapproval.

The curious choice of Leni Riefenstahl to film the party rally proved inspired, or nearly so. *Victory of Faith* was long thought to be a lost film, and, when it was, Leni dismissed it as a "thankless task" and "only an imperfect fragment, not a motion picture." Her comments not only served to minimize her early involvement with the party but expressed genuine dissatisfaction with the film itself. Her achievement, in spite of the praise from the Nazi press, was fitful and uneven, especially compared with what would come later. Except for Allgeier's opening sequence of Nuremberg awakening—also soon to be surpassed—*Victory of Faith* is technically unsure and exposes the rally as a messy, amateurish affair rather than the demonstration of precision and efficiency it was meant to be. Discipline among the crowds was a chronic problem, marred by public drunkenness, smoking, and nightly mass pilgrimages to Nuremberg's red-light district, few of which were visible on film but all of which would be officially forbidden whenever future cameras were turning. The film is full of disordered milling about, and neither Leni's editing skills nor Speer's monumental décor succeeds in dispelling an impression of ragged disarray. Pointless or incomplete panning shots, shaky camera moves, uncertain focus, and badly framed compositions preclude stylistic unity. Even Hitler is photographed unevenly, looming heroically on some occasions and, on others, looking like a thick-waisted middle-aged man nervously combing windblown hair with his fingers as the elements ruffle the ritual.

It is finally an hour and four minutes of marches, banners, and speeches with none of the bayonet-edged precision and lockstep monumentality suggesting disciplined invincibility that today seems an integral part of the Nazi legacy and is almost wholly the product of Leni's subsequent attempt "to glorify the party and to glorify the strength of Hitler's power," as Speer put it.

Her editing of *Victory of Faith*, as even Fanck was forced to recognize, was her most notable achievement. It was not compromised, as on *The Blue Light*, by vanity and fascination with her own image. This time the only image that mattered was Hitler's, assembled to rhythms she had learned from feature films and could create from strips of celluloid at her editing table. In the end, *Victory of Faith* was more than a sketch but less than a portrait. Still, it was something new, a tentative joining hands of fiction and reality techniques in a trial run whose importance lay less in what it accomplished than in what it anticipated. And without it as a kind of dress rehearsal on film, Leni could never have realized the still-startling achievement about to follow.

TEN

TRIUMPH

Whoever has seen and experienced the face of the Führer in Triumph of the Will, *will never forget it. It will haunt him through days and dreams and will, like a quiet flame, burn itself into his soul.*

—Joseph Goebbels

It doesn't contain a single reconstructed scene. Everything in it is true. . . . It is history. A pure historical film.

—Leni Riefenstahl

Leni Riefenstahl was not ordered. . . . She asked *to do this picture.*

—Walter Traut, production manager

LENI LATER WROTE THAT SHE suffered a nervous collapse after shooting *Victory of Faith* and another after its release. Though she had the stamina and physical hardiness to see her through a trying century, breakdowns were to become near rituals following virtually every film she completed and some she didn't. Even Hitler took note of them. If she had a failing, the Führer said, it was "that she took her work too seriously and was sick for months after every film."

She wore her breakdowns as badges of honor. They gave her work an aura of heroic endeavor and cast her, like Junta, as defenseless against the demands of such powerful forces as creativity, beauty, and Hitler. Creativity was both curse and reward, though there were also tangible compensations.

When *Victory of Faith* was still in rough cut, Hitler acknowledged the distinction she was bringing to propaganda. By mid-October 1933, he decided she should repeat her task for the 1934 rally, for which Speer was redesigning the Nuremberg site on a more imperial scale. The appointment would not be officially announced for months, but Leni had assurance as she edited her first film for the party that a second was hers for the taking. By spring, she had taken it. A letter in the Ufa files dated April 19, 1934, cites her "appointment by the Führer" for "artistic and technical responsibility" for the film he personally would title *Triumph of the Will*. The April appointment provided months—not days, as she would later insist—to plan and prepare. It guaranteed her a vastly expanded staff with unlimited resources and freedom of movement under the personal patronage of the Führer.

Immediately after Hitler's decision in October, Goebbels summoned Leni to his office, she wrote in her memoirs. Enraged that she had complained to the Führer of humiliations she had suffered from his underlings on *Victory of Faith*, Goebbels told her in cold fury that "if you weren't a woman, I'd throw you down the stairs. How dare you tell Hitler such stories about my staff. I am the boss. You are to report to me."

No reference to any such scene survives in the Goebbels diaries or elsewhere, but, if true, Goebbels—wittingly or unwittingly—presented her with almost ideal grounds for extricating herself from a task she would later claim she found intolerable from the outset. It is unlikely Hitler would have incarcerated her had she declined to make *Triumph of the Will*, any more than he had when she refused to make the Horst Wessel film. But Goebbels alone was not enough to make her reject the commission or the prestige that went with it. "Tell me one person who would not make this film under these conditions," she challenged an interviewer much later, though the tears she claimed to have shed over letters from colleagues in flight or exile must have hinted broadly that there were many persons who would not or could not.

The conditions she viewed as irresistible included absolute freedom in making the film, an assurance that she would never have to make another for the party, and a guarantee that her company would be producer of record, to which copyright was linked, at least on paper. Any reluctance she may have felt was augmented by an unexpected reawakening of her acting career at about the same time.

Ten days after the *Victory of Faith* première, Leni left for a skiing holiday in Switzerland after leaving the matter of "the Jew Béla Balács [*sic*]" and her power of attorney in the hands of Julius Streicher. While in Davos with her lover Walter Prager, she received an inquiry from a second-tier Berlin film company called Terra about making a nonmusical film based on *Tiefland* (*Lowlands*), a popular 1903 opera by Eugen D'Albert that she may have known was a lifelong favorite of Hitler's. *Tiefland* was based on a nineteenth-century Spanish play and, like *The Holy Mountain* and Leni's other Alpine films, contrasts the purity of the highlands with the sordidness of the low. An idealized shepherd named Pedro embodies virtue, while a corrupt landowner, Don Sebastian, is the emblem of evil. The two vie for the love of a beautiful Spanish dancer, to be played by Leni.

Terra's inquiry quickened Leni's interest in financial matters, and so did her negotiations for the second Nuremberg film. She felt stung by Harry Sokal's flight into exile with *The Blue Light* under his arm, leaving her with no return on the picture, though she would soon find a way to amortize her investment and exclude Sokal from the proceeds when she did. *Victory of Faith* had been financed entirely by the Nazi Party and—except for the gray Mercedes convertible Hitler gave her as a personal thank-you gift— she received a fee of only twenty thousand reichsmarks, which, while modest, was a third of the film's budget, or around five thousand American dollars at the height of the depression. In agreeing to "artistic and technical responsibility" for *Triumph of the Will*, she insisted that production credit go not to the party but to her L-R Studio-Film GmbH (renamed Reich-Party-Rally-Film-GmbH) in order to establish copyright and a percentage of the profits, which she would collect—or try to collect—until the day she died. The party was financing *Triumph,* but surreptitiously. Theatrical distribution was awarded to Ufa in a business deal that was, according to documents, personally approved by Hitler. Public perception was thus created that Ufa and its still considerable prestige were financing the film, freeing it from any taint of party propaganda. Ufa agreed to pay a distribution advance of three hundred thousand reichsmarks—five times the total cost of *Victory of Faith*—which was made immediately available for preproduction expenses, with further financing to be funneled through the Reich Film Credit Bank, newly formed by Goebbels to control which "privately" produced films got financed and which ones didn't. Though Ufa would not be fully nationalized until later in the decade, its activities were already effectively under the fiscal control of the propaganda minister. The star of *Triumph of the Will*—the Führer himself—and hundreds of thousands of extras would be provided at no cost, as would the costumes, props, technical apparatus, services provided and paid for by the city of Nuremberg, as well as the sets and locations under construction by Speer, making any accurate budget or cost accounting literally incalculable.

In financing *Tiefland,* Leni maneuvered cannily enough to win the admiration of a Hollywood or Friedrichstrasse mogul. She told Terra she would discuss the film on her return to Berlin, but before leaving Switzerland, she secretly bought the film rights to *Tiefland* herself. "Then I spoke with Terra and we made a very good agreement," she said. "I wanted it that way—to be free. But it was *my* production. Leni Riefenstahl—L.R. Studio-Film—my own. I put up some money, but most of it was paid for by Terra."

Simultaneously, she began work on *Triumph of the Will* by engaging filmmaker Walter Ruttmann as her codirector. Ruttmann had worked with Fanck on the film of the 1928 Winter Olympics, and his widely seen full-length documentary *Berlin: Symphony of a Great City,* of 1927, had

TRIUMPH   149

pioneered techniques Leni and Allgeier adapted for *Victory of Faith*'s morning-in-Nuremberg sequence. Though alleged to be a Communist, Ruttmann was not averse to turning out propaganda for the Reich and would produce a "culture film" about aviation in 1934 called *Metal from Heaven* (*Metall des Himmels*), one in a series of short subjects made for commercial distribution that, in the words of German film historian Klaus Kreimeier, "educated for war."

Leni ordered Ruttmann's Berlin preparations for *Triumph of the Will* to go forward with Allgeier as his chief cameraman, while she prepared *Tiefland* in Spain. For her Spanish vehicle, she persuaded Hans Schneeberger once again to film her; engaged the popular German film and stage actor Heinrich George to play Don Sebastian; and cast Sepp Rist, her leading man from *Mont Blanc* and *S.O.S. Iceberg*, as Pedro. Other Riefenstahl alumni included Guzzi Lantschner and Walter Riml as production assistants, who were supported in their location search by Günther Rahn, the tennis pro, who was now living in Madrid. To direct scenes in which she was on-camera as the Spanish dancer, she hired actor Alfred Abel, best remembered from Fritz Lang's *Metropolis*. In Spain, she organized a production schedule that revolved around Heinrich George's theater commitments, which left him a window of only twenty-one days in which to film his role as Don Sebastian.

Ruttmann, meanwhile, was in Berlin writing and directing a prologue for *Triumph of the Will* that would precede footage of the rally itself. Contemporary news reports and interviews make clear that the concept resembled the "film about my movement" that Hitler had proposed to Leni a year earlier. Ruttmann planned to use montages of photographs, newsreels, placards, and docudrama reenactments to "revisit all the movement's historic venues and the stages in its development."

Leni, meanwhile, traveled to England to lecture the German Club at Oxford on *The Blue Light* and "the spirit of the New Germany." She returned to Spain to discover that, in spite of her participation as star and director, Terra had been unable to fully finance the production. When the last possible start date to accommodate Heinrich George's schedule came and went without a camera's turning, she collapsed and checked into the German hospital in Madrid. The picture collapsed with her, though that was very far from the end of *Tiefland*.

Recuperating from her Spanish debacle, Leni turned her attention to *Triumph of the Will* when Ruttmann traveled to Majorca to report to her on his progress. She later claimed she was uneasy with the results and so unhappy with his footage when she saw it on her return to Berlin—footage on which she charged he had spent a full third of the Ufa advance (or one hundred thousand marks)—that she had no choice but to fire him and assume full control of the film on the eve of the rally.

But focusing on *Triumph of the Will* in summer 1934 was a different challenge than in April when she had accepted the commission, for the political landscape had been dramatically altered in the meantime by two events that would make her second Nuremberg film vastly more important than the first. It became instead a vital and unprecedented opportunity for transforming images into myth and for aestheticizing power, challenges she met so brilliantly that her film itself would enter history.

The second of these two linked events was the death, at age eighty-six, of President Hindenburg on August 2, a month before the rally began. He had been a towering figurehead for the military as supreme commander of an aristocratic officer corps that distrusted Hitler because of his toleration of the SA, the paramilitary storm troopers who posed a threat to the military's desire for a return to power under (they vainly hoped) a restored monarchy.

The SA—the notorious brownshirts—constituted a private militia that had been vital in bringing Hitler to power through street violence and intimidation. Under the command of Ernst Röhm, the SA was a force of two to four million mostly unemployed thugs restless for spoils of victory that had thus far eluded them. They were increasingly given to random acts of violence against Jews and eager to challenge the role of the traditional army, which they outnumbered by a ratio estimated as high as forty to one. As a political force, the SA had outlived its purpose of agitation and intimidation the moment Hitler assumed power. As a destabilizing force, it remained potent and dangerous.

The Führer had few colleagues in the party of more enduring intimacy than Röhm, whom he had known since before joining the party. A
predatory homosexual whose meaty, bullet-scarred face gave him a look of
brutality that matched his reputation, Röhm was said to be the only party
member who spoke with Hitler on the familiar *du* basis, and their close
relationship had been conspicuous in *Victory of Faith*, where the two old
comrades appeared repeatedly, shoulder to shoulder.

To assuage Röhm's ambitions for an SA ministry with which he could
effectively supplant the military, Hitler named him to his cabinet—without portfolio—at the end of 1933 and on New Year's Day 1934 wrote him
a widely publicized letter employing the *du* form, acknowledging his
"imperishable services" to the movement and the German people. He
ended with gratitude "that I am able to call such men as you my friends and
fellow combatants."

Röhm was viewed as Hitler's chief rival within the party, and the public
praise was prelude to what may have been the most ruthless act of Hitler's
career prior to his invasion of Poland and the start of the Second World
War, an act linked both to the military's wariness of his regime and to the
rapidly declining health of the aged president.

Hitler had long planned to assume total power on Hindenburg's death,
consolidating the offices of president and chancellor and making himself
sole dictator. He had privately discussed this agenda with Goebbels just
before the Nuremberg rally of 1933 and met secretly with the generals in
April 1934 to overcome their skepticism and win their support for his
ambitions. His quid pro quo for the generals' backing was the notorious
"Night of the Long Knives," the purge that solved the Röhm and SA
problems in blood.

The action began in the early-morning hours of June 30, 1934, in Bad
Wiessee, the Bavarian resort town to which Hitler had ordered Röhm and
his closest SA associates on holiday furlough. Acting on the invented pretext
of an SA putsch against the army and himself, Hitler traveled secretly to
Bavaria with Goebbels and others. They arrived at Röhm's hotel at dawn,
where Hitler—"whip in hand," according to his chauffeur—personally

awoke his *du* friend and informed him at gunpoint that he was under arrest. The astonished Röhm was swept off to a cell in Munich's Stadelheim Prison. Two days later, he manfully declined the offer to commit suicide tendered by Theodore Eicke, SS commandant of Dachau. Eicke and his deputy murdered him on the spot.

The generals had been forewarned of the action but were allowed to remain aloof from it, gloves unsoiled. They were told that the SS, formerly an elite unit within the SA under the command of Himmler, would take their part in halting the alleged putsch. Across Germany, the SS led round-ups of SA leaders they forced to the wall and shot without charges, evidence, or explanation. The exact number of victims has never been determined, though it likely rose into the hundreds as the corpses continued to turn up for weeks in woods, streams, and alleyways. Nor did the slaughter end with the SA. Hitler seized the opportunity to settle old scores with political rivals such as Gregor Strasser and Gen. Kurt von Schleicher, his predecessor as chancellor and an obstacle to his rise. Both men—along with von Schleicher's wife—were murdered as the sweep of summary executions continued.

"The blood-lust had developed its own momentum," Ian Kershaw notes, and, as it continued, Hitler returned to Berlin, where orders were issued that "all documents concerning the action of the past two days are to be burned." On July 3, he retroactively legalized the purge. "The measures taken on June 30, July 1 and 2, to suppress treasonous assaults," he decreed, "are legal as acts of self-defense by the State."

It was not until July 13 that he publicly addressed the purge and the "horror at the butchery" its headlines had produced. In a two-hour oration before members of the Reichstag, he justified the bloodletting on grounds of treason and Röhm's perversions. "I became the supreme judge of the German people," he declared. "I gave the order to shoot the ringleaders in this treason, and I further gave the order to cauterize down to the raw flesh the ulcers of this poisoning of the wells in our domestic life." He added with crystal clarity, "Let it be known for all time to come that if anyone raises his hand to strike the state, then certain death is his lot."

Hitler's speech unmistakably endorsed murder in the interest of the state. Hindenburg praised Hitler's actions from his deathbed as "gallant personal intervention" that "rescued the German people from great danger." The military, in spite of the murders of General von Schleicher and other army officers, seconded Hindenburg's sentiments—"We love him because he has shown himself a true soldier," a general announced—and congratulated themselves that, by eliminating Röhm, Hitler had unwittingly disarmed himself and was now at their mercy.

The generals were mistaken. They had colluded with Hitler when fore-warned of the purge, technically guiltless but up to their epaulets in moral compromise. And Hitler knew, in the words of one historian, that "if the army would stand for the murder of army men, he had achieved the break-through to unlimited control." Only days after his speech to the Reichstag, Hitler detached the SS from the SA—"especially in connection with the events of June 30"—making the SS independent of the SA *and* of the army. He had purged and weakened the SA but supplanted it with an armed SS answerable only to himself that would prove a far more lethal instrument of power and terror than what it replaced.

The nation largely accepted the conspiracy theory—"the Röhm putsch," it was labeled. If doubts lingered, they were stilled by Hindenburg's death, the day after Hitler paid him a deathbed call. The dying old man mistook the chancellor for the former kaiser, addressing the upstart he had once derided as "the Bohemian corporal" as "Your Majesty."

Hindenburg's death inspired nationwide outpourings of grief. He had been, as the official death proclamation intoned, "the national myth of the German people," a leader who had presided over the dissolution of the Weimar Republic he had sworn to uphold and had "opened the gates of the Reich for the young National Socialist Movement." Hitler announced that he so honored the "greatness of the departed" that he could not accept the title of president himself. Instead, he simply merged the offices of president and chancellor into that of the Führer and, with the support of a now mollified and subservient military, became sole head of both government and state.

The day of Hindenburg's death, the military—as a measure of gratitude and political blindness—declared its unconditional loyalty to the
Führer it had once hoped to displace. What had been the army's oath of
allegiance to "nation and fatherland" became an oath "by God" to "render
unconditional obedience to Adolf Hitler, the Führer of the German Reich
and people, supreme commander of the Armed Forces." Pledged to Hitler
personally, rather than to the state, each member of the military vowed "to
risk my life at any time for this oath." A civilian version of the pledge
would soon be required of all government officials. After little more than
a year and a half, Hitler stood unchallenged as leader of state, government,
and military. The seizure of power was complete. "Up to then," Joachim
Fest writes, "illusions about the nature of the regime had still been possible."

Restoration of illusion was already under way. The public's "power of
forgetting is enormous," Hitler had noted in *Mein Kampf*, and he could
now count on Leni's filmmaking to help them forget. In full charge of
Triumph of the Will, she could restore and extend the myth of a gallant but
decisive leader who struck down the Reich's enemies in self-defense while
declaring murder a legitimate tool of domestic policy.

Uniting the nation and soothing public apprehension in the wake of the
blood purge gave *Triumph of the Will* immense purpose. It was no longer
a mere rally film, but a vehicle to apotheosize Hitler as absolute leader and
make him safe for Germany as successor to the revered Hindenburg, even
after the seismic shocks of the Röhm affair. "The bond between the Führer
and the people was of supreme importance," Leni told an interviewer.
"Showing this, expressing it, is one of the tasks I have set myself." The
word she favored for her task was "glorification."

Victory of Faith—so inconveniently compromising in its repeated
views of Röhm laughing or marching at Hitler's side—was withdrawn
from circulation. Its suppression and subsequent disappearance for almost
half a century permitted Leni to assert that it was nothing more than a
"film fragment," a hastily composed snapshot of an event that contained
"several shots" of Röhm at the rally (it has dozens). The film's recent

rediscovery revealed that the Hitler-Röhm relationship was so central to the film that it could not be ignored and made hollow her denials that the purge—of which she claimed ignorance due to her illness in Spain—had anything to do with the raison d'être of *Triumph of the Will*.

Minimizing and distorting *Victory of Faith* was of a piece with her postwar claims that Hitler compelled her to make *Triumph of the Will* and that the latter film was overemphasized in her body of work, having taken up a scant "six days." Six days was the length of the rally, but the film would consume a year of her creative life. Walter Frentz, who had worked on *Victory of Faith* and *Triumph*, recalled details in an unpublished interview forty years later. "We were planning many weeks before the rally to arrange certain requests with the architect [Speer] and the technical staff," he said. "The program of the rally came from the propaganda ministry [but] we knew the program *exactly*. Every minute, every second. Leni Riefenstahl made a plan from the program. By [the rally's opening,] the technical preparations were complete, including where our camera positions would be. This had been arranged some weeks before."

Walter Traut, production manager on *Triumph of the Will* as on *The Blue Light*, confirmed technical readiness "many days before" the rally began. A fierce Leni loyalist, Traut credited the smooth organization to her having had "a conception *before* the event which guided her in finding the best camera positions" and volunteered that "Leni Riefenstahl was not ordered" to make the film. "She *asked* to do this picture."

A book titled *Behind the Scenes of the Nuremberg Rally Film* (*Hinter den Kulissen des Reichsparteitag-Films*) that detailed the production was published under Leni's name in 1935. The text affirmed the months "since May" that she and her collaborators had prepared. After World War II, she would disavow the book—which generously thanked not only the Führer but also Goebbels and Streicher—claiming it had been written by Ernst Jäger of *Film-Kurier*, the friend and effusive reviewer of *The Blue Light* who had urged her to attend her first Hitler rally in 1932. "I didn't write a word of it," she later stated, "and couldn't even read it" because of its style. Whether Jäger ghostwrote the text or not, it is unlikely Leni never read or approved it if only because of its thirty-seven photographs of herself, more than the Führer gets. She took credit as the author in 1935, listing it among her annual professional achievements for the Reich Culture Office. Nor did ghost authorship inhibit her inscribing presentation copies for members of Hitler's personal staff, such as Martin Bormann, his personal secretary and leader of the party organization, who would prove crucial to her as a source of funds at the height of World War II.

Leni pursued her work obsessively, brooking no obstacles. Her secretary called a cameraman named Emil Schünemann regarding his availability, to which he replied, "I would not do that on principle, it is below my dignity." Leni wrote the film division (the same organization she normally accused of obstructing her) calling Schünemann's comment "a belittlement of my work, with which the Führer has entrusted me." The cameraman responded that he merely meant he would not work for a woman. "Herr Schünemann's comment," she replied, "amounts to a boycott against the Führer. The Führer has given me overall artistic responsibility and I therefore feel duty-bound to hire cameramen and other crewmembers who are answerable to me in artistic matters. If the Führer does not feel it beneath his dignity to give me overall artistic responsibility for this project, it is curious, to put it mildly, if Herr Schünemann feels it beneath his dignity to recognize that fact."

Though Leni was justified in her fury at Schünemann's hostility toward women (an attitude universal within the party), her letters betray a readiness to trade on her relationship with Hitler that verged on political denunciation, a tactic she would resort to within her own family. And her displays of self-righteous entitlement would grow and be remembered by colleagues, not all of whom would remain silent loyalists.

She arrived in Nuremberg in August to take command—with equal measures of steel and elation—of a production staff of more than 170, including sixteen cameramen and sixteen camera assistants operating hand-cranked cameras under the direction of Sepp Allgeier. Nine aerial photographers supplemented those on the ground, as did another twenty-nine cameramen from the newsreel divisions of Germany's Ufa and Tobis film companies, as well as their counterparts from the European subsidiaries of Fox and Paramount, whose footage would be at Leni's disposal during editing. A technical staff of ten was complemented by a lighting crew of seventeen, two full-time still photographers (one of them personal), twenty-six drivers, thirty-seven watchmen and security guards, a sound crew of thirteen, two office workers and their assistants, including her skier-lover Walter Prager working with her secretary, Erna Peters, and Guzzi Lantschner and his brother Otto, both avid National Socialists. Hans Schneeberger's new wife, Gisela, prepared publicity stills, and, to ensure ideological integrity, the staff accommodated Dr. Herbert Seehofer, propaganda consultant of the National Socialist Party.

Such lavish support is not unusual for a major studio film but was unprecedented in reality-based filmmaking anywhere in the world, signaling the importance of the project and Leni's stature, now light-years beyond anything she had known—or perhaps dreamed—as a young dancer or actress. A week after the rally ended, she would appear on the cover of *Newsweek* as "Hitler's Friend," and Janet Flanner, writing in *The New Yorker*, would be struck by the mere fact of her celebrity as she moved in her white greatcoat among the storm troopers and SS men, a "professional woman on her job, and so rare a sight in masculinized Germany today that among the quarter-million spectators assembled, there wasn't a person who didn't know who she was. She is unique, and the white-skirted figure couldn't have been anybody else."

Leni met logistical challenges that would have defeated any film director without her sense of organization and entitlement. She drew again on her experience with Fanck, who had captured images from the edges of cliffs or from deep within glacial clefts. To ensure a variety of perspectives in Nuremberg, she secured vantage points on rooftops and from man-deep trenches and extendable ladders supplied by the Nuremberg fire department. She sent cameramen aloft in planes for aerial views and laid tracks on the ground for cameras to glide on while photographing Hitler—

always from below—or clamped roller skates on her crew so they could execute moving shots that, in a studio, would have required rubber-wheeled dollies. To keep her cameramen from capturing one another in cross shots (though they can be spotted throughout the film), she dressed them in designer-made uniforms of light gray—not in SA uniforms as is everywhere reported—so they might blend into the crowd and still be distinguishable from the black- or brownshirts when she needed to find them. Fireworks, magnesium flares and torches, and smoke pots and braziers full of flames dramatized nighttime shooting, suggesting ancient rites made modern by wave after wave of flags, undulating oceans of them emblazoned with the swastika, the most recognizable and potent political symbol of the twentieth century.

Fortuitously, all Leni's Nuremberg films were built around predetermined programs of events she could use as narrative armature. In compressing a week's events into two hours, she omitted some and reordered others for rhythm and impact, some atmospheric, some ideological. The schedule of the "Party Rally of Unity and Strength" (its official title) from September 4 to 10 provided her with obligatory scenes such as the introduction of more than fifty thousand new Labor Service recruits who displaced the labor unions Hitler had abolished, all of them wearing green uniforms and carrying spades as if they were rifles. There were the ritual scenes repeated from *Victory of Faith*, now cleansed of Röhm and more elaborately staged, most memorably the ceremony to honor the war dead. Where Hitler and Röhm had marched side by side as a duo, the Führer now walked alone at the apex of a triangle, followed by the new and deferential leader of the SA, Viktor Lutze, and Heinrich Himmler of the SS, the trio flanked by massive blocks of tens of thousands of uniformed party faithful on either side of their path. Leni filmed their processional from a tiny elevator Speer built at her request to run up and down one of the huge flagpoles supporting the three swastika banners at the edge of the field (it can be seen moving in the film). Her camera's high, soaring view is the only one that makes visual sense for a ceremonial that was visually meaningless at ground or even stadium level and is key testimony to the rally's having been designed as much for its photogenic potential as for its participants.

Parades and ceremonies contained their own small narratives of ritual and response, making plentiful use of the Nazi iconography of eagles, standards, helmets, belts, boots, and flags. Speeches somberly noted the death of President Hindenburg, though the entire rally can be read as a celebration of his passing. Oratory reassured the one hundred thousand rank-and-file members of the SA of "unity and strength" in the aftermath of "the Röhm putsch," alluded to only as a "dark shadow" now dispelled.

Other scenes included the opening ceremonies; sound bites from the speeches of Goebbels, Streicher, and other power players; nighttime torchlight parades and serenades; the quasi-religious consecration of regional swastika banners with the so-called Blood Flag, a bullet-torn relic of the failed putsch of November 1923; and, finally, military parade reviews in Nuremberg's Central Market Square, now renamed Adolf-Hitler-Platz. At intervals came Hitler's speeches. Leni's cameras sought out and found "the power and passion" that historian Gordon Craig cited after watching the finished film, with Hitler's "breaking down the emotional resistance of his audiences, in driving them to transports of rage and exaltation, in forcing them to merge their wills with his own." Rudolf Hess sang out the rally's theme at the emotional closing ceremony: "The Party is Hitler. But Hitler is Germany, as Germany is Hitler. Hitler! *Sieg Heil!*"

Principal photography ended when the rally did, on September 10. Before leaving Nuremberg, Leni attended a tea party at the Grand Hotel hosted by Julius Streicher, who raised a glass to "all the difficulties" she had overcome in pursuit of her "achievement." Leni graciously acknowledged that "this time it had gone a thousand times better than it had in the previous year" and hoped aloud she might be given the commission for another rally film that would "go even more smoothly," a wish soon to be granted.

Though production had taken place mostly during the six-day rally, Leni was not limited by that agenda and shot material before and after, such as the atmospheric views of Nuremberg, its statuary and landmarks bettering similar passages in *Victory of Faith*. The opening ceremony in vast Luitpold Hall (which conveyed "something of the mysticism and religious fervor of an Easter or a Christmas Mass in a great Gothic cathedral," according to William L. Shirer, reporting back to America) is composed of fragments of speeches delivered at various times and excerpted with considerable political sophistication or, as with the previous film, redelivered after the rally on studio sound stages. But two major sequences stand out for their departure from the calendar and from documentary reality.

The more famous of the two would come at the very beginning and lacks any objective authenticity, though it indelibly sets the metaphoric mood for everything that follows. Hitler's arrival by air in Nuremberg immediately follows the opening credits and introductory titles (written by Walter Ruttmann) with their quasi-religious language invoking recent history:

> Twenty years after the outbreak of the World War,
> Sixteen years after the beginning of Germany's suffering,
> Nineteen months after the beginning of the rebirth of Germany,
> Adolf Hitler flew to Nuremberg to review his faithful followers.

The titles fade as cloud banks loom and drift apart to make way for a small airplane gliding through steep billows to an orchestral version of the Horst Wessel song. As the clouds part, sunlight floods the heavens until, finally, the plane—the camera—begins its descent. From the aerial point of view (the passenger is never seen), the camera looks down on medieval Nuremberg, wreathed in mists that dissolve to reveal rooftops, towers, and cathedral spires festooned with swastika banners. Troops—tiny as toys—pass through narrow streets as if marching to greet the plane, which glides over them like an eagle as the music soars, its shadow like a cross.

The imagery is lyrical, expansive, unmistakably messianic. The sequence segues to Hitler's motorcade through Nuremberg and is constructed not on documentary techniques but on those of fiction films.

Hitler stands solitary in his open Mercedes, photographed mostly in half-profile medium shots from behind (by Walter Frentz) as his car glides along the parade route like destiny—"a Roman emperor," according to Shirer. Architectural details, fountains, and statuary are intercut as visual emblems uniting the Führer with the German past. The *Volk,* in alternating shots suggesting his point of view, cheer ecstatically, their arms thrust high in the Hitler salute. The throngs are anchored and personalized by the occasional blond and comely figure in medium close-up—usually a woman or a child—implying eye contact with the Führer and conveying joy through order, discipline, and grateful submission. Shot and countershot continue. A cat on a windowsill (again) glances up as the procession continues to the Führer's hotel, where SS men grip one anothers' leather belts to form a human chain and lightbulbs spell out HEIL HITLER. The sequence occupies a full one-tenth of the film's length and is one of the most elaborate star entrances in film history. Ian Kershaw calls it "a celluloid exposition of the Führer cult," but others have characterized it as a love story, one with a single star consummating his seduction of a supporting cast of hundreds of thousands, an entire nation.

The carefully choreographed consecration of the new Labor Service to the Führer later in the film is similarly constructed and cut on a fiction-film model.

The leader of the Labor Service calls out: "My Führer, I announce that 52,000 Labor Service workers have answered the summons." Hitler responds, "*Heil,* worker volunteers!" The men of the labor corps (there are no women) respond in unison, "*Heil,* my Führer!" They shoulder their spades. The leader calls out: "Here we stand, ready to carry Germany into a new era." A liturgical call-and-response begins, faces and voices of the choir expertly intercut:

LEADER: Where do you come from, comrade?
CORPSMAN: I come from Friesland.
LEADER: And you, comrade?
CORPSMAN: From Bavaria.

LEADER: And you?

CORPSMAN: From Kaiserstuhl.

ANOTHER: From Pomerania.

OTHERS: From Königsberg . . . from Silesia . . . from the
   Baltic . . . from the Black Forest . . . from Dresden . . . from the
   Danube . . . from the Rhine . . . and from the Saar. . . .

LEADER: One People, one Führer, one Reich!

The faces are carefully lit, intercut with shots of Hitler, Nazi banners, and Speer's wooden eagle, the swastika clutched in its talons. As the choral recital continues, the rhythm becomes mechanical in its precision, as synthetic as a chorus number in a Hollywood musical. Together with the speeches, it is one of the few sequences shot with direct sound, technically impossible without rehearsal, and, according to Speer, "This was certainly rehearsed—fifty, a hundred times." Like Hitler's plane descending through the clouds, the sequence belies Leni's contention that *Triumph of the Will* is "a pure historical film" without "a single reconstructed scene."

These passages achieve their power and coherence through editing, which is, by definition, reconstruction. Leni began editing in Berlin in September, and it was not until the process was well under way that *Triumph of the Will* found its form, what Leni called its "architecture" and cited as her starting point, though it clearly was not. The task of cutting four hundred thousand feet of raw footage to one-fortieth that length, or about two hours, was formidable, and Leni cited twelve-, then fourteen-, then sixteen-hour days, including holidays and weekends. She devoted herself obsessively to making and remaking the film on the editing tables trying to find it. Speer recalled, "She was working to exhaustion, working from day to night."

She began editing to meet an initial release date of December 1934 in conditions that were anything but spartan. She had a prior relationship with the Geyer film laboratories in Berlin from *The Blue Light*, and Dr. Karl Geyer, genuflecting to her status, provided her with state-of-the-art facilities that came to include offices as well as four editing rooms modeled on Fanck's, in which film strips hung from hooks against backlit translucent opal-glass walls so they could be quickly identified for content or light/dark densities. There were separate rooms for sound editing, developing, and making of dupe copies, as well as a private screening room, a lounge, and even a private canteen. No director in Germany—perhaps anywhere—had ever been provided such lavish private facilities.

She also had Walter Ruttmann.

Far from having fired Ruttmann months earlier as she later claimed, she worked with him on the picture as late as February 1935 (it finally opened in March), when press reports still referred to him as codirector. Excerpts from his script for the history-of-the-party prologue were published in early October, suggesting it was still current weeks after the rally, and trade papers confirmed later in the month that "Leni Riefenstahl and Walter Ruttmann are directing the shooting in the [Babelsberg] studio" with actors. The studio shooting was graced by a visit to the set by Goebbels, the SA's Viktor Lutze, Nazi press chief Otto Dietrich, and others. Further shooting with actors was announced for November, indicating that the "architecture" for *Triumph of the Will* was far from final and may have remained elusive until December 6, when Hitler himself viewed the assembled footage.

What Hitler saw in the projection room almost certainly included staged material Leni and Ruttmann shot together, those re-creations of recent party history that—with Röhm so publicly dispatched—can only have been artful exercises in elision and evasion. Nor did documentary recapitulation glorify Hitler as Führer. His myth did not need Ruttmann's summing up; it needed Leni's vision of "the new god" (the phrase is Ian Kershaw's) descending from the clouds.

Leni may well have disagreed with Ruttmann's approach from the beginning, as she later insisted, though, as producer, she appears to have rejected it very late in the day, perhaps at Hitler's insistence. Ruttmann was not, after all, the first Riefenstahl collaborator to be expunged from her memory and the credits. She consistently sought to present her work as hers alone, springing fully formed from dream images as with *The Blue Light*— "These things basically come from a gift that one has or does not have," she

explained. But with or without collaborators, form—architecture—
evolved from painstaking trial, error, and attention to detail. As Speer
observed, "It was not done in the way of a genius who could just say
simply, 'Oh, this is it!' It was hard work."

She finished editing and recording sound and music in time for the
première on the evening of March 28, 1935, at the Ufa Palast am Zoo (its
façade redesigned for the occasion by Speer). She later claimed that no one
but her assistants had seen the film and that she refined it until the last possible moment, not even taking time to have her hair done for the première.

Her sense of drama overwhelmed accuracy. Goebbels, Lutze, Hess,
and Hitler himself had made visits to her cutting rooms. The Reich's censors had seen the finished film and issued an official approval. She even
lectured about it two days before the première at a press conference organized for her by Goebbels's propaganda ministry.

She arrived late to the première with Alfred, Bertha, and Heinz and,
despite some appealingly modest smiles for the cameras and murmurs of
anxiety to well-wishers, must have been suffused with elation, knowing
that she had crafted a work of unique power and resonance, the definitive
aesthetic expression of a Führer myth that did justice not only to her subject but to her own self-estimation and sense of personal potential. The
proof came in waves of ovations that washed over her at evening's end.
When her Führer presented her with a large bouquet of lilacs on stage,
again she swooned.

Most of Germany swooned. Press headlines hailed the film as "A
Symphony of the German Will" or "The Soul of National Socialism" or,
as the official party paper, the *Völkischer Beobachter,* put it, "the greatest
film we have ever seen." No one failed to praise the music by Herbert
Windt, who had also scored *Victory of Faith* and whose wide-ranging,
heroic orchestrations—partly conducted by Leni herself in the recording
sessions to match musical rhythms to those in the editing—freely quoted
from Beethoven, Wagner, and the Horst Wessel song, heightening the
film's emotional impact.

Ufa took daily ads in the trade papers to trumpet record-breaking attendance as the film opened nationwide on April 5. In its first three weeks in Berlin, one hundred thousand spectators crowded the Palast am Zoo. As it continued to break box-office records, its portrait of the Führer was recognized as so definitive and desirable that newsreels and even amateur films with rally footage were officially forbidden from exhibition.

No one heaped more praise on the film than Goebbels, who noted correctly, "Whoever has seen and experienced the face of the Führer in *Triumph of the Will*, will never forget it. It will haunt him through days and dreams and will, like a quiet flame, burn itself into his soul." On May Day, he awarded it the National Film Prize for 1935, describing it as "forged to the tempo of marching formations, steely in conviction, glowing with artistic passion."

Leni's passion, though not intended for international release, traveled well. It won one of several gold medals at Mussolini's 1935 Venice Film Festival and the Grand Prix of the Paris Film Festival from a right-wing jury in 1937, an honor Leni would cite forever after to prove that the film could not be propaganda.

Ordinary Germans' response to *Triumph of the Will* was the measure of homeland success. The picture played in major theaters and minor, in school auditoriums and assembly halls, in churches and barracks. Its final revenues are not known, but Ufa reported that the film had earned back its advance and gone into profit just two months after its release, and it continues to impress audiences and make money today (though not in Germany, where its public exhibition is forbidden) from rentals and sales of videos and DVDs. Its ideological success cannot be precisely measured, but, to Leni, her exertions were resoundingly vindicated. Agreement was all but universal that, at only thirty-two, she had created a new kind of heroic cinema. With art and craft, she had wed power and poetry so compellingly as to challenge the artistry of anything remotely similar that had gone before. Her manipulation of formal elements was virtuosic, her innovations in shooting and editing set new standards and remain exemplary for filmmakers seven decades later, when the controversy the film continues to generate is, in itself, testimony to its effectiveness.

It is, in a sense, two films. Those who saw it in the 1930s, ignorant of things to come, lived in its moment, whether ecstatic, uneasy, or uncertain. They did not view it through the haunting and obscene images that color its grandiosity for later viewers: images of Auschwitz, Dachau, and Bergen-Belsen, of Dresden, of the courtrooms of Nuremberg.

Leni was not directly responsible for those images, and whether they might have been avoided if she had never made the ones she did is beyond speculation. What is undeniable is that she used her century's most powerful art form to make and propagate a vision that eased the path of a murderous dictator who fascinated her and shaped a criminal regime she found both inspiring and personally useful. Her lifelong pose of naïveté about them is not credible, which is not to deny her the right to any political enthusiasm or, as she liked to claim, none at all. Nor does that make *Triumph of the Will* "a pure historical film" or one that merely captures a moment in time; it glorifies what it depicts and in doing so lulls and deceives.

There is justice, of course, to her protestation that she could not have known what lay ahead. Nor could she have imbued Hitler with messianic qualities in a culture unwilling to find them there. She drew on what a noted historian calls "popular sentiments and quasi-religious levels of devotion that could not simply be manufactured." But her later disavowals are consistent in one regard: Whatever degree of veracity they may contain, they are as opportunistic as her making of the film. She sought credit for art and craft while rejecting to the end of her life all moral responsibility for content or consequence. One thing counted: She made a landmark film. It is full of seductive images that, however troubling to our eyes, have not dissipated with time. They survive the ashes and graves that may fairly be judged as part of their legacy.

ELEVEN

THE OLYMPIC IDEA

I don't do things by halves. I hate halves.
                                    —Leni Riefenstahl

Germany is supposed to be "like an open book"—but who chose and prepared the passages at which the book lies open?
                                    —Victor Klemperer, August 13, 1936

NO OTHER SUCH HITLER FILM was ever made. No other was needed. But not everyone rhapsodized over Leni and *Triumph of the Will.* The generals did not, their discontent fed not by what was in the film but by what was not. Apart from passing glimpses of an officer or two, the professional military was ignored in favor of the SA, the SS, the Labor Service, even the apple-cheeked schoolboys of the Hitler Youth. Minister of War Gen. Walther von Reichenau, who had professed his love for Hitler when Röhm was murdered "because he has shown himself a true soldier," grew steely and demanded to see Leni's Wehrmacht footage while she was still editing. Claiming it had been ruined by bad weather and brushing it aside as useless, she inflamed the general's displeasure, which he communicated to the Führer.

Whether bad weather destroyed footage or not, it was unsurprising that *Triumph* deemphasized the Wehrmacht. The Versailles Treaty prohibited a postwar German army of greater than one hundred thousand and was still in force when the film was made. Hitler renounced the treaty on March 16, 1935, two weeks before the première, and, until he did so openly, strategy dictated concealment of the secret military buildup.

But now that the Versailles Treaty was dead, the Wehrmacht demanded a film of its own. Leni fell into line. She had expressed her hope for another rally film to Streicher, but this one came just as she was negotiating with Goebbels for another project that would prove the biggest commission of her life, and pliability was good policy. She embarked on her third Nuremberg film, to be called *Day of Freedom* (*Tag der Freiheit*) in recognition of Hitler's liberation of Germany and its military from the Versailles prohibitions so profoundly resented since 1919.

After the challenge of *Triumph of the Will*, *Day of Freedom* seemed a chore, a mere finger exercise to satisfy military vanity. Leni referred to it that way, claiming "the only thing we had to shoot was the army exercises, which took place on a single day."

But that single day required extensive and exacting preparations. *Film-Kurier* reported on September 17, "Just like last year, Leni Riefenstahl is absorbed in her work. Since the first days of September, she begins her daily work with her collaborators in the early morning hours, only to rest for a couple of hours late at night, after the day's shooting, and when she has finished giving assignments for the next day in every detail."

After the Second World War, she minimized *Day of Freedom*, confident she was safe from rebuttal because, like *Victory of Faith*, it was believed lost. At only twenty-eight minutes, it was the least of what has been called her "Nuremberg triptych" but was not negligible, for it boldly depicted the resurrection of a military machine that would soon overwhelm Europe. *Day of Freedom* was guaranteed a broad general audience by its release on the same bill with Ufa's *The Higher Command* (*Der höhere Befehl*) featuring Lil Dagover, a star epic of the 1930s built on a patriotic theme. Leni's attempt to distance herself from it or from anything concerning the 1935 party congress was prudent. The rally would enter history with what historians have called "the most murderous legislative instrument known to European history," the notorious Nuremberg racial laws, which deprived German Jews of their citizenship and the right to vote (among other measures) in the first legal step toward more final solutions.

Leni's film is devoted solely to the military and ignores the Nuremberg Laws. It builds to the oratory at its center that Leni to the end of her life privately called "the most beautiful Führer speech of them all," though it was never clear if she was referring to its military implications or the aesthetic qualities she lent Hitler as he addressed the Wehrmacht while swastika banners whipped in the wind.

What is striking about *Day of Freedom* is its assured mastery of rhythm and how relaxed it looks in comparison to the sometimes oppressive control of *Triumph of the Will*. It begins (again) in the Nuremberg morning, this time in the tent city housing rally participants after an ornamental title sequence of glinting crossed bayonets. Shaving, sausages, and horseplay fill the screen before the tanks, planes, and cannons roll out for the war games that make up the bulk of the film.

The military maneuvers were shot not in one day but during repeated practice sessions, largely before the rally began. Trenches were dug for perspectives of tanks rolling "over the camera," and towers were built for crowd scenes, high elevations, and close views of the Führer in full oratorical cry. Most impressive were the air displays, culminating in fighter planes in a swastika formation against the clouds. *Day of Freedom* is a minor work and, like *Victory of Faith,* served as a technical rehearsal for cameramen she had assembled for her next commission, the larger one she was discussing with Goebbels at the same time.

Her passion for athletics—for movement and physical beauty—easily outweighed whatever affinity she felt for tanks and bayonets. Skiing was a "joy" that allowed her "to forget everything that previously dejected me, forcing even my professional plans to take a back seat." Scaling cliffs in the "magic garden" of the Dolomites made her "freer and healthier," and climbing "drove out all other thoughts."

After the opening of *Triumph of the Will* in March 1935, she had traveled to Davos and the high-altitude apartment she had rented there for herself and Walter Prager, though she found herself again alone. Prager, out of place as an assistant on *Triumph,* had grown restless in the months Leni sat preoccupied at her editing tables and, like Schneeberger before him, left her for a less driven companion. Believing she was still in love with him, Leni felt wronged but didn't grieve. She took a new friend to ski with, Guzzi Lantschner, now a fledgling cameraman and fervent fan of the Reich. She tanned on her balcony with Guzzi, his equally political brother Otto, and their sister Hedi, a quartet of ski aces glowing with sunburn and optimism in the bright, pure atmosphere of Davos—"no air like it anywhere else in the world."

Thoughts of other spheres did not intrude except for intermittent visions of a film starring herself based on Kleist's *Penthesilea,* a notion that had intrigued her off and on since that chance meeting ten years earlier with impresario Max Reinhardt, who told her she looked the part. Leni had then never heard of *Penthesilea* but soon became familiar with Kleist's savage Amazon queen and her love affair with Achilles. She could visualize herself on film—naked on horseback, hair streaming in the wind as she plunged into battle, spear in hand. Why not? She was as daring, as bold, as beautiful. And more than one Achilles had succumbed to her spell. But *Penthesilea,* like *Tiefland,* could wait. She had other tasks to fulfill for her Führer—the Wehrmacht film in the fall—and then the great, unprecedented one whose dimensions were as vast as her ambitions.

If *Triumph of the Will* made Hitler safe for Germany, a film of the 1936 Olympics in Berlin could make him safe for the world. Leni's Nuremberg films celebrated the "New Germany" for her compatriots, but an Olympic film could define the new order for an international audience not yet fully persuaded that Hitler meant it when he said, "Germany needs peace and desires peace!" The spectacle of the Olympic Games could add imagery to the rhetoric and dazzle the world with Third Reich modernity, efficiency, and healthy goodwill.

Certainly Hitler grasped the propaganda potential—"Who else but

you could make a film of the Olympics?" he asked her—though he had
not the slightest personal interest in athletics. In October 1933—at about
the same time he commissioned *Triumph of the Will*—he reviewed the
proposals for the 1936 games and committed to the building of the vast
new Sport Forum in Berlin. It would be the largest and most up-to-date
athletic facility in the world, with a stadium to seat more than one hundred thousand spectators, splendid arenas, tracks, fields, pools, and an
artificial lake surrounded by woodland. An Olympic Village of 160 buildings and thirty-eight dining halls would accommodate the five thousand
athletes expected to attend from nearly thirty countries. "If one has
invited the world to be one's guest," he explained, "something great and
beautiful should be built." When he saw it, he would complain that it was
too small, for he was convinced, as he told Speer, that after 1940, no
Olympics would be held anywhere else for the next thousand years.

Even as he laid plans in 1933 to welcome the world, he was only hours
away from withdrawing from the League of Nations. The elimination of
Röhm, the repudiation of the Versailles Treaty, and the reintroduction of
universal military service followed. Then would come the occupation of
the Rhineland, the murder of Austrian chancellor Engelbert Dollfuss,
the intimidating denunciations of Austria and Czechoslovakia, and the
Nazi pledge of the airborne Condor Legion to support Franco's forces in
the Spanish Civil War—all of them occurring in worldwide headlines as
the new Sport Forum rose in peace-loving Berlin. It may have seemed a
particular irony to Hitler—the *New York Times* pointed it out—that the
games would begin on August 1, 1936, twenty-two years to the day from
the outbreak of the Great War in 1914.

Cities host the games, not states, and Berlin had been named site of the
1936 games by the International Olympic Committee in 1931, before
Weimar had succumbed to the swastika. A host city approved in one era
aroused controversy in another. Articles began appearing in England
with titles such as "Under the Heel of Hitler: The Dictatorship over
Sport in Nazi Germany," and boycott movements were threatened or
mounted in Sweden, the Netherlands, and Czechoslovakia.

The United States was the largest and most successful competitor in the modern games, and there protest swelled. Opposition to the Third Reich's racial policies roused public sentiment to relocate the games or avoid them altogether. The Amateur Athletic Union voted to boycott unless the German government guaranteed that Jewish athletes would be allowed to compete, especially after the Nazis deposed the Christian president of the German Olympic Committee because his grandmother was Jewish. Few had done more to secure the games for Berlin than Dr. Theodor Lewald, and his removal shocked the international sporting community. The Nazis hastily made him an "honorary Aryan" (a "temporary Aryan," Count Harry Kessler predicted darkly) and gave him the title of "adviser." As such, he reassured the world that Jews would compete "as a matter of principle," though how they were to train was a mystery. Jews had been legally excluded from German playing fields since June 1933, gratifying Julius Streicher, who editorialized in *Der Stürmer* that "Jews are Jews and there is no place for them in German sports."

In June 1934, the American Olympic Committee, at the urging of its president, Avery Brundage, tentatively agreed to participate. Brundage— later a member with Charles Lindbergh of the America First Committee, which, until Pearl Harbor, opposed aid to U.S. allies at war with Nazi Germany—made a personal fact-finding trip to Berlin. There he accepted the German government's assurances that a select number of Jewish athletes had been nominated to train on German teams. Brundage was satisfied with German pledges, though none of these athletes ever appeared at the games. "Politics has no place in sport," he announced, adding that "certain Jews must now understand that they cannot use these Games as a weapon in their boycott against the Nazis." The secretary of the American Olympic Committee said that "Germans are not discriminating against Jews in their Olympic tryouts. The Jews are eliminated because they are not good enough as athletes. Why, there are not a dozen Jews in the world of Olympic calibre."

Two of the "not a dozen" were originally German and were publicly welcomed back to compete and provide spin for the fatherland. Jewish ice hockey player Rudi Ball, who had fled to France in 1933, and half-Jewish fencer Helene Mayer, a student and resident of Los Angeles, would both compete wearing swastika jerseys. Mayer would win a silver medal in fencing and deliver a "*Heil,* Hitler!" salute when she did.

Boycott pressure grew vehement in the United States when the Nuremberg racial laws were announced. Nevertheless, the executive board of the Amateur Athletic Union met in New York in December and—again at the urging of Brundage—voted by a razor-thin margin to send an American team to Berlin in spite of petitions bearing half a million signatures asking them not to. The president of the AAU resigned in protest and was replaced by Brundage, who immediately requested the resignations of all board members who had voted "anti-Olympics."

By then, Leni was advancing plans for her Olympics film. She had just returned to Berlin from Davos in the early summer of 1935 to prepare *Day of Freedom* when Dr. Carl Diem of Germany's Olympic Organization Committee approached her, telling her that his admiration for *Triumph of the Will* persuaded him that she should film the Olympic Games for the world.

A onetime runner, classical scholar, and ardent Olympian, Diem was "a perfect miracle of channeled energy," as someone called him. His sincerity and courtliness conquered Leni's reluctance to consider another documentary with *Tiefland* in cold storage and *Penthesilea* still a fantasy. But Diem had a passionate vision of a footrace: young runners in relays carrying a burning torch from Greece's ancient Olympia across modern Europe to the new stadium in Berlin, where it would ignite the Olympic flame to open the games. Leni was stirred by a classical allusion from her childhood—"Athens on the Spree!"—and by what Diem referred to as "the Olympic idea."

She consulted with her old mentor Fanck, who had filmed the 1928 Winter Olympics at St. Moritz. Though Fanck had no interest in a Summer Olympics film, he prepared a thirty-seven-page detailed analysis for her of the problems and commercial potential of such a film. His conclusions were negative to equivocal and left her unsatisfied. "I do not like doing things by halves," she liked to say. "I don't do things by halves. I hate halves."

"The Olympic idea" stirred fantasy, as did Diem's torch race, which built a human bridge between classical Greece and the New Germany. "I could see the ancient ruins of the classical Olympic sites slowly emerging from patches of fog and the Greek temples and sculptures drifting by," she explained. "That was my vision of the prologue to my *Olympia*." It was almost precisely the way the film would begin three years later, though the sculptures would dissolve to living nudes and then to a map of contemporary Europe with a swastika representing Germany, and then, through bells pealing in celebration, to a close-up of the Führer, personification of the fatherland's classical renaissance.

Leni was adamant to the end of her life that her commission to film the Olympics came directly from Diem, but the commission was never his to give. In a flouting of Olympic principles that barred political activity or influence, the Reich had relieved the German committee of decision-making power when it demoted Lewald from president to adviser. His replacement was the Reich Sport Leader (*Reichssportführer*) Hans von Tschammer und Osten, a hard-core party follower of Hitler's since 1922 who reported directly to another "old comrade," Minister of the Interior Wilhelm Frick. Diem was invited to join Lewald on the sidelines, stripped of authority "because of his strong involvement with the former political system." As a figurehead and spokesman, Diem could recommend whatever he wanted, but the power to award a film commission resided where all film power resided in the Third Reich, in the hands of Goebbels.

Leni later told of securing financing for the filming herself, going first to Ufa, which turned her down because the film had no love story and could not be released until after interest in the games had faded. She said she went to Ufa's competitor Tobis, where production chief Friedrich Mainz was enthusiastic and contracted to finance the filming for 1.5 million reichsmarks. But the contract with Tobis was not signed until

December 1936, four months after the end of the games, and was an advance against distribution that guaranteed only half that sum, or 750,000 reichsmarks. If Leni's Tobis story had been true, *Olympia* might never have been made. Fortunately, she had negotiated with Goebbels the full 1.5 million she said she needed a full year before the games began.

Goebbels was impressed enough by her Olympic plans on August 15, 1935, to note in his diary, "She's a clever thing!" By October 4, she was making demands. "A woman who knows what she wants!" Ten days later, he recorded, "Contract with Leni Riefenstahl re the Olympics film approved." By November 7, it had been delivered: "Fräulein Riefenstahl gets her Olympics film contract. Transaction: 1.5 million. She is overjoyed." Delight was fitting. Her production budget was triple that of the typical German feature film of the mid-1930s. Her personal fee of 250,000 reichsmarks was equivalent to half the cost of the average studio's star-oriented drama, comedy, or musical.

Goebbels had worked swiftly, securing Hitler's approval for the full 1.5 million reichsmarks by August 21, the day before Leni's thirty-third birthday, with the total budget charged to the propaganda ministry. Direct financing by the Reich was "certain to bring revenue," as a finance ministry memo predicted. It would also provide Goebbels with oversight of Leni's accounts, with unexpected consequences.

A bureaucratic obstacle remained: preserving for the International Olympic Committee the appearance of political independence. Funding through the Film Credit Bank, which Goebbels controlled, was permissible only to private ventures. Compliance was achieved by Leni's establishing Olympia-Film GmbH on December 9 as the nominal private entity producing the film, and Goebbels announced her project the next day with appropriate fanfare. Internally, the ministry spelled out that the Olympia-Film company was "founded on the instigation of the Reich and with funds provided by the Reich. All funds needed by the company for making the film will also be made available within the Reich budget. The founding of the company is necessary because *the Reich does not wish to be seen openly as the maker of the film*" (italics added).

Leni and her brother, Heinz, were the sole stockholders of Olympia-Film, which would be "solely responsible for the general artistic direction and overall organization of the Olympic film." The company was to be liquidated and signed over to the Reich when production was complete, a transfer of rights that Leni later said she agreed to on the advice of lawyers as part of a sophisticated tax scheme she didn't understand. If true, she was the only one involved who did not know that the Olympia-Film company was a front for the Reich from its inception.

If she was as naïve about financing as she claimed—or confused about the nature and date of the Tobis contract—she could hardly have been clearer about them a month after the games concluded, when she wrote Paul Kohner, now an important agent in Hollywood. She suggested that he might care to elicit a modest offer from MGM for her "magnificent sports film." She added that "within the next few weeks we will decide whether Ufa or Tobis obtains the film. The ultimate determination on who gets the film belongs to Reichsminister Dr. Göbbels [sic]."

The size of the budget underlined the significance the Reich placed on the Olympics. Leni admitted it was "a sensational amount," and Goebbels's having secured it for her marked a level of support and cooperation unlikely to survive their mutual wariness, and—miles of film and mounting expenses later—it would not. But preserving the games on film was a key element of Goebbels's broader propaganda campaign to present the New Germany to the world in a positive light, deflecting attention from repressive racial policies by emphasizing Strength through Joy (*Kraft durch Freude*). Goebbels's *Der Angriff* lectured its readers on Olympic hospitality: "We must be more charming than the Parisians, more easygoing than the Viennese, more vivacious than the Romans, more cosmopolitan than London, and more practical than New York."

To ensure Berlin's image as a "model city" with streets safe for tourists as the games drew near, the police bundled vagrants, pickpockets, and public nuisances behind bars, shielding them from temptation in "preventive custody." On July 16, two weeks before the games opened, the Gypsies of Berlin—who, like Jews, had been declared persons of "alien blood" and deprived of their citizenship under the Nuremberg Laws—were rounded up and relocated far from tourists' eyes on sewage-disposal plots in the Berlin suburb of Marzahn. The measure was temporary, just for the Olympics, but lasted until the Gypsies were resettled again, most of them to Birkenau and Auschwitz. It is a largely unnoticed irony that the first racially defined detention camp of the Third Reich was prompted by the Olympics, and, though she cannot have known it, Leni's future would include some of the very Gypsies forcibly relocated to Marzahn as she prepared her film.

Elsewhere, posters that once warned "Jews: Your Entry Is Forbidden" were placed in storage, as in Garmisch-Partenkirchen, where the winter games were held in February. William L. Shirer, still covering Germany for the American press, reported, "The signs that last summer bellowed 'Jews Get Out' and 'Jews Unwanted' have been quietly removed," and "Jew baiting is officially off in Germany during the Olympics," causing the propaganda ministry to threaten him with expulsion. *Der Stürmer*, with its "Jews Are Our Misfortune" slogan, was ordered under the counter on city newsstands. Berlin was on its best behavior, smiling, friendly, and festive with swastika banners fluttering from shop and tenement windows—except those of Jews, who were forbidden by the Nuremberg Laws to fly the German flag and displayed the Olympics flag instead, a subtle gesture of defiance the Nazis tolerated for the duration and no foreign correspondent seemed to notice.

The games were scheduled for August 1–16. Leni had been preparing since *Day of Freedom*, months before the November contracts were signed. She embarked on a punishing schedule that took full advantage of her obsession for organization. She had assembled the camera team for *Day of Freedom* with an eye to the Olympics and encouraged them to work on the propaganda ministry's Winter Olympics film in Garmisch to get the hang of photographing athletes in motion. In Garmisch, the star attraction on ice was Norway's Sonja Henie, winning her third figure-skating gold medal in a row, but Leni—a much bigger celebrity—reigned on the slopes, posing for a *Time* magazine cover on skis in her bathing suit.

"I went with a few of the cameramen," she explained later. "Maybe four, maybe there were six, some other young boys, I don't know. But Guzzi and Otto Lantschner, Hans Ertl and Walter Frentz, these four I do remember exactly. And we went just to look at all the sporting events, to study, to *see*, because many of us were not interested in sports before. Sometimes we made tests with film, but most of the time I helped them so they would be able to work with a camera without thinking. All this was training for the camera, and for moving. Not *only* to look. You must try whatever is possible with the moving camera in this sport art. We trained for this like you train athletes in the circus."

No film had ever been made to document an entire Olympics at full length, and there were no precedents for logistical challenges that seemed to increase exponentially the moment solutions were proposed. Camera placement, as always, was a major issue and fixation. The summer games were slated to be held not only at the new Sport Forum in Berlin but in outlying or distant locations as well, none of which could be neglected. Boating events were scheduled in Kiel, on the Baltic (yachting), and in suburban Grünau (canoeing and rowing). Bicycle racing, the marathon, equestrian events, and the decathlon would literally cover the map.

Each event required not only ideal camera placements but also the ideal cameras, film stocks, filters, and cameramen. Photographic tolerances were limited in an era of slow film speeds and cumbersome sound cameras with minimal portability. Color was investigated, then rejected as too slow and unpredictable. "I would have had to change my style," Leni said. Cameras ranged from the fastest in the world for slow-motion photography to the smallest in the world for candid shots of spectator reactions (including the Führer's), supplemented by the world's longest telephoto lenses for close-ups of athletes in performance when proximity was forbidden, which was most of the time. Film stocks and filters were tested for rendering faces, architectural elements, and grass and foliage. Because no single stock was suitable for every purpose, reserves of a dozen different types—as much as fifty thousand feet a day—were made available for distribution to cameramen at a moment's notice based on the events, on weather and light conditions, or on Leni's orders or whims.

Events—and their trial heats, which were also photographed—were scheduled concurrently in different locations, some at considerable distances from Leni's command post in the main stadium. Many events demanded multiple cameras of different types and speeds, especially in track and field, where focus was intense on African American Jesse Owens, "the fastest man in the world," who was a living challenge to the racial theories of his hosts. In Berlin—within range of Leni's cameras and to Hitler's fury—Owens would become one of the great legends in the history of the modern games.

Not all 136 Olympic events could be included in the film, but all had to be covered, for Leni's contract charged her with preparation of a sports film archive from which short films could be made for educational use. Her order to her crew of forty-five cameramen (plus their assistants and drivers) was that "everything would have to be shot and from every conceivable angle." All she required, as she paced among them in flared slacks and silken blouse, was "making the impossible possible." All she demanded was "to shoot the Olympics more closely, more dramatically than sports had ever been captured on celluloid." As insurance, her contract put the footage of all newsreel companies covering the games—domestic and foreign—at her disposal, at nonnegotiable prices to be determined for her by the cost-conscious bookkeepers of the Reich.

Cameras flew overhead in dirigibles, light planes, and free-floating balloons when the games opened on August 1. Automatic cameras were cushioned in rubber and fastened to horses' saddles or were suspended in tiny baskets from the necks of marathon runners and aimed at their feet as they pounded concrete roadways. Trenches were (again) dug for low-angle views; steel towers (again) erected for high. The committee forbade positions that might interfere with athletes' concentration, and Leni admitted privately that "actually, any camera inside the stadium was disruptive," which did not dampen her near-fanatical desire to be there.

Testing from February to August, Leni stockpiled images.

Preshooting joined reshooting in a shrugging aside of purist rules of documentary practice. She filmed trials and training sessions, during which close-ups could be made for later intercutting with competition footage to suggest straining muscles and grimacing faces at the instant of victory or defeat. After winners were declared, she persuaded them to reenact their feats for her cameramen, sometimes, as with pole vaulting and the long jumps, into the night when spectators had departed and the stadiums were empty but for Leni, her cameramen, and the athletes.

Territorial conflicts occurred hourly with Olympic Committee watch-dogs, stadium officials, referees, roaming newsreel crews, wire service photographers, and—inevitably—the propaganda minister. Goebbels was making the Berlin Olympics the first ever to be televised—live from enormous electronic cameras in the stadium and almost-live from spe-cially designed television vans. Film cameras photographed from platforms on top of trucks; their footage was fed directly into the vehicles' interiors, where technicians developed their images as the vans raced through Berlin to television studios for broadcast to eighteen public "tel-evision halls" around the city only minutes after exposure.

The press made much of Leni's innovations, though not all were suc-cessful. Some were disallowed by the Olympic Committee, notably the "catapult," a robot camera designed by Hans Ertl to hurtle along track railings just ahead of the runners. Others never worked, such as the cam-eras in the free-floating balloons, which descended on vacant lots or rooftops with unusably shaky footage. Camera pits were sometimes dan-gerous for the athletes and ordered filled (Jesse Owens almost tumbled into one while winning four gold medals and breaking two world records). Steel camera towers weighing almost a ton were dismantled and repositioned daily, only to be declared off-limits by the committee once they were in place.

For every misfire, an experiment worked, none more brilliantly than Hans Ertl's solution for the diving competitions. He built an underwater housing for his Sinclair camera that enabled him to shoot divers poised on the high board from his water-level vantage point and then—without a break in his filming—to follow their dives in flight, to submerge with them underwater, and to rise again as they burst to the surface in jewell-like constellations of bubbles. Any single shot required continuous manual focus *and* exposure adjustments as his camera tracked the movement. Most of his shooting was done before or after the actual competitions, but nothing like it had ever been attempted, let alone achieved. Ertl's inventiveness and manual dexterity were as remarkable as any of the athletic feats he photographed.

The ingenuity of Leni's crews testifies to the creativity she could generate along with the labor and sweat. She was amassing torrents of footage in hopes of discovering an "architecture" for the film that was elusive and, for an unnervingly extended time, was limited to the classical prologue stimulated by Diem's vision of the torch race. The prologue would be almost entirely the work of one cameraman, the eccentric and exacting Willy Zielke, who later complained about chronic overshooting, saying, "It was just throwing away money," but her response was unvarying: "No, shoot it," and "we'll see later if it can be used."

She knew the value of unlimited footage for editing from *Triumph of the Will* and brushed aside suggestions of uncertainty: "The moment I had a clear picture of the film in my head, the film was born. The structure of the whole imposed itself. It was purely intuitive." But the clear picture was slow to focus, and none of her interviews at the time allude to a final shape or structure, intuitive or otherwise. As with *Triumph,* it would come in the editing, and its conception harkened back to Fanck.

When she had approached him for advice early on, he had advised that she had two options: a purely aesthetic film devoted to the body in motion or a series of long films (he suggested six) that would comprehensively document the games. She wanted both. In her Nuremberg films she had demonstrated mastery at compressing "everything" from "every conceivable angle" into concise dramatic form at the editing table and was confident she could do so again. But, as a former dancer and connoisseur of beautiful athletes, she was drawn to the sensual qualities of grace and movement, too. She would combine Fanck's approaches in two separate full-length films. The first, with its classical prologue and competitive events that she called "the struggle," would be titled *Olympia: Festival of Nations*. The second, *Olympia: Festival of Beauty*, would focus on "poetics," beginning idyllically with naked athletes in a lakeside sauna and culminating in divers soaring against the sky in a dramatic ballet of anonymous physical perfection. "You only see the beauty," she exulted.

A preview of the sensual, even erotic quality that pervades much of *Olympia* came in July when she and her assistants flew to Greece to film the lighting of the torch for the prologue. The torch race (which survives to the present day) would take twelve days and 335 runners in relays across almost two thousand miles from Mount Olympus to Berlin, but Leni needed only the beginning. Cameraman Willy Zielke had preceded her to Greece and already filmed the Acropolis in mists he manufactured with smoke pots and filters. When she joined him there with her publicity chief, Ernst Jäger, and a select group of journalists and personal photographers, she was dismayed to discover that antiquity was overrun with automobiles and souvenir hawkers. Athletes in modern Greek dress clashed with her vision of clean-limbed classical youth. Crowds and police interference prompted a move to quieter Delphi, site of the now-silent oracle, where an olive-skinned adolescent caught her eye. Here was her ideal Greek runner, quickly stripped down to almost nothing for a simulation of the lighting of the torch and commencement of the race. Henry von Jaworsky recalled her shouting, "Shoot more of him, shoot more of him! Shoot everywhere more of him, he is beautiful!"

Her classical Greek runner was neither classical nor Greek. His name was Anatol Dobriansky and he was the son of Russian immigrants, but he captured Leni's fancy so completely she was willing to pay his bewildered parents two hundred reichsmarks to take him back to Berlin with her. She briefly made him her lover and arranged acting lessons for him at Tobis while he struggled to learn German.

Anatol could not long compete with Leni's obsession for work or Berlin's flesh-and-blood Olympians. Her affairs with Fanck, Trenker, Sokal, Schneeberger, Allgeier, Ertl, Lantschner, Prager, and others (even

Zielke was said to be in love with her) left her vulnerable to ribald jokes of the "glacial crevasse" variety that placed her in the beds of Hitler, Göring, and Goebbels—or didn't. "She didn't need Hitler," went one of them. "She had five gold medal athletes every night, why should she look at Hitler?" While bawdy quips were the good-natured currency of canteens and beer gardens, at least one Olympian rumor had substance.

Leni's affair with America's decathlon gold medal winner Glenn Morris began with a single glance, after which, she said, "we both seemed transfixed." The folie à deux went public at the decathlon medal ceremony. The chiseled American with the gold medallion around his neck descended the steps of the victors' dais and "grabbed me in his arms, tore off my blouse, and kissed my breasts, right in the middle of the stadium, in front of a hundred thousand spectators." Newspapers (oddly) remained silent, but when gossip reached the Olympic Village, it inspired young Anatol to defend Leni's honor with his fists.

Leni was so smitten she was oblivious to Anatol's bloody-nosed chivalry. "Never before had I experienced such a passion," she rhapsodized about Morris. "I had lost my head completely. I forgot almost everything, even my work." As Leni's cameramen confirmed in photographs that Leni would later claim as her own, Morris was superbly photogenic, whether pole-vaulting, hurling a javelin, or stretched out in lean and lanky repose on the stadium grass. Hollywood would acknowledge his looks after the games, putting him in a loincloth to play Tarzan at Twentieth Century–Fox.

When not quickening pulses among Olympians, Leni barked orders as their general. This was evident in the stadium and in the converted castle-in-a-park five miles from the Sport Forum that was off-site headquarters for the crew. Castle Ruhwald ("peaceful woods") housed some three hundred people with offices, film and equipment storage areas, camera repair shops, sleeping rooms, a cafeteria known for the best breakfasts in Berlin, plus a scale model of the Sport Forum that Leni used to plot camera positions for the next day's work in after-dinner strategy meetings that often lasted well past midnight.

Her public persona was sunshine and modesty, with two full-time personal photographers trailing her wherever she went. Her professional demeanor was steel. The Riefenstahl work habits were detailed in *Film-Kurier* early in the games and did not minimize the strain her command could exact. "She has allocated seven hours for this important afternoon of the third day, discussed five different takes with each of 34 cameramen, as well as talking to each of them for an extra ten minutes about material, filters and apertures," the report noted. "That makes a total of 510 minutes during the morning and midday for organizing the afternoon . . . eight hours of conversation at [a Jesse] Owens–like pace. No wonder the sparks fly if one of her team is unable to cope. She works and treats her cameramen as if she were possessed."

Berlin columnist Bella Fromm etched a vignette of Leni at work not unlike the one Janet Flanner had contributed to *The New Yorker* two years earlier. Fromm—Jewish and never a fan—wrote: "She wears a pair of long, grey flannel trousers and a kind of jockey's cap and is unpleasantly conspicuous wherever one looks. She attempts to give the impression of untiring activity, thereby underlining her importance. Meanwhile her colleagues calmly and expertly get on with the job at hand."

Hans Ertl later offered his own critique. "Egocentric, as was her nature, she again and again offended the public as well as, if I am honest, some of her co-workers, because she ran—even during the tensest events—from one camera to another, and with large gestures, acted as if she was giving real director's orders. Like a shadow, her personal photographer Rolf Lantin followed, shooting publicity pictures. She only came up to me one time, as my unequivocal 'Don't bother me!' even attracted the applause of a referee standing nearby."

The correspondent of the *New York Times* noted, "Her word is law in the matter of all picture taking anywhere at the games. Any cameraman who puts himself anywhere that Miss Riefenstahl thinks he should not be is swiftly approached by an attendant who hands him a pink slip. It says in effect: 'Remove yourself from where you are now —Riefenstahl.' "

It was inevitable that Leni's proprietary attachment to the games would conflict with Goebbels's. On the fifth day of events, a referee ordered Guzzi Lantschner off the field as he was photographing the hammer throw. Leni threatened to "drag" the referee "by the ears to the Führer's box, you swine!" When the referee filed an official complaint of abuse, Goebbels demanded she apologize publicly and threatened her with removal from the stadium. Anger spilled into his diary for the first time. "I dressed Riefenstahl down for her incredible behavior. Hysterical woman! Certainly no man!" As if on cue, Leni "cried bitter tears."

Her tears may have been real, but they were strategic, too. Both Nazi culture and the world of filmmaking were profoundly antifeminist, but no more immune to tears than her father had been when she was determined to get her way. "For everything you see that was shot inside the stadium," she told an admirer, "I had to get permission and if I had been a man, I wouldn't have gotten it. So, it was easy. I was a nice young girl, so I said, 'Please let me do it. Please let me do it. Please let me do it.' " Three decades later Harvard documentary filmmaker Robert Gardner recounted being "in her presence with a producer and she wept until the man was so beside himself he didn't know how else to deal with her and said, 'Go ahead, Leni, go ahead and do it.' She was an actress, after all," Gardner observed, "and willing to be shrewd, to cajole, to weep to get her way."

Her crews sympathized with her ambitions and pressures, but they, too, were subjected to outbursts of anger or tears. Her methods of filmmaking demanded perfection, a goal they respected and shared, but perfectionism encouraged the proliferating excess that Zielke and others considered wasteful and indulgent and would come back to haunt her. The skills of command without which she could have accomplished little were easy to resent, though film directors are not known for laissez-faire coddling, nor can they be. Their jobs are too enormous.

So, sometimes, are their egos. And command skills are not the same as budgetary skills. "I didn't have a talent for business," she admitted, though she would soon prove how shrewd she could be when it mattered. She had never made a film on a studio budget or one with conventional balance sheets, cost reports, or daily accounting, but she knew that the larger the budget, the greater the likelihood of slippage and the harder the assignment of accountability for overage or excess. The resources of Nuremberg had been bottomless and available as needed, as free-flowing as her demands, as plentiful as the supply of swastika flags and torches.

The Olympic funds, on the other hand, were taxpayer monies— "within the Reich budget"—and the accountants of the Reich were keeping meticulous books. The approved 1.5 million reichsmarks had begun to flow in November 1935 with a start-up disbursement of 300,000, followed by another 700,000 on April 1, 1936. The final 500,000 reichsmarks were reserved for editing and postproduction. "Making the impossible possible" drove costs into overages on a daily basis. By the end of the games, she had spent four-fifths of her budget—all but 300,000 reichsmarks—with a year and a half of postproduction still to come. Her contract stipulated that she was "solely responsible" for the filming and "for the disbursement of the 1.5 million reichsmarks by presenting receipts." Goebbels, growing impatient, ordered a surprise audit.

He had been angered by the incident with the referee and with the Olympic Village brawl involving Anatol Dobriansky, which brought to light Leni's having paid his parents to permit him to leave Greece (now interpreted by the family as kidnapping), an expense she had charged to the picture. Moreover, party functionaries at all levels were complaining that she spent too much time after hours photographing American athletes such as Glenn Morris and, during events, blacks such as Jesse Owens.

The money drain slowed with the Olympics' closing night of August 16, when Speer's searchlights encircled the stadium and were aimed at the heavens in the great Cathedral of Light for which Leni would later claim credit. Shooting of medalists continued postgames in Berlin as Zielke photographed the remainder of the prologue on the Baltic Sea coast, including a group of nude female dancers and a difficult dissolve from Myron's marble *Discobolus* to German athlete Erwin Huber as the statue's flesh-and-blood manifestation. Leni visited Zielke on the Baltic dunes to evaluate his work before traveling to the resort island of Sylt for a holi-day with Margot von Opel, daughter-in-law of the German automobile magnate. In early September, she dropped in on Ertl at the 1936 Nuremberg rally, where he was filming for the propaganda ministry and had promised to make some pickup shots she could splice into *Olympia*.

Leni's attempt to piggyback on the rally production precipitated a violent tug-of-war for Ertl's services between Leni and Goebbels's unfriendly deputy, Hans Weidemann. Goebbels's fury at their clash made its way into his diary following her stormy complaints back in Berlin. "Riefenstahl makes accusations against Weidemann. But she is completely hysterical. Further proof that women can't handle such tasks."

Leni was arming herself against what she believed was Goebbels's intention to take the film away from her and give it to Weidemann to edit now that shooting was completed. Her timing was poor. Gross irregu-larities in her accounts had been called to Goebbels's attention the day before her "hysterical" accusations and accelerated the audit. This inva-sion of a sensitive domain may explain Leni's boundless animosity toward Goebbels, who had again and again been more supportive than not. It would be easy to attribute malice to his actions if his response to many of the bookkeeping irregularities had not been so relaxed. "Let's not be petty," he scrawled across one of the auditors' reports, though he had much to chew on when the full fourteen-page summation reached his desk suggesting both incompetence and "a remarkable amount of white-collar crime."

He froze her funding.

Leni claimed in her memoirs that the report cited a shortfall of a mere eighty reichsmarks, but there was much more. Irregularities involving the odd bottle of schnapps were one thing, but the purchase and disposal of motorboats, automobiles, and furniture "for business purposes" were something else again, as were camera and film tests that had mysteriously taken place in Davos rather than Berlin and included months of travel and personal allowance payments to Guzzi Lantschner (among others) at the time he was still Leni's lover. Petty cash in the thousands of reichsmarks was carried around in the pockets of Leni's disbursement agent and doled out on demand without vouchers or receipts. The report concluded that the books were such a shambles it was impossible to reconstruct what had happened to the money. Goebbels angrily condemned it as "a pig sty of a mess" ("*Sauwirtschaft*") and cracked down with a permanent monthly audit that Leni resisted "with all the means at her disposal," insisting that "she must have independent control" and threatening to appeal directly to the Führer.

Film budgets are notoriously subject to creative accounting, but the very real uncertainties of production offer a reasonable line of defense. At the least, unpredictability is the rule, not the exception. It is even possible to find a comic aspect to the banality of dueling egos of the Third Reich crossing bayonets over receipts and petty cash, but the amounts were not negligible and came at a crucial moment. Leni had just begun to review her 250 hours of exposed film and only now discerned the "clear picture" of two films instead of one, though she would make it almost canonical that she had conceived of two films from the beginning. This new and unprecedented plan might have met resistance at any time, let alone in the midst of a crisis brought on by overbudget costs and financial mismanagement that jeopardized her completing even the one film Goebbels had agreed to.

The atmosphere was poisonous, laced with renewed rumors about Leni's possibly Jewish ancestry. She was forced to fire her publicity chief, Ernst Jäger, whose all-but-estranged Jewish wife made him politically unreliable in spite of their open marriage. Speculation percolated again about the nature of her relationship with Hitler; the less well connected glowed with schadenfreude and spoke sagely of hubris. Leni, never more willful than when thwarted, indignantly charged Goebbels with "insolence" that she would not forgive for the next seventy years. She felt persecuted and described her fate as "tragic." To make matters worse, reports began to circulate that her miles of footage were mediocre.

She went directly to Hitler. "I began to weep unrestrainedly," her memoirs relate. She emerged red-eyed but triumphant. She painted

Goebbels's attempts to discipline her as harassment and persuaded Hitler to shift oversight of *Olympia* to Rudolf Hess. Instead of a reprimand for financial mismanagement, she got the additional half million reichsmarks she wanted to complete her two full-length films, a scheme that, however audacious it was creatively, infuriated Goebbels when he learned of it on November 6: "Riefenstahl demonstrates how hysterical she is. There is no working with this wild woman. Now she wants another half million for her film and to make two films out of it. It stinks to high heaven in her shop. I remain cold-hearted. She weeps. That is the final weapon of a woman, but it doesn't work anymore on me. She should tend to business and keep her house in order."

Keeping footage in order was the higher priority. Leni and her editing staff of twenty spent eight to ten hours a day for the next two and a half months viewing 1.3 million feet of film. When the last frame had run through the projectors in January or February 1937, she declared 70 percent of it unusable. Of Ertl's swimming and diving footage, only 5 percent passed muster, but that still left her with seventy-five hours of footage from which to fashion two films of roughly two hours each.

The translucent glass walls of her state-of-the-art editing rooms at Geyer were hung with thousands of strips of celluloid cascading to the floor. Each was indexed by event, participants, angle, lens, focal length, film speed, camera speed, cloud and sun positions, weather conditions, tonal densities, and other notations that might help locate a given strip of film months after it had been approved. Though rough assemblies had been made of some events shortly after they were shot, Leni announced that she could not deliver the finished films before February 1938.

Press coverage of *Olympia* was suspended until a première date could be set, which Leni interpreted as a ban by Goebbels on her carefully cultivated personal publicity. Their conflict mysteriously leaked into headlines in June. Tabloid items in France, Switzerland, and Austria reported that Goebbels had publicly labeled Leni a Jewess and banished her from a dinner party attended by high Nazi magnificoes. Goebbels termed the reports "mean vilification" in his diary and issued "a very sharp denial" that any such incident had ever occurred.

To undo the damage, the Führer ordered a photographic session at the luxurious new villa Leni had been building for herself in the Berlin suburb of Dahlem ever since work on *Olympia* began. His personal photographer, Heinrich Hoffmann, spent a July afternoon photographing her with Goebbels and the Führer chatting amiably in her garden, with Leni's mother, brother, and sister-in-law supplying smiles from the sidelines. The photos, including Goebbels's presenting Leni with a massive bouquet of roses as a housewarming gift, were widely reprinted, and Leni carried proofs with her to refute rumors and demonstrate how harmonious life was at the apex of the Third Reich.

She took a holiday after editing part one, *Olympia: Festival of Nations*, to attend the 1937 Paris Exposition as a representative of the Reich. French president Édouard Daladier presented her with a gold medal for *Triumph of the Will*. *The Blue Light* and a teaser film about the making of *Olympia* also received awards. After a mountain-climbing breather and a detour to Berchtesgaden to visit Hitler at his mountain retreat overlooking still-independent Austria, she returned to Berlin and her editing tables.

Goebbels kept a close eye on Leni's progress, though she was now officially under Hess's supervision. Unless Goebbels was a pathological liar even to himself, his diary brims with unqualified praise for her work. In late November, he and Magda spent an evening with her and saw some of the completed first film. "Indescribably good," he recorded, and then went on to describe it. "Ravishingly photographed and mounted. A very major achievement. In some places deeply moving. Leni is unquestionably capable and I am enthusiastic." Two days later, he decreed in his official capacity that Jews could no longer attend the theater or other cultural events and dined with Hitler, to whom he conveyed his enthusiasm for *Olympia*. The Führer "is overjoyed that it is such a success," he told his diary. "We want to do something to honor Leni. She has earned it." And then, perhaps unable to restrain a sardonic flick of the pen, added, "She has denied herself fame and recognition for so long."

Leni had completed editing the first part of *Olympia* in five months, two months of that time reshaping Zielke's classical prologue from dreamlike dissolves to routine motifs he considered crude, obvious, and cause for lasting grievance. "It had no architecture," Leni said, justifying her handiwork. "I made and I unmade." Editing of the "poetic" part two, *Festival of Beauty*, went swiftly, taking a mere two months, with only four days devoted to the justly famous diving sequence near the end.

"I could have edited the film in half the time," she explained, "if I hadn't been so thorough, but I had to try everything, every kind of cross-cutting experiment. Once I had edited a section or a sequence, for instance the marathon, it ought to have been finished and okay. But then I started wondering whether it couldn't be done still better, so I made perhaps one hundred, two hundred or more trial [edits]."

Solutions that retrospectively seem elegant and inevitable had, in fact, been elusive and had evolved sequence by sequence, frame by frame. She talked about architecture but likened the process to creating music, too, saying, "As a composer composes, I made everything work together in the rhythm," though finding the rhythm was a matter of improvisation, of trial and error.

She talked so easily about "intuition" that it was not always clear what she meant, though a hint survives in a private interview she gave when almost seventy. She revealed that she had conceived of her film version of the marathon long before the games began. "I *am* the marathon!" she had exclaimed to herself while watching a particularly radiant sunset in the Harz Mountains. Her version of the race, she confirmed, was somehow based on that moment of epiphany. Attaching tiny cameras to the runners' necks to film their feet pounding the paved marathon course captured their ordeal subjectively. It was ingenious and innovative and, ironically, independent of any personal experience of the race or the runners. Leni never saw a moment of the marathon except on film. The sequence is extravagantly and justly admired even today but is less about the race than about filmmaking. It grew from a self-projection, a preconceived notion of struggle—exalted, radiant, and heroic, but anonymous—like the diving sequence. "You only see the beauty."

Intuition needed finally to be translated technically, and, apart from editing the images, no challenge was more demanding than fitting sound to picture, and particularly music. Pop composer Peter Kreuder had scored *Day of Freedom*, but *Olympia* needed a score that was more heroic and transcendent. Nazi Party member Herbert Windt, as on *Victory of Faith* and *Triumph of the Will*, would be her composer.

It was "a nightmare." Direct sound had been recorded during the games, but—except for Hitler's brief speech opening the games—all of it proved unusable. The entire final sound track of almost four hours had to be manufactured artificially with a team of sound engineers using technology that would be considered impossibly primitive today. Chief sound editor Hermann Storr surmounted the difficulties and—a "sensitive man," she called him—replaced Glenn Morris in her affections, remaining her lover until shortly after the outbreak of war.

Building a sound track from scratch before the invention of magnetic tape meant that every footfall, gust of wind, cheer, sigh, starter's gun, and diver's splash had to be recorded separately on optical film, which then had to be developed and printed in the laboratory before it could be heard. Each track was then painstakingly mixed with other tracks and rerecorded—still on film—to a then maximum of eight tracks, though Leni often demanded as many as sixteen. This meant recording and rerecording to the maximum of eight, then combining composite tracks to make a single omnibus track containing up to sixteen different tracks competing with one another. An error or a mishap at any stage of the process destroyed the utility of all and required starting over again from step one.

Four sound engineers worked for six weeks recording and mixing tracks, including those for on-screen and voice-over sports announcers filmed in the studio after the games were finished in the four languages in which different release prints with slightly varying messages were to be made—German, English, French, and Italian.

Herbert Windt recorded his score in January 1938, conducting the Berlin Philharmonic Orchestra and a chorus of 340 voices. Leni and Hermann Storr worked for another two months combining music and effects tracks, reducing a maddening hum that Leni likened to "a waterfall," balancing competing aural elements, and finally arriving at an acceptable sound track in early March.

The propaganda ministry had announced an *Olympia* première for early February, then mid-February, then early or mid-March. When March arrived, the opening—at last in sight—was abruptly put on hold. Leni later accused Goebbels of vindictively thwarting her première schedule, though sound-track problems made final prints unavailable until late March in any event. Finally, an achievable date was agreed upon, one that linked *Olympia: Festival of Nations* and *Olympia: Festival of Beauty* more closely than ever to the man who had sponsored and financed them: April 20, 1938, the Führer's forty-ninth birthday.

Before the première, Leni vacationed in Davos and relaxed from her three years of *Olympia* labor by writing a first-person testimonial for *Film-Kurier* that had nothing to do with the film. Her words revealed, however, the reason for the première's delay, which was to avoid conflict with the establishment of "Greater Germany," a geopolitical concept that Leni as a loyal artist of the Reich was eager to endorse. Her claim of ideological naïveté was no impediment to her impassioned plea for the Führer's expansionist agenda, couched in aesthetic terms. She wrote:

Years ago the Führer once said, if the artists knew what great tasks were reserved to them in a more beautiful Germany, they would come to the movement with greater enthusiasm. Today every artist knows, just as it has become clear to every German: reality yields more than even artistic fantasy could imagine. Greater Germany has become a reality; we have seen it grow from year to year with increasing certainty and emotion. The creator of Greater Germany is at the same time its most artistic man.

She segued to the language of mobilization and obedience:

> Time after time during these years the voice of the Führer has called
> to us, "Begin!" and time after time artists have obeyed the call to fall in
> with the troops of millions to declare their allegiance to the Führer and
> his deeds for Germany's freedom, honor and greatness. The vote on
> the tenth of April will be a unanimous affirmation of our Führer
> Adolf Hitler.

The affirmation Leni urged was in the matter of the Austrian
plebiscite that, after murder and intimidation had prepared the way,
would legitimize the *Anschluss,* the annexation of Hitler's homeland to the
Reich. The campaign was aided not only by Leni's exhortation to the
readers of *Film-Kurier* but also by a special rerelease of *Triumph of the
Will* on the screens of no fewer than seventeen cinemas in Vienna alone
to ensure the outcome of the plebiscite. *Olympia* was at an end, and so
was Austria, even as a place-name; it would be known henceforth as the
Ostmark. Greater Germany—and Leni—confidently anticipated the
dawning of their most dazzling hours.

TWELVE

TOMORROW THE WORLD

Carefree and unaware, I accepted all the tributes paid to me.

—Leni Riefenstahl in America, 1938

Pretty as a swastika.

—Walter Winchell

THERE HAD NEVER BEEN and would never again be a film première quite like it. It combined the glamour of an opening night with the pomp of a state occasion. The façade of Berlin's Ufa Palast am Zoo had been redesigned with an eye to metaphor and the monumental: floodlit red-and-black swastika banners marched in lockstep with white flags bearing the five linked rings of the Olympics. Twin towers simulating the entrance to the Olympic stadium rose over the theater entrance to circlets of laurel leaves between which the film title appeared as if carved from stone. Massive, three-dimensional Olympic rings crowned the marquee, where LENI RIEFENSTAHL blazed in electric lights.

Expectations were high after the long delay, but the première date marked, as every German knew, the Führer's forty-ninth birthday. When he entered the crowded auditorium shortly before seven, Goebbels at his side, the audience rose to its feet, arms outstretched in the now-mandatory Hitler greeting. The guests in dress uniforms and evening clothes constituted the most formidable gallery of political, military, industrial, theatrical, and social luminaries convened in Berlin since the monarchy at its height, and no such congregation would come together again. A more contentious assembly was only five months away in Munich that would end in headlines trumpeting "Peace in Our Time" only ten months before night fell and tanks rolled over Poland.

Inside a decade, many of the high-living celebrants at the Palast am Zoo would survive only in memory. A dozen of the powerful heads that nodded to one another above the flash of medals and jewels would end in the noose at Nuremberg, and another dozen first-nighters would be in solitary cells, condemned as war criminals and enemies of mankind. No presentiments of such destinies shadowed the brilliance of the evening.

The world's diplomats were there in full official force. Ambassadors from Italy, France, Turkey, Chile, Brazil, Argentina, Great Britain, Spain, Japan, and the United States rose to their feet to honor Hitler alongside envoys from Lithuania, Switzerland, Greece, Ireland, Finland, Portugal, Uruguay, Iraq, South Africa, Afghanistan, Yugoslavia, Hungary, Belgium, Estonia, Panama, Sweden, the Netherlands, Guatemala, Venezuela, Iran, and Siam, their applause mingling with that of representatives of the Dominican Republic, Colombia, Cuba, Peru, Romania, Egypt, Denmark, Bulgaria, Luxembourg, and fretful, friendless Czechoslovakia.

Hitler acknowledged the standing ovation with his bent-elbow salute as he entered his private box with Goebbels and Reich Sport Leader von Tschammer und Osten, occupant of the seat of honor as organizer of the games. Filing into adjacent boxes were cabinet ministers Wilhelm Frick (interior), Joachim von Ribbentrop (foreign), and Walther Funk (economics), sharing the feverish gaze of spectators with Heinrich Himmler of the SS, Viktor Lutze of the SA, Baldur von Schirach of the Hitler Youth, and Reinhard Heydrich, the "Blond Beast," who was an accomplished violinist, future protector of Bohemia and Moravia, and the partly Jewish author of the final solution yet to come. Sepp Dietrich, commander of Hitler's SS bodyguard, was there, as were Streicher and Speer (soon to be elevated to minister of armaments), and dozens of other high officials of the Reich. Orchestra seats cushioned the industrialists, the bankers, the financiers and their wives, who had found Hitler so fascinating from the beginning. The field marshals and generals—harder to win over but no less seducible in the end—were there: General Wilhelm Keitel, who would meet the following day with Hitler to finalize Case Green, the invasion plan for Czechoslovakia, and General von Reichenau, whose old-school military vanity had resulted in Leni's making *Day of Freedom*. Conductor Wilhelm Furtwängler was on hand, adding his prestige to the glamour of film stars Lilian Harvey, Willy Fritsch, Emil Jannings, Lída Baarová (Goebbels's mistress), Gustaf Gründgens (director of the state theater and the model for Klaus Mann's *Mephisto*), Mathias Wieman (Leni's leading man in *The Blue Light*), and the beautiful Anny Ondra, who had once worked for Hitchcock and was escorted by her husband, heavyweight champion Max Schmeling, a world celebrity since he gave Joe Louis the first defeat of his life in 1936. Finally, there was Leni, whose labors had brought them together. She arrived late, wearing a smart evening gown and a slightly distracted demeanor, as if she were a starlet and not the Führer's favorite. She scurried with a smile of becoming modesty past the photographers and the swastika and Olympic flags and under her name in electric lights, into the cinema lobby, and up the staircase to the gilt dress circle beyond, followed at a tactful distance by her mother, father, and brother.

The performance began with Herbert Windt conducting the Berlin Philharmonic in the music he had composed for the marathon. Four hours and an intermission later, cheers exploded as the Führer presented Leni with a massive bouquet of white lilacs and red roses onstage. They were joined by the Greek envoy, who gave her an olive branch from the sacred grove on Mount Olympus. Festivities moved on to the reception in Leni's honor hosted by Goebbels at his ministry, where no one's praise was more sincere or unrestrained than the host's. "A masterly achievement by Leni Riefenstahl," he confided to his diary. "One is electrified by the power, the depth, the beauty."

Leni was cheered, envied, and swept aloft by adulation and applause. It is likely that if there was any single moment that marked the zenith of her days, any single event that confirmed her inexhaustible belief in herself and fully gratified her self-esteem, this was it. Just fifteen years after she had dared fortune as an unknown young dancer with upstart ambitions, she had become the most celebrated woman in Nazi Germany, and the most euphoric.

Newspaper reviews the next day appeared on the front pages (at the personal request of Goebbels), all without qualification or quibble. The following day the propaganda minister presented the filmmaker with a bonus of one hundred thousand reichsmarks "she had earned" and that made her "quite happy." On May Day, knowing that the rest of the year could produce nothing more worthy, Goebbels awarded *Olympia* the National Film Prize for 1937–38 before either of the Olympic films had gone into general release (part two, *Festival of Beauty*, would not be seen publicly until June). The prize was as satisfying as the bonus was generous, but it was only a beginning.

No *Olympia* opening lacked splendor. Leni was the dazzling centerpiece of gala premières in Munich, Vienna, Graz, Baden-Baden, Zurich, Paris, Brussels, Copenhagen, Stockholm, Helsinki, Oslo, Bucharest, Venice, and Rome. She gave lectures about art and film, was photographed and newsreeled, submitted to press interviews in languages she didn't know, and spoke into radio microphones as simultaneous translators conveyed her every word to foreign ears. She met and was fêted by the kings of Denmark, Sweden, Norway, and Belgium (the last of whom flirted and made a date with her to go climbing), was guest of honor at state dinners attended by hundreds of dignitaries in white ties and medals of state among whom she was the only woman present except for her mother, now her beaming chaperone and confidante on a triumphal tour with no precedent in living memory. In Venice, Leni and *Olympia* (in its Italian version) won the film festival's first prize, the Coppa Mussolini, triumphing over Walt Disney's *Snow White and the Seven Dwarfs* and Marcel Carné's *Quai des Brumes*.

Her European tour attracted sellout crowds everywhere *Olympia* was shown and was expected to stimulate interest from distributors in England and America. She traveled the Continent from June to September, collecting clippings that called her "genius" and "goddess," reassuring herself that "the unpolitical shape of the film conquered all prejudices."

She pointed out correctly that *Olympia* did not disparage foreign competitors or favor German athletes, did not even allude to Germany's cumulative Olympic supremacy with a total of 239 gold, silver, and bronze medals. She cited the dominant (and inescapable) role on camera of America's Jesse Owens as evidence of the film's independence from Third Reich racial policies. While all of this was accurate, it was also in alignment with the official orders of the propaganda ministry to the German media. "Jesse Owens has been repeatedly attacked and his behavior treated critically or ironically in the German press," the ministry observed in one such directive. "Such criticism does not have a favorable effect in foreign countries, because the impression is produced that Germany was forced to have consideration for its guests during the Olympic Games." Goebbels personally forbade press reporting of the point lists that ranked national victories, for "it is not nations that compete, but persons" and—more to the point—"the International Committee has already complained officially."

The "unpolitical shape" of *Olympia* did not violate Goebbels's Olympics script but was in strict accordance with it in presenting the New Germany in a light that obscured policy and camouflaged such realities as the removal of anti-Semitic postings and the internment of Gypsies. Contemporary admirers of *Olympia*'s technical achievements often resist labeling it propaganda, even when acknowledging its clandestine financing and sponsorship. But the airbrushed portrait of the New Germany was widely recognized abroad for what it was and was rejected by audiences Leni most hoped to win, particularly after the crises involving Czechoslovakia and the Sudetenland unfolded while she was on her triumphal tour.

Distributors in England had been lukewarm about the film (and

Germany) since the annexation of Austria. Hitler's saber rattling in Munich over Czechoslovakia sharpened their wariness. *Olympia*'s winning the Mussolini Cup in Venice (not the Golden Lion, as Leni would later misstate) did little to reassure them of the film's political neutrality. In October, Tobis sent a sales representative to London, prompting comment in the British trade press that *Olympia* was "blatant and undisguised German propaganda." In spite of box-office success on the Continent, not even the German ambassador's opinion-maker screenings at the London embassy could overcome anti-German sentiment. The abundant artfulness with which the film was made hinted at some unsportsmanlike cunning. *Olympia* failed to find distribution in Great Britain and would not be shown there publicly until after the world war that, to the film's early antagonists, justified their opposition.

England's rejection of *Olympia* was an affront to Leni, who took herself seriously as "an ambassador for Nazi Germany," as a friendly English periodical styled her. She was touring to promote her films and herself but was a conscientious representative of her Führer (her travel was coordinated through official channels), and Goebbels himself might have scripted her public statements, which mostly restated longtime fealty to the cause. When she went to Oxford and Cambridge in 1934 to lecture students about *The Blue Light*, she had described Hitler to a British reporter: "To me he is the greatest man who ever lived," she said. "He is really faultless, so simple and yet so filled with manly power." She continued and clarified: "He is beautiful, he is wise. Radiance streams from him. All the great men of Germany—Frederick, Nietzsche, Bismarck—have had faults. Hitler's followers are not spotless, only he is pure."

Such effusions were both sycophantic and sincere. The stage of history beckoned, and she could find drama almost anywhere. She believed, for instance, that she had been an unwitting diplomatic courier when summoned to Rome by Mussolini in early 1936. Il Duce was hoping she might be persuaded to make a film about his swamp-reclamation projects, but Leni—like the heroine of *Mademoiselle Docteur*—saw through his pretext. The point, she decided, was her transmitting back to Hitler personal greetings from Mussolini that seemed innocuous but were, in fact, coded messages of state. Perhaps they were.

If England was not to add to the laurels of Leni's tour, there was richer, more opportunity-laden territory across the Atlantic in a land that had welcomed German film people with open arms and checkbooks since Lubitsch arrived there in the early 1920s. Emil Jannings had reigned over a German colony in pretalkie Hollywood that included Pola Negri, Lya de Putti, and F. W. Murnau. They had been greeted as artists, and those who remained or came later still were. Dietrich was there; so were Fritz Lang, Peter Lorre, Billy Wilder, Kurt Weill, Lotte Lenya, E. A. Dupont, Wilhelm (William) Dieterle, the great Max Reinhardt, and dozens more. Some had fled the Reich, it was true, but Leni failed to see how that had anything to do with her or her work.

A visit to the United States and Hollywood was the trip "I had dreamed of," and Goebbels had dreamed of it, too. She sailed to New York on the German luxury liner *Europa* on October 29, booking herself as "Lotte Richter." She brought along three prints of *Olympia* and seventeen pieces of luggage, along with presentation copies of *Beauty in the Olympic Games* (*Schönheit im Olympischen Kampf*), the sumptuous book of sport photographs that she signed as her own, though they were the work of her cameramen. Soon impatient with being incognito, she left her *nom de voyage* in Cabin 142 on A Deck and ventured forth to become the shipboard celebrity she already was.

"Even the dishwashers in third class" knew she was on board, one witness reported, and she traveled with an entourage: Ernst Jäger, her onetime ghostwriter and publicity chief on *Triumph of the Will* and *Olympia;* and Werner Klingeberg, a member of the German Olympic Committee for 1940, who had attended the 1932 games in Los Angeles and later studied at the University of California at Berkeley, where his English acquired an American accent. He had been a Nazi since 1931 and may have been a member of the German Secret Service as well. Though the trio traveled as private citizens, the Reich was fully financing the trip and would require receipts to justify expenditures.

Going to America was daring, a display of what Leni's target audience in Hollywood might have called chutzpah. The American film industry was heavily Jewish, and while Leni claimed to have wept for her Jewish friends, she deftly concealed her emotions. Just before embarking for America, she capitalized on the success of *Olympia* with a rerelease of *The Blue Light* coolly purged of credits for her Jewish collaborators— Balázs, Mayer, and Sokal. Nor would any of them share in receipts of the rerelease, hailed by the Nazi press now that "non-Aryan sectors" that had precluded success in 1932 were no longer a box-office factor.

Leni thus had two hit pictures for shipboard companions to gossip about on the *Europa*. She charmed Americans she met on board and in her stateroom made notations about the wealthy and well connected among them on maps of the United States as if she were organizing a campaign or a production. Among those she particularly noted were Conkey P. Whitehead and his wife, Emmy, major stockholders in Coca-Cola, whom she had met in Berlin through Heinz; Mr. and Mrs. Frank H. Powell of the Portland Cement Company; and young Frank T. Ryan, a wealthy New Yorker related by marriage to the president of Chase National Bank.

The crossing was uneventful, and the *Europa* docked in New York on November 4, where Leni was greeted by press photographers alerted by an article about her arrival in the *New York Times*. She posed on piles of suitcases with a silver fox fur around her neck, flashing her legs like the movie star she had been. She "giggled" when asked if she was "Hitler's honey" and said that they were "just good friends." Though she was now thirty-six, readers of the *Daily News* learned that "the child is charming," and, though he wasn't there, Walter Winchell reported in his widely read column in the *Daily Mirror* that she was "pretty as a swastika."

She checked into the Hotel Pierre on Fifth Avenue and went to the Stork Club, El Morocco, the Museum of Modern Art, and Harlem. She visited Radio City Music Hall, where interest in *Olympia* was (at first) so high that a plea for its booking would be made by management directly to Radio City's landlord, John D. Rockefeller. Leni lingered long enough to sign autographs for the Rockettes, thinking they were Ziegfeld girls.

Three days into her mission in America, unpleasantness stirred. Her well-publicized arrival brought a warning on November 7 from the Non-Sectarian Anti-Nazi League that she intended "to flood the United States with Nazi doctrines." The league claimed a membership of one hundred thousand, including prominent religious figures of all faiths and New York mayor Fiorello La Guardia. Most prominently, it had the support of Judge Jeremiah T. Mahoney, the former head of the Amateur Athletic Union who had opposed sending an American team to the Berlin Olympics and had been defeated and deposed by Avery Brundage in 1935. "The importance of the games from an athletic standpoint was forgotten," Mahoney now charged. "The games were for Nazi propaganda."

That same day, a seventeen-year-old German-Jewish refugee shot and killed the third secretary of the German embassy in Paris while trying to assassinate the ambassador, eliciting howls of outrage from Goebbels and triggering "spontaneous" anti-Semitic demonstrations in Germany. Two days later, on November 9, the anniversary of Hitler's 1923 putsch, retaliation against Jews began, organized by Reinhard Heydrich, who issued a secret directive ordering, "As many Jews, especially rich ones, are to be arrested as can be accommodated in the existing prisons." Synagogues were torched in towns and cities, and Jewish shop windows shattered across the fatherland. The sound of breaking glass provided Goebbels with a label for the firestorm that his oratory and Heydrich's efficiency had fanned: *Kristallnacht.*

The shattering glass initiated a "night of horror" and "human misery" that shocked the world. Thirty thousand Jews were arrested and herded into concentration camps. At Buchenwald, 244 were murdered. Scores, perhaps hundreds more were killed defending their property, while dozens committed suicide in terror or despair. Property damage—including the total destruction of 267 synagogues—amounted to hundreds of millions of reichsmarks, for which Hitler, on November 12, held the Jews responsible, "guilty of their own persecution," as Ian Kershaw has phrased it. Insurance companies were forbidden to honor claims of Jewish victims, who were instead fined a total of one billion reichsmarks, collected by compulsory confiscation of 20 percent of the property of every German Jew.

If a hallmark of the successful opportunist is an instinct for timing, for knowing what to say and when to say it, Leni's abandoned her in New York. Anyone less self-absorbed might have taken the international revulsion *Kristallnacht* produced as a cue to alter strategy or remain silent. Instead, Leni claimed not to believe the news that in a matter of days generated more than a thousand editorials in American newspapers. It was all "slander," she announced, libelous attacks on her homeland and "the greatest man who ever lived."

Refusing to believe news reports that no one in Germany was denying, she remained "carefree and unaware" because of "all the tributes paid to me" by such admirers as film director King Vidor, though Vidor was later to deny ever having met her. "It was only on coming back to Germany three months later," she said, "that I found out things that I would never have believed possible," and "had I believed the press reports I would never have set foot on American soil," somehow implying that the American outcry was more regrettable than the horrors that produced it.

Her disbelief was a pose, surprisingly crude and unsubtle. She had been personally advised by the German consul in New York and by embassy deputies of the propaganda ministry in Washington to return to Germany and avoid the "hurricane" swirling around her, especially when, on November 14, President Roosevelt recalled Ambassador Hugh Wilson from Berlin. Leni defied advice to retreat after consulting Gestapo agents in New York, who had been vetting business prospects for her in the United States. If one can credit Ernst Jäger's reports, she was cool and determined. "I have to wait till the storm dies down," he recalls her saying. "If only this damned Jewish question would get out of the headlines. The American public would quickly forget about the whole business if they had a new sensation to talk about. They can't put the blame on me for what happened," she said, adding her familiar rationale: "I wasn't even in Berlin at the time."

She traveled by train from New York to Washington the day after

Roosevelt recalled Wilson (permanently, as it turned out), where she overnighted at the Vanderbilt mansion that was Reich ambassador Hans Dieckhoff's residence until he was recalled to Berlin (also permanently) three days later. She omits this visit entirely in her memoirs, stressing instead the "cheerful atmosphere" through which she moved and blaming the outdated newspapers available on the *Europa*, though the pogrom occurred after her arrival in New York.

Kristallnacht proved the irreversible turning point in the world's awakening to the plight of Germany's Jews, but it was culmination, not revelation. A drive to "Aryanize" Germany had been under way since spring, forbidding Jews to practice medicine or law. An identifying "J" was required on Jewish passports and official documents, as well as the addition of "Israel" or "Sarah" to birth names. The synagogues of Munich and Nuremberg escaped *Kristallnacht* because they had already been demolished in June and August, the first as an obstacle to traffic where there was none, and the second because Julius Streicher found the temple an offense against "the beautiful German landscape." Entrepreneurial opportunism ran rampant as non-Jews took over Jewish businesses and properties at fractions of their worth and non-Jewish professionals—including doctors and lawyers, like practitioners of film, theater, music, and other arts before them—eagerly filled positions barred to Jews who once held them. The smashing of storefront windows and looting of Jewish shops had taken place in Berlin as early as May, giving authorities an excuse to place victimized (and protesting) Jewish business owners in the protective custody of Dachau, Buchenwald, and Sachsenhausen. This was not yet the final solution, but as Goebbels remarked, "A start has to be made somewhere."

The magnitude of international protest over *Kristallnacht* had no observable effect on Leni's agenda. She left Washington on November 16 for Chicago, where she had a warm reunion with the Olympic Committee's Avery Brundage, always sympathetic to Germany (he would be buried there). He introduced her to prominent Chicagoans, including Mrs. Claire Dux Swift, former wife of German film star Hans

Albers and now married to the American meatpacking heir. Brundage agreed to arrange a private screening of *Olympia* in Chicago, while Leni made a brief detour to Detroit on November 18 to meet Henry Ford, who had recently accepted a decoration from the German government and was vocal in his admiration of Hitler. What she thought Henry Ford could do for *Olympia* is uncertain, but he was gracious and saw to it that a subordinate gave her a deal on the rental of a new Ford.

Brundage came through. He hosted a private screening of *Olympia* at the Chicago Engineers' Club on November 20. The handpicked audience numbered thirty-five, seven of them from the German consulate. Leni made a speech about the "unpolitical" nature of her films and the next day telephoned Ambassador Dieckhoff, just leaving Washington for Berlin, to say that he could inform Hitler on his arrival that the screening had gone well and she was optimistic about success.

She left Chicago for California with Jäger and Klingeberg on the *Super Chief*, arriving at Los Angeles's Union Station on November 24. The welcoming committee, even allowing for Thanksgiving Day, was nothing like the one that had greeted her in New York. Waiting on a virtually empty platform was Dr. Gyssling, the German consul in Los Angeles, accompanied by a single member of the press, the editor of the German-language *California Staats-Zeitung*. Also on hand was a friend of Leni's from Berlin and the Olympics, an American named Hubert Stowitts.

Gyssling would be Leni's liaison with movie industry figures considered friendly to Nazi Germany. More important to Leni was Stowitts, who had contacts at MGM, where he had worked as a dancer and set designer, most recently in 1934 on *The Painted Veil* with Greta Garbo, with whom he claimed to remain friendly.

The Nebraska-born Stowitts had been a student at Berkeley and captain of the University of California track team when he saw his first ballet in San Francisco. He threw himself into dance, eventually appearing with Pavlova and headlining at the Folies Bergère in Paris. By the early 1930s, he had mostly given up dancing for painting and costume and set design. He prepared a suite of fifty-five canvases of nude male athletes titled "The American Champions," which he submitted to the American Olympic Committee for an art exhibit at the 1936 games. His work so shocked the Americans that he was forced to send it at his own expense to Berlin, where nudity shocked no one and had become a cliché in monumental statuary and painting of the Third Reich. Stowitts's nude athletes on canvas were well received in Berlin until the blacks and Jews among them attracted the attention of Alfred Rosenberg, the viciously racist party "philosopher" who was as outraged as the Americans had been shocked, and the exhibit was ordered closed.

Leni saw Stowitts's graphic depictions of male beauty while preparing *Olympia* and contacted him to see if there was some way to incorporate them into her film. There was not, but his work may have influenced the prologue, where nudity—male and female—was central to the classical concept and introduced the theme of erotically charged, even prurient physical perfection that marked *Olympia* and work yet to come.

Stowitts was a Riefenstahl acolyte, the kind of quietly worshipful, compliant man she often took as a lover, and he might have played that role had he been heterosexual. Instead, he decorated her new villa in Dahlem and nagged her about her figure, forcing her to diet on salad greens while editing *Olympia*. Leni gave him access to her editing rooms as *Olympia* took shape and helped him find work at Ufa as choreographer and dancer in a musical film starring Lilian Harvey, thus prolonging his stay in Berlin.

Stowitts returned to America before *Olympia* opened. There he received a print of the film from Leni in early March, together with her permission to screen it quietly for selected audiences. He showed it to sports-minded audiences that included American Olympians at the Wilshire Ebell Club in Los Angeles and elsewhere in Southern California prior to Hitler's or Goebbels's having seen it. Leni's motive for authorizing these secret, prerelease screenings is obscure, though Cooper C. Graham of the Library of Congress, in his comprehensive *Leni Riefenstahl and "Olympia,"* suggests she may have hoped to please American athletes she knew from Berlin, including Glenn Morris. She may also have hoped to exploit Stowitts's connections at MGM with an advance copy of the film since she had known for more than two years that her letter to Paul Kohner inviting him to offer *Olympia* to MGM had elicited no interest. Stowitts became, with Jäger and Klingeberg, a fixture of her California entourage.

If the meager welcome in Los Angeles did not hint that her visit there might be troubled, Consul Gyssling did. He informed her that demonstrations had already occurred at the Garden of Allah, the celebrity-studded Sunset Boulevard hotel she had chosen for her stay. Arrangements were quickly made for a secluded bungalow at the Beverly Hills Hotel, where she waited for invitations that Stowitts assured her were forthcoming from Louis B. Mayer, Gary Cooper, Greta Garbo and her paramour Leopold Stokowski, and others. And she waited.

Five days later, the storm broke. The trade papers *Daily Variety* and the *Hollywood Reporter* carried full-page advertisements paid for by the Hollywood Anti-Nazi League for the Defense of American Democracy. The headlines read: "POST THIS ON YOUR BULLETIN BOARD!"

The text reminded readers that the league had a year earlier protested the visit to Hollywood of Vittorio Mussolini, "son of Il Duce, collaborator of Adolf Hitler," and announced that now "LENI RIEFENSTAHL, Head of the NAZI FILM INDUSTRY [*sic*], has arrived in Hollywood." It continued with emphatic typography:

There Is No Room In Hollywood For LENI RIEFENSTAHL!

In this moment, when hundreds of thousands of our brethren await certain death, close your doors to all Nazi Agents.

Let The World Know

There Is No Room In Hollywood for NAZI AGENTS!!

The ad concluded with an appeal for an economic embargo against Germany. Only three weeks after *Kristallnacht*, the advertising was a well-timed blow to Leni's hopes of conquering official or unofficial Hollywood with nothing more than beauty, charm, and talent. The league, formed in 1936, included such prominent left-leaning members ("premature antifascists" many would be labeled by the House Un-American Activities Committee) as Fredric March, Eddie Cantor, Oscar Hammerstein II, Salka Viertel, Dorothy Parker and her husband, Alan Campbell, Dudley Nichols, and Donald Ogden Stewart, who served as league president.

Leni was flabbergasted and incensed as the full-page ads became news around the world, but she was not without American friends of influence, thanks to Avery Brundage. After the Chicago screening of *Olympia*, Brundage had written William May Garland of the American Olympic Committee in Los Angeles that he had just seen "the greatest sports film ever made" and encouraged Garland to extend his hospitality to the filmmaker. Garland did so, taking Leni and Klingeberg to the Notre Dame–USC football game and hosting a private dinner for her at his home with carefully selected guests, noting to Brundage that "the Jews of Hollywood are hostile to Leni." He amplified: "Well time marches on and perhaps some time in America they may get what is coming to them."

Garland arranged a screening of *Olympia* at the exclusive California Club in Los Angeles and enlisted the support of his brother-in-law Harrison Chandler, son of the owner of the *Los Angeles Times*, whose warm opinion would not harm her in the family newspaper. On her own, Leni contacted her *Europa* shipmates, the Powells of Portland Cement, hoping they might exert influence on her behalf.

The California Club screening was held on December 14. Leni took the precaution of submitting the version she brought from Germany that deleted scenes of Hitler. The audience consisted mainly of club members and their friends, plus Olympic athletes past and present, including young diver Marjorie Gestring, who had been a crowd-pleaser in Berlin, most of the American track-and-field team, and athletes-turned-Tarzans Johnny Weissmuller and Glenn Morris.

Garland asked that the screening and its auspices remain confidential, but the *Hollywood Citizen-News* carried a review the next day calling *Olympia* "the finest motion picture I have ever seen." The reviewer emphasized that "it is not propaganda, but a magnificent filming of the greatest meeting of athletes in the history of the world. . . . If it is not shown to the youth of this country, the youth of this country will be the loser . . . its only message is the joy and the glory that comes from the development of a superb body." The same day, the *Los Angeles Times* reported that *Olympia* "is in no way a propaganda production"; rather, "it is a triumph for the camera and an epic poem of the screen."

Such notices would have been prelude to an avalanche of invitations in ordinary times, but not as 1938 drew to a nervous end and not in Hollywood. Invitations promised or offered were withdrawn or never materialized. Former Riefenstahl friends and associates such as Sokal and Kohner did not call. Josef von Sternberg remained silent. Veteran producer Hal Roach hosted a private reception that turned into "a fiasco," scuttled, according to screenwriter and novelist Budd Schulberg, by an industry-wide anti-Nazi telephone campaign.

Long-remembered slights suffered by American companies and cameramen at Leni's hands in Berlin that had made little impression when reported in the *New York Times* surfaced to haunt her in the pages of *Daily Variety* and the *Motion Picture Herald*. Readers were reminded of "the manner in which the American newsreels were taken over the bumps at the Berlin Olympics."

Her sole inroad on household-name Hollywood was a private visit to Walt Disney at his studios, where the animator, whose *Snow White* she had beaten out for the Mussolini Cup at Venice, gave her a tour of his facilities and showed her animation sketches of Mickey Mouse intended for *Fantasia*. Disney expressed a desire to see *Olympia* in his own screening room but backed off in the end, citing fears of a boycott of his films by left-wing union projectionists should the screening become public knowledge.

Leni left Los Angeles after the presentation at the California Club for the first of several trips to Palm Springs, where, according to Jäger, she had taken a new lover of unknown identity; then up the Pacific coast to Santa Barbara and San Francisco, stopping off to visit Spanish missions and pose in cowboy hat and boots for photographers who found her news value as "Hitler's girl friend" undiminished. When Goebbels's notorious affair with Czech actress Lída Baarová erupted as an international scandal that had caused a rift between the propaganda minister and his Führer, Leni became a willing source for journalists, grateful that the press was sniffing elsewhere for notoriety. "It is all so absurd," she told reporters. "Like such absurd stories they tell about me."

In San Francisco, she showed *Olympia* to World's Fair representatives, who offered and then withdrew an exhibition contract after she refused to make cuts they requested. She returned to Hollywood via Yosemite, where she and Stowitts spent a day skiing and hiking. Just before New Year's Day, producer Winfield Sheehan, said to be "a friend of Germany" and married to Viennese opera singer Maria Jeritza, hosted a reception for Leni, Klingeberg, and Consul Gyssling at his home. Sheehan had been head of production at Fox until it merged with Twentieth Century; Leni's *Europa* shipmate Frank T. Ryan may have helped smooth the introduction, as his brother-in-law, the president of Chase National Bank, had helped broker the merger that created Twentieth Century–Fox. Sheehan and his wife were enthralled by what they saw of *Olympia* in their private projection room and offered help in obtaining distribution through their industry contacts.

Their contacts laid low. No amount of private or press enthusiasm for *Olympia* could overcome news of anti-Semitic brutalizing in Germany that Leni continued to deny or claimed that, as an artist, she could not be expected to know about, even if the rest of the world did. "There are four walls about me . . . when I am at work. I work always. It is not possible for me to know what is true [or] what is a story," she told a *San Francisco Chronicle* reporter.

Politics alone did not account for Hollywood's resistance. The motion picture industry—which Irving Thalberg had alerted to a murderous

Nazi threat as early as 1934—could always rise above conviction if there
was money to be made, but the economic prospects of *Olympia* looked
dubious. At four hours and in two parts—with no stars but Jesse
Owens—*Olympia* would have deprived at least two of the studios' conventional features of valuable playing time. The $250,000 purchase price
that Leni had suggested to Paul Kohner was far from insignificant when
full-length films rarely cost more than half a million, and, although there
had been commercially successful documentaries in the past, such as
Nanook of the North in 1922, they were regarded as flukes in a fickle marketplace.

Still, Leni's persistence, monomaniacal as it seemed, did not lack for
method. She was aware that MGM, Paramount, and Twentieth
Century–Fox still had distribution offices in Berlin they were eager to
maintain. It was reasonable for her to suppose that she might leverage
their anxieties: first, to benefit *Olympia* and, second, to the advantage of
the grandiose project she was already preparing and took care to mention
in her interviews with American media. Like all film directors, she knew
that financing of her next project was dependent to some degree on the
success of the last, and *Olympia*'s prestige and box office were important
to her plans for 1939. Her project was not a documentary but an expensive
epic that could not break even in German-speaking territories alone and
had the narrative dimension to further Goebbels's goals of penetrating
the international market. It was, at last, *Penthesilea*, a vehicle to return her
to the screen as director, producer, writer, and star of a monumental feature film that would secure what she saw as her rightful place in film
history.

Berlin approved a two-week extension of her California visit that
resulted only in more frustration. Leni packed her tent and left Los
Angeles for New York on January 13 after a bon voyage tea party for two
hundred "friends of Germany" hosted by Consul Gyssling. Before she
embarked on the *Hansa* on January 19 for the sea voyage home, there was
a sudden flurry of interest in British and American distribution from the
British Gaumont firm that did not, in the end, materialize. One more

bitter pill remained. To her credit, Leni had defended Ernst Jäger, getting him reinstated as her press chief after Goebbels removed him because of his Jewish wife, Charlotte. Leni may have needed him because he had dealt with Hollywood executives while at *Film-Kurier* or because his mixed marriage, however "open," might have produced sympathy from Hollywood's Jewish community. But now, in spite of a relationship that predated, indeed triggered Leni's first infatuation with Hitler, Jäger chose to remain in America—sans Leni, sans visa, sans job, and sans Charlotte, who, at her own request, stayed in Berlin in the embrace of her Nazi Party protector.

Several versions of Jäger's motives made the rounds. In one, Maria Jeritza persuaded Leni that he had been an American spy ever since a trip to the United States in 1935. In another, more credible version, he had been job hunting during the American tour, a theory that arose from expenses he incurred during a never-explained private trip to Cleveland in early January. Jäger claimed he had conducted business in Ohio for Tobis, but Tobis—whose American offices in New York had been shuttered months earlier—could not corroborate his claims. Whatever Jäger's motives, his last-minute failure to board the *Hansa* effectively ended his relationship with Leni, except for the eleven-part series of tabloid-flavored articles he published in the *Hollywood Tribune* under the scandal-sheet title "How Leni Riefenstahl Became Hitler's Girlfriend."

Leni returned to Berlin via Paris, where she lectured on "Is Cinema Art?" and illustrated her talk with film clips not from *Olympia* but from *Triumph of the Will*, fitting perhaps for an audience assembled by future *collaborateurs* during the Vichy regime to come. Back in Germany, she gave press interviews. "I visited New York, Washington, Chicago, Detroit, and Los Angeles," she told readers of Hamburg's *Tageblatt*. "With the sole exception of Hollywood, I was received everywhere in the friendliest manner and was astonished at the heartfelt hospitality of the leading American circles. In Hollywood, naturally, I ran into resistance from the Jews who, on my arrival, had already published a giant advertisement in several newspapers that—under the headline 'There is no place in Hollywood for Fräulein Riefenstahl'—demanded a boycott against me. Numerous American film directors didn't dare to receive me because of their financial dependence on the Jewish moneymen. An honorable exception [was] Walt Disney, creator of Snow White, [who] warmly welcomed me and showed me his extensive studios and even his latest work. It was gratifying to learn how thoroughly proper Americans distance themselves from the smear campaigns of the Jews."

She told Goebbels much the same when she spoke with him in Berlin on February 5. He noted their Sunday meeting in his diary: "In the evening, Leni Riefenstahl reports to me on her trip to America. She gives me an exhaustive description, and one that is far from encouraging. We shall get nowhere there. The Jews rule by terror and bribery. But for how much longer?"

Leni had no time for reflection. Failure to secure distribution for *Olympia* in the English-speaking world was a blow but had no effect on her status in Berlin except to burnish her aura as a martyred victim of American Jewry. Certainly nothing about her financial dealings suggests that she felt diminished in entitlements by America's rejection.

On March 6, ten days before Hitler seized Czechoslovakia and made it a Reich protectorate under Reinhard Heydrich, Leni applied to Goebbels for payments of five thousand reichsmarks per month for travel and publicity, retroactive to the *Olympia* première. She requested additional reimbursement for costs of her wardrobe because "I had to change it repeatedly" for press photographs. "My complete expenditures in the last year amounted to 99,000 Marks," she declared, neatly reducing Goebbels's lavish postpremière bonus by 99 percent.

Even Goebbels, now in total control of a fully nationalized film industry, may have been startled at what followed. "In order not to burden further the overhead of the Olympia-Film [company]," she suggested, "I recommend that these wages including February 1939 be paid, and to grant me a share, for my further activity as head of the firm, of 20%" after recoupment of costs. She was thus renegotiating with the man she portrayed as her nemesis to secure a personal profit participation in the

Olympic films beyond what she had already received or would receive from the ongoing preparation of short subjects assembled from the Olympic footage.

Goebbels reminded her evenly that wardrobe costs had already been covered by the advance of ninety thousand marks she had received from Tobis. Then—astonishingly—he agreed to her profit participation request even though the Reich had totally financed her work. There was no question the Olympic films would go into profit. Nor was there any doubt that Leni was already using her *Olympia* staff and facilities to prepare *Penthesilea*. Granting her the profit participation would smooth the way for the dissolution of the sham Olympia-Film company, which would in turn get her preparations for *Penthesilea* off the Reich payroll. The propaganda ministry prepared documents spelling out that once Leni's contractual obligations were concluded, "The Olympic films are Reich property."

The dissolution contract, made official on January 9, 1942, provided that "20% of the remaining net proceeds are to be paid to Fräulein Riefenstahl." No statement regarding ownership could have been clearer: *Olympia* was the property of the Third Reich, and that—as long as the Third Reich existed—was that.

But personal profits and reimbursement for wardrobe did not exhaust Leni's needs or even the generosity of her patrons. Foremost among her concerns was *Penthesilea*, which troubled Goebbels as a commercial subject and was unexpectedly taken out of his hands by the Führer. "He [Hitler] wants to finance the *Penthesilea* film of L. Riefenstahl himself," Goebbels noted in his diary on June 21, adding, "Good. I can't do it out of my funds and have no real faith in the project." Hitler's extraordinary gesture effectively granted Leni unique independence in an otherwise nationalized film industry that was controlled—financially and in virtually every creative aspect from script to casting—by Goebbels. Nor did the Führer's largesse end there.

On March 8, two days after her reimbursement petition to Goebbels, Speer, still active as Hitler's architect, began scouting sites for the construction of a film studio for her personal use near her villa in Dahlem. The facility would house her new company, Leni-Riefenstahl-Film GmbH, providing her with 28,000 square meters (more than 300,000 square feet) of offices, workrooms, cutting rooms, projection rooms, canteens, kitchens, air-conditioned archival and storage spaces, and a common room to double as a gymnasium. A shooting sound stage and processing laboratory would be housed in separate buildings on land summarily appropriated from the present owners by Hitler's first secretary, Martin Bormann. The cost of the state-of-the-art complex—fully financed by the party—was just under two million reichsmarks, and Leni's personal workroom was to be fitted with a massive retractable picture window four meters wide by three meters high (roughly thirteen by nine feet), a near duplicate of the one at Hitler's aerie above Berchtesgaden that overlooked what had once been Austria.

Acquisition of land and drawing up of plans (the principal architect was Ernst Petersen, Fanck's nephew and Leni's onetime costar in *The Holy Mountain*) occupied the spring and summer of 1939 as Leni busied herself with preproduction on *Penthesilea*. She traveled to Sylt to work on her script and, now that she was almost thirty-seven, to train for the physically demanding role of an Amazon by learning to horseback ride and throw a spear. She would shoot interiors and work on postproduction in her new private studio.

Penthesilea would be her first picture in color, and exteriors would be shot in Italian-controlled Libya. Battle sequences would feature a thousand horses and horsemen supplied by Italo Balbo, now Italy's governor of Libya, who had been Italian minister of aviation when Leni met him in Berlin in 1932 and who had subsequently pursued her brazenly at the Venice Film Festival in 1938.

Citing her preoccupation with *Penthesilea*, Leni turned over the film project that Speer offered her about Hitler's monumental capital-city-to-be—"Germania"—to Fanck, a project financed by the Reich but produced by Leni's company. Fanck, the founding pioneer of Alpine films, joined the Nazi Party on April 1, 1940, to shore up his credentials and went to work as an employee of the woman who had once been his protégée.

No film director in history has ever enjoyed such unlimited protection and lavish resources. She had earned her unprecedented rewards through the very work that Hollywood and London spurned, but Julius Streicher once consoled her with assurances that her service to the Reich and her Führer was her "great calling. Here you have found your heaven and in it you will be eternal," he had said, and heaven seemed very close at hand, if Hollywood was not.

Ground breaking for the Leni Riefenstahl Film Studio was scheduled for the end of August 1939. The ceremony was mysteriously postponed. Three days later, on September 1, Hitler put Case White into motion. German troops marched into Poland and plunged the world into war for the second time in a generation.

Where Hitler went, the faithful would follow.

Three

AFTERMATH

Is propaganda a means or an end? It is a means and must therefore be judged with regard to its end.

—Adolf Hitler

Is there really no one in Germany who does not feel a pang of conscience? Once more: Machiavelli was mistaken; there is a line beyond which the separation of morality and politics is unpolitical and has to be paid for. Sooner or later.

—Victor Klemperer, September 3, 1939

THIRTEEN

LENI AT WAR

Close your hearts to pity. Act brutally.
> —Adolf Hitler, August 22, 1939

In Poland, I never saw a corpse, not of a soldier, not of a civilian.
> —Leni Riefenstahl

"I SHALL GIVE A PROPAGANDIST REASON for starting the war, no matter whether it is plausible or not," Hitler told his commanders in chief at the Berghof, his mountain retreat in Berchtesgaden, on August 22, ten days before he invaded Poland. "The victor will not be asked afterwards whether he told the truth or not. When starting and waging a war it is not right that matters, but victory," he said. "Close your hearts to pity. Act brutally."

Leni reported that "the world collapsed for me" at the thought of war, partly because she had been with Hitler twice in Berlin shortly before the invasion and he had spoken fervently of peace. Except that he wasn't in Berlin and neither was she. They were both in Berchtesgaden, where Hitler delivered his speech to the commanders (on her thirty-seventh birthday, as it happened). In the Berghof's screening room, Leni watched films with Hitler, Goebbels, and Speer, including newsreels of Stalin. The Soviet leader's face on-screen looked trustworthy and reassuring to

Hitler, though he had reason to credit the power of film images to deceive. He saw in Stalin's face what he needed or wanted to see, even as the Nazi-Soviet Nonaggression Pact was being negotiated in Moscow.

Leni left Berchtesgaden to attend a Berlin reception celebrating that surprising alliance on August 23. Foreign Minister Joachim von Ribbentrop, just back from Moscow, passed on to her a handwritten letter of admiration for *Olympia* from Stalin himself. Mingling with top party officials and diplomats evidently gave her no inkling of coming events. She left Berlin for a mountain-climbing holiday in the Dolomites near Bolzano, "happy and filled with dreams of the future."

She first learned of the imminence of war, she said, on August 31. A telephone call had come from soundman Hermann Storr, whom she still called her lover in spite of long separations and short dalliances. Storr was with the Lantschner brothers, Guzzi and Otto, in Berlin, a city roiling with rumors of mobilization.

Leni claimed that after Storr's call, she somehow drove overnight from the Alps to Berlin, arriving in time to be among the official guests admitted to the Kroll Opera House for Hitler's address to the Reichstag at 10:00 a.m. "This night for the first time Polish regulars fired on our own territory," he announced. "Since 5:45 a.m. we have been returning the fire, and from now on bombs will be met with bombs." The Nazi press trumpeted the invasion as a "counter attack," but two days later, on September 3, England and France demanded a withdrawal of German troops and, when Hitler refused, honored their obligations to Poland with a declaration. World War II had begun.

William L. Shirer, broadcasting from Berlin to CBS Radio in America, noted the subdued reactions of Berliners as they heard the news from London and Paris crackling over loudspeakers in Indian summer avenues. "They listened attentively to the announcement," Shirer reported. "When it was finished there was not a murmur. They just stood there like they were before." He detected a shrugging off of the "Polish thing" by the man in the street but also noted the profound alarm in President Roosevelt's appeal to Hitler "not to bombard open cities or the civilian population." FDR's plea gained urgency when, three days later, Shirer reported that "not only the Polish army is fighting, but that Polish civilians—men, women and even boys—are fighting desperately from house to house." Hitler promptly declared that the Poles' civilian resistance was criminal and a violation of international law.

Leni at first considered becoming a nurse at the front but came to her senses and took charge of her troops. She would save Storr, Allgeier, and the Lantschner brothers from conscription by launching a combat photographic unit. Her request for war correspondent status was approved in twenty-four hours at the Reich Chancellery, she said, by an unnamed "high-ranking Wehrmacht officer," but such assignments were not so casually obtained, even for Leni. Almost certainly Hitler approved her commission—perhaps had done so in Berchtesgaden ten days earlier— and so must have Goebbels, whose military propaganda units of radio, press, and film personnel had been rehearsing for duty in the field since the annexation of Austria and the Spanish Civil War.

A "Special Riefenstahl Film Unit" (*Sonderfilmtrupp Riefenstahl*) was fully accredited and its itinerary recorded in propaganda ministry files by September 10. That it was "special" (*sonder*) was evident from its staff composed of handpicked film personnel who were Leni veterans: as cameramen, the Lantschner brothers and Sepp Allgeier, plus Fritz Schwarz and Heinz Kluth of Tobis; longtime production manager Walter Traut; personal still photographer Rolf Lantin; personal projectionist Hans Kubisch; with Hermann Storr operating mobile sound equipment on loan from Tobis.

Before Leni's unit left for the front on September 10, the Wehrmacht had entered Warsaw and Germany had suffered its first home-front casualty, a worker in Dessau executed by firing squad for refusing defense work. Leni and her team departed Berlin at seven in the morning outfitted in silver gray uniforms, pistols, and gas masks. They traveled via Breslau for Poland in a convoy of two Mercedes sedans, a BMW motorcycle with sidecar for transporting exposed film back to Berlin, the sound truck from Tobis, three drivers, and an SS captain as military escort.

The Nazi press, meanwhile, blazed headlines—"TERRIBLE BESTIAL-ITY OF THE POLES" and "RED CROSS NURSES MURDERED"—in a barrage of propaganda to justify sending fifty-three German divisions to confront a Polish army defending itself mostly on horseback. Ferocity and superior forces would decimate Poland inside of three weeks, by which time the Soviet Union, pursuing a secret protocol in the Nazi-Soviet Pact, invaded from the east. The taking of Warsaw—claiming an estimated sixty thousand victims—would be completed by the German Tenth Army under the command of Gen. Walther von Reichenau, whom Leni knew from *Day of Freedom*.

The Special Riefenstahl Film Unit arrived on September 11 to report to Reichenau in Konskie, a small Polish town of around nine thousand inhabitants, two-thirds of them Jewish. German forces had occupied Konskie for five days, and Hitler had passed through earlier the same day on his three-week tour of the front by armored train and automobile. Leni's itinerary and Hitler's were imperfectly synchronized but almost certainly coordinated. She asserted as much while en route to Konskie, when her caravan paused near the frontier at Lublinitz. There she told Gen. Erich von Manstein, later strategist of the invasion of France, that she was "following the Führer's trail," filming at the front "on Hitler's orders." She made an impression on Manstein. In his wartime memoir, he sardonically recalled: "She looked pretty and daring, a bit like an elegant partisan who might have obtained her outfit on the Rue de Rivoli in Paris. Her beautiful hair swirled around her interesting face with its close-set eyes like a blazing mane. She was wearing a kind of tunic over breeches and soft, high-top boots. A pistol hung from the leather belt around her hips, and her combat gear was supplemented by a knife stuck into her boot-top, Bavarian style. My staff, I must admit, was a bit per-plexed by this extraordinary vision."

In Konskie, General von Reichenau may have taken pleasure in informing Leni that no accommodations were available for her use but the military parking area outside the village. She pitched her tent and, on the morning of September 12, awoke to gunfire shredding the canvas. "I hadn't imagined it would be this dangerous," she admitted. That same day, with apt but coincidental timing, the German News Bureau (DNB) enunciated the Reich's policy regarding Jews and Poland: "We promise the Germans that never again will Polish Jews come to Germany. The solution of the Jewish problem in Poland will contribute to ordered relations between Germans and Poles."

As September 12 unfolded, Leni heard rumors that Polish partisans in Konskie had killed and mutilated a German officer and four soldiers. The victims were laid out in the square before Konskie's five-hundred-year-old town church, where she observed German soldiers supervising the digging of a burial pit by Polish civilians, who looked, she thought, "terrified they were digging their own grave."

She remembered a German police officer admonishing the soldiers to maintain discipline, telling them, "Soldiers, cruel as the deaths of our men may have been, we do not want to return like for like." The police officer ordered them to bury their fallen comrades themselves. But instead of dispersing the gravediggers, the soldiers struck out at them, kicking them back as they tried to scramble out of the burial pit.

Leni said she cried out, "Didn't you hear what the officer told you? Are you German soldiers?" causing one of them to shout, "Punch her in the mouth, get rid of the bitch." Another yelled, "Shoot her down!" and someone aimed a rifle at her. At that moment, an amateur photographer captured her reaction—unmistakably distraught—on film.

A shot rang out from somewhere on the square, then more. Onlookers scattered at the burst of gunfire (machine-gun fire, according to some reports). During the confusion, Leni said she went to General von Reichenau to express her outrage at the breakdown of military discipline. The general appeared suitably incensed, she said, and assured her that a court-martial would ensue. He explained that a Luftwaffe officer had fired a rogue shot, setting off a panic in which soldiers opened fire on the fleeing gravediggers they assumed were guilty of the killings and mutilations. Leni said she learned that in the mêlée that followed, some thirty Polish civilians (some accounts cite upwards of forty) were killed and four German soldiers were wounded. She may also have learned that the Konskie synagogue was set on fire and its rabbi taken hostage with other town officials until Konskie's Jews paid a fine for the massacre, for which they were held responsible.

She later wrote, "I was so upset by this experience that I asked the general to allow me to terminate my film reporting [as] I wanted to get back to Berlin as soon as possible." The general agreed.

The massacre at Konskie, less than two weeks into the war and more than two years before articulation of the final solution in January 1942, was not an isolated incident. What Ian Kershaw calls an "orgy of atrocities" had begun in the first days of the invasion through executions carried out mostly by SS and SD (Security Police—*Sicherheitsdienst*) task forces (*Einsatzgruppen*) to meet Hitler's demand that "the nobility, clerics, and Jews must be done away with." Predominantly Jewish communities such as Konskie were special targets. Another was Wloclawek, birthplace of Bertha. Shortly after Konskie, the SS sought to arrest the entire Jewish male population of Wloclawek that had not already been shot "while trying to escape." When a Wehrmacht officer challenged the arrests, the SS commander informed him, "They will all be shot in any case." Numerous similar incidents were reported before Warsaw fell, though they are less well known than later actions involving whole populations.

But if Konskie was no more than a pinprick on the map of the Holocaust to come, it would not go away. The snapshot capturing Leni's distress in the town square would surface after the war and be published as evidence that she had witnessed murders of unarmed civilians prefiguring murders that would number in the millions. Leni denied the charge and sued for libel, the first of scores of lawsuits she would bring to defend her reputation or to deny allegations about her conduct during the Third Reich.

The Konskie incident would thus remain a central exhibit in inquiries regarding her credibility. Her narrative is confused (how could Reichenau have explained events as they were occurring?), but there were other observers present that day whose accounts supply details missing in Leni's version. The most striking difference (it is inescapable) is that only Leni fails to mention that *all* of the Konskie gravediggers were Jews. Second, the surviving snapshots do not suggest any threat to her safety from the soldiers around her. On the contrary, the men appear protective and sheltering as they, too, glance off-camera at whatever it is that has so distorted Leni's face.

All of the eyewitnesses report unambiguously that Leni witnessed the massacre or said that she did at the time. The testimony of military radio operator Horst Maetzke, for example, states: "I was [in Konskie] with several other radio operators when Leni Riefenstahl arrived and wanted to film the twenty to thirty Jews digging a grave in front of the church, some with shovels and some with their bare hands. An officer of the Wehrmacht dispersed them, saying we will bury our comrades ourselves. Everybody got out of there fast. Suddenly a woman in a window fired a shot at the German soldiers and, at that moment, a lieutenant ordered the soldiers who were standing there to fire. The Jews who had been fleeing the scene fell in the street, shot down by the German soldiers. Leni Riefenstahl was standing in her car in front of the church, and when she saw the massacre happen, broke into a sobbing fit."

An aide to General von Manstein, the officer who had noted Leni's appearance en route to the front, testified in Manstein's war crimes trial that "one day the film actress Leni Riefenstahl approached [Manstein] in a distressed condition. She had been assigned to the Tenth Army as a film reporter. She described the shootings of Jews at Konskie and declared that she could not continue her work in such circumstances."

Manstein confirmed this version in his memoir: "There had been shootings during the occupation of Konskie in which civilians were involved. An assembly in the marketplace led, as a consequence of the edginess of a gunnery officer, to an outbreak of unjustified panic and senseless shooting that claimed numerous victims. The film troop witnessed this regrettable scene and our lady visitor took her leave, thoroughly shaken."

Leni may, as she said, have gone to Reichenau to protest, but it is unlikely she did so as the action was taking place. Reichenau may well have assured her that a court-martial would follow, and one did, though the errant officer's punishment was never carried out. This was not surprising given Reichenau's directive during the occupation "for the severe expiation against the Jewry." Though the SS then and later spearheaded the Jews' "expiation," the regular military carried out the butchery of Konskie. Such incidents were frequent enough and criminal enough that they were protested by the Wehrmacht command, resulting in Hitler's amnesty decree on October 4 justifying the violations as retaliation "out of bitterness for the atrocities committed by the Poles." Two weeks later, he removed the SS and police entirely from Wehrmacht oversight.

German film historian Rainer Rother is as clear-eyed as anyone writing about Leni and is surely correct in noting, "There cannot have been many war correspondents who protested against cruelty and shootings." But she did not protest against shootings. She denied she had witnessed anything but a breach in military discipline aimed partly at her, and she believed the claim important enough to reiterate it almost half a century later in the closing pages of her memoirs: "In Poland, I never saw a corpse, not of a soldier, not of a civilian."

Whatever the truth, resigning her commission resulted in neither an end to "following the Führer" nor a return to Berlin as she claimed. After her meeting with Reichenau, she drove with Tobis's cameraman Heinz Kluth from Konskie to Lublinitz, where she related what had happened to General von Manstein and his aide. With Kluth still in tow, she boarded a military plane for Danzig, the Baltic port free city whose reunification with Germany had been a primary focus of Hitler's offensive.

Hitler arrived in Danzig on September 19 to find Leni still there. At the luncheon he gave for his officers to celebrate the "liberation" of Danzig at the Casino Hotel in nearby Zoppot, Leni was seated at his left (the wife of Danzig's gauleiter sat on his right). Hitler expressed shock and anger at her report about Konskie, she said, and assured her that

Hitler addresses the masses in *Victory of Faith* (1933),
Leni's first film for the Nazi party.

The masses in Nuremberg as seen by Leni's cameras in *Triumph of the Will* (1935),
still widely considered the greatest propaganda film ever made.

Goebbels, Minister of
Propaganda and
Leni's purported nemesis

Hitler and Ernst Röhm, supreme leader of the Storm Troopers,
just months before Hitler had Röhm murdered

Julius Streicher, anti-Semitic publisher
of *Der Stürmer*, reenacting his speech
in studio retakes

Architect Albert Speer,
who built the set, pretends to listen.

Leni (seated left) claimed Goebbels (standing at right)
spoiled the Berlin Opera's *Madame Butterfly* for her with his roving hands.
Magda Goebbels (seated center) and others appear not to have noticed.

August 1934:
Hitler and Leni in
Nuremberg discuss
final logistics for
Triumph of the Will.

Leni's supporters for her three Nuremberg films included such party figures as the Führer's deputy Rudolf Hess (to her right) and Hitler's secretary Martin Bormann (behind her, partly obscured).

Leni's literal cast of thousands, Nuremberg 1934. She can be seen in her trademark white coat beneath the speaker's platform.

Leni's cameras were everywhere in Nuremberg: even high on
fire ladders courtesy of the city fathers.

Leni, seated at center in her white greatcoat, is surrounded by
massed symbols of the Reich that made her Nuremberg films possible.

The Messianic cloudscapes
of *Triumph of the Will*

The death's head flag of
Victory of Faith

A Hitler Youth in
Triumph of the Will

Cavalry on a bridge in
Day of Freedom (1935)

Film imagery of helmets and bayonets in *Day of Freedom* (1935)
vividly repudiated the Versailles Treaty of 1919.

A Riefenstahl dissolve: warriors in *Day of Freedom* merge with the swastika.

Leni worked sixteen-hour days preparing for
the Berlin première of *Triumph of the Will*,
for which Albert Speer redesigned the cinema façade, 1935.

After the première: the Führer, flowers, and a filmmaker

Leni achieves international fame
on the cover of *Time*, February 17, 1936.

The Olympic torch
(carried by Anatol Dobriansky)
begins the relay from
Mount Olympus to . . .

. . . Berlin's new Olympic stadium, 1936.
Both images are from the portfolio Leni privately made for Hitler.

Leni eagerly takes command of the vast logistics of *Olympia*.
Cameraman Walter Frentz stands at her shoulder.

The director and Frentz shoot from a moving dolly during the games.

Olympia's prologue
(shot by Willy Zielke)
evokes antiquity as statues
of ancient Greece dissolve to
become flesh and blood.

An American champion: Jesse Owens won four gold medals
and immortality as the living refutation of Hitler's racial politics.

Leni discusses plans with the American track team.
Facing her directly is decathlon victor and love interest Glenn Morris.

Regimental calisthenics reminiscent of the
massed figures in *Triumph of the Will*

Leni and Hans Ertl shoot Olympic trials
that will be cut seamlessly into
competition footage.

Ertl built his own waterproof camera
housings for diving and swimming
competitions.

Ertl shooting the high-diving trials that would form *Olympia*'s
most beautiful and famous sequence.

An image from the portfolio Leni made for her Führer

Leni and her admirer at her villa in Berlin in 1937

Hitler ordered photographs taken in Leni's garden by his personal photographer to scotch rumors that Goebbels and Leni were feuding because the propaganda minister believed she was Jewish.

Leni in America to sell *Olympia* on the heels of *Kristallnacht* in 1938.
Among the few to welcome her was the scion of the *Los Angeles Times*,
Otis Chandler (tall man at right).

Leni, boycotted by Hollywood:
all dressed up, nowhere to go

punishment would be swift and harsh. He then invited her to hear his Danzig victory speech, which blamed England for the war on Poland.

Only then did Leni return to Berlin, and so did Hitler, waiting for the news of September 27 that Warsaw had capitulated. On October 5, Leni was in the fallen city for the massive military parade celebrating Poland's ceasing to exist and the invincibility of the Reich. It was the only victors' parade Hitler attended during the war, and it was filmed by personnel of the Riefenstahl unit. Leni watched the parade at the elbows of Sepp Allgeier and the Lantschner brothers as their cameras whirred near the Führer's vantage point on his reviewing tribune.

What the Riefenstahl unit was charged with filming in Poland is not known, but simple newsreels were unlikely objectives. Five propaganda ministry units were already shooting newsreels in Poland when she arrived. She claimed that before hostilities broke out in the west, Goebbels asked her to make a short film about the Siegfried Line, the fortified border between Germany and France, but she declined. (Goebbels's deputy in charge of newsreel units, Fritz Hippler, had in fact already made such a film.) It is probable that her mission was another Führer film on the order of *Victory of Faith*, this time glorifying the political leader as warlord. Footage from the cameramen of the Riefenstahl unit turned up in films such as *Feldzug in Polen* (*Campaign in Poland*), though Fritz Hippler, the Goebbels deputy who made that film—and the virulently anti-Semitic *The Eternal Jew* (*Der ewige Jude*) as well—confirmed that Leni had nothing to do with it: "We would have lost the battle of Poland, because the armies would have had to march *her* way or not at all."

But Konskie remained a problem that would, in time, resurface. If she witnessed the massacre and protested, as the testimony indicates, why not take credit for denouncing brutality? If she did not witness the slaughter, as only she maintained, was a breach of military discipline so shattering that she had to resign as a combat correspondent? The answers may lie not in Konskie but elsewhere and in events soon to follow, for if she conceded witnessing the massacre, her claim to naïveté was fatally compromised. Truth and advantage beckoned unequally, and ignorance became strategy—a defense in which millions of her compatriots indulged, eyes carefully averted—as the Nazi catastrophe ran its course. Naïveté—or its simulation—was too easy, too useful, too soothing, too self-exculpatory to relinquish.

If a terrible ambiguity shadows Konskie, nothing that happened there disillusioned her about her Führer. Nine months later, on June 14, 1940, she sent him an effusive personal telegram. He was in Paris, fulfilling a dream that had eluded Kaiser Wilhelm II before him. He was viewing as conqueror the great capital of a traditional enemy, a city that had fallen with speed that stunned the world. Leni telegraphed:

> With indescribable joy, deeply moved and filled with burning gratitude, we share with you, my Führer, your and Germany's greatest victory, the entry of German troops into Paris. You exceed anything human imagination has the power to conceive, achieving deeds without parallel in the history of mankind. How can we possibly thank you? To express congratulations is far too inadequate a way to convey to you the feelings that move me.
>
> [signed] Your Leni Riefenstahl.

There is hyperbole here, for all her admiration, for what moved her most profoundly was her filmmaking. If the first casualty of Hitler's war had been the traditional one, the second, from her self-absorbed point of view, was her Amazon queen. Assembling one thousand horses and riders in the Libyan desert for *Penthesilea*, plus a cast, film and construction crews, an eminent stage director to guide her in speaking verse on-camera, and full office and support staffs, and shipping them across the Mediterranean with sets, costumes, props, cameras, lights, and sound equipment was out of the question in wartime.

Giving up *Penthesilea* was not painless; she would never cease regretting its lost opportunities. She had seen it as her masterwork, building on "all the artistic challenges" already met. It was to have been spectacular *and* profoundly personal. Her fascination lay not in Kleist's poetry—most of which she planned to render in pictorial equivalents—but in his outsize heroine, with whom Leni identified almost mystically. Because the film was never made, in years to come she became ever more effusive about what she had lost in ways that are more revealing than her sentimental affection for the realized but—by contrast—insipid Junta in *The Blue Light*.

"Penthesilea and I formed an indivisible entity," she said. "Each of her words, each of her expressions—I had the feeling of having already lived them myself." Her description limns what sounds like an idealized self-portrait: "She is both goddess and human, full of royal dignity, but also unrestrained, uncontrolled, savage, and feline, flying from one extreme to another."

The extremes were fabulous and luridly photogenic, especially in the romantic arena. Here Leni muted any personal resemblances to Penthesilea, as if glancing over her shoulder at the hit-and-run casualties of her past. Her contemporary, the poet Gottfried Benn, probably neither knew nor cared about her identification with the Amazon queen, but in 1936, he described the drama in sensationally high relief as "a play about a woman who loves a man, Achilles, kills him, and tears him apart with her teeth. Tears him apart!"

Hitler's war put an end to all that and, whatever the blow to Leni's ambitions, may have come as a secret relief. She accepted being thwarted, for once, without bitterness or complaint, acknowledging expense and the insufficiently patriotic nature of such a production at such a time. But *Penthesilea* was foundering even without a war, teetering between grandiose pretensions and creative blockage. She had been talking publicly about the film since 1935, had announced the start of production for April 1939, then for summer, then for August. She had trained physically and taken voice lessons to soften her hard-edged Berlin accent for her first real speaking role; she had arranged through Italo Balbo the horses and horsemen and permits to shoot in Mussolini-controlled Libya; she had secured financing through the personal generosity of the Führer; she had even cast some prominent roles in the film, though not—as she briefly fantasized—the attractive King Leopold III of Belgium as

Achilles. But for all her talk and plans, by September and the invasion of Poland, there was no screenplay to film, not a word.

She had been caught up in the size, the look, and the feel of what her epic might be. She had attended meetings of the Kleist Society to familiarize herself with poetry she didn't know and wrote elaborate notes about adapting verse to dialogue. She had added physical action and talked about incorporating episodes from *The Iliad* to make Achilles and the Trojan War compelling for audiences accustomed to comedies, musicals, and sentimental melodramas. Ideas tumbled.

She had envisioned action (the Amazons "at a gallop, throw their battle-axes in the air and catch them again"); atmosphere ("the earth must be covered in great clouds of dust rising from the pounding hoofs of the horses"); props ("on poles symbolic heraldic figures—images of gods—that during attack are carried at the head of the army"); sets ("rough, natural and primitive in character—in part, cave dwellings"); costumes ("silver armor and [for] Penthesilea golden armor"); animals on leashes ("mastiffs and leopards"); and herself in compositions that suggested a female version of *Triumph of the Will* ("the shining sun rises out of the sea, and Penthesilea, sitting on her white horse, stands like a statue against the sun on the edge of a hill and looks down upon the Greek ships").

She had seen "the harmonious fusion of optical, acoustical, rhythmical, and architectonic factors." She imagined "a fresco" or maybe "a great film opera," so stylized that "not a single scene in the film dare be realistically photographed." She conceived of a struggle between "the demonical and the classical" in "an ecstasy of beauty" that sounded sometimes like *Olympia* and sometimes like kitsch: "Every thigh, every arm, every neck must be beautiful—beautiful, not in the ordinary sense of a popularized sort of beauty—but beautiful as Michelangelo created his sculptures—beautiful, just as everything in creation."

What she had not seen was a script. Her gift was for visual moods and motifs, for dynamic compositions and juxtapositions, for rhythmic counterpoints of picture and sound discovered through trial and error at the editing tables. She had a flair for the stunning image and the histrionic episode, but none for sustained dramatic narrative. Without a Balázs or Mayer to guide her, she had compiled laundry lists of scenes and effects. A colleague remembered that "she was always working on it somehow," but the obsession with detail was also a way of compensating intellectually. "She wasn't so educated or from an educated family and what she had to know about, she *learned*." If abandoning *Penthesilea* robbed her of a transcendent creative experience, as she believed, it may also have spared her the frustration and humiliation of a vision beyond her reach.

Ambition and energy needed an outlet, and there was one, less elevated and less Michelangelo than manageable and immediate. Tobis announced plans to revive the same *Tiefland* she had worked on in 1934 before making *Triumph of the Will*. She declared her interest reawakened but admitted privately that she "no longer felt close to it." Still, she had creative investment in it, and financial interest, too, from her purchase of the film rights six years earlier. The melodrama of the corrupt aristocrat from the lowlands and the noble shepherd from the high vying for the beautiful Gypsy dancer restated the highlands/lowlands theme of her Alpine films. It was kitsch with castanets but suggested Goya and El Greco to her, and the opera on which it was based was one of Hitler's personal favorites. To the consternation of Wagner aficionados, the Führer had selected it the year before for the command performance by the Vienna Opera to celebrate his annexation of Austria.

Leni's production manager, Walter Traut, negotiated a uniquely advantageous deal with Tobis, for Leni needed no financing. The funds the Führer promised for *Penthesilea* would now go to *Tiefland,* dispersed not through Goebbels or the alert bookkeepers of his ministry but by Martin Bormann. A Tobis memorandum noted that the party would supply finance "allegedly stemming from the Führer's funds" and would do so covertly (*"schwartz"*). Leni's company would receive 85 percent of the profits and Tobis 15—a full 20 percent less than the fee it had received for distributing *Olympia*. Leni would also recoup forty thousand reichsmarks from Tobis for the film rights she had purchased in 1934.

She was, as Goebbels had learned, a disorderly but determined businesswoman. Economically the outbreak of war had little immediate effect on her circumstances, but she had seldom shown indifference to her financial well-being. Her fiscal self-interest may have been the inevitable lesson of the tenements of her childhood or an inheritance from Alfred, whose modest plumbing business had grown and prospered as Riefenstahl Heating and Sanitation GmbH. The firm flourished in peacetime on subcontracts from the architectural offices of Ernst Petersen and in war from Speer with installation contracts worth more than a million reichsmarks at prisoner-of-war camps outside Berlin and in southern Russia, projects that had the added advantage of keeping Heinz, now married and the father of two, ineligible for combat duty.

Leni's Olympia Film Company continued operations until its formal dissolution in January 1942, when her 20 percent of *Olympia* profits became official, after having carved short films from Olympics footage for a total of eight of the twenty shorts originally envisioned. These would go into release as late as the end of 1943, with a handful of other subjects that Leni-Riefenstahl-Film produced for the Reich, such as *Mountain Farmers* (*Bergbauern*) and *Paradise on Horseback* (*Höchstes Glück der Erde auf dem Rücken der Pferde*).

She retained her commission for the archiving of footage—used and unused—from the Olympics and the three Nuremberg party rallies (she was a meticulous archivist, with her own system of color coding). These were lucrative bread-and-butter jobs in addition to the film Fanck was making for her company about Hitler's vision of "Germania," *The Führer Builds His Capital* (*Der Führer baut seine Hauptstadt*). The project would remain active until 1943, when "Germania" was overwhelmed by the rubble produced by Allied bombardments. From the footage assembled before then, Fanck would salvage two short films for Leni's company about Hitler's favorite sculptors, *Josef Thorak: Workshop and Work* (*Josef Thorak: Werkstatt und Werk*, 1943) and *Arno Breker* (1944).

The films Leni's company produced were routine propaganda chores, but not compulsory; they were commissions that kept things humming.

Fanck, for example, was earning four thousand reichsmarks per month (about which Leni would bitterly complain in days to come), enough to buy himself a villa in the fashionable Berlin suburb of Wannsee. The property, ironically, would be earmarked for destruction to make way for the postwar grandiosity of "Germania," which was the subject of his film. Speer intervened to avoid disruption of his schedule, suggesting helpfully that Fanck might find a suitable replacement residence among the many villas recently confiscated from wealthy Jews.

Nor did the coming of war threaten Leni's projected studio complex, to which Speer approved a final addition of 11,000 square meters (120,000 square feet) in July 1940, shortly after Hitler's entry into Paris. Development of the studio would be halted only in August 1942, by which time Hitler—now at war with both the United States and the Soviet Union—had elevated Speer from architect to minister of armaments.

Leni had always been independent of the German film industry and remained so though the film landscape had changed around her. Goebbels had been nationalizing the industry since 1936, and by 1939, the three major companies—Ufa, Tobis, and Bavaria—had been fully absorbed by the Reich, soon followed by smaller companies such as Terra, Wien in Vienna, and Prag-Film in the former Czechoslovakia. By January 1942, the creation of Ufi (Ufa-Film GmbH), Goebbels's personally controlled monopoly for film production, was announced. Only three private companies were permitted during the war to remain independent: that of the popular Austrian director and star Willi Forst in Vienna; the Berlin firm of industry pioneer Carl Froelich, who was also president of the Reich Film Chamber; and Leni-Riefenstahl-Film, the most autonomous of the three. Fritz Hippler, Goebbels's deputy, corroborated Leni's unique self-determination. "No one else in Germany had the right to decide alone what to film."

Deciding alone was a lonely luxury. Her fiercely preserved autonomy shielded her from an entire creative community, and her relationship with Hitler created envy and hostility. Her intuitive approach had always been at odds with the collaborative nature of professional filmmaking. Her technicians and crews were not colleagues, they were employees; routine obstacles were obstructionism, and workaday disputes were personal attacks. Her bitter quarrels with Goebbels were almost always over routine practical matters such as access or money and rarely, if ever, over creative issues. She was justified in defending her creative independence—any director would be—but her exploitation of her unique status often grew imperious and looked like mere arrogance or egomania, especially in areas in which she was not gifted, such as acting and writing. *Penthesilea* might have exposed those weaknesses; *Tiefland*, a far more modest project—for which she would don the mantles of producer, director, writer, and star—would, ironically, confirm them.

When she turned to *Tiefland* after Warsaw, she found herself dissatisfied with the script of 1934 and undertook to write a new one. She rented a ski cottage near Kitzbühel, where Alpine slopes proved enticing and seclusion for writing proved elusive. She took up with Harald Reinl, a freshly minted lawyer she had known since *Storm over Mont Blanc* in 1930, when he worked as an assistant to Fanck. She discussed her ideas for *Tiefland* with him in Kitzbühel, suggesting he might avoid the war by working as her assistant, an "essential industry" exemption she would invoke successfully on behalf of her favorites until the very end of the war, when even ten-year-olds were pressed into military service. Reinl abandoned law to work on *Tiefland* and became a prominent director in postwar Germany, often called a Fanck successor because of his mountain films.

Leni and Reinl wrote the *Tiefland* script together in six weeks (though Reinl received no script credit), introducing a social conflict to the story. In their new version, the corrupt marquis diverts the region's water from agriculture to his fighting bulls, leaving none for the peasants whose livelihoods depend on it. This subplot gave the beautiful Gypsy girl Martha something to do beyond dancing and exciting lust (she sides with the farmers) and allowed for bullfighting scenes that had nothing to do with the narrative and, though shot, would not survive the final cut.

Otherwise the script told the opera's story—minus the music—of the struggle between the shepherd and the aristocrat, with the Gypsy dancer as the trophy.

Leni claimed she didn't want to play Martha at first, but the part, while little more than decorative, was catnip to a former dancer. As before, she enlisted a personal director for her own scenes, a major name who had briefly defected to Hollywood and lost Goebbels's favor as a result: G. W. Pabst. His direction of Leni in *Piz Palü* had produced her one good screen performance, and his agreeing to take part in *Tiefland* may have helped in casting other actors, especially Bernhard Minetti, a classically trained stage star, who had been a celebrated Richard III and could embody the arrogant and cruel Don Sebastian with ease and flourish.

Always alert to handsome young men, she saw a face that cried out to her "This is Pedro" on the ski slopes of St. Anton. She impulsively engaged twenty-three-year-old Franz Eichberger as her highlands shepherd in spite of an Austrian accent so thick Reinl said he couldn't understand it. Eichberger was blond, bronzed, and Viennese; had no acting experience; and was on active military duty, posted in the Alps as a Wehrmacht ski instructor. Leni could take care of the Wehrmacht as she had for Reinl, though it was later charged (and denied) that she had selected her Pedro from some two thousand troops who auditioned by repeatedly marching past her in full military formation. All Eichberger had to do in the picture was look pure and unspoiled, gaze rapturously at Martha, and strangle a wolf threatening his sheep in the opening, which would foreshadow his strangling of the wicked marquis in the closing.

Tiefland was dated and banal (Leni told Fanck that it was "dusty"), but it allowed her "the fairy tale quality" she always favored. She obsessed over photographic effects, seeking to re-create the picturesque look of *The Blue Light*, even ordering from Agfa the same raw stock the company had supplied in 1932. She had planned *Penthesilea* in color, but color stock was rationed, and *Tiefland*'s moody melodrama seemed better suited to black and white in any case. She chose to imply color through the use of filters and manipulations of the gray scale as if she were making art photographs—an album of silvery images whose subtleties might distract from the creakiness of the drama. Her chief cameraman would be Albert Benitz, another onetime lover she had known since *The Holy Mountain*, a man as willing to avoid the front lines as Reinl and Eichberger.

By spring, she had packed her bags for Spain. When she showed her script to Goebbels as a courtesy on April 2, he was already anticipating wartime "difficulties." He confided to his diary, "I won't let myself get too drawn into this affair," but he was impressed with Leni's preparations and—in a comment that may reveal more about his taste than hers—thought her script "first rate." Two days later, his apprehensions about wartime production were confirmed. "Leni Riefenstahl may not go to Spain," he noted. "Things are too uncertain in the Mediterranean. The Führer believes that Italy will soon step into the war. God willing!"

Tiefland thus encountered the first stumbling block in an obstacle course of challenges that would result in one of the most extended production periods in all film history. The war was a factor, of course, but seldom directly. Mishaps, illnesses, miscalculations, and Leni's recurrent personal preoccupations dogged the production more extensively and to greater effect, until a small picture she thought might take six months to shoot would not be finished after five years. The end of principal photography in late 1944 and a chaotic race to finish before the Allies annihilated or occupied the Reich pushed the film into a decade of limbo and reworking before it could reach the screen. *Tiefland* would become one of the most expensive pictures ever made in Germany (perhaps *the* most expensive), a project that could not conceivably have been permitted to continue churning money and manpower but for the indulgence Leni enjoyed as Hitler's filmmaker. Goebbels, unsympathetic as he may have been, was prescient in sniffing trouble.

Difficulties snowballed, some inevitable and some stemming from the independence Leni demanded so that her innovative ingenuity and originality might roam freely. She had never collaborated with any art director but Speer and, in late spring 1940, sent industry veteran Erich Grave to Spain to make architectural sketches and gather props and impressions. His stay was cut short by the outbreak of war in France, and when he returned to Berlin via Italy, Leni was unhappy with his sketches. She sought advice from Ernst Petersen, then designing her film studio, who assigned the design of the Spanish village to Isabella Ploberger, a young architect in his office who had never done film work but whose costume designer husband encouraged her in putting her ideas on paper. The new sketches pleased Leni, who hired the inexperienced Ploberger as art director for the production, alienating the more experienced Grave.

Ploberger's sketches were converted to wooden miniatures that Leni approved as guides for construction and sent to the Alps. Unable to shoot in Spain, she chose to build the fictional town of Roccabruna in a village called Krün nestled in a high mountain plateau near Mittenwald in the Bavarian Alps, an area that resembled Spain as little as a dirndl resembled a mantilla. When Leni arrived there in June to begin shooting, she was horrified. The wooden models she had approved had been translated into full-scale conventional buildings, not films sets, allowing her none of the flexibility for camera placements she insisted on, especially not the perspective of village, castle, and fortress in a single establishing shot that she maintained was vital to the whole mise-en-scène and would, in the end, never appear in the finished film. She ordered the entire village razed and rebuilt. Before a camera had turned, *Tiefland*'s budget and schedule were rendered irrelevant. The cost of reconstruction was half a million reichsmarks, the budget of a full-length feature film in Berlin.

Leni summoned Ploberger and Fanck from Berlin to supervise the reconstruction. Ploberger knew Fanck only as Petersen's uncle and was eager to learn from him how sets should be "built for the camera." Instead, she found herself buffeted between Leni's demands and Fanck's resentment at being summoned from his "Germania" film like an employee. Leni countered that that was exactly what he was and was baffled by his ingratitude. Nevertheless, he had once been her mentor, and always eager for praise, she sought his approval of her script. He scrawled in the margins, "*This* is supposed to be a gypsy?" and said he thought that the improbably chaste dancer Leni had written for herself should change her name from Martha to "Touch-me-not" (*"Rühr mich nicht an"*).

Pouring oil on Fanck's inflamed sense of grievance, Leni insisted he accompany her to the Dolomites and direct for her scenes of Pedro's strangling the trained wolf on loan from a Berlin zoologist. Fanck's footage—"except for two takes," she later said—left her "aghast" when she saw it. Fanck argued that the wolf was dangerous and the scene recklessly conceived; he chortled with vindication after the first animal died and a second had to be shot, forcing Leni finally to film the scene herself using a trained dog.

Back in Krün, Fanck gave Ploberger practical training by laying camera tracks in the reconstructed village sets and experimenting with lenses and focal lengths to map a shooting plan. Leni coolly accepted his camera plot when she and Benitz returned from the Dolomites. They could afford to be gracious, as they arrived with luminous footage of mist-shrouded mountains that didn't recall Goya or El Greco so much as they recalled Fanck's Alpine films, which only underscored (to Fanck) his onetime apprentice's creative debt to him.

Before going back to Berlin, Fanck bent elbows and ears at a rowdy dinner with crew members, many of them Fanck alumni who had worked on *The Blue Light*. Fanck remembered: "And Leni said to them, 'Oh, you were there, and you were there,' and I said, 'Yes, and *I* was there, too.' And she said, '*You?* What did *you* have to do with *The Blue Light?*' And I said, 'Well, I think that I did all of the cutting for you on that film.' And she said, 'Oh, yes, I recall that you did change a *few* splices.' Typical Riefenstahl!"

Isabella Ploberger remained behind in Krün after the initial shooting was completed and the crew were temporarily released, though still on payroll. "Then the winter came and the winter is very rough in the mountains," she recalled. "Leni lived and relaxed close by in one of the hotels there and took a vacation. She wanted me to come and talk with her about the sets we had to build in the studios in Berlin. So I stayed in the mountains, where the Roccabruna set was now covered with snow and icicles. I made a drawing and she had it printed up for Christmas cards. It was lovely."

Despite the early setbacks in production, Leni had exposed enough footage to give Goebbels a preview when she left the Alps for Berlin to prepare for studio work at Babelsberg. On December 6, 1940, the propaganda minister recorded in his diary that "Leni Riefenstahl gives me a report on her work on the *Tiefland* film, which is very big and expensive. Still, she has some splendid footage to show for it. She has something going there, and when she's properly situated, gets results."

Goebbels did not note precisely what he saw, but we know that in October, after her return from filming Pedro and the wolf in the Dolomites, she shot scenes of her Gypsy dancer in the village among extras. Though she had counted on Pabst to direct such scenes, he remained in Berlin, having objected to her casting of Pedro. Leni turned instead to her old friend Mathias Wieman to guide her. A self-styled "soldier of art" for the Nazi regime, Wieman had recently been honored as a state actor and knew Leni's strengths and weaknesses as an actress, having worked opposite her as Vigo in *The Blue Light*.

Leni's first scenes as Martha introduced her as the idol of Roccabruna's street urchins, less a wildcat Gypsy than a gracious ballerina on donkey-back. But the Moorish arches and wrought-iron filigree of Roccabruna required "Spanish flavor." Mountain farmers from the Sarn Valley who had lent their weathered dignity to *The Blue Light* were recruited again to play peasants, but their blond, blue-eyed wives and children made unlikely Spaniards. Fortunately, extras who looked Spanish were available just outside of Salzburg in Maxglan, within driving distance of Krün. Maxglan was a transit or collection camp for German Gypsies destined for cattle cars to the east. Here, behind barbed wire, her moral vision blinkered by self-interest and obsession with her film, Leni found all the "Spanish flavor" she needed.

Maxglan was sometimes called Camp Leopoldskron because it was a stone's throw from Schloss Leopoldskron, the castle presented to Max

Reinhardt as a personal residence when he founded the Salzburg Festival there in 1917. Reinhardt, who was Jewish, had been forced to turn the castle—and his theaters in Berlin and Vienna—over to the Nazis in 1938 and flee to New York. Pasturelands near the castle were turned into a confinement camp for Gypsies who worked as forced labor building roads or maintaining the huts in which they were crowded until they could be transported east—most of them, in the end, to Auschwitz.

The Nuremberg Laws had deprived Gypsies—or Sinti and Roma—of citizenship and the right to vote, but, unlike Jews, they were not a clearly defined racial category and were therefore secondary targets in the Nazis' hierarchy of victims. Objects of persecution for centuries, German Gypsies (Sinti) were "undesirables" considered "asocial and criminal" and had been interned in camps such as Marzahn in Berlin since the 1936 Olympics, though official Gypsy policy was not formulated until December 1938 by Himmler. The fall of Poland triggered the general arrest decree of 1939, administered by Heydrich. So-called collection camps (*Sammellager*) such as Maxglan were established to deal with "the Gypsy plague" by assembling and isolating whole communities prior to their transport to the General Government, as Nazi-occupied Poland was called. Sterilization and shipments by rail to the east began in the first weeks of the war and continued into 1940 and beyond. "The final solution of the Gypsy question" was deferred until Heydrich and Himmler developed a comprehensive approach to the more pressing issue of Jews, especially in conquered territories. Maxglan and Marzahn were holding pens for the Holocaust.

In late September 1940, under armed guard and on orders of SS commandant Anton Böhmer, the approximately 270 Gypsies interned at Maxglan lined up for a *Tiefland* casting call. Leni would later maintain she never visited Maxglan personally and that Harald Reinl and production manager Hugo Lehner selected extras while she was "location hunting in the Dolomites," though her locations there had been fully secured by June or July. A number of Gypsies who worked on the film and survived Auschwitz later testified that they had first seen her at Maxglan, wearing slacks and carrying a briefcase in the company of two men (presumably Reinl and Lehner) with police or SS guards. In choosing her extras, they said, she used her thumbs and forefingers to "frame" their faces as if looking through a viewfinder. A then seventeen-year-old Gypsy girl named Rosa Winter recalled, "We were all there in the camp. And then she came with the police and chose people. I was there with a lot of other young people and we were what she wanted." A Gypsy boy named Josef Reinhardt, then thirteen, recalled overhearing her tell an official, "I can't take these people like this; they need to be re-clothed."

If Reinhardt can be believed, the comment testifies to Leni's unblink-ered perception of camp conditions. Maxglan was a collection of "primitive huts," according to SS commandant Böhmer's own descrip-tion, built in "mud up to the ankles," surrounded by barbed-wire fences five feet high, and overseen by armed guards stationed in watchtowers. A review of camp conditions by a Salzburg police commission a month earlier found them "appalling" and cited the need for immediate rebuild-ing of inmate housing, as well as erection of a second barbed-wire fence to protect locals from the Gypsies "until their final departure."

Such dire conditions suggest the motivation for Leni's adamant claims that she never personally visited the camp. Her having done so was legally irrelevant and might even have allowed her to claim credit for mit-igating—however briefly—the appalling circumstances of the Gypsies she selected to work on *Tiefland*. But that would have compromised her deniability about the Nazi camps she chose them from and returned them to, just as the massacre in Konskie—if admitted—would have compro-mised her claims of naïveté about the occupation of Poland and the fate of its Jewish population. Even if she never personally visited Maxglan, as she maintained (postwar judges dismissed her claim: It was difficult to imagine so obsessive a personality allowing assistants to select her extras), she cannot have been blind to the nature of the camp if only because of the provisions of the formal contract signed on September 24, 1940, between Leni-Riefenstahl-Film and Böhmer.

Terms included "strict isolation" of the extras from other personnel ("especially from prisoners-of-war") under continuous observation of armed police from the camp in Salzburg to prevent "escape attempts." Rules and punishments on the set were to conform to those of the camp, with activities such as smoking and use of latrines under strict regulation and oversight, especially at night. The film company was responsible for housing, feeding, and transporting the extras (housing provided in barns or stables). Compensation for labor was set at seven reichsmarks per day per adult (three children counted as one adult), and the contract directed that these sums *"may not be paid to the gypsies directly"* (italics added) but to the Gypsy General Fund in Salzburg, to defray overhead costs at Maxglan, especially during the coming winter should the Gypsies' "resettlement" to Poland and points east be delayed.

Leni requisitioned twenty-three Maxglan Gypsies (Nazi thoroughness certified they were "not from Jewish tribes"), fifteen of them children (the youngest was three months old), who arrived on October 4. She would call on them again when she resumed shooting in Krün in September 1941. In Berlin, when the *Tiefland* company moved to the Babelsberg studios on April 27, 1942, she requisitioned sixty-eight adults and children from Marzahn, the camp built on sewage flats outside the city at the time of the Olympics. Among the adults invoiced for the film was a Gypsy grandmother in her sixties named Charlotte Rosenberg, who had been in confinement at Marzahn with her entire family since 1936. As with Maxglan, the Gypsies were not paid directly. Leni-Riefenstahl-Film tendered payment for their services to the Marzahn authorities on April 6, 1943, a month after they had been deported to Auschwitz-Birkenau, where many of them died.

Leni later characterized Maxglan as a "welfare and care camp" and claimed that the Gypsy children she worked with there were the "darlings" of the company. This is easy to believe: On film, they are winning, and Böhmer's files attest to Leni's particular pleasure with the youngsters of the Reinhardt and Winter families. She remembered their calling her "Aunt Leni" and boasted of rewarding them with chocolates, pocket money, and the odd article of clothing to demonstrate her pleasure and satisfaction. Though she would later deny giving them false hopes for the future, Böhmer, who visited her in Krün at least three times during the shooting, complained about her urging Josef Reinhardt's fourteen-year-old sister Antonie to seek stage and film training. Such niceties and tender mercies did nothing to alter the fact that the Gypsy extras of Maxglan and Marzahn were unpaid forced labor, however willingly they may have performed for the cameras.

The Gypsies themselves were under no illusions about their status and few about their futures. Most had already been shuttled from camp to camp: The Reinhardt family's downward trajectory had led from police confinement in Dorfgastein in 1939 to horse stalls at the Salzburg racetrack in 1940 until they were transferred to the mud of Maxglan. Camp regulations at Maxglan provided for individual or collective punishment for infractions, "according to necessity." Punishments included "political corrective measures" or "deportation to concentration camps." These rules were "made known to all gypsies" orally and through posted notices.

Leni agreed to observe and enforce these regulations as stipulated in the contract with Böhmer, but, according to Josef Reinhardt, she behaved with what looked and sounded like sympathy. "My father said to me," he remembered, " 'If this woman is so nice and good, ask her if she can't do something for us. We have a good reputation, none of us has been convicted of anything, maybe she can do something to get us freed.' So I did," Reinhardt continued. "She said she wanted to try to get our family to Berlin and freedom. We waited painfully long while nothing happened. No letter, no thank you. Then in May 1943 the camp was closed and everyone was sent to Auschwitz. . . . Maybe twenty came back. All the rest died there. From one family that worked as extras—father, mother and seven children, the oldest nine years old—just one returned. The others are all dead."

Leni was not responsible for what happened to the Gypsies after she released them, nor was she likely to have known such then-obscure place-names as Auschwitz, Birkenau, Treblinka, and Sobibor, which had not yet begun to haunt civilized memory. The Gypsies' availability, rather than their cost, was certainly the decisive factor in using them, for money was no object on the film even at the very end of the war. It would have been possible to obtain Mediterranean-looking extras from Italy or Sicily, though perhaps not without red tape or delays. And strict cooperation was more likely with hostages of the Reich than with free agents.

Leni later claimed, "We saw nearly all of [the Gypsies] after the war" and they remembered the experience as "the loveliest time of their lives," especially as "nothing happened to a single one of them." It is not hard to imagine that a busy film set was preferable to barbed wire, but at no time does it seem to have occurred to Leni that there was anything morally questionable about contracting with the Reich for the forced labor of a defenseless minority the Reich openly despised. No word of remorse ever passed her lips, for, in her view, none was required. She saw herself as the Gypsies' benefactor, and self-reproach was as foreign to her nature as self-scrutiny. "No doubts or qualms, no shadows or misgivings darkened my creativity," she explained. "The artist knows but one struggle—the struggle for perfection of his own work. He knows only one freedom—the unifying of his *idea* with his creation."

The freedom and struggle the Gypsies knew was another matter, and a bill of particulars could not be permanently avoided. Near the end of her life, she was forced to confront the death lists of Auschwitz and Birkenau. There in black and white were the names—ghost names now—of her darlings, proving that doubts or misgivings might not have been idle or out of order. Through a spokesman, she issued a generic statement of regret "that Sinti and Roma had to suffer under National Socialism," as if she had not known that at the time, any more than she had known about the corpses of Konskie.

FOURTEEN

GOODBYE TO ALL THAT

Just imagine what would happen if, a thousand years from now, people could see what we have experienced in this era.
—Adolf Hitler to Leni Riefenstahl, 1942

An end with terror is preferable to terror without end.
—A White Rose student resistance leaflet

TRAGEDIES LARGE OR SMALL were not the stuff of Leni's lavish obsessions. They may have furrowed her brow, but her heart belonged to art and *Tiefland*. War mattered, when it did, because of its potential to disrupt, delay, and thwart her plans.

She labored under authentic difficulties such as the loss of Spain as a primary location, but the setbacks were mostly temporary, clouds passing before the sun. Hitler's military successes in the west made travel viable soon enough, and by 1942, she could shoot her shepherd's mountain scenes in Italy and, in 1943, her marquis's bullfights in Salamanca, though the six hundred bulls she charmed from the owner of "the largest *finca* in Spain" (he had "a soft spot for Germans") would not appear in the finished film.

Even with open borders, roadblocks appeared and were swiftly vanquished. Her departures for Italy and Spain were frustrated by currency restrictions imposed by Minister of Economics Walther Funk. She appealed directly to Martin Bormann, who, with Hitler redrawing the maps of Europe (the word *blitzkrieg* entered every language), handled his affairs, maintained his isolation by building "a Chinese wall" around him that was impenetrable without his approval, and spoke for him—or claimed he did. "No one was more powerful," notes a historian, and "no one was more hated." But if even Goebbels, Göring, and Speer were wary of Bormann, Leni used him.

As administrator of the Führer's personal funds, including monies earmarked for *Tiefland* and the Leni Riefenstahl Film Studio in Berlin, Bormann was more potent as her enabler than Goebbels had ever been as her adversary. When he intervened on her behalf with Minister of Economics Funk, he did so using his patron as his hammer: "Riefenstahl Film GmbH was founded with the special support of the Führer," he wrote, "and the Führer has instructed that the costs of the *Tiefland* film . . . be borne from the funds managed by me. . . . I have shown the documents to the Führer, who has decided that the currency payments requested by Riefenstahl Film GmbH should be made available if at all possible."

Leni was later to complain, "This Bormann was such a primitive man," but she boasted to her *Tiefland* cast and crew that she had "direct access" to him. She proved her readiness to use it when Terra tried late in the war to enforce its contract with Albert Benitz to photograph an important color feature (to be directed by Arthur Maria Rabenalt, who directed some of Leni's scenes in *Tiefland* without credit). She claimed Benitz was indispensable for shooting the final scene of *Tiefland* on sets built in Prague simulating mountains he had shot in Krün five years earlier. Invoking Bormann as *her* hammer, she wrote Dr. Max Winkler of the Reich's film office: "Before I inform Herr Reichsleiter Bormann of this new threat, I would respectfully like to ask you, Herr Dr. Winkler, to use your personal influence in order to avoid any such catastrophe." Winkler yielded; Terra gave up both cameraman and production.

Even with Bormann's support and protection, Leni maintained contact with Goebbels. Domestic film production was a priority for the propaganda minister with his steady release schedule of escapist musicals, comedies, and melodramas to divert the home front from the realities of war. Conflicts with his productions—real or imaginary—triggered Leni's always quick sense of injury. When she shot *Tiefland* interiors at Babelsberg studios in Berlin after Krün, the "thrilling" Alhambra-like sets designed by Isabella Ploberger were abruptly dismantled in midproduction. Leni later raged that Goebbels had taken them down as "revenge" for her refusal to make the propaganda film about the Siegfried Line that his deputy Fritz Hippler had made almost two years earlier. She was victimized, she charged, in favor of two historical dramas of greater home-front propaganda value than *Tiefland,* but neither film she cited was in production then or there. When she communicated her outrage to Goebbels, he dismissed her as "an hysterical person" with "every day something new."

Thirty years later, Hippler, who had issued the order to strike the sets, claimed that he had done so because Leni haughtily ignored the studio's schedule. "The difficulties that Riefenstahl says she had are now slanted in a political direction," he said. "She had the protection of Hitler. We didn't make any trouble. If we had done so, she would have gone to Hitler and we would have been ordered to stop. She had difficulties with Goebbels? That sounds very good *now.* I can only laugh."

Her sets were rebuilt and photographed without incident, but being thwarted brought on a physical crisis that further delayed production. "I was so upset that I fell ill," she wrote, suffering a recurrence of the bladder ailment that had prompted her return from Greenland and *S.O.S. Iceberg* ten years earlier. Whether physical or psychosomatic, her illness forced repeated production shutdowns from mid-1941 until late 1944, when the film's final scenes were shot (by Benitz) in Prague. Goebbels acknowledged her physical distress with solicitous concern: "I advised her urgently to convalesce before taking on further work," he told his diary. At the same time, he grumbled about the "welter of consequences" ("*Rattenschwanz*") that her work habits seemed always to entail and congratulated himself on having "nothing to do with this disagreeable project and . . . bear[ing] no responsibility for it." His annoyance was palpable when he went on to note that "already over five million [reichsmarks] have been thrown away on this film that will take another year before it is ready." The completion date he projected of 1943 would prove wildly optimistic, and if "over five million" was an accurate figure, *Tiefland* was well on its way to becoming one of the most expensive motion pictures in German film history, possibly more costly than Goebbels's spectacular color epic *Münchhausen* of 1943 or even the cast-of-thousands *Kolberg*, his eleventh-hour attempt to rival *Gone with the Wind* and rally domestic morale as the Reich was literally collapsing around him in 1945.

Film budgets are almost always more about time than anything else, and Leni was establishing with *Tiefland* a production schedule that remains unsurpassed. Wartime conditions inevitably ground work to an occasional halt, but Leni's erratic health and personal life were the major factors keeping technicians and actors more often idle than engaged over a record-breaking five years of production. They remained on payroll and worked on other pictures (Benitz shot an entire feature during one hiatus), unable to shoot around their ailing producer-director-writer-star. When possible, she directed from a stretcher, pumped full of painkillers and homeopathic remedies, and when that was too exhausting, she shut down production altogether and hospitalized herself for treatments from a succession of doctors, including acupuncturists and Hitler's personal physician, Dr. Theodor Morell, who tended to her in both Munich and Salzburg.

The Führer himself emerged from warlord isolation to bring flowers to her bedside, where he speculated not on *Tiefland*'s future or the one engulfing the German people but on preserving his film image for their descendants. "Just imagine what would happen," he mused, "if, a thousand years from now, people could see what we have experienced in this era." The notion cheered and revived Leni, who had her own designs on posterity: "The optimism he displayed did not fail to have its effect on me," she said.

Shooting, when it resumed, was slowed by her apprehensions about working again before the cameras, whether speaking lines or dancing, ill or convalescent. At almost forty, she was preoccupied with her appearance and was able fifty years later to reproduce the exact lighting setups she devised to bathe Martha in an incandescent glow of youth. She was dismayed that Pabst, who had guided her so surely in *Piz Palü*, seemed "dour, almost cold, and nothing was left of his excellent eyes" when he directed her in Berlin, a withering of gifts she attributed to his brief and unhappy sojourn in Hollywood in the thirties, though he was to do admired work (for Goebbels) immediately after she dismissed him from *Tiefland*. She replaced him with the "extremely empathetic" Arthur Maria Rabenalt, whom she credited with teaching her how to handle actors (though her gratitude would fade when he asked to borrow Benitz in 1944). Modern dancer Harald Kreuzberg helped choreograph her dances, though illness left her looking strained and fragile when she clicked her heels and castanets on a smoky café set full of Spanish peasants played by Gypsies requisitioned from Marzahn.

If the predicaments of war, ill health, and a film growing ever more grandiose and undisciplined were not daunting enough, there was a new diversion, a new obsession: Leni was in love. His name was Peter Jacob, and he was a first lieutenant in the Wehrmacht. Leni wrote in her memoirs that she first encountered him while crossing the Brenner Pass on a midnight train from Berlin. His gaze into her compartment from the adjoining corridor was enough to melt glass. To her surprise, the hot-eyed stranger materialized in Krün as an equestrian stand-in for *Tiefland*'s cruel marquis. There he broke down her reserve and the doors of her hotel room with the force of his passion. Isabella Ploberger told a more prosaic version of the tale, for she had known Peter Jacob before knowing Leni. She introduced the two, she said, when it was apparent that the darkly attractive lieutenant had caught Leni's eye among extras recruited at no cost from mountain troops (*Gebirgsjäger*), whose military headquarters in nearby Mittenwald had helped determine the choice of Krün in the first place.

Leni had been romantically uninhibited and sexually liberated since her self-scripted deflowering at twenty. Many of her affairs had been professionally advantageous, but there had been powerful physical attractions, too, to boys such as Anatol Dobriansky and men such as Glenn Morris whom she pursued with a modern sense of sexual parity. Her affairs with crew members and cameramen were mostly recreational episodes that filled empty hours on location and nourished the narcissism that had been apparent since adolescence, when, in her telling, suitors threatened suicide or splintered doors in passionate frenzies to possess her. Even with Hitler and Goebbels, she painted herself as an object of desire, though chastely demure in the one case and a model of offended virtue in the other. If she lacked the innocence of Junta or the man-eating ferocity of Penthesilea, she was never pliant or passive. If she inflicted the occasional scar, she bore few or hid them well. Her long-term relationships were placid but negligent interludes with such submissive men as Schneeberger and Storr, who behaved more like subjects than lovers and were remarkably willing to look the other way when she strayed. And when they left her, she was always astonished, but always resilient.

Peter Jacob, on the other hand, was independent, dashing, and, at thirty-two, seven years younger than Leni. He had the glamour of a uniform and medals (won in the French campaign) and the aura of courage and destiny that attaches to a soldier in wartime. He was also a notorious womanizer whose infidelities would challenge Leni's own, which may have been the secret of his appeal.

Once smitten, she tried to establish control by integrating Jacob into her sphere of filmmaking. She met with little resistance, for he had acting ambitions he would indulge on the stage after the war. In Krün, according to Ploberger, Leni coaxed him to spend "hours upon hours every night in the projection room. And he helped her cut the film. He was very interested and I think he was quite gifted, too, because she could talk with him about all her problems."

He moved his kit bag into Leni's lodgings at the Hotel zur Post in

Krün, where the two enjoyed an ardent period of Bavarian domesticity before he was ordered back to the front in late 1941. Separations thereafter were frequent as he was ordered to Berlin, Greece, and Russia, with brief, often unannounced furloughs spent with Leni in Bavaria or Berlin. Sometimes he spent them elsewhere. He rested his head on assorted perfumed pillows while telling Leni he was in a convoy en route to the Russian front or at sea in the icy Arctic Ocean. His affairs in Berlin with women Leni knew (he was drawn to actresses) were too brazenly conducted not to be reported, and the news caused Leni "emotional suffering," which worsened her physical ailments. Neither painkillers, injections, nor hypnosis relieved her distress, but frontline love letters—weeks or months in transit—did.

"I clung to his every word [and] drew hope from them for a new life together," she said, though fresh rumors left her "haunted by tormenting images." Declarations of passion and fidelity from the Russian front "worked a miracle" with their assurances that "you've made a new man out of me." When Jacob appeared on leave in the Dolomites in August 1942 and placed a ring on Leni's finger for her fortieth birthday, she surprised no one more than herself by accepting his proposal. Still, her fiancé—now a major in the Wehrmacht with a Knight's Cross for heroism pinned to his tunic—remained an "enigma," especially when he whiled away their engagement evening playing cards and drinking beer with an elderly Tyrolean lodge keeper.

Leni returned to Berlin when Jacob was called back to the eastern front, where Stalingrad and the Russians were turning the tides of winter and war against the Reich. Aerial attacks on Berlin were escalating as well, damaging Leni's seldom-inhabited villa in Dahlem and turning to ash the blueprints for the Leni Riefenstahl Film Studio. With marriage as much on her mind as *Tiefland*, she turned her attention to her family and real estate.

Her father's weak heart forced him to retire with Bertha to their country house in Zernsdorf, twenty-five miles east of Berlin. Heinz succeeded his father and remained shielded from combat duty as head of a firm employing more than two hundred essential workers, thanks to the war contracts facilitated by Speer. Heinz was a casual manager by all accounts, distracted by divorce proceedings and an active social life. A custody battle loomed for his two children—Eckart, five, and Uta, three—with implications for property and inheritance issues that quickened Leni's territorial instincts and encouraged her to test her influence with Bormann in a personal matter.

Heinz and Ilse Riefenstahl had married in 1935, their union most notable to some observers for having separated "Berlin's Most Beautiful Siblings," as Leni and Heinz were described by the boulevard press. Heinz's young-man-about-town persona lit up Berlin, its luster undimmed by marriage and fatherhood, while Leni introduced unsophisticated Ilse to life among the privileged, even taking her to the Chancellery for a personal introduction to the Führer. Leni invited her to locations such as Krün, where she and her children vacationed when shooting began on *Tiefland,* allowing Heinz to remain in Berlin running the business and keeping city lights bright between blackouts. In 1942, when the marriage foundered after separations resulting in episodes of mutual adultery, it was Leni—not Heinz—who informed Ilse that her marriage was over, *"kaputt."*

Leni discussed the marriage's end in her memoirs, where, intentionally or not, she conflated the divorce and the custody issues it raised with Heinz's unexpected induction into the Wehrmacht in spite of his exempted status as head of an essential enterprise.

Heinz received his notice ordering him to the eastern front in May 1943. He was eventually assigned to a punishment battalion or, as Leni called it, a "death commando." This assignment, she asserted, was the result of Heinz's denunciation by "his best friend" for "buying meat on the black market and making disparaging remarks about Hitler." The denunciation and draft notice were linked, she implied, to Ilse's having "planned to divorce him, taking full custody of their children, whom he adored," though Heinz had initiated the divorce action, which had already been finalized in December 1942, six months before his induction.

Leni contended that an SS officer, with whom Ilse "was friendly," threatened Heinz's life if he would not give up custody of the children and had arranged his being drafted and forced to serve on the eastern front. There was such an SS officer. His name was Karl Wolff, former adjutant to Himmler, now Hitler's liaison officer. But Wolff was close to both Ilse *and* Heinz and, according to Ilse, tried to get Heinz's induction notice rescinded in 1943 and, having failed, tried again in 1944 to have Heinz recalled from the front after his promotion to SS general. Custody of the children had been an emotional issue but was never legally challenged. Ilse had granted Heinz custody before the divorce was filed following his threat to charge her publicly with adultery while denying his own infidelities, a tactic that would, if successful, have deprived Ilse of all rights regarding her children as well as any entitlement to alimony.

There had been a last-minute legal wrinkle: a sentimental reconciliation that included sexual relations, a circumstance that under German law automatically nullified a divorce petition. In spite of that, when Heinz and Ilse arrived at Berlin's Palace of Justice on December 19, 1942, for their previously scheduled preliminary hearing, they were informed that the divorce had already been granted on orders from "on high" ("*höheren Orts*"). Ilse was unshakably convinced that Leni had arranged the outcome through Speer or Bormann or both.

Before he was officially drafted, Heinz discovered that custody of two young children cramped his social style. By April 1943—still a month before his induction notice—he voluntarily delivered Eckart and Uta to Ilse, now living alone in a small flat in Berlin. Ilse felt "like a lamb led to the slaughterhouse" because she lacked legal rights to her children but was expected to care for them on a token alimony of 375 reichsmarks per month, set to expire in 1944. She regretted, not without bitterness, that she had suppressed evidence against Heinz at the time of the divorce that might have altered everything. Since 1939, she claimed, he had been conducting an affair with the Jewish wife of a diplomat stationed in Berlin and was thus guilty of "racial defilement"—*Rassenschande*—a grave violation of the Nuremberg Laws, even with protectors "on high."

Heinz's military records do not note grounds for his induction or postings, but news of his military service aroused intense curiosity in Leni's circle, for she was correctly credited with sufficient influence to keep her personal favorites safe from the front. Some observers, such as Harry Sokal, later professed bewilderment at her apparent detachment, while others assumed she had resigned herself to sacrifice for the fatherland. Few things would have been more out of character. She privately asked Speer to intervene for Heinz as he had done sometime earlier for Fanck. When Speer disappointed her, she tried again a year later, urging him to get Heinz an early leave from his officer training at the front. Speer told her a furlough was out of the question. Chief of the general staff Gen. Kurt von Zeitzler had informed him that Heinz's officer candidacy had been terminated because his performance in combat was "every bit as bad as" it had been in training camp. Speer delivered this harsh message, which Leni would guard to her grave, on what came to be known as D-Day, June 6, 1944.

The war in the east had already been lost by the time Heinz was stationed there in late 1943. More than a quarter of a million German soldiers had fallen or been taken prisoner in the Stalingrad campaign alone, shocking German expectations of an unbroken string of victories and heartening the rest of the world as evidence that Hitler's military invincibility was as hollow as his greatness as a statesman. Nevertheless, fanatical hopes for victory would keep the death machinery rolling for another two years and inspired Goebbels's infamous "total war" speech on February 18, 1943, in the Sportpalast in Berlin, where Leni had first heard Hitler speak a dozen years earlier.

Defiance, not despair, was Goebbels's mood in crisis. "Stalingrad was and is," he trumpeted to fourteen thousand spectators, "the great call of destiny to the German nation." He ranted on for two hours, demanding, "Is your trust in the Führer greater, more faithful, and more unshakeable than ever? Is your readiness to follow him . . . absolute and unrestricted?" The prescreened audience interrupted him more than two hundred times to affirm their loyalty and readiness for "total war." It was a masterpiece of agitation that solicited from the nation what one appalled observer called a " *'Ja'* to self-destruction."

Resistance existed. In Munich that same day, the Gestapo arrested Hans and Sophie Scholl, brother and sister members of the White Rose student movement, for distributing leaflets opposing Hitler and the war. Hans Scholl and his circle were medical students on leave from the eastern front, where they had observed atrocities against civilians not unlike those that had occurred in Konskie. They claimed to speak in the name of "life itself" and charged that silence was "complicity in guilt" and that "every people deserves the government it is willing to endure!" Their courage was undaunted by the terrible risk of their dissent. "An end with terror," they pamphleteered, "is preferable to terror without end." They were beheaded four days after their arrest, their families ordered to pay court costs and execution fees.

Leni traveled to Spain that summer to shoot her bullfight footage, gratified "by the pro-German attitude of the [Spanish] people, and by their kindness." Her spirits were lifted, too, by Peter Jacob's appearance on another surprise leave from the front. When shooting ended in Spain, the two traveled to an increasingly dangerous Berlin to move Leni's company and personnel to safer Austria. They left the capital in late October, traveling via Nuremberg so Leni could introduce Jacob to Julius Streicher, no longer Gauleiter of Franconia but still publisher of *Der Stürmer*.

Streicher—"a caricature of a lecher posing as a man of wisdom," as the examining psychiatrist at Nuremberg would describe him—was so corrupt in helping himself to property expropriated from the Jews that he had been removed as gauleiter in 1940 following revelations of greed and sexual excess extreme even by Nazi standards. Leni's visit to him in 1943 continued a friendship that had begun ten years earlier during the filming of *Victory of Faith*. Her memoirs gave Streicher the briefest of mentions, hardly more than a paragraph in which her "blood ran cold" when she first laid eyes on him in Nuremberg. She denounced him to his face, she wrote, telling him she found his publication "loathsome." But, if

such a confrontation ever occurred, Leni overcame her distaste sufficiently to give Streicher a private preview of excerpts from *Olympia* in
Berlin, to enjoy being his houseguest in Nuremberg, and to extend handwritten invitations to film premières ("You absolutely must be there or I'll
be sad"). Giving him her power of attorney "in the matter of the Jew,
Béla Balács [*sic*]" may have been a legal matter, but their social encounters left a paper trail of cordiality and goodwill. After Streicher attended
her housewarming in Dahlem, he wrote her in the familiar *"Du"* form,
advising her to ignore her critics and the jokes they told at her expense.
"You will always be alone," Streicher had written her in 1937. "That is
your fate . . . but this fate is also your happiness." Filmmaking, he had
noted shrewdly, was her true joy and passion: "Go laughing down the
way of your great calling. Here you have found your heaven and in it you
will be eternal."

If only a social call in wartime (carefully noted by the Gestapo), Leni's
visit was also the final reunion of two key mythmakers of the Third
Reich. Three years later—on October 16, 1946—Streicher would die on
the gallows at Nuremberg. The British prosecutor trying him for crimes
against humanity noted: "It may be that this defendant is less directly
involved in the physical commission of crimes against Jews [than others,
but] his crime is no less the worse for that reason. No government in the
world, before the Nazis came to power, could have embarked upon and
put into effect a policy of mass extermination without having a people
who would back them and support them. It was to the task of educating
people," he charged, "that Streicher set himself [and that] made these
things possible—made these crimes possible—which could never have
happened had it not been for him and for those like him."

Leni and Jacob left Streicher and Nuremberg for Kitzbühel, where,
with the aid of Bormann and Speer, Leni requisitioned a spacious tim-
bered chalet known as Seebichl Haus. The three-story structure sat on the
edge of a small lake called the Schwarzsee on a hill that gave it unob-
structed views of the Alps in one direction and of gently sloping paths to
the center of town in the other. Leni turned bedrooms into offices and

social rooms, installed a new heating system, a screening room, cutting rooms, and sound-mixing facilities. The physical amenities lacked a kitchen, but that presented no hardship, as she arranged to have three meals a day catered by local hotels and restaurants for herself and the staff Goebbels had authorized her to evacuate from Berlin, including secretaries, editors, and the technicians essential for finishing *Tiefland*, supplemented by Ploberger and later by Bertha, who would live there with them until the end of the war.

Kitzbühel, known as "Kitz" to socialites and winter sports enthusiasts then as now, had advantages beyond its scenic charms. It was near Innsbruck, provincial capital of the Tyrol and site of military troops and installations, and was plentifully supplied with SS elements. The area was considered the center of the Alpine Redoubt by the American and French forces when they arrived a little more than a year later and arrested Hermann Göring, one of the Nazi officials seeking refuge in Kitzbühel's five-star Grand Hotel.

As a favorite of the Führer who enjoyed direct support of two ministers of the Reich and authorization from a third, Leni relocated with full military assistance for the transport of staff, equipment, and much of the physical inventory of her archives: "negatives, positives, lavender prints, duplicate negatives—not only of *Tiefland*, but also foreign-language versions of *Olympia* and *Triumph of the Will*, as well as *The Blue Light* and many short subjects and sports films." This was her life's work, proof of everything she believed about herself as an artist and the only annuity she might have if Hitler and the Reich were to fall.

What had not already been secured in military bunkers in Berlin-Johannisthal was stored in the ruins of a castle near Kitzbühel or in Seebichl Haus itself. Materials in active work were installed in the new cutting and storage rooms. Editing proceeded on *Tiefland* through the winter, as Ploberger designed a set for the picture's final scene, which "required an enormous sound stage" to accomodate Leni's desire for "a stylized mountain landscape with a beam of light, something not to be found in nature." The scene, a single silent shot of Martha and Pedro ascending in exaltation from lowlands to high on a flower-strewn path, would be photographed in Prague at the Barandow Studios in the fall, bringing the almost five-year shooting schedule to an end.

Before that could occur, on the first day of spring 1944, Leni married Maj. Peter Jacob in Kitzbühel. They arrived in deep snow by horse-drawn sleigh at the local registry office for the civil ceremony, witnessed by Leni's parents visiting from Berlin. Reception guests at the Grand Hotel in Kitzbühel included Hans Schneeberger and his wife, Gisela, Leni's former photo assistant; plus Ploberger and other friends and colleagues fortifying themselves against the cold with German *Sekt*. The magistrate performing the ceremony had, by coincidence, been Jacob's messenger at the front. His officiating may explain a curious irregularity in the occasion's documentation that was allowed to stand. The license, confirming that Jacob had been born on December 30, 1909, and christened "Eugen Karl Jacob," omitted mandatory information about the bride's parents, though no such gap existed for the parents of the groom. Such details were required in the Third Reich as indexes to genealogical data and racial purity. The omission regarding Alfred and Bertha Riefenstahl may have resulted from oversight, but it veiled information much as Leni's substitution of grandmothers' names had done when she prepared her official documents of descent in 1933.

After the wedding and her parents' return to Berlin, Leni Riefenstahl-Jacob, as she now began signing herself, continued with plans for shooting in Prague. She saw Speer from time to time and accompanied him at least once to Berchtesgaden, though Hitler was not in residence. She later wrote that she had last seen the Führer there—or anywhere—shortly after the wedding, when he asked to meet her groom, who was then slated for duty on the Italian front. The occasion was less than festive. The host's grandiloquent monologues gave way to incoherent rages about Italy and England. "I noticed Hitler's shrunken frame," Leni remembered, "the trembling of his hand, the flickering of his eyes; he had aged years since our last meeting. Yet despite these external signs of decay, he still cast the same magical spell as before."

Hitler's aging and decay were less surprising in early 1944 than any putative interest he might have had in newlyweds. But Leni's presence at the Berghof was almost certainly timed so she could present him—as she had for *Triumph of the Will* and *Olympia*—with a luxuriously boxed, hand-crafted portfolio of nearly four dozen oversized and mounted stills from the unfinished *Tiefland*. It was a one-of-a-kind offering to its one-of-a-kind financier, suitably inscribed: "To my Führer on his birthday in fidelity and devotion. 1944. Leni Riefenstahl."

On July 16, Leni rushed to Berlin when news arrived that her father had died of heart failure in Berlin's La Charité Hospital. Speer promised to attend burial services with her on July 20, but as Leni and her mother stood at Alfred's graveside, the armaments minister was called away. A bomb had exploded at 12:42 p.m. at the Wolf's Lair, Hitler's military headquarters in East Prussia. It was the fifteenth in a series of assassination attempts, and Hitler regarded his escape with minor injuries as "a miracle," further proof of his ordination by Providence. The failed assassination and coup (called Operation Valkyrie) had been organized by Count Claus Schenk von Stauffenberg of the army high command and other officers who were persuaded that killing Hitler was the only means of saving Germany. Stauffenberg and his principal coconspirators in the "officer clique" were executed that night or shortly thereafter. "I want them to be hanged, strung up like butchered cattle," Hitler had ordered, and he was furnished with home movies of their executions for his private viewing.

Leni learned of the assassination attempt after Alfred's burial, but more grievous news arrived. At about the same time her father was interred in Berlin and the assassins' bomb exploded in East Prussia, a grenade splintered in Lettland, killing Heinz Riefenstahl so efficiently he could not be buried. He died *"für Führer, Volk, und Vaterland,"* read the official letter, which was addressed to Alfred and arrived ten days later. Reflecting on her beloved brother's fate, Leni voiced a rare regret: "I still cannot forgive myself for failing to approach Hitler just once in connection with a personal matter; all because I felt inhibited about turning to him in this difficult phase of the war." She had chosen silence that day at the Berghof, even before she had learned the unwelcome truth about Heinz's failings as a soldier from Speer. "I held my tongue," she said of a moment of remarkable restraint for a woman so rarely reticent.

The almost simultaneous deaths of Alfred and Heinz raised inheritance issues. The family business, thriving on maintenance contracts for war-damaged and prisoner-of-war facilities, passed on July 16 to Heinz and on July 20 to his heirs, the children who had been in Ilse's de facto custody since early 1943. As surviving parent, Ilse now secured their legal guardianship, grateful that both were safely out of Berlin, Uta in Oberstdorf, in Bavaria, with her and Eckart in Zernsdorf, outside of Berlin, with Bertha. When Ilse arrived there to retrieve the boy, caretakers refused her entry and told her Bertha had left, taking Eckart with her and leaving no forwarding address.

This was untrue. Bertha would not leave Zernsdorf until February 1945, shortly after the firebombing of Dresden and then accompanied by Speer, who personally drove her from Berlin to Kitzbühel. But Eckart was, as Ilse guessed, already in Kitzbühel by September, in care of a governess hired by Leni, who had departed for Prague to shoot the final takes for *Tiefland*. Ilse made her way to Kitzbühel, where she threatened to press charges of kidnapping. Local authorities declined to honor guardianship documents issued in Berlin, but two weeks later and without explanation, Leni's longtime personal photographer, Rolf Lantin, also a resident of Seebichl Haus, delivered Eckart to his mother in Oberstdorf.

By November, Leni was back in Berlin at the Hotel Adlon, attempting to overturn Heinz's will. Ilse's lawyer, Dr. Hertha Curtius, was acting as trustee of the Riefenstahl firm and hoping to sell it to its caretaker management before it could be destroyed by Allied offensives or seized in an occupation by the approaching Red Army. Leni's attempts to gain custody of the children and, through them, control of the firm failed. She returned to Kitzbühel.

Back at Seebichl Haus at the end of the year, she doggedly continued plans for dubbing and scoring *Tiefland* there. Despite widespread hopes for a last-minute miracle weapon or some sudden, providential reversal, the outcome of the war seemed grimly inevitable. Paris, whose occupation Leni had called "a deed without parallel in human history," had been liberated in August, Italy had fallen in September, and the U.S. Army had taken Aachen in October, just as the Russians reached East Prussia in their push to Berlin. By March, the Americans would be crossing the Rhine.

Leni's monomaniacal concern for *Tiefland* struck even her as "absurd and inexplicable" but kept fear and panic at bay. She drove herself and her assistants; tried and failed to get sound engineer and former lover Storr assigned to her staff; edited compulsively; recorded actors' voices and then rerecorded them; and supervised scoring by Giuseppe Becce, who had composed the music for *The Blue Light*. She bombarded Berlin with demands for continued draft deferments of her technicians at a time when young boys and old men were being drafted into civilian militias armed with shovels. Almost all deferments were rejected or rescinded, including the one Speer had obtained for Fanck, now well over fifty.

Allied bombers flew in nightly armadas over Seebichl Haus on missions to Munich, making her feel "as if we were on a ship that was slowly sinking into the waves." Fearful for her husband's safety, she impulsively left for Italy now that her film was almost finished, hoping to locate him or learn of his fate. Her access to high-ranking personnel remained as effective as ever. Through an adjutant of General Field Marshal Albert Kesselring, she secured transportation in a supply column to the front and, eventually, to the hospital in Merano where she found Jacob, bedridden with a crippling attack of rheumatism.

With her husband still alive and the dubbing on *Tiefland* mostly complete in January (though she would still be sending telegrams to her actors in April), she was free to leave Kitzbühel for Berlin in February for another attempt at overturning Heinz's will.

According to Ilse, now remarried to a frontline war photographer, Leni went to Speer and his deputy Karl Hettlage to denounce her former sister-in-law as "defeatist" even as Berlin was collapsing in ruins and civilians were building barricades in the streets with mattresses and kitchen chairs in frantic preparation for a suicidal "fight to the last man." Ilse saw the denunciation in her personal file and claimed that her lawyer, Dr. Curtius, was warned by Leni's lawyer that "if you refuse to sign the documents [relinquishing guardianship and custody], the matter will be referred to the Reich's Chancellery and Martin Bormann." If appeal to Bormann became necessary, the lawyer continued, the likely outcome would be Ilse's assignment to a concentration camp and a sentence at forced labor for her attorney.

Lawyer and client stood firm. Ilse later claimed that Dr. Curtius was, indeed, sentenced to a munitions factory in Spandau, the sentence suspended only because she was pregnant. The Riefenstahl firm was lost and would shortly cease to exist in any event, but Leni's attempts to disinherit her niece and nephew would continue for another half century. For now, even as the Reich was collapsing and talk of suicide was rampant among loyalists unable to imagine life without their führer, Leni remained determined to use whatever influence remained to her. She had, incredibly enough, telephone access to Hitler's bunker through a direct line from Kitzbühel belonging to the wife of his personal aide, Julius Schaub. With most of Germany paralyzed and an estimated seventeen million refugees roaming bombed-out roads on foot, she was still able to obtain gasoline for personal use from the military and arrange—courtesy of the Brown House in Munich—removal for safekeeping of her archive of Nuremberg negatives to Bolzano.

When Schneeberger, now over fifty, appealed to her for help in evading service in the civilian militia in Vienna, she obtained his release to shoot titles for *Tiefland* through a personal appeal to the offices of Vienna's gauleiter and former head of the Hitler Youth, Baldur von Schirach. When Schneeberger's half-Jewish wife, Gisela, was jailed in Innsbruck for an anti-Hitler tirade on a train full of wounded soldiers, Leni persuaded the local Gestapo chief to release her. Her efficiency at wresting favors from a regime from which she claimed to be disengaged was as remarkable as ever, though her Hitler card was nearing expiration.

Leni's patron issued his scorched-earth policy on March 19, ordering destruction of bridges, water and power plants, and factories, the very infrastructures on which the existence of the civilian population depended. "It is not necessary to worry about the basic things the German people will need for its most rudimentary survival," he explained, since "only those who are inferior will remain after this struggle, for the good have already been killed."

Leni's last view of Berlin was "like the end of the world," she said. Kitzbühel was no longer a haven, but a target for American and French occupation forces. She fled with the original negatives of *Olympia*, driving with the Schneebergers and their daughter Billie to the village of Mayrhofen in the Ziller Valley. Though she later portrayed leaving Kitzbühel as a dramatic overnight escape, Isabella Ploberger, who stayed behind at Seebichl Haus with Bertha and the staff, said Leni lived with the Schneebergers in Mayrhofen for "some weeks" in late April, until news came on April 30 that the Führer had committed suicide in his bunker. "Hitler is dead—he's dead!" exulted Gisela, while Leni was seized by a "chaos of emotions" and took to her bed, weeping.

The next day, Leni later wrote, the Schneebergers abandoned her as they sought refuge deeper in the Alps. Lacking enough gasoline to return the seventy miles to Kitzbühel, she followed their trail and was bewildered by their icy reception when she found them at a provincial hotel owned by a relative of Schneeberger's, who tried to bar her way, telling her, "I don't take any Nazis."

Infuriated, Leni shoved him aside and confronted Hans and Gisela in their rooms. "Are you here?" Gisela asked her in astonishment. "Are you crazy? Did you really think you could stay here with us?"

The proud and celebrated woman to whom the doors of chancelleries and palaces had been open wide was speechless at Gisela's ingratitude and effrontery. She turned to her former lover for support. He remained passive and silent as his wife shook with righteous rage.

"You thought we'd help you?" Gisela cried. "You Nazi slut!"

More than an era had ended.

FIFTEEN

PARIAH

*Peace is visible already. It's like a great darkness
falling; it's the beginning of forgetting.*
　　　　—Marguerite Duras, *The War: A Memoir*

She did all the talking.
　　　　　　—*Revue* magazine, December 11, 1949,
　　　　　　　　on Leni Riefenstahl in court

"A WORLD HAD COLLAPSED INSIDE ME," she said, stung by the
"Nazi slut" accusation and wondering in a daze "what could have
changed" to have brought it about. She was frantic to get back to
Kitzbühel, fearful that her film might be seized by French or American
occupation forces or that she might be captured and find herself "at the
mercy" of the victors, with "no legal protection of any kind."

Her protectors were of no use to her now: the Führer dead; Goebbels
a suicide in the bunker; Bormann in flight (his suicide not established until
1972); and Speer branded a criminal with an appointment in Nuremberg.
Even Nazi symbols—the swastika flags and emblems she had fixed as if
forever on film—vanished. Banner-bearers of the thousand-year tomorrow ran for cover or willed themselves into forgetfulness. "With the end
of Hitler," Ian Kershaw notes, "the outward signs of National Socialism
also disappeared, seemingly overnight, from the face of the earth." Victor

Klemperer told his diary in early May that "the Third Reich is already almost as good as forgotten; everyone was opposed to it, 'always' opposed to it."

She traveled by foot, by wagon, and finally on a rickety bicycle traded for the crocodile cosmetics case she had snatched up in panic—leaving behind the negatives to *Olympia*—when she fled Mayrhofen and Gisela Schneeberger's blistering personal attack.

She was intercepted on the road to Kitzbühel by American troops and taken to a detention camp where G.I.'s too young to remember her face on the covers of *Time* and *Newsweek* examined her identity papers. Her anonymity may have been fortuitous but was a blow to her vanity, too, one assuaged by Austrian detainees who recognized her and crowded around in an echo of more halcyon days. She made what she called "my first escape" the following morning by walking through a break in an unguarded barbed-wire fence and continuing on the road to Kitzbühel.

She was picked up again, detained again, and walked away again, oddly indignant at the Americans' lax sense of security until she neared the shelter of Seebichl Haus, where the Stars and Stripes rippled from her roof. A tall, mustached American officer in his midthirties approached her on the path, introducing himself as Lt. Col. Milton H. Medenbach.

Colonel Medenbach had never heard of Leni Riefenstahl, but as Allied administrator of civilian affairs in Kitzbühel, he felt no animus toward survivors of the Reich. He spoke fluent German, learned as a student in Vienna in the early thirties, and viewed Leni as a woman in distress, disheveled but handsome and, in spite of her fatigue and agitation, capable of charm. The United States Army, he informed her, had temporarily requisitioned her house at the suggestion of Kitzbühel's mayor. But her mother was safe, relocated to the nearby vineyard estate of Joachim von Ribbentrop, the former Nazi foreign minister.

Medenbach delivered her to her mother at the Ribbentrop estate and gallantly yielded to anxious entreaties to find her husband. Calls to nearby detention camps located Jacob only a day before he was scheduled with other prisoners of war for release and dispersal into the general population. The colonel short-circuited his release, claiming he needed a driver and translator, and reunited the Wehrmacht major with Leni and Bertha in the comfort of their former lodgings with wine and *"Willkommen."*

Medenbach assuaged twinges of unease he felt over occupying Seebichl Haus, with its "magnificent leather club chairs and shelves of leather-bound books," by inviting the trio—and members of Leni's live-in staff, including Rolf Lantin and Waldi Traut—to socialize when an occasion warranted. When old friends from Berlin came to Seebichl Haus looking for her, she was allowed to entertain them there with the aid of the Romanian girls who had been her maids. She impressed the G.I. staff as an obsessively dedicated artist and businesswoman who talked of little but her work and hinted darkly that all her woes—past, present, and perhaps those to come—were because of "the Jewish element." She held court in lively broken English while Bertha, "a lovely woman" who spoke only German, became *"Mutti"* to American boys homesick for maternal warmth. Peter Jacob, "an attractive guy" in laborer's smock and shorts, made himself useful as an all-around handyman they called "Jake."

Denazification was in progress, and not even Leni's chivalrous "Herr Colonel" (as she styled him) could subvert the bureaucratic machinery of occupation. She was taken by Jeep to Salzburg Prison, formerly administered by the local SS, which had helped her cast extras for *Tiefland* at nearby Maxglan. "I found myself in a prison cell," she recalled, though Medenbach later protested that she was never incarcerated, merely held for questioning or placed under house arrest. Still, she was treated without deference, strip-searched, and transported in the open back of an armored truck to the detention camp of the Seventh American Army in Bavaria. There she was comfortably housed with Hitler's senior secretary, Johanna Wolf, and caught glimpses of other guests of the Seventh Army's hospitality milling in the courtyard, including Hermann Göring.

She was forced to look at photographs, images of Dachau. "I hid my face in my hands," she recalled, as if the ordeal of viewing them equaled the horrors they depicted. She was not permitted to look away from the "gigantic eyes peering helplessly into the camera" from the hells of Dachau, Auschwitz, Buchenwald, Bergen-Belsen, and other death camps of which, she told the Americans, she had known nothing.

These were revelations that shocked the conscience of the world. If anything could have stirred amnesia or struck dumb the fictions of self-justification, these images—the legacy of the Reich she had used and served—ought to have qualified. Instead, she scrambled to shield herself from their "incomprehensible" testimony with the names of Jewish friends—a personal physician, Manfred George, Josef von Sternberg—and did not shrink from claiming Béla Balázs among them. It was a litany of names she would recite so automatically in years to come that the German magazine *Der Spiegel* would refer to it as her list of "alibi Jews."

When interrogated about her relationship to the party, she claimed that she had been a recognized artist "before the world ever heard the names of Hitler and Goebbels" and, except for unavoidable professional contact with the latter ("He was cold and forbidding toward me, I almost hated him," she said), she had "no contact whatever" with other party officials. "I saw them occasionally at official celebrations," she allowed, but "I never received an invitation from any Party man, and if I had I would have rejected every one of them."

She acknowledged friendships with World War I flying ace Ernst Udet, the earliest of the inner-circle suicides, and with Speer, and admitted to "a certain admiration for the personality of the Führer." This sounded candid and forthright, emboldening her to add, "If that was a crime, then many people in the democratic countries are guilty too, because they have committed the same crime during the years from 1933–1939." The interrogating officers recorded her claim that she "never thought about the Führer's policy, because she did not have the slightest idea about these things." Or about the camps. "I knew nothing about them," she repeated, and "when I hear all these dreadful things which happened in Germany, I could cry. And I cannot grasp how any of the people who shared Hitler's political ideas have the courage to continue living. I would have committed suicide had I felt that I shared the responsibility for these crimes."

Her interrogators were American officers born in Germany, still fluent in the language. One of them, Ernest Langendorf, would stay behind as a journalist in Munich, where he remained casually friendly with her and even helped hang pictures in her postwar Munich flat. But when she submitted to their questions in late May 1945, she was "difficult to recognize" from photographs of the once vibrant film star and seemed "a broken human being." It appeared as if recent events had "strongly affected her mental state," though she was self-possessed enough to tell them that "if I have a conviction [it is] my conception of the art to which I have dedicated myself, and for which I have lived."

The official report contains minor errors about the German film industry, is tentative rather than penetrating, and accepts at face value her assertions that "money was of no importance to me" and "had I ever had the impression that my freedom as a creative artist would be limited, I would have gone abroad." She was an artist *über alles,* rehearsing the first draft of the self-exonerating legend to come. She gave "the impression of honesty," her interrogators allowed, without necessarily being "reliable." Nevertheless, she seemed "sincere," and they judged, "It is possible that she actually was not aware of what went on. That was," however, "her sin of omission, which appears all the more serious due to the fact that she, more than any other person, had the opportunity to get to the truth. She is a product of the moral corruption which characterizes the Regime."

They rejected any notion that she was merely an opportunist or a "fanatical National Socialist who had sold her soul to the regime," focusing instead on "her lack of moral poise." In conclusion, they wrote a kind of epitaph: "If her statements are sincere, she has never grasped, and still does not grasp, the fact that she, by dedicating her life to art, has given expression to a gruesome regime and contributed to its glorification."

Leni was mollified by their courtesy and their questions, which suggested what they knew and what they didn't know. No one mentioned Konskie or Gypsies or Warsaw or effusive telegrams to Hitler or details about finance. There had been humiliations, to be sure. A medical doctor had attempted to ask her about Hitler's sexuality and the appearance of his genitals. The obvious inference outraged her, though the indignity was self-inflicted. She had always denied to the press that she was "Hitler's honey" or "girlfriend," while trading on the sexual glamour such rumors contributed to her reputation.

After her exposure to the concentration camp photos, she tried to reconcile their evidence with "Hitler, as I knew him." His secretary Johanna Wolf, who had taken his dictation since 1929, sobbed, "He can't have been informed about those crimes." They must have been the doing of "Himmler, Goebbels and Bormann." Leni temporized, deciding Hitler must have been schizophrenic—or maybe just lonely. "After all, he wanted to be honored and loved, but in his voluntary isolation there were no more human relationships." Only when he realized victory would elude him did he become "spiritually anemic and finally inhumane."

It was a sentimental view of the author of the Holocaust, a self-serving analysis. Any harsher verdict would have compromised her work, her claims to naïveté and lack of ideological awareness, and there is evidence she believed what she said and identified with it. Her every public utterance on the subject stressed Hitler's personality and distanced her from the consequences of his politics. "Hitler, as I knew him" was ideologically neutral, requiring no renunciation, no remorse.

She freely acknowledged his seductive charisma, for which she— among so many—could hardly be held responsible. Privately, she continued referring to him as "the Führer" and "the greatest man of his time." Her loyalty to the myth she had helped create was unswerving and so impermeable it could inspire laughter. After the war, she and Jacob visited what was left of Hitler's mountaintop hideaway at the Berghof with Friedrich Mainz, the Tobis executive who had distributed *Olympia* and facilitated *Tiefland*. He thought Leni "a foolish Nazi: a Nazi for Hitler, *not* for the Party," but when he remarked in Berchtesgaden that Hitler had been "an idiot," Leni was so incensed she stormed off into the cold and snow. "After about two hours she came back frozen," Mainz recalled, "and said quietly, 'Excuse me, but you *must* accept that he was a very powerful man. He ruined all Europe!' " Mainz deadpanned, "I accept *that*," but she failed to appreciate his irony.

On June 3, 1945, she received clearance from the Seventh Army. She was released three days later "without prejudice" and returned to Kitzbühel, where the Americans, transferring administration of the area to the French, restored Seebichl Haus to her, together with its contents and household staff so she might complete work on *Tiefland*.

Her U.S. Army documents were valid for all occupation powers, but an uneasy Colonel Medenbach advised her that, with administration changing hands, she should consider relocating to the American zone in Bavaria. "Jake" departed with Medenbach, but Leni stayed behind in Kitzbühel. Surely the many prewar honors she had received from the French for *Triumph of the Will* and *Olympia* were positive omens, harbingers of favor.

She miscalculated.

The French had not forgotten their own occupation and insisted on fresh interrogations. She was detained, transported to Innsbruck for questioning, and confined in a local resort hotel until the French officially declared her "undesirable" and gave her twenty-four hours to leave their zone. She contacted Jacob and Medenbach for help in packing and transporting her belongings, but the order to leave brought on an attack of the old bladder complaint that seemed always to accompany stress, and she checked into the Kitzbühel hospital as the French clock ticked. Jacob was delayed by an automobile accident in which Medenbach was injured, and, when he finally arrived, there was time only for essentials, which meant leaving *Tiefland* behind. On exiting Kitzbühel, their car was intercepted by French officers (the deadline had expired) and driven to Innsbruck, where Leni blacked out and was taken to the hospital ward of the Innsbruck women's prison.

She was treated and released, partly due to the intercession of Colonel Medenbach before he returned to America. In spite of her classification as "undesirable," she returned to Kitzbühel and Seebichl Haus to finish *Tiefland*, her travel documents signed by the French commander in chief in Austria, Gen. Antoine Bethouart. Rumors quickly circulated—and were quickly denied—that the cost of French protection had been a hasty love affair with the *général*.

She was a lightning rod for gossip and for schadenfreude. Budd Schulberg, the American author of *What Makes Sammy Run?* (and later screenwriter of *On the Waterfront*), tracked her down at Seebichl Haus. He was nearing the end of his army duty and searching for pictorial material that could be used as evidence in the Nuremberg trials. Though prosecutors had a print of *Triumph of the Will* confiscated in America, he was hoping to unearth *Victory of Faith* and *Day of Freedom*, neither of which had been seen in the United States.

Schulberg had grown up in Hollywood as the son of the Jewish head of Paramount Pictures and prided himself on having "done my bit" in the anti-Nazi campaign protesting Leni's visit there in 1938. Now that the war was over, he was curious to meet the object of his boycott and traveled from Berlin to the "gingerbread houses" of Kitzbühel. A French major who had already interrogated her there responded to his inquiries by asking, "Why should anyone want to find a third-rate movie actress?"

At Seebichl Haus, Schulberg was admitted by "Jake," who seemed to be acting as a houseman or butler. Leni made an artfully delayed entrance, tanned and wearing "yellow corduroy slacks with a golden-brown leather jacket." She reminded Schulberg of "I don't know how many actresses of her age I had met before, fading beauties who try to compensate in grooming, make-up and animation for what they begin to lack in physical appeal."

Willing to "frighten or flatter her," as he wrote in the *Saturday Evening Post* under the sardonic title "Nazi Pin-Up Girl" in 1946, Schulberg played at their being "just a couple of artists" talking of her films while a housemaid prepared tea and cakes. When he mentioned *Triumph of the Will*, Leni's tan went pale. "Why do you want that one?" she asked, denying it was propaganda and displaying the French diploma she had won for documentary to prove it. She brushed aside the other films as of no interest, and, anyway, they were hidden in a tunnel somewhere near Bolzano.

She changed the subject to the horrors of being Goebbels's victim. "I was even afraid he might put me into a concentration camp," she said, causing her visitor to ask why she should fear concentration camps if she had never heard of them. Leni poured more tea and turned to the future. She asked if her name was on a blacklist and if Schulberg thought *Tiefland* would be boycotted in America. She was deeply concerned about postwar Germany. Though she had never been a Nazi, she was troubled that "the concentration camp Germans will be in power."

Schulberg was a disappointment to her, wanting in gallantry. He even declined her request for a can of gasoline. "Just one liter, so we can get into town and back?" she pleaded. "Not allowed," he told her, noting "something queer about [her] smile; it was intimate and appealing, and yet clearly designing. That must have been the way she looked at Hitler when she wanted him to make Goebbels back down." In disappointment, it was a face "unmasked and heavy with self pity."

Leni's reprieve in Kitzbühel was short-lived. She was still officially under house arrest, but the most crippling blow came when the French seized her bank accounts. Her personal account held thirty thousand marks, but her *Tiefland* production account totaled, by her own estimate, more than three hundred thousand marks, a fortune in postwar Europe and enough to finance a modestly budgeted feature film. These were Bormann-supplied monies from the Führer's personal funds, and they introduce a mystery never solved. The work remaining on *Tiefland* was too minor—final editing and preparation of a release print—to require significant cash outlays. The existence of such an opulent "cushion" suggests possible scenarios, but budgetary thrift on Leni's part is not one of them. It is likely that either Bormann's or Leni's accounting was less than meticulous—or Hitler's patronage was generous beyond even her worst enemies' estimates.

She would never see this money again, in spite of efforts to reclaim it. Aside from the villa in Dahlem, which would not be legally restored to her by the Allies until 1952, she had no assets but her films. She learned to her bitterest horror that the *Olympia* negatives she had hastily left behind with the Schneebergers in Mayrhofen were now under their control as French-appointed trustees of her firm. She still had—or assumed she had—the Nuremberg films, but their copyrights were in doubt and their economic value dubious to nil.

Her one real asset was *Tiefland*, effectively removed from her control when French authorities once again declared her "undesirable" and again ordered her to abandon Kitzbühel for the French-administered zone of Germany, allowing her the standard single piece of luggage and forty marks pocket money. When she arrived with Bertha and Peter Jacob in Freiburg, the hometown of Arnold Fanck, she was "aghast" that her onetime mentor "refused to have anything to do with me." Because safe haven with Fanck was no option, the French assigned her to nearby Breisach, where the mayor provided lodgings in a small, bomb-damaged hotel. Under house arrest and ordered to report to the French police twice a week, she was confined to narrow quarters with her mother, her cutter, her secretary, her bookkeeper, and her wandering husband, now the object of what she called her "love-hate."

Life in Breisach was "intolerable," she said, for its "undignified circumstances." She grew depressed, wrote letters to authorities that went unanswered, was subjected to questioning that was "relentless mental torture." She was finally relocated with her mother and husband to Königsfeld, in the Black Forest, and required to report to the police in nearby Villingen, where French denazification hearings would soon focus on her Third Reich history.

Leni's hardships and humiliations were no more (and often considerably less) than those suffered by thousands—even millions—of Germans at the end of the war, but they were debilitating to a woman so accustomed to deference and authority. Frustration and depression produced what she termed "chronic paranoia" and "persecution mania." She had lost so much—property, money, films, staff, status, and independence—that she contemplated suicide. But most tormenting of all were Jacob's continuing infidelities. He was "a nymphomaniac," she told Gitta Sereny years later, misusing the term but making clear the grounds for her distress.

When she learned that everything left behind in Kitzbühel, including *Tiefland* and all of her elaborate technical equipment, had been removed by French authorities to Paris, she wept. "My life's work seemed destroyed." Overwhelmed at last by misfortune, she filed for divorce in May 1947 and submitted to medical treatment.

In one version she told, she was locked away in an "insane asylum" in Freiburg "at the orders of the French military government." There she was subjected to electroshock therapy for three months while the French conspired behind her back over ownership of her films. In another, less colorful rendering, she was a live-in patient for four months at a private psychiatric clinic in Freiburg overseen by a Dr. Beringer.

Whichever version is closer to the truth, her breakdown appears to have been genuine. Whatever stability she regained from psychiatric care, at least one goal was achieved: She was no longer Leni Riefenstahl-Jacob. At forty-five, she was independent again.

But to do what, now that *Tiefland* was lost? The future seemed darker and emptier of promise than at any time in her life when a stranger unexpectedly appeared. An unlikely deus ex machina, he introduced himself as Jean-Pierre Desmarais and threw her what looked like a lifeline.

Desmarais claimed he had been born a Jew named "Kaufmann" in Germany and had escaped the Third Reich to become a French citizen and film producer in Paris. He knew, he said, the whereabouts of *Tiefland*, had even seen it at the Cinémathèque Française, and was prepared to become Leni's partner in recovering and distributing it. Moreover, he said he could arrange lifting of her house arrest through his Paris lawyer. In return, he wanted her power of attorney, a share of her profits, and control of all her film and book projects for the next ten years.

"I would have signed just about anything to regain my freedom," Leni later explained and agreed to her benefactor's terms, telling him, "I don't care about the money. You can have it all," though her gratitude left her unable a dozen years later to recall his name when a London journalist pressed her for details. In early 1948, as Desmarais had promised, his Paris lawyer, André Dalsace, was successful in bringing her house arrest to an end. Dalsace was also attempting to recover *Tiefland* and the cache of funds French authorities had seized from her Austrian bank accounts. Just as success seemed imminent, he sent word that restitution had been rescinded "by orders from above."

Hitler had risen from the dead. French cooperation vanished with sensational headlines announcing publication of *Le Journal Intime d'Eva Braun*, the diary of Hitler's mistress. The existence of such a document had been widely unsuspected, but the ninety-six-page manuscript (unsigned and perfectly typed) came with assurances of authenticity from none other than Luis Trenker, Leni's old costar and sparring partner. The sensation it caused would not be equaled until the 1990s, when Hitler's "private journals" emerged from nowhere and were published with authentications from scholars whose infallibility was equaled only by their gullibility.

Eva Braun's putative prose told of hot nights in the Berghof and her jealousy of females close to Hitler, especially Leni, who was described as temptress, manipulator, upstart, and ruthless opportunist. Excerpted widely, the diary generated headlines promising glimpses of "LENI'S NAKED DANCES FOR ADOLF" and predicting "MARLENE TO PLAY LENI" in a movie version. Hitler's quoted remarks ran the gamut from "She has a beautiful body" and "is a great artist and important person," to complaints that she was "all instinct," an exhibitionist who "can't help wiggling her behind," a meddler who "bitches about people" and "gives herself airs and graces." If she was "the 'secret queen' " of the Nazis when dancing nude at the Berghof, her host "ridicule[d] her whenever she talk[ed] politics."

This was an irresistible gloss on history, so transparently bogus that many assumed it could only be genuine. Leni viewed it as "criminal," which had justification, and said it made it "impossible for me to practice my profession as a film director," which did not. Still, such defamation—obvious hoax or not—came at an inconvenient time for recovering funds of uncertain provenance from the French government. Lawyer Dalsace agreed the diary was a "gross fabrication" but left it to Leni to extricate herself from its fallout, while Desmarais beat a hasty retreat to Canada.

The diary was a malicious forgery, but Leni's quashing it was not as simple as invoking the names of Hitler and Bormann had once been. Luis Trenker was clearly behind the hoax but remained at home in Italy, safely beyond reach of a German lawsuit. He wrote Leni, lecturing her that "you as an artist were very prominent during Hitler's regime [and] people in the public eye are always exposed to distortions and defamations." He preempted any charge of malice by adding that he had "long since buried any personal grudge against you."

Leni had no funds to pay a lawyer but joined Eva Braun's family in their suit against a German publisher, the action financed by legal aid that Braun's sister advised was available for the needy. The Brauns had retained Dr. Otto Gritschneder, a dedicated anti-Nazi who had been barred from practicing law during the Third Reich because he was "professionally qualified, politically unreliable."

Certified to practice since July 1945 by the American military government, Gritschneder branded the Wehrmacht (in which he had served) a "criminal enterprise" and called Nazi judges "terrorists." Until his death at ninety-one in 2005, he honed his reputation as a champion of truth and justice without regard to the political bona fides of his clients. In 1948, he was willing to take on what looked like and was a clear case of defamation and swiftly obtained an injunction against further publication. Leni wrapped herself in his political prestige, noting in her memoirs that he facilitated the legal aid with which she paid his fees in "over fifty" cases yet to come. She called him "the lawyer who has defended me against libel for decades," long after he ceased personally to represent her.

She became a shrewd student of litigation and aid that permitted her to sue without cost. With the legal expertise of Gritschneder or his partners (and others as well), she would employ access to the courts—often on technical grounds—to seek justice, vindication, and income.

Her most critical postwar legal proceeding was one she had no control over: denazification. Hearings to investigate and classify degrees of complicity with Hitler's regime had been conducted by the Allies for more than three years by the time she appeared before her first tribunal in

Villingen at the end of 1948. The hearings were mandated by the Allies
but conducted by German judges, some unimpeachable, some highly
sensitive to judicial sins committed by their predecessors under the
swastika banner because, as Alfred Polgar noted after attending one of
Leni's hearings, "so many of the successors and their predecessors are
identical." (A recent study estimates that 75 percent of German judges
hearing postwar cases against the Third Reich's legal system had themselves served on the Nazi bench.)

Leni's denazification hearing attracted attention because of her notoriety, but the evidence presented was limited to a survey of party
membership lists on which her name did not appear and affidavits she
submitted from friends and colleagues (in and out of the party) attesting
to her political purity. The thoroughness of the investigation may be
judged by the official conclusion: "Not a single witness or document
could be found that would indicate a close relationship between Frau
Riefenstahl and Hitler." Elsewhere the judicial finding summarized
defenses made under oath that were a mixture of the true, the arguable,
and the false: She made documentaries, not propaganda; she was coerced
by Hitler into making *Triumph of the Will;* she was not responsible for
uses the party made of her work; *Olympia* was an international project
that had nothing to do with the party; she had many Jewish friends but no
party associations beyond the professional; she did not require her
employees to greet her with the Hitler salute. Her not having been a
party member was considered decisive, and the tribunal pronounced her
free of "political incrimination"—"*nicht betroffen.*"

The French military government immediately appealed the verdict to
a chorus of German press approval, and she was remanded to Freiburg
for a second tribunal conducted by the state of Baden in July 1949. Again
she was judged unimplicated, and again the decision was appealed. The
Baden State Commission on Political Purgation scheduled a third hearing
for December, while letter and editorial writers continued vociferous
campaigns protesting indulgent court decisions.

If Leni was not the principal target of such protests (there were many candidates to choose from), she became a prime focus when charges appeared in the popular illustrated weekly *Revue* that she had used Gypsies as slave labor on *Tiefland*. Leni sued the magazine for libel in November, and the case was under appeal in Munich when the Baden tribunal met in December for her third denazification hearing.

Abstractions about the blindness of justice seldom conform to the unruly realities of open court. Certainly the November trial concerning the Gypsies could not help influencing the December tribunal in Baden, if only because of Leni's courtroom performance (there is no other word) in Munich, where Gritschneder represented her against *Revue* publisher Helmut Kindler, who had printed an array of accusations, some accurate, some not, but all provocative and potentially damaging.

Kindler had purchased photographs taken in Krün that pictured Leni with Gypsies characterized in captions as "film slaves" and claimed she had personally selected them from a "concentration camp" in Salzburg. The magazine charged that the still-unfinished film had been financed with seven million marks of public funds administered by Martin Bormann and that Leni had selected her leading actor from a troop of two thousand *Gebirgsjäger* forced to parade before her in a casting call. While some of Kindler's sources were well informed, his principal witness, the woman who had taken the Krün photographs, admitted basing her allegations largely on location hearsay.

Leni arrived in court smartly dressed in a hat and jacketed suit of navy blue over a white silk blouse that epitomized Paris's "new look." She announced that she was defending herself at the insistence of Allied officers sympathetic to her upcoming denazification hearing in Baden. In an apparent bid for sympathy at odds with her chic appearance, she told the court that reduced circumstances forced her to seek legal aid. Having set the scene, she proceeded to direct it. One news source thought her postwar tribulations had only sharpened her instincts "to make herself the center of attention," to choose "when and at what time she has to explode" or "don her thick, horn-rimmed glasses to read aloud from documents with a little 'triumph of the will.' "

She overplayed her role from the start, heatedly contradicting Kindler's cost estimate for *Tiefland* of seven million marks. It was "only" five and a half million, she rebutted, and was "only a loan." She denied that troops had paraded before her or that she had personally selected Gypsy extras, who were, as she put it in an odd choice of words, "glad to escape" and work for her. Kindler produced some of them as witnesses. They testified that they had been treated "like dogs" or "pigs" and had later been "better cared for in the concentration camps." Journalists cited "fierce" disputes and "duels of words as sharp as knives." A defense attorney sarcastically asked if the Allied adviser insisting she go to trial was President Truman and suggested that *Tiefland* ought never be released, as she was "the devil's director," which elicited an outburst from Leni so "violent" that the judge had to order a recess.

News accounts called the entire proceeding "a carnival" and cited "laughter and outbursts [from spectators] not once objected to by the court," and noted that Leni "wildly" justified herself with anger and tears, "never allowed the defendant [Kindler] to finish a full sentence," and would not permit her own attorney to interrupt her. "She did all the talking." This was not the demurely winning Leni Riefenstahl heretofore on public display. This was Goebbels's "hysterical person" who abused referees at the Olympic Games and threatened party officials who dared to thwart her. There was "coldness" in her "eyes and expression," though a visitor noted, "When she spoke Hitler's name—and she often did—it fairly melted on her tongue."

The cost of *Tiefland* and whether the funds were or were not a loan (*all* movie funds are loans to be repaid from proceeds) and whether or not she had personally selected her extras were irrelevant to the central assertion that the Gypsies were slave labor, easily proved by documents from Maxglan (and Marzahn) that would not come to light for almost another forty years. The court found Kindler's claims "unsubstantiated and exaggerated," though he quickly filed an appeal. In the end, the court ordered him to pay Leni six hundred marks on a semantic technicality: Camps such as Maxglan were not officially designated "concentration camps" until March 1943, when the random transporting of Gypsies to Auschwitz and other death camps became systematic. *Tiefland* had begun shooting in 1940, when Maxglan was still nominally a "collection camp," and Kindler's terminology was therefore faulty and defamatory.

In the avalanche of press coverage of Leni's startling performance (two-thirds of the spectators were journalists), hardly anyone focused on the Gypsies at the heart of the matter. One who did was critic-essayist Alfred Polgar. He called the proceedings a "tragic farce" and noted that "one matter remained an insignificant detail: the fact that, shortly after having the pleasure of serving Riefenstahl's cinematic art, the extras— including women and children—were shipped off to the gas ovens."

The Baden commission, meeting only weeks after the raucous trial in Munich, concluded that Leni, though innocent of specific crimes, had consciously and willingly served the Reich. They reclassified her as a "fellow traveler" (*"Mitläuferin"*), the next-to-lowest of the five degrees of complicity. The designation was milder than some had hoped, and, while it fell short of exoneration (and she would challenge it in still another hearing), it ended uncertainty about legal status that had bedeviled and threatened her for the four and a half years since VE Day.

She was not without supporters. As many observers applauded her stand in silence as were vocally appalled by it. She resented, not unreasonably, that others equally cooperative with Hitler's regime came away unmolested by the press or the courts and had been working freely since the end of the war. Historians agree that in all fields and professions, many with dubious pasts "were able wholly or in part to avoid serious retribution for their actions—in some cases building successful post-war careers for themselves." Nor was her self-righteousness singular. "Few of those forced to account for their actions under Hitler showed remorse or contrition, let alone guilt."

Even so, Helmut Kindler and *Revue*, attuned to scandal and public accountability, would not let her get on with her life in spite of the disappointing judgment regarding the Gypsies. In spring 1952, Leni initiated a final hearing in Berlin in order to recover her villa in Dahlem, held by the Allies (and accumulating property taxes) since the end of the war. Two days before the hearing, Kindler and *Revue* struck again, editorializing that her "fellow traveler" classification (on which recovery of the property hinged) made a mockery of the denazification process because "Leni Riefenstahl is one of the few German women who not only knew about [atrocities], but also saw them with her own eyes." The subject this time was Konskie.

Kindler published photographs of Leni in Konskie and of Jews digging their own graves or gunned down in the streets, the snapshots taken during the massacre of September 1939. *Revue* did not accuse Leni of pulling triggers, but the photographs, definitively associating her with an atrocity involving Jewish civilians only days into the war, clearly mitigated her repeated claims of naïveté and ignorance. With the memory of *Tiefland*'s Gypsies still fresh in the public mind, *Revue*'s charges aimed at dominating the Berlin hearing and did.

She could not deny her presence in the photographs but attempted to discredit the images by producing a letter proving they had been offered to her a year earlier by a blackmailer and charging that *Revue* was acting in concert with the same tainted source. She claimed, as always, that she had not witnessed the massacre and that, when she learned of it after the fact, she "gave up [her] newsreel assignment that very same day and left the military zone," forgetting her flight to Danzig courtesy of the Luftwaffe and her subsequent visit to Warsaw to celebrate and film Hitler's Polish victory at his side, events unknown to Kindler and the court.

The man who had taken the Konskie photographs was a Wehrmacht radio operator named Stubbening who fell on the eastern front sometime after the Konskie incident. His snapshots mysteriously turned up in a document center in Hamburg where they had gone unnoticed, and how they came to the attention of *Revue* remained Kindler's secret. That they were genuine was never contested (duplicates would later be found in the files of the East German State Security Police). Leni produced eyewitnesses who testified she "had nothing whatsoever to do with those events." The court's decision, delivered by a Jewish judge named

Levinsohn, was noncommittal about "those events" but ruled, "Frau Riefenstahl is not incriminated by the photographs in question." Her "fellow traveler" status was upheld and the Dahlem property returned to her, together with tax liens and the squatters who were living in its wreckage. A developer was willing to take it off her hands for a distress price of thirty thousand marks.

The issues raised by Konskie, for all their troubling implications, had been, strictly speaking, irrelevant to the property issue before the bench. Leni claimed victory and threatened to sue Kindler and *Revue* for defamation. She estimated that "the moral damage" to her reputation ran "into the millions," but she settled out of court for ten thousand marks.

She won, however, a potentially more important concession. As part of the settlement, Kindler agreed to withdraw an exposé he was preparing for *Revue* regarding the secret financing of *Tiefland*. How much he knew beyond Bormann's role as disbursement agent is uncertain, but he knew that much and let it be known he already had a provocative title for his story: "Leni Riefenstahl's Millions."

If Kindler knew and had published the story of Hitler's personal financing of *Tiefland*, the earlier court's findings that "not a single witness or document" could testify to a "close relationship between Frau Riefenstahl and Hitler" could hardly have withstood scrutiny. And that, in turn, might have led to a fuller comprehension of Leni's relationship to the party on *Olympia* and to a revised picture of the "coercion" involved in the making of *Triumph of the Will* and the other Nuremberg films.

Those questions would not go forever unanswered. Fresh court battles lay ahead, but the vital matter of her postwar classification was at last settled. Being a "fellow traveler" was more than she was ever willing to acknowledge publicly as a moral judgment, but it had one clear advantage: It carried no prohibitions or penalties whatever.

She was free to work again.

SIXTEEN

SURVIVOR

No one needs to know who I really am.

—Leni Riefenstahl

She is, after all, an actress.

—Friedrich Mainz

WITH MORE THAN HALF HER LIFE yet to live at midcentury, Leni believed she had outrun, even conquered, the notoriety of her past. She seldom missed an opportunity to aggrandize her postwar ordeal as an indication of her fitness and moral entitlement to take on challenges of the future. "Anyone like me," she said in 1951, "who spent years in prison, suffered rumors and trials and highly painful hearings—not to mention my activities as a potato peeler for the armies of occupation—will know how to overcome obstacles and opposition." But the challenges to come carried unfamiliar imperatives.

American and British military governments had early in the occupation enacted laws "to promote a healthy German film industry based on democratic principles." Goebbels's Ufi had been dismantled and reduced to a patchwork of underfunded companies struggling to cobble together private finance. Germans were divided by checkpoints and ideologies (though not yet by a Wall), and in the West, they debated the effects of materialism on German culture and the German soul even as they reveled in their "economic miracle."

Films from West Berlin, Munich, and Vienna repented the Nazi past in narratives more candid and probing than one might have predicted, or regressed into nostalgic costume epics about pretty, pre-Nazi empresses or inane musicals aimed at pubescent audiences with no idea who Leni Riefenstahl was. That she was a prodigious creative figure of high ambition compared to all but a few postwar filmmakers was a futile distinction. Few remembered her scrambling over glaciers in her Alpine films, and her directorial achievements—especially *Triumph of the Will*—were forbidden by a republic that banned images of the swastika in an attempt to erase all vestiges of National Socialism and prevent its return.

If Leni's work was all but impossible to view, her self-exoneration was on permanent display. She had relished her role near the center of a great historical drama and would not meekly relinquish the spotlight. She miscalculated the public mood in her claims of naïveté, assuming they would inspire sympathy and respect from those who claimed the same. In some quarters, they doubtless did, but most ordinary Germans trying to remake their lives did not want to be reminded of their own indifference and evasions. They knew shame and assumed that, as a privileged member of a privileged elite, she *must* have known something. As for her suffering, house arrest was not Dachau, and few of the *Trümmerfrauen*, housewives working in bucket brigades or filling wheelbarrows to clear rubble from city streets, equated her hardships with theirs.

She had boasted during a recess of the boisterous Gypsy trial that, though indigent and relying on legal aid, "her pockets were full of foreign contracts." This was face-saving bravado. She had received feelers about filming the 1952 Olympics but otherwise was idle in straitened circumstances with her ailing mother in Munich. To pay bills and keep up appearances, she tried to borrow money from former employees such as cameraman Richard Angst, who refused and rebuked her, or from film executives such as Friedrich Mainz, who loaned her ten thousand marks to purchase a top-floor apartment in an elegant new building in Schwabing, a flat she would use as her Munich residence and office to the end of her life.

Her belief that enemies took pleasure in her predicament was not paranoid fantasy, though she failed to intuit (or admit) how many of her present enemies were former associates. The quick rejections from Fanck, Angst, the Schneebergers, Rolf Lantin (who betrayed her to the French, telling them that everything in Kitzbühel had been paid for by Bormann and Hitler), and soon even faithful Waldi Traut signaled old grievances slow to die. They no longer had to subordinate their careers to her ambitions or sacrifice their egos to her narcissism. Comeuppance was satisfying.

As Friedrich Mainz put it, "She had no talent for making friends." He, like the others, admired her enormous gifts and acted as a character witness when she needed one. But his private judgment epitomized the ambivalence she aroused. "She spent millions and millions on nothing," he explained. "She made pictures that could not be budgeted because she always had a new idea or would wait for the right sky over the mountains." He thought her "*very* egocentric. She makes her own laws" but is "the best in the world of her kind. *Nobody* can do what she has done.

"She always had enemies because she was always fighting," he continued. "She mixes lies with truth and sometimes she is terrible, going on about money, money, money. . . . If you need something from her, she is sick. She had an accident or her mother is dying. Always something. But if she needs money, she is fresh as a god. And she is going to make *such* a picture! She is, after all, an actress."

Mainz knew her fawning and her rage and had the wary respect of one who has lived to tell the tale. Her tactics of allure titillated him as much as they exasperated him; he was convinced that her story of shrinking from Hitler's advances in 1932 was the opposite of what transpired in life. As her primary creditor, he viewed her stratagems with rueful resignation. "I asked my lawyer, 'Can I take her to court? She owes me 80,000 Marks.' And he said, 'You will win, but she will say she has no money. Then what can you do? You will wind up paying court costs and her lawyer.' "

Mainz's mixed feelings were widely shared. Even the most loyal of her longtime employees, production manager Waldi Traut, admitted, "She hasn't many friends. You can hate her if you have worked for her for many years because you are like a slave. She has a passion for film and there's no compromise. It's *her* way and if you are even a little intelligent you know it's not the only way. Perhaps, you think, it is the *wrong* way."

There were those, such as Harry Sokal, back from exile in America, who tempered their schadenfreude now that she seemed diminished. Leni was still outraged that he had sold the original negative of *The Blue Light* without paying her, though she never offered to share the proceeds of the 1938 rerelease from which she had removed his name. He was now in Munich producing a studio-based, papier-mâché remake of *Piz Palü* with Mainz. The picture starred Hans Albers, still Germany's biggest film star, and when Leni visited the studio to give advice on screen tests, Albers lashed out that he would not work as long as "that woman" was on the lot.

Sokal was hard-pressed to defend her. He had known her longer than anyone and thought "she still mourned the loss of the Führer and the Thousand Year Reich." But in spite of personal scars and professional resentments, he defended her talents. "I made pictures with her because she was an excellent collaborator," he said, and credited his producing career to what he had learned from her as *she* was learning.

He offered her three thousand marks for the remake rights to *The Blue Light* if she would withdraw the earlier version, but she refused, "unable to sacrifice my favorite film no matter how high the sum." Such a sacrifice would not remain forever unthinkable, but Sokal's offer was both paltry and an affront. And sparked a plan. *The Blue Light* had already been reworked once without the original negative, why not again? It could become activity and income, and—most important— remind the world that she had had a life and an art before Hitler.

She seized on the legend of Junta as the story of "my own destiny" as the innocent martyr persecuted by philistines unable to appreciate her dedication to art and beauty. The bombproof bunkers in Berlin, where much of her property had been stored since the end of the war, yielded everything she needed: 1,426 canisters of film, including a dupe negative and outtakes from the original *Blue Light*. She could edit a new version of the picture—and obtain, too, a new copyright that need not include her former partners Sokal, Schneeberger, or Balázs.

Energized and revitalized, she dusted off a ski film idea she had talked about since the early thirties, visualizing it now in color. At first, she toyed with a biographical picture about the skiing Lantschner brothers, Guzzi and Otto, and even hired a scriptwriter, though the brothers' card-carrying enthusiasm for the Nazis was an inconvenient story element. The notion evolved into something less likely to raise hostile eyebrows titled *The Red Devils* (*Die roten Teufel*), about a race featuring a famous ski team from Innsbruck (called "the red devils" because of their uniforms) and a female team from Norway she thought of as Amazons (in blue) and an Italian team (in yellow), tracing multicolored patterns in the snow while loudspeakers played music to pace their rhythms on the slopes. She boasted of it as a reworking of the old *Penthesilea* dream, as if adapting classical verse tragedy about love and death to romantic comedy on skis were not, as one observer put it, "positively grotesque."

Raising money on her name in Germany proved impossible. Even among the sympathetic, her never having been part of the industry was held against her, just as insiders deplored her reputation for extravagance and shied from her tainted past as if she were radioactive. The Italian industry was less skittish. It was also flush with investor confidence after the worldwide success of neorealists such as Roberto Rossellini and Vittorio De Sica, who had taken to the streets with nonprofessional actors to create such classics of anti- (or post-) fascist compassion as *Open City, The Bicycle Thief*, and *Umberto D.*

She could even shoot *The Red Devils* in Italy, in and around Cortina d'Ampezzo. She obtained seed money from private investors in Rome and started negotiating with hotels, location sites, and technicians even before she had the screenplay she assigned to her former assistant Harald Reinl and Joachim Bartsch. She colored her hair blond to give a lift to the approach of fifty and haunted Rome's Cinecittà, visiting film sets and being photographed in gold hoop earrings with Gina Lollobrigida and Vittorio De Sica. She told the Roman press that De Sica would act in her film alongside others yet to come, including a young and unknown Brigitte Bardot.

While waiting for the *Red Devils* script, she recruited Otto Lantschner to help prepare the new version of *The Blue Light* (with more money from Italy), using equipment loaned by Arri (Arnold & Richter), the Munich firm that had revolutionized cinematography in 1938 with its portable Arriflex camera. She installed editing tables and projectors in the Breitenhof Hotel in Thiersee in the Tyrol and went to work, not far from where she had shot the original picture twenty years earlier.

It was a new age of new tensions, but *The Blue Light* had never reflected any reality beyond Leni's fantasies. It had aspired to the poetic and the timeless, qualities that might—paradoxically in the gritty age of neorealism and the Cold War—seem aesthetically fresh again. "It was not made for the moment, to be forgotten again by tomorrow," she reminded the curious. "Perhaps romanticism will again overcome realism, haste, restlessness and the modern, technical tempo." She had rhapsodized twenty years earlier about "the redemption of realism . . . through romanticism" and now redeemed realism by eliminating it altogether.

She cut away the framing story in which contemporary urbanites arrived in Santa Maria in a touring car wearing goggles and dusters to be greeted by locals hawking souvenirs of the beautiful Junta. The excision was judicious: It removed details that dated the picture and did away with the merchandising of Junta's legend, which, with Leni everywhere identifying with Junta, might suggest the marketing of her own.

Press releases heralded *The Blue Light* as "a standard work in German film history," but the new version—shortened from eighty-six to seventy-three minutes—was a different work and effectively *re*wrote the history it graced. The names of "the Jewish element" had been long since erased, but in 1951, the picture acquired a new and irreducible possessory credit: "A Mountain Legend by Leni Riefenstahl."

Leni's Italian bankers presented the picture with its new edit, score, and sound track in Rome in November 1951 at what she called "a dazzling gala screening," but dazzle was not enough for a picture that had struck many as dated even in 1932. No Italian distributor expressed interest in a second showing. It finally opened in Germany in early April and ran briefly in Austria under the title *The Witch of Santa Maria* (*Die Hexe von Santa Maria*), which neatly undermined any interest students of film history might have had in the original work, which no longer existed anyway. *The Blue Light* flickered weakly as a nostalgic curiosity and went out. To add ironic insult to economic injury, the Italian bankers tried to sue her to recover their losses.

The Red Devils was still alive, but—suddenly and providentially—so was Leni's most substantial bid for future and reputation. After five years in Paris under the curatorial eye of Henri Langlois at the Cinémathèque Française, *Tiefland* was now in Vienna before the courts, entangled in competing bureaucratic claims that it was German—possibly Nazi—property seized by French authorities on Austrian soil. Leni's only hope for its recovery lay in establishing that it was hers, not the party's and certainly not Hitler's, which would have consigned it, like the copyright to *Mein Kampf* and the rest of the Führer's personal property, to the state of Bavaria, which administers it (and collects royalties) to the present day.

Leni had taken the precaution of filing a claim of ownership with the Bavarian Restitution Office and received confirmation "that no Party funds had been involved in my firm." This was technically correct. The analysis rested entirely on the documentation she supplied, which, though partial, enabled her to establish a provisional title claim. Austrian authorities, more open to her petitions than the French, released *Tiefland* to her in early 1953, eight years after she had last seen it in Kitzbühel.

When she inspected the hundreds of cans of film turned over to her in Vienna, she claimed it was a devastating blow to discover that four reels of negative were missing, perhaps stolen by the French, including footage she had shot in Spain. A trip to Paris and a scouring of the vaults of the Cinémathèque failed to turn up the bullfighting and drought sequences, and she said she was forced to assemble her long-delayed final cut without them.

Distribution agreements for Germany, Austria, and even America were negotiated while Leni and her assistants worked for months in up-to-the-minute cutting rooms provided by Arri a few blocks from her new flat in Munich. Herbert Windt, composer for *Olympia*, wrote a new score (replacing Becce's) incorporating themes from the opera on which the film was based and conducted recording sessions with the Vienna Philharmonic.

The world première of the ninety-nine-minute *Tiefland* took place in Stuttgart on February 11, 1954, fourteen years after the first camera had turned. Leni described it as a "dazzlingly festive" occasion on which she took "countless bows," though even she could see that what she had once described to Fanck as "dusty" was "long out of date." Her most agonizing disappointment came in observing herself on-screen as Martha. Her performance left her feeling "quite sick."

Surprisingly, she considered the critics' mixed reactions "objective" when she read them; a film made without conviction had not been saved by passionate intensity. Almost all reviewers acknowledged photographic effects of unusual beauty and praised her direction. Most of them tactfully ignored her work as an actress, but not all did. "When one sees her dancing here," an acerbic critic wrote, "one suspects that the world of ballet was only too happy to lose her to the world of film; when one sees her act, one concludes that, in fact, she should have stuck to ballet." A serious film journal, anticipating a theory yet to come, credited her "as an author, director and director of photography [*sic*] for achieving a perfect triad."

Tiefland's release inevitably reawakened speculation about her role in the Third Reich, especially with all those Gypsies on view. "No lie was too big," Leni railed about the tempest in the press, but she directed her litigious energies against her own distributors when they began canceling contracts due not to her renewed notoriety but to its inefficiency in filling empty cinema seats. Even so, the Association of Survivors of

Concentration Camps announced it would boycott the film no one was going to see. She accepted the challenge of meeting its representatives and produced affidavits, letters, and denazification documents to prove that rumors about slave labor and concentration camps were "inconsistent with the facts." This was enough to clear the way for a personal appearance tour in Austria by Leni and Franz Eichberger, her Vienna-born Pedro, which she recalled as "a roaring success."

If the tour was successful, *Tiefland* was not. Seen today, it is a kitsch curiosity, as nearly unwatchable as any film ever released by a world-class director. It is stylistically a silent film with sound effects, studded here and there with dialogue as basic as intertitles. It labors under a florid acting style from one-dimensional characters whose melodramatic lack of nuance defeats any sense of human dilemma or sympathy. It has moments of stunning photographic distinction—many—but the luminous compositions are beautiful backgrounds that pauperize their human foregrounds. One is reminded of a critique of Leni's early dance performances: In spite of the obsessive pains taken with costumes, sets, atmosphere, and photography, *Tiefland* lacks soul.

Leni's multiple functions add up less to a "perfect triad" than to a kind of unwitting self-sabotage. Filmmaking is a collaborative art, fashionable theories notwithstanding, and while Leni never shrank from erasing the fingerprints of collaborators, on *Tiefland* she came as close to total control as any director ever has. It is not unreasonable to judge the picture's lifelessness as the consequence of a "perfect quartet": a star, writer, producer, and director impervious to suggestion or criticism.

No work of such a tortured production history can escape lingering questions. Whether it would be a better or different film with the footage Leni claimed the French lost or stole (they denied her charges) is unknowable. What is curious is that she quietly deposited a quantity of unused *Tiefland* footage with the German national archives (*Bundesarchiv*), footage that has not been seen and remains sequestered. Speculation has suggested that it may contain Gypsy material that, after postwar charges and trials, seemed better removed but that the archivist in Leni-could not bear to think of as permanently lost or destroyed. Nothing is certain but that the film she envisioned is not the film that exists and the one we know offers, together with *The Blue Light,* little justification for mourning a career in dramatic filmmaking that ended with its failure.

Tiefland became something quite curious in a revisionist view of the 1990s. Apologists promoted a new reading that ignored its origin in preexisting material and saw its true value as psychobiography. In this view, the film is not failed melodrama but political allegory, nothing less than a subversive anti-Nazi film. The malevolent marquis is a Hitler figure and Martha a stand-in for Leni-the-repentant, an unfortunate tempted and ensnared by opportunism. The marquis's murder by good shepherd Pedro is an act of "tyrannicide." The notion plays on Hitler's code name—"Wolf"—and the on-screen predator of Pedro's sheep with whom the tyrant is visually identified. Pedro strangles one wolf to save his flock and throttles the other to save Germany. The message hidden in symbols is Leni's rejection of Hitler, an interpretation whose aptness may be judged by her astonishment—and stony silence—when she heard it.

But allegory and beauty depend on the beholder. When Jean Cocteau saw *Tiefland* in Munich, he was struck by its "Breughel-like intensity" and "the poetry of the camera." As chairman of the 1954 Cannes Film Festival jury, the aging enfant terrible tried to persuade the West German government to make the film its official entry and offered to write French subtitles for it himself. Bonn, unsurprisingly, expressed "very serious reservations" about its suitability "to represent the cinema of the Federal Republic of Germany." Cocteau, who had been accused of collaboration in Vichy France and was an extravagant admirer of Hitler's sculptor Arno Breker, screened the film out of competition, anyway, where it did not distract attention from the festival's most admired films, *Gate of Hell* from Japan and *From Here to Eternity* from the United States.

Cocteau told Leni, "You and I live in the wrong century," and proved it by proposing that he star for her in a costume film about Friedrich the

Great and Voltaire in which he would play both parts. Leni was delighted with the possibility of "satirical and effervescent dialogue" in French *and* German, but in the end, Cocteau settled for promoting his protégé and companion, Jean Marais, for the lead in *The Red Devils,* telling Leni that Marais was "the only man I can imagine in the role."

But the ski picture Leni planned as a "symphony of colors, rhythm and music" collapsed with the failures of the new *Blue Light* and *Tiefland,* and with reports that *The Red Devils'* financing would be supplemented by funds from Austrian taxpayers. Leni called this "a bare-faced lie," but it was not. Austrian permits and discounts for lodging and services were, in effect, subsidies extended by a conservative government in Vienna intimidated in the end by innuendos in the press that equated their support with that of Leni's previous political sponsor, also an Austrian.

She was in her early fifties now and, with her ex-husband's help, continued to care for her unwell mother. She persuaded underemployed writers to work on ideas no one wanted until, finally, frustrated by inactivity and indifference, she accepted an invitation from Günther Rahn, her old Berlin tennis pro of the twenties, to visit Spain. She packed her Leicas and a borrowed 16-millimeter Arriflex and drove herself and a secretary south and west, searching for a subject. She photographed the running of the bulls in Pamplona and monuments of Spanish architecture from Madrid to Majorca. She told reporters she was location scouting for a new dramatic film and told others that she wanted to make a documentary about Spain and call it *Sol y Sombra* or, perhaps, *Bullfights and Madonnas* (*Kampfstiere und Madonnen*). Spanish censors hinted that Franco's regime was unaccustomed to her kind of creative independence, and she returned to Munich, her passion for filmmaking alive but adrift.

The running of the bulls had suggested Hemingway, and, when his *Green Hills of Africa* was published in Germany, she devoured it overnight. The Dark Continent had long been an exotic lure. Udet had flown there; Dr. Morell, Hitler's physician who treated her during the war, had worked there; a cameraman who photographed her in *The Holy*

Mountain had roamed its savannas and veldts. More recently, Hemingway's *The Snows of Kilimanjaro* had been a hit film in 1952 with Gregory Peck and Ava Gardner (featuring Germany's young Hildegard Knef), and when Leni read a United Nations account of African slave trade in the twentieth century, she discovered a new and compelling subject for a comeback.

She persuaded Munich dancer-choreographer Helge Pawlinin and screenwriter Kurt Heuser to fashion a dramatic script: A female scientist in Africa (she would play the part) searches for her husband, who has gone missing on an anthropological expedition. Together with a British agent, she discovers that traders have murdered her husband and enslaved the primitive tribe among whom he lived. After freeing the natives, she and the agent are rewarded by them with the treasure her husband sought, a secret cave filled with ancient hieroglyphs revealing the tribe's history and beliefs.

The story line was a cobbling together of *S.O.S. Iceberg* and *The Blue Light*, but London's Anti-Slavery Society furnished her with research materials on Africa and the modern slave trade. A big-game hunter's popular nonfiction account of the same subject titled *Hassan's Black Cargo* supplied anecdotal details and a film title: *Black Cargo* (*Schwarze Fracht*).

"I was obsessed with my project," she said, and rashly persuaded herself that, with lightweight Arriflex cameras and a small crew, she could make a full-length color feature in 16 millimeter for two hundred thousand dollars, low enough to attract financing. With any luck, she might even reawaken interest in *The Red Devils*, a film she was determined not to abandon. She and Waldi Traut established Stern Film, in which Traut personally invested two hundred thousand marks (about fifty thousand dollars) as preproduction money, a figure that would double, while he tried to raise the balance from Gloria Film in Munich, where he was a house producer. Leni forged ahead, contracting with an English safari firm in Kenya that offered location services and equipment equal in value to Traut's investment. That the firm had handled operations for

Kilimanjaro and *King Solomon's Mines,* another big-scale international hit set in Africa, buttressed her optimism about *Black Cargo.*

She flew to Nairobi via Khartoum in April 1956 without script, financing, or budget, much as she had gone prematurely to Cortina five years earlier. On arrival, she was heady with euphoria that recalled her first view of the Alps. Far from "the plague of civilization," she felt "intoxicated, yet aware of everything," especially the faces and bodies of the natives, the first blacks she had encountered since filming Jesse Owens at the Olympics. "They seemed to float on a cushion of warm air," she said, her pictorial sensibilities fully engaged, "detached from the earth like a mirage. They moved in slow motion, the sun behind them. The black faces, swathed in white cloths, the relaxed, walking figures, their wide robes blowing about them, moved towards me as in a profound dream."

It was "a vision of strangeness and of freedom which affected me like a drug," but enchantment was shattered after a single day. The Land Rover her English guide was driving swerved to avoid a leaping antelope on the road from Nairobi to Somalia and careened off a bridge into the dry riverbed below, sending driver and passenger through the windshield. Leni suffered head injuries, broken ribs, and a punctured lung. After four agonizing days waiting for transportation, she was flown in critical condition back to Nairobi in a single-engine sport plane. She spent six weeks in the European Hospital regaining strength for "a new life." In June, she returned to Munich via Rome, hobbled by pain but convinced "I could uproot trees."

Her passion to conquer Africa was only slightly dimmed by Traut's report that Gloria Film's interest in *Black Cargo* hinged on tax credits that required the use of German actors for all roles, including those of natives. This was unacceptable (as was perhaps intended), but Leni had already begun exploring other sources in April, before leaving for Nairobi. She had cast her net in the unlikely direction of Hollywood.

She was still angry at her onetime publicity chief Ernst Jäger and his postdefection tabloid articles about her but overcame her bitterness to solicit his advice about money contacts in California. Interest in the subject matter was expressed by Paramount, though only for distribution, not production. By July, she had an American ally in Kurt Kreuger, a German-born, Swiss-raised actor she knew from Rome and Switzerland. Kreuger had built a minor Hollywood career playing handsome Nazis at Warner Bros. and Twentieth Century–Fox and was, like Leni, an athlete and a skier. She offered him the leading male role in *Black Cargo* if he could deliver financing through his American contacts. She dangled before him a role in *The Red Devils* as well.

Kreuger knew financing was impossible without a completed script and guarantee of distribution, though, to his surprise, interest in the skiing film materialized almost at once. He found distributors ("fully Jewish, by the way," he wrote her) willing to buy or invest in *The Red Devils* on condition that she remove her name from it. He told her that Paul Kohner had gotten wind of her attempts to raise Hollywood money, and "you can imagine what *that* let loose." To facilitate financing stymied by mere mention of her name, she insisted over Kreuger's objections that he identify her as "Helene Jacob," the name on her passport. "No one needs to know who I really am."

An executive at Universal Studios named John Bash quickly expressed interest in *Black Cargo* if "Helene Jacob" would agree to a second, English-language version with an American cast—including leading lady—and an American director working from a screenplay Universal could preapprove. The screenwriter would be Robert Hill, who had written a steamy B picture for Universal and Joan Crawford called *Female on the Beach*. Universal proposed a letter of credit for $50,000 (which could be borrowed against) toward the now projected budget of $175,000. A list of suggested names and figures followed:

American director (Victor Stoloff, an assistant of German-born director William Dieterle): $5,000
American actress (Viveca Lindfors, Signe Hasso, or Andrea King—none of them born in America): $3,000
Travel expenses: $8,000

Housing and expenses: $8,400
Script (by Robert Hill): $3,000

Leni was slightly abashed, as she had convinced herself the actresses would include Ingrid Bergman and Katharine Hepburn. These meager numbers hinted at the level of Universal's enthusiasm and did not include finder fees or acting and coproducing fees for Kreuger. At a total of $27,400, Universal's conditions consumed more than half its proposed investment and upended the nature of the production. This was the clash of corporate financing and creative control that Leni had been able to circumvent all her professional life, made more galling by the subterfuge of anonymity she felt forced to hide behind. Nevertheless, she was prepared to move forward with the deal if Universal would bear the cost of its own conditions outside of her original budget and guarantee her 100 percent of the revenues from German-speaking territories, with a fifty-fifty split from the rest of the world.

Having agreed in principle, she returned to Africa in early August, taking two German cameramen with her. Inside of a month, they had exposed ten thousand feet of color film in Uganda, Zanzibar, and on the Kenyan island of Lamu in the Indian Ocean, mostly landscape and animal footage with doubles standing in for actors who could later be cut into the colorful footage. Without a signed deal from Universal, this was impulsive, even reckless, but for most of her life, she had willed or raged obstacles away, and the results had almost always justified the leaps of faith.

"Africa had embraced me—forever," she exulted. Her fascination with the natives made her eager to begin casting and photographing them in Nairobi. The area was teeming with restless Mau-Mau and Masai warriors, whose "unapproachable arrogance" stimulated and challenged her. She overcame their mistrust in isolated tribal visits and persuaded a dozen of them in and around Mombasa to accept clothing and trinkets as good-faith payment for services to be rendered at the base location near Nairobi.

The natives seemed unsure that the white woman with a camera was not selling them into the very slavery her film intended to expose. They were bewildered by the mysterious filmmaking equipment and refused to expose themselves to crocodiles and bathing elephants when Leni improvised scenes she was confident she could somehow work into the script. She was not asking them to do anything more dangerous than the mountain stunts she had performed thirty years earlier under Fanck, and she found their reluctance to endanger themselves for her incomprehensible.

By the end of September, war had broken out in the Suez Canal zone, delaying equipment en route from Germany and setting her back weeks, still without a full script or financing. Not until November could shooting begin in Queen Elizabeth National Park in Uganda, where bad weather and unrest among native extras added to pressures aroused by Traut's increasingly urgent cables requesting footage to show potential backers. Defections of the natives in the dead of night stopped production cold.

Traut cabled that the money—all of it his—had run out. There was barely enough left to get Leni back to Munich and none to transport her crew. The English safari company reconsidered its commitment and bailed out, seizing cameras, lighting equipment, and fifty thousand feet of unexposed film stock as security.

Leni returned to Munich in a state of collapse. Hospitalized with a "nervous condition," she was given tranquilizer injections and narrowly escaped addiction to the morphine administered to ease pain from the Land Rover accident and her perennial stress ailments. Traut's funds were exhausted, and Universal's remained just out of reach. John Bash insisted on coming to Munich to see footage before finalizing the deal, now redefined as a negative pickup, in which the letter of credit was useless, as it could not be issued until delivery of the full negative.

Even from a hospital bed, Leni refused to entertain the notion of defeat, certainly not one she was responsible for at any rate. She admitted she had "been wrong to think that one could shoot a feature in Africa on our shoestring budget," but she was a victim, more sinned against than sinning. She indignantly attributed the collapse of *Black Cargo* to "a Judas in the person of a production manager" hired by Traut who fired off "venomous remarks" to Munich that "blamed all the problems on me, saying I was over demanding and claiming that the film could be salvaged only if I were fired as producer and director."

Traut had needed no reports from the front lines to tell him that his investment was driving him to what he later termed "financial death." His years of loyalty gave way to bitterness: "She didn't feel it; she doesn't know it; she doesn't *want* to know it," he insisted. He had indulged her because he believed in her as an artist but knew, as a skilled manager, that her reputation for organization was mythical. It was confined to the minutiae of photographic techniques and editing or to the deployment of resources so vast that they obscured waste or profligacy. But in production, where time ruled everything, she was willful and arbitrary. Even under the Nazis, he reflected, "She had all the possibilities and all the money, but the way she works is too expensive because she takes too long. *She needs time.* And nobody can tell her how to make a picture."

Traut was injured in a near-fatal automobile accident shortly after Leni's return from Africa, releasing him from a ruinous lost cause. Leni exchanged ever more desperate letters and cables with Kreuger in Beverly Hills about Universal or other backers who might yet save *Black Cargo*, but no one would invest without a completion guarantee, a standard but expensive insurance policy to supply finishing funds even if the budget ran out. In February 1957, Universal revised its potential investment upward to seventy-five thousand dollars, but with Traut's money gone and no other investors on any horizon, *Black Cargo* sank and, with it, any lingering hope of resuscitating *The Red Devils*.

Not all was lost. Almost two years later, Kreuger cabled Leni that a major Hollywood firm was interested in buying her African footage. The firm was MGM, then preparing *Tarzan, the Ape Man* to star UCLA basketball player Denny Miller with a script by the same Robert Hill who was to have rewritten *Black Cargo*. The producer wanted Leni's African footage for rear-projection use before jungle sets in Culver City. Leni authorized Kreuger to negotiate and, if possible, get her a job at MGM shooting additional footage, anonymously if necessary. The deal was abruptly canceled when someone at MGM realized who "Helene Jacob" was. *Tarzan, the Ape Man* used outtakes from *King Solomon's Mines* instead.

She had had two fiascoes in a row and had made a shambles of an ill-conceived low-budget feature. Her desk drawer contained other projects she had toyed with or talked about over the years—a van Gogh picture about "how a genius expresses himself," and a script titled *Three Stars on the Cloak of the Madonna* for Italian actress Anna Magnani, whom she'd met in Rome. Magnani turned Leni down in favor of Tennessee Williams. She went to Hollywood to work opposite Marlon Brando in *The Fugitive Kind* and Burt Lancaster in *The Rose Tattoo*, for which she won a Best Actress Academy Award.

Leni's options had dwindled. There was one possibility she refused to credit but could no longer ignore. It was spelled out to her in a stark letter from her German distributor at the time of the Austrian flap over *The Red Devils*. "The opposition to you, personally," it read, "is so strong that—forgive me for telling you the truth—you can never practice your profession again."

SEVENTEEN

COMEBACK

Leni Riefenstahl is one of the greatest filmmakers in the world, and certainly the greatest female filmmaker in history.

—John Grierson

She is a monument. She is a mountain. She is a genius.

—Jonas Mekas

"THERE MUST BE AN ORGANIZATION," Leni decided, and expanded on this theme in 1971 to an American admirer. "And this organization is very powerful. And this organization was against me in 1938 in Hollywood. This organization is made up of Jewish people, yes? I think they have a blacklist. And on this list is my name."

But any blacklist, formal or informal, had long since expired. Her gifts, ambitions, and need for vindication had not. She always felt most creative when "a new life" beckoned as escape from the martyrdom of an old, and Africa, the arena of the newest of her lives, asked no questions, hurled no charges, and permitted her to shed her skin. "When I am in Africa I am a different person," she explained. "My vitality returns. I am freed from the here and now to do what I want." Returning there after the debacle of *Black Cargo* would require ingenuity, but she had spent much of her life "making the impossible possible," and, as sixty approached, she was determined to do so again.

If the films that made her famous were banned in her homeland, the world beyond stirred with curiosity. Not even her harshest critics denied her achievements; it was the power of her work that perpetuated opposition to it and kept it alive. *Triumph of the Will* played for eight months in a single cinema in San Francisco in the 1950s. A long run at the New Yorker theater on Manhattan's heavily Jewish Upper West Side roused more unease than protest, though someone tried to burn down an exit door. When Venice held a Riefenstahl retrospective in 1959, admirers thronged the Lido as they had in the Mussolini heydays of the 1930s.

Olympia, now almost two decades old and never as controversial as *Triumph of the Will*, had been largely unseen in English-speaking countries (it played briefly in New York in 1940) and was for many a revelation of powerfully innovative film technique when screened at New York's Museum of Modern Art in 1955, minus three minutes of Hitler footage Leni had agreed to excise for West German television ("to make some money," she told a friend). An American critic hailed it as "history, aestheticized," and the expurgated version elicited similar responses in London. It achieved classic status the same year when American film directors, many of whom had boycotted its exhibition in 1938, named it one of the ten best films ever made, alongside *Battleship Potemkin* and *Citizen Kane*.

Among those most eager to reevaluate Leni's work after *Olympia* played in England were the cinéastes at London's British Film Institute. In April 1960, they invited her to lecture at the National Film Theatre on "My Work in Films" as part of a series of celebrity screenings that was ecumenical enough to include leftist director Ivor Montagu, winner of the Lenin Peace Prize, and actor Peter Sellers, not yet an international star and known mostly for *The Goon Show*.

Leni's inclusion may have guaranteed controversy (Montagu withdrew; Sellers did not), but the storms of dissent would have been less indignant had the biographical material sent out about her not avoided any mention of *Triumph of the Will*, an oversight that could hardly have looked more devious. Montagu publicly denounced *Triumph* as "that brilliant, but evil, obsequious and blood-curdling piece of hero-worship." A spokesman for the National Film Theatre countered with bravado that "Satan himself is welcome at the NFT, provided he makes good pictures." Outbreaks of swastika graffiti and the vandalizing of Jewish graves in London and Manchester aroused alarm, causing the BFI to withdraw its invitation in the interests of "public safety," a move that looked craven and inspired fresh choruses of disapproval or defense.

Among Leni's defenders was the venerable documentarian John Grierson. He announced that during the war, as a propagandist for the British, he, like Luis Buñuel in America, had attempted to recut Leni's Nuremberg films to turn their imagery against the Nazis and came away awed by their artistry. He frankly labeled Leni "the propagandist for Germany" but offered to show reels of *Olympia* on Scottish television (and did) to demonstrate that she was "one of the greatest filmmakers in the world, and certainly the greatest female filmmaker in history."

Leni's response to the withdrawal of the BFI's invitation was uncharacteristically muted. She claimed that she "did not care to go where I was not wanted," though she inundated the British press with affidavits and denazification documents. Privately, her lawyers put the BFI on notice (inaccurately) that she held the copyright to her films and that screening them without her consent would trigger "appropriate proceedings." Much more was at stake than a BFI speaking engagement.

A few months earlier, a young film editor named Philip Hudsmith had contacted her with an ambitious plan to remake *The Blue Light* in the style of *The Red Shoes*, which had sparked international interest in ballet films. Hudsmith, who had worked on a film about the Bolshoi, offered her thirty thousand pounds plus 25 percent of the profits and promised a production in color and wide screen with a script by W. Somerset Maugham.

A plan to adapt *The Blue Light* into a ballet for the stage in Paris had fallen through two years earlier, sabotaged, Leni reported darkly, by "an influential person." But her anxieties about the scenic and economic constraints of theater had led to her writing worried analyses that looked to Paris like meddling. A film, it was clear, need not suffer from limitations of proscenium or spectators. Maugham, in his early eighties, declined the script assignment, and the job went to L. Ron Hubbard, an American living in England. Hubbard was touted as having written major scripts in Hollywood, though his official résumé boasted only shared credits on Poverty Row serials of the 1930s such as *The Great Adventures of Wild Bill Hickok*. His controversial distinction as science fiction writer and the founder of Scientology lay in the future, but he had a comfortable flat in London where Leni was welcome to stay and advise on the script he would write with Hudsmith.

Hubbard mysteriously decamped to South Africa on other business, leaving Leni and Hudsmith to tailor a screenplay for Italian actress Pier Angeli in Leni's old role and Lithuanian-born actor Laurence Harvey as Vigo. When not in London, Leni kept busy bringing libel suits against publishers on the Continent, usually settling out of court for unreported sums and retractions of the familiar charges that she had been a Nazi or Hitler's mistress. Among her litigation targets was the French publisher Plon, which issued an Adolf Eichmann biography claiming she had made documentaries in death camps. This new charge, though wholly invented, was inflammatory enough in the wake of the BFI controversy to threaten the work permit for *The Blue Light* that Leni was required to obtain from the British government.

She succeeded in getting a temporary injunction against the Eichmann book in Paris, her lawsuit financed by Hudsmith, and returned to England to meet John Grierson after his defense of her on television. He reportedly kissed her foot in public and urged her to use the money he was paying her for *Olympia* excerpts to sue London's *Daily Mirror* and its columnist "Cassandra" after they recycled charges (complete with photographs) about Konskie. Leni hired solicitors in London, one of whom "refused to believe I had known nothing about the extermination camps [until] I lost my temper and furiously jumped at his throat." She later said she settled out of court with the *Daily Mirror,* but this was untrue: British courts found her charges "groundless" and dismissed them.

Hudsmith, meanwhile, pleaded with her to meet the British press face-to-face to counter allegations that endangered issuance of her work permit, which required trade union consent. At a press conference in December, London's *Evening Standard* thought she appeared "pathetically anxious to win approval." The event was abruptly terminated when a reporter refused to shake the hand that had shaken Hitler's and she broke down in tears, sobbing that everything written about her was "lies, all lies." The *Standard* remarked that, however unhappy or well meaning she might be today, she was "responsible for one of the most morally perverted films ever made." Such "unfortunate scenes need not be repeated," the *Standard* lectured, "if Fraulein Riefenstahl would go back to Germany and stay there."

"Everywhere else in the world I am accepted as an artist," she lamented. "But in England, no! In England any German who did not actually kill Hitler is still regarded as a Nazi criminal!"

The BBC had earlier produced a forty-five-minute television interview with Leni in conversation with Derek Prouse that was aired in England shortly after the disastrous press conference. Attempting to create clarity, it merely aroused fresh criticism for publicizing "this Ophelia among the storm troopers." If even the BBC came under fire for consorting with her, trade union approval for her work permit was out of the question. *The Blue Light* ballet film withered in the glare of hostile public opinion. A newspaper in Germany seemed to approve: "The denials came too late and tears were no argument."

Fifteen years into the postwar era, it was clear that the centerpiece of her life's work would accompany her to the end like some awful celluloid albatross. While the achievements of others were touchstones for awards and retrospectives, hers were turned against her. To make matters worse, others were profiting from them while she remained humiliated and unemployed, a casualty of fate deprived of honor and income.

Excerpts from *Triumph of the Will* had been turning up since the early fifties in films about the Nazis. English film historian Paul Rotha, a fierce detractor who grudgingly called Leni "one of the most brilliant [talents] ever to be concerned with film," paid her for footage he used in a documentary about Hitler. In 1953, a German film titled *Until Five Past Twelve* (*Bis fünf nach zwölf*) incorporated scenes from *Triumph,* causing Leni to sue for compensation. She received a small settlement, which she said she donated to charity for repatriated prisoners of war.

In 1960, however, a Swedish film by Erwin Leiser played to large audiences in Germany under the title *Mein Kampf* and made extensive use of footage from *Triumph of the Will.* Leni was observed in a Munich cinema with her cutter, secretary, and a stopwatch, clocking shots that she claimed totaled more than two thousand feet (about twenty minutes), though they amounted to a little more than half as much. That Leiser's film was a denunciation of everything Leni's film glorified might have induced quiet circumspection, but she was incensed that "*Mein Kampf* was a box-office hit—at least partly with the help of my footage." She sued, demanding one hundred thousand marks and 10 percent of the profits.

That "my financial problems were acute" seemed justification enough. She was responsible for her own and her mother's medical bills, had debts that were long overdue, and any return to Africa was stalled without funds. Her suit claimed that *Triumph of the Will* was her copyrighted property, and she won a temporary injunction against *Mein Kampf*'s German distributor. The Swedish company that produced the film, Minerva, derided her claim, saying "they had no need to buy anything from the beneficiaries of the Third Reich in order to make a film about that Third Reich." The German distributor, loath to withdraw a solid hit, voluntarily agreed to pay her thirty thousand marks for Germany and another five thousand for Austria, but her suit against Minerva remained unresolved. To pay debts (including five hundred marks owed to Fanck, who was threatening to take her to court), she assigned future proceeds in the *Minerva* suit to Friedrich Mainz, canceling her debts to him and ensuring he would carry the case—and its costs—forward.

A technical issue of copyright infringement might normally have gone unnoticed. But because it concerned Leni and *Triumph of the Will*, it excited the press, which detected whiffs of greed. Headlines spoke of "The Reward for Immorality" and "Dirty Money," or caustically referred to "Her Struggle" ("Ihr Kampf"). A Berlin daily styled her "the poet laureate of the Nazi regime" and wondered why she "did not just go quietly home and hide her shame." A Frankfurt editorial deplored her "lack of political and moral instinct," while a Swedish daily pointed out her "want of remorse." The broad consensus held that she not only refused to repudiate her past but was capitalizing on it, once again making—or trying to make—money from the Nazi Party.

Litigation in the *Minerva* case crawled at a bureaucratic pace, complicated by West Germany's refusal to recognize copyrights on films produced by the Reich. It had created a firm called Transit-Film GmbH to administer such films on behalf of the Federal Republic. After examining the documentation on *Triumph,* Germany's highest court ruled irreversibly that the party—not Leni—had produced the picture (as the credits clearly stated) and that all rights therefore resided with Transit.

Leni was "stunned" by what she termed "a miscarriage of justice"* and later devoted an entire chapter of her memoirs to disputing the court's finding. She attempted to frame the argument around who *made* the film rather than who owned it, though her creative responsibility had never been at issue and, to many observers, confirmed the moral case against her. She produced witnesses and affidavits during the hearings to misrepresent the roles of Ufa and the propaganda ministry, none more ironic than Arnold Raether, the erstwhile lieutenant of Goebbels's who had insisted in 1933 that Hess investigate rumors about Leni's ancestry. Raether submitted that *Triumph* could not have been a party production because he, in his official capacity under Goebbels, would have had to approve it, thus sliding over Hitler's personal commissioning of the picture, which made Goebbels, the propaganda ministry, and his own bureaucratic function irrelevant.

The vital issue had nothing to do with authorship and everything to do with distribution and exploitation rights. Both were tied to copyright and, as a result of the *Minerva* decision, were assigned to Transit, which held similar rights to *Olympia*, granted after the television broadcast for which Leni had agreed to cut images of Hitler surrounded by swastikas.

Olympia was a more critical issue than *Triumph* because its commercial value was greater and because it mitigated the notion that Leni was nothing more than the Führer's glorifier. Questions about it were freighted because the International Olympic Committee had been blind to the Third Reich's sponsorship of the film. Olympic officials such as Dr. Diem, who had urged her to accept the 1936 assignment in the first place, testified on her behalf and presumably did so in good faith. They had themselves been duped, unaware that Goebbels's meticulous files would expose Leni's Olympia Film Company as a sham "founded on the instigation of the Reich and with funds provided by the Reich," which did "not wish to be seen openly as the maker of the film." Such "irrefutable evidence," the court ruled, proved "that the copyrights and exploitation rights to the Olympia films were really held by the German Reich, and that [Leni Riefenstahl] only held the shares to Olympia-Film in trust."

Leni wanted to know, "What kind of people were they to be denying my ownership of *Olympia* after thirty years!" having forgotten, perhaps, that she had signed away all rights in 1942 in return for 20 percent of the Reich's profits. When confronted with the paper trail of "irrefutable evidence," she claimed she had never seen the documents in question, or they were fictional, or they had been prepared by Goebbels as a tax dodge on her behalf that she had never understood.

Transit won decisively with both *Triumph of the Will* and *Olympia*. Leni's ownership rights were nonexistent and her moral claim to autonomy vis-à-vis the party seriously impaired, if not in ruins. Which is what made the sequel to the legal wrangling so extraordinary. In spite of the courts' irreversible rulings, Transit contracted with Leni, stipulating, "Both parties pledge to keep the contents of this agreement secret."

Transit had won something it didn't want, much as the state of Bavaria rued its role as de facto literary agent for Hitler's *Mein Kampf*. The Federal

Republic of Germany sought to distance itself from its Nazi predecessors, not identify with them by exploiting works as tainted as *Triumph of the Will*. Though forbidden for exhibition at home, *Triumph*'s exploitation abroad—complete or in excerpts—could provoke the same charges of profiteering that the press had leveled at Leni, or worse. *Olympia* was a lesser problem of political public relations, but one compromised by the documentation that Leni's claims of obliviousness failed to rewrite.

Transit's self-extrication from this dilemma (and from the prospect of ongoing confrontations with a litigious filmmaker) was bizarre but pragmatic. In early 1964, a secret agreement was reached giving Leni the right *"to describe herself* [italics added] as the owner of the exploitation rights [to *Olympia*] when signing contracts relating to exploitation." Transit (that is, the Federal Republic) retained copyright, and Leni's new rights were to expire in thirty years, or in 1994, though they remained in force until after her death in 2003, when the International Olympic Committee acquired rights to the film from the German government for a reported two million dollars. In the meantime, Leni received 70 percent of all profits, with 30 percent going to Transit.

Triumph of the Will was dealt with in a separate agreement in 1974. Profit participation was moot in Leni's homeland because of the exhibition ban, but beyond German borders there was no such prohibition, and she was able to make minor recdits in the film and, on the basis of revisions and new subtitles, obtain fresh copyright in her name in the United States, enforceable around the world.

The advantage she gained regarding *Triumph* at home was control. The exhibition ban had exceptions for institutional purposes that, under the Transit agreement, could not be invoked without her express permission. In 1979, for example, she was able to bar Germany's liberal Free Democratic Party (FDP) from showing it as part of a program condemning the rise of neo-Nazism. When she did agree to its exhibition at film museums or universities, she dispatched emissaries to mingle with the crowds and monitor remarks made by programmers that might require rebuttal or fresh rounds of litigation.

These lucrative victories ensured a stream of income for the rest of her life, but the decades of unsympathetic scrutiny—or frank revelations— by the courts and press amounted, she said, to "systematic character assassination" and made her feel she had been "crawling about in the dirty mire of human nastiness." Escape beckoned undiminished from Africa, one of the few places on the planet where the past did not matter, where "nobody knows that I am Leni Riefenstahl."

What she would do there after the collapse of *Black Cargo* in the 1950s was unclear. A brief flurry of activity in 1961 swirled around a low-budget documentary about the Nile to be financed by Japanese entrepreneurs, but the erection of the Berlin Wall brought business reversals that forced them back to Tokyo. She tried and failed to get financing from Goebbels's stepson Harald Quandt of BMW and from Alfried Krupp von Bohlen und Halbach of the Krupp armaments dynasty. She tried to raise funds from Adolf Vogel, the Salzburg "salt king" who built her apartment house in Schwabing, and from Emmy Whitehead, the Coca-Cola millionairess she knew from Berlin and her American *Olympia* tour. Finally, she got a travel loan from the German distributor who had told her she would never work again. It would prove an investment with dividends.

She was, she allowed, "Africa crazy." Her fascination with "the dark, mysterious and still barely explored continent" had been kept alive over the years by a photograph she said she had torn from a copy of the German weekly *Stern* during her recovery from the Land Rover accident in Nairobi. But that was in 1956, and she had seen the photograph and quietly tracked down its maker half a decade earlier. It pictured a majestic African athlete, naked but for a single earring, riding on the shoulders of his defeated rival after a tribal wrestling match. It was black and white and had the heroic, erotic force of the Olympics photographs of 1936. The naked tribesmen looked "like a sculpture by Rodin or Michelangelo."

The photograph had been published in *National Geographic* in 1951, the work of George Rodger, the British photojournalist who cofounded Magnum with Robert Capa and Henri Cartier-Bresson. Rodger had been the first photographer to enter Bergen-Belsen in 1945; after six years covering the war for *Life* magazine, he found himself "subconsciously arranging groups and bodies on the ground into artistic compositions in the viewfinder . . . treating this pitiful human flotsam as if it were some gigantic still life." Shocked at his aestheticizing of the Holocaust ("so horrific that pictures were not justified"), he renounced war photography and turned to Africa, to "get rid of the stench of war that was still in me."

His portrait of wrestlers resulted from that retreat and so struck Leni that she wrote him in 1951, offering a thousand dollars if he would introduce her to his subjects. He wrote back: "Dear Madam, knowing your background and mine I don't really have anything to say to you at all."

Leni never mentioned the offer she made to Rodger, though she acknowledged his impact on her imagination, and it is not impossible that it had sparked the obsessiveness with which she worked on *Black Cargo*. His photograph served her self-narrative as the equivalent of the dream images she tirelessly cited as catalyzing inspirations for *The Blue Light* and for the prologue to *Olympia*. Apart from a caption identifying the wrestlers as Nuba tribesmen of Kordofan Province in Sudan, "there was no other information," she said. Leaving her ailing mother in the care of her ex-husband, she set out at sixty "to track down the Nuba."

There was, in fact, considerable information available, including the maps and text accompanying Rodger's Nuba photos in *National Geographic* and the book he published about them in 1955. There were numerous well-known scholarly works about the Nuba, and even Merian C. Cooper, the creator of *King Kong*, had published an extended photo-essay about them in *National Geographic* in 1929.

The various Nuba tribes lived a few degrees north of the equator, south of Khartoum and east of Darfur in highland villages that were isolated and remote; they had, from tribe to tribe, different languages, rituals of mating, manhood, and death. The Nuba of Kordofan Province (the Mesakin Qsar Nuba that Rodger had photographed) lived in thatched-roof mud huts perched in crannies of the red granite hills they had retreated to centuries earlier to escape slave traders. They were strong, lithe, and peaceful (Cooper thought them "dirty, savage, and suspicious"). They lived as farmers, raising cattle and goats and planting sorghum, tobacco, peppers, and beans. They decorated their shaven bodies with ash, oil, paint, and elaborate scar-tattoos, and made music on drums, lyres, and animal horns.

The end of joint British-Egyptian administration of Sudan in the mid-1950s threatened their indigenous culture. The detribalizing Arab-Islamic influence of the successor regime was well under way when Leni arrived in 1962, Rodger's now-famous photo in hand. An official glanced at it and brusquely informed her, "You are ten years too late."

More eager than ever to locate them, she despaired that "not even a travel bureau could tell me how to reach the Nuba," but Dr. Oskar Luz of the University of Tübingen could and did. An anthropologist and founder of the German Nansen Society (named for Norwegian explorer Fridtjof Nansen), Luz was then mounting a five-man expedition "to make a record of the primitive cultures of the Nuba people before progress further impairs their way of life" and "to make the information collected available to scientists and research institutions." Leni met with Luz. She later claimed she had "no notion other than to get to know the people," but she had already commissioned Kurt Kreuger to raise sixty thousand dollars in Hollywood for a 35-millimeter color film about a people she had never seen except in Rodger's photograph and—not for the first time—before she had a script or clear idea of what her film would be. She secured a berth with the Nansen expedition by promising them 30 percent of her profits, which she wrote Kreuger seemed "a very good deal."

The Nansen expedition, partially underwritten by Lufthansa, left for Khartoum in September 1962. Leni followed in November, but without the funds she had hoped to raise in the meantime and without the 35-millimeter cinema cameras Luz insisted were too bulky for vehicles loaded with provisions. She would have to make do with stills and leave motion pictures to Luz's son Horst, an architect acting as the expedition's photographer.

The team was delayed in Khartoum by rain, a period of frustrating idleness during which Leni toured bazaars, marveled at minarets, dined with German diplomats and expatriates, and cultivated Sudan's minister of tourism, Ahmed Abu Bakr, the key to travel permits and political favors. She noted that Luz and his son were "usually grumpy and unfriendly." When the rains ended in December and the expedition left for the interior, Leni volunteered her expertise to young Luz as he manned his movie camera. She was taken aback that "all he said was he wouldn't work with me: He took the camera off the tripod, packed up everything, and left me standing there."

As the sole woman among scientists, she may have stirred some sexist resentment, but her independence was disruptive. Her fervent search for images of "what is beautiful, strong, healthy," conflicted with the anthropologists' goals of methodical, unmediated documentation. She was open about her disinterest in natives wearing ragged, Islamic-issue gym shorts that made them look "no different from the blacks in the big cities." The ideal she had preconceived finally appeared in the Eden of the Nuba hills: "A young girl sat on a boulder, swinging a switch. She was naked. Only a string of red beads adorned her black body. She stared at us, terrified, scared, and vanished into the bushes like a gazelle." Oskar Luz thought the girl looked like a girl: "a black nymph on a pedestal."

Leni's dramatic sense of imagery permeates her journal's version of what she saw next: "One or two thousand people are swaying in the light of the setting sun in an open space surrounded by many trees. Strangely painted, fantastically adorned, they appear like creatures from another planet." In Luz's calmer and less artful account of the same moment, expedition members merely walked to a cluster of huts and introduced themselves to the village elders with the aid of a tape-recorded message that explained their purpose in the local dialect.

The expedition had been officially cautioned against exploiting Nuba nudity, but nudity was an inescapable, if not invariable, fact of village life, and Leni ignored the warning, as did Horst Luz. Young Luz mostly documented mud-hut architecture, pottery making, farming, and other aspects of daily life, while Leni, asserting that "what is average [and] quotidian doesn't interest me," sought out colorful rituals of tribal dancing, wrestling, bloody body tattooing, and funerals. Leni's and Luz's subjects sometimes overlapped: Individual natives recur in their photographs with subtle but striking differences. Luz's work documents; Leni's dramatizes and transforms. She spoke of a "tableau" here and "a thrilling motif" there and, on one occasion, described "an army camp of fantastically adorned people—an endless tide of flags and spears," which sounded uncannily like an image from her European past.

To the Nansen Society, Leni's pursuit of tableaux and motifs was intrusive and unprofessional and resulted in an "angry argument" with Oskar Luz in full view of the bewildered Nuba. By the end of the expedition, she had stopped speaking to the Nansen group, and they to her, the relationship "shattered." Leni stayed on in Africa for another eight months, learning enough Nuba dialect to make friends of natives willing to pose for her cameras in exchange for beads and other trinkets she did not regard as payment or bribes. They called her "Leni," taught her native dance, and made her promise to return when she left in August 1963. There would be a curious postscript in 1966: a twenty-eight-page account by Oskar Luz in *National Geographic*, handsomely illustrated by Horst Luz's color photographs. The article alluded in not a single syllable to Leni's presence during the expedition's seven weeks in the Nuba hills.

The collaboration of celebrity filmmaker and anthropologists had been curious from the start and was not the last of its kind. Two years later, she would make a similar alliance with Robert Gardner of Harvard, whom she met on an Ibiza holiday after her second trip to Sudan and who had made groundbreaking ethnographic documentaries in Africa and New Guinea. When she accepted Gardner's invitation to lecture on her Nuba photographs at Harvard's Visual Arts Center, she persuaded him to join her in a partnership to distribute her old films in America and raise funds for her Nuba documentary. In the meantime, Milton Fruchtman, head of Odyssey Productions in New York, advanced sixty thousand marks for production and pledged postproduction costs and financing for three more films to be shot in color and CinemaScope. "It was the chance of a lifetime," Leni exulted, but one that collapsed when she was unable to deliver the Nuba film on schedule.

Gardner observed ruefully that "she couldn't collaborate with anybody." On Ibiza, he had seen "the charm of an eager child . . . unencumbered by doubt." He thought her "gullible and self-centered" but "gentle." Their brief association exposed him to her cajoling and weeping on cue when she wanted something, and he reminded himself, as others had done, "She is an actress." He concluded many years later that he had "admiration for the technical (optical) quality of some of her work, but no enthusiasm whatever for her as an artist." In the end, he altered his earlier view that she was "gentle" to "Oh, she's tough."

Toughness had served her well from the tenements of Wedding forward and was vital now, for Leni was truly alone for the first time in her life. During a second brief visit to the Nuba, her mother died in Munich, her heart weakened by a long struggle with cancer. Leni broke off her safari and returned to Germany in January 1965, arriving four days after the funeral. Bertha had been the one absolute in her life, both goad and coconspirator since the days of defying Alfred in Leni's adolescence. Bertha was the enabler—unconditional and steadfast—and may have been the only person Leni ever loved without reservation because Bertha loved *her* without reservation. She mourned the maternal loss as "one of the worst blows ever dealt to me by fate" and lamented that "I couldn't envision life without my mother." A week later, as Bertha might have applauded, she was back in Africa.

There could be no successor to Bertha, but a substitute for her uncritical constancy appeared in 1968, as Leni was preparing yet another trip to Africa. Horst Kettner was tall, slim, blond, and twenty-four years old. He spoke halting German, having been raised in Czechoslovakia by German parents, and had never heard of Leni Riefenstahl. As an out-of-work auto mechanic with an interest in Africa and a gift for cameras, he signed on to Leni's expedition and life as her assistant in all things—her cameraman, her cook, her gatekeeper, her live-in companion—devoted to the end in spite of the forty-two-year difference in their ages.

Between 1962 and 1977, Leni made half a dozen excursions among various Nuba tribes on visits ranging from a few days to the better part of a year. Her expeditions began as solo excursions with the bare essentials of folding cot and spirit stove and grew to elaborate treks with Horst, Land Rovers, Toyotas, and Unimogs (military trucks provided by Volkswagen) hauling as many as thirty-five crates of photographic and recording equipment weighing in at a ton and a half. Her resources expanded from personal loans and the money from Odyssey to financial backing from magazine publishers such as *Stern* and *GEO* and equipment provided by Dr. Arnold at Arri. She graduated from a still camera around her neck to an Arriflex on her shoulder (though Horst did much of the filming), or she carried a clutch of motorized Leicas with telephoto lenses that compensated for the reluctance of skittish or superstitious subjects engaged in violent or intimate rituals. When most women in their sixties and seventies were nursing infirmities, she was on camera safari in a land torn by civil war (since 1964) with the self-punishing single-mindedness and stamina that had made her a mountain star in her twenties. If Gardner and the Nansen group saw her as grasping and manipulative, she saw herself as a romantic seeker, a preservationist pioneer, and unblushingly compared herself to another European in Africa, Dr. Albert Schweitzer.

Africa was "paradise," she said, rejuvenating and inspiring. "Nowhere in the world have I become so healthy and young so quickly," she wrote Kreuger, and she fantasized living out her days in a simple mud hut, surrounded by tribesmen who "come to me in my dreams, not as human beings, but as strange impalpable creatures fashioned by artists."

It was, however, their human palpability she was capturing with her cameras, and it had market value. She had been selling stills from the beginning to raise money for the Nuba film. She tried in vain to interest major illustrated magazines in Germany, such as *Stern* and *Bunte,* and settled in 1964 for selling a handful of photographs to the less prestigious *Kristall*. A few more were included in a Time-Life book called *African Kingdom*. On her visit to Gardner and Harvard in 1966, she made a side trip to Rochester, New York, and George Eastman House, where a slide show she gave Eastman Kodak executives did not persuade them to underwrite her film costs. She had more success stimulating interest at *National Geographic* (just then planning the article about the Nansen expedition) but would not agree to its financial terms.

Though economically important, her images had still greater value. They were the artifacts of her new life, instruments for comeback and rehabilitation. She conceived of them from the start as analogues to the Olympic photographs, but their warriors covered in ash and their dancing girls glistening with oil resonated with echoes of unrealized projects such as *Penthesilea* and had other purposes as well. They could demonstrate to a skeptical world how truly distant she was from the racial policies of the Third Reich. She made this explicit by citing her photographs of Jesse Owens at the Olympics whenever possible and boasted of rejecting an offer from L. Ron Hubbard to collaborate on a project in South Africa because of apartheid, though she tactfully refrained from mentioning that racist policy to Hubbard in declining his invitation.

After her early harvest of motion picture footage was ruined by laboratory mishaps in Germany and refilming proved only marginally satisfactory, placement of her stills became more urgent. A striking selection appeared in the *Sunday Times Magazine* in London in 1967, where past acrimony had been forgotten, and, in 1969, Germany's *Stern* reversed its earlier rejections and published a fourteen-page color layout just before Christmas, with an African cover announcing "Leni Riefenstahl Photographs the Nuba: Photos No One Has Ever Seen."

The reaction was electric. If the nudity was startling, the statuesque bodies in classical, heroic poses and saturated colors were dramatic and sensuous, the compositions immediate and timeless, primitive and majestic. Their impact was still greater when published in opulent book form in 1973 as *The Last of the Nuba*, a selection of 126 large-format color photographs of tribal life and death, with emphasis on wrestling and mourning. *The Last of the Nuba* was followed three years later by an equally sumptuous volume on the so-called South-East Nuba from the villages of Kau, Nyaro, and Fungor titled *People of Kau*, devoted primarily to tribal face painting of patterns whose abstractions recalled Picasso. There were layouts anatomizing erotic "love dances," body-scarring tattoo rituals, and lacerating bracelet combat, two-man events that tested warrior survival and supremacy fought with curved knives attached to the wrist.

Both books were publishing sensations in Germany, then in England, France, and America. *Newsweek* called *The Last of the Nuba* "the year's most compelling picture book in any category," one that is "deeply romantic—but never romanticized" and is "monumentally moving." Eudora Welty in the *New York Times* cited its "absorbing beauty" and "cumulative power." Jonas Mekas, a onetime refugee from the Nazis, wrote that Leni's photographs "can cut through your heart" and solemnly declared, "She is a monument. She is a mountain. She is a genius."

There were dissenting voices, disturbed and not always measured. Henri Cartier-Bresson viewed Leni's work among the Nuba and observed that his friend George Rodger had photographed them earlier and "with infinitely more humanity." Anthropologists and ethnographers studied her photographs and methods and saw exploitation where Leni and others saw art.

The huge success of the Nuba books made them an easy target, but Leni had invited backlash by suggesting to the press that she was a distaff Livingstone or Schweitzer. She sent out hundreds of autographed postcards of herself in safari garb with naked Nuba babies—usually named "Leni," she said—pressed to her cheek. She transformed her shortcomings of scientific objectivity into personal drama by describing her departures from Africa as "real tragedy" for those she left behind. "The children cried, the people cried, and when I came back, they had feasts and celebrations." No one would likely have held her to academic standards but for her boast to the press that *The Last of the Nuba* "has a scientific text which I've written myself. And I was the only person who could do this because scientists had not yet researched the Nuba."

Scientists who had done so in scrupulous but unsung detail were accustomed to being neglected, but not so cavalierly denied. The Nansen Society had already lodged its protest of silence in omitting Leni from accounts of its Sudan expedition, but her claims of discovery and authenticity raised hackles among academic researchers even before the Nuba books saw print.

Ethnographer James C. Faris, professor of anthropology at the University of Connecticut, had studied the Nuba in Sudan over a three-year period beginning in 1966 and was lecturing at Cambridge and London when asked by Leni's prospective English publisher to write an introduction for what would become *The Last of the Nuba*. He was given a mock-up of the photographic layout together with an unsigned text written by Leni with the help of Speer, now a bestselling author with his monumentally successful memoir-history, *Inside the Third Reich*. Unaware of the text's authorship, Faris pronounced it "drivel" and "hopelessly racist" and declined the publisher's assignment.

Faris resumed fieldwork among the Nuba while teaching at the University of Khartoum. The result was *Nuba Personal Art*, a scholarly, handsomely illustrated volume with color and black-and-white photographs supplemented by maps, tables, and line drawings. Published in 1972, Faris's book was a study of the arts of face and body painting among the South-East Nuba of Kau, Fungor, and Nyaro, and it drew Leni to those villages in 1974 (though typically she claimed, "I had a dream") and inspired the strikingly Picassoesque face- and body-painting photographs that were the heart of *People of Kau*.

When *The Last of the Nuba* was published in America in 1974, Faris recognized the layouts he had seen in London. The book's introduction—"How I Found the Nuba"—was new (he thought it ghostwritten) but "condescending" in tone and in its constant references to " 'my' Nuba." *Newsweek*, whose reviewer had found the book "monumentally moving," printed Faris's accusations that "her facts are fabrications, her interpretations obscene and racist and even many of her photographs [are] complete distortions."

These were serious charges against a work that boasted "permanent anthropological and ethnographic importance," and Faris added to them. He had been made aware of Leni's earlier forays in Sudan by Nuba tribespeople who told him that she had paid for photographs, rejected clothed or aged subjects, used telephoto lenses to photograph rituals they had forbidden her to record, and employed generator-driven flashes and electric lighting. When Leni learned of Faris's comments, she admitted having heard of his work but denounced him as "driven by revenge" because of "the sensational success of my Nuba books in America."

But Faris's criticisms predated by two years the publication of *People of Kau*, over which he might justifiably have experienced professional envy. When *Kau* was published in 1976, he issued new objections, charging that Leni was "ignorant of [Nuba] society" and had introduced European cosmetics and lip glosses to the Nuba in order to achieve her striking color effects, making a mockery of tribal customs in which colors and patterns were honorifics, signifiers related to status and age. Her photographs were, he said, "a grotesque perversion" that "profoundly misrepresent[s] local life" and "grossly distorts the customs and lifestyle of the Mesakin and south-east Nuba."

Others raised more objections, including a scholar-protégé of Faris's named Oswald Iten, today a prominent Swiss journalist, then in Sudan as a Ph.D. candidate at the University of Zurich to research his dissertation in economic anthropology. Iten encountered Leni and her Land Rovers— supplied by the government of Sudan and the nature magazine *GEO*—in Fungor in 1977. He remembered that, in contrast to the primitive isolation in which Leni claimed to work, her party was encamped in "a large compound fenced with thorns and grass that served as a photographic field studio and was equipped with a generator." He wrote in the Swiss and German press that she made payments in cash or goods for stage-managed photographs on commission for *GEO*, whose editor was one of her party; that dissension was open with natives trying physically to block her photography; and that she violated burial grounds in the Land Rovers from which she and Horst raised sacred dust while photographing tribal rituals out of the windows with telephoto lenses.

Though Faris and Iten took and published photographs themselves, they had profound reservations about the invasive nature of photography, which too easily became voyeurism dignifying itself as art. "There is something appalling about photographing people," Cartier-Bresson once acknowledged, "some sort of violation." The camera aestheticized, as Rodger had discovered at Bergen-Belsen, reduced people to curiosities and commodities, to decorative figures in blighted landscapes. To Faris, Leni's Nuba photographs, with their melodramatic sensuality, typified exploitation that claimed benevolence while subjecting peoples of lesser power to value systems they were ignorant of and helpless to protest. "It is as if we (the West) are to be admired and lauded for having appreciated them, or for having felt sorry for them or for empathizing with them," he said. "We will not leave them alone, not take their own positions at face value—their histories become myth," defined by outsiders, and "their subjecthood is reinforced, reproduced."

Such charges were largely confined to academic journals or symposia, though Leni—an obsessive collector of her personal press—noted them and retaliated in her memoirs. She pursued Oswald Iten through his Swiss landlady, masquerading behind her "Helene Jacob" persona, and concluded that he, like Faris, was "eaten up with envy." In spite of what she called "slander [that] couldn't get any filthier," she decided in the end not to sue "this young student."

It was more difficult to dismiss the critique by Susan Sontag in the *New York Review of Books* in February 1975. Sontag—writer, critic, and occasional filmmaker—had written a decade earlier that "to call Leni Riefenstahl's *The Triumph of the Will* and *The Olympiade* [*sic*] masterpieces is not to gloss over Nazi propaganda with aesthetic lenience. The Nazi propaganda is there. But something else is there, too, which we reject at our loss." Almost alone, Sontag acknowledged both the artistry *and* the advocacy. But the "disquieting lies" she detected in *The Last of the Nuba* required comment and annotation. Sontag used the book's American publication as the pretext for her widely read essay "Fascinating Fascism," in which Leni's life and work became central exhibits in a rigorous attempt to define and condemn a fascist aesthetic.

Sontag immediately acknowledged that *The Last of the Nuba* was "certainly the most ravishing book of photographs published anywhere in recent years." She further allowed, "*Triumph of the Will* and *Olympia* are undoubtedly superb films," possibly "the two greatest documentaries ever made." But, she noted, *The Last of the Nuba* (even its dust jacket) avoided mention of *Triumph of the Will* or any hint of Leni's role as propagandist for the Third Reich, making the Nuba enterprise part of a dishonest campaign to rehabilitate reputation by rewriting personal history. Sontag recapitulated that history with an efficiency one German critic called "mercilessly clever," making minor factual errors along the way that would later be acknowledged and corrected.

Sontag defined Leni's *Last of the Nuba* as "the third in her triptych of fascist visuals," in which the "aloof, godlike Nuba" incorporated themes that were "continuous with her Nazi work." While acknowledging the photographs' appeal, Sontag argued that "when people claim to be drawn to Riefenstahl's images for their beauty of composition . . . such connoisseurship prepares the way for a curiously absentminded acceptance of propaganda for all sorts of destructive feelings—feelings whose implications people are refusing to take seriously." The Nuba photographs, she wrote, endorsed "a primitivist ideal" of physical perfection wrapped in "a sanctimonious promotion of the beautiful." Ravishing the photographs may have been, but to discuss "aesthetic merits" and ignore content, as Sontag herself was mistakenly thought to have done ten years earlier, was "to filter out the noxious political ideology." She now wrote that "more than beauty is at stake in art like Riefenstahl's," for "fascist art glorifies surrender, it exalts mindlessness, it glamorizes death."

Asserting the moral significance of content was a departure for a critic who had made her reputation by privileging style over content in her early work, but "the context has changed," she wrote. "Art that seemed

September 1939:
Leni "follows the Führer's trail" to Konskie, Poland,
just days after the outbreak of World War II.

Polish Jews, ordered by German soldiers to dig pits
in the Konskie town square

Leni is captured in a snapshot at the moment gunfire begins.

The victims of the Konskie atrocity Leni claimed she never saw

Leni in Warsaw, chatting with a Wehrmacht officer at Hitler's victory parade celebrating the fall of the city in October 1939

Leni and her own Wehrmacht officer: Maj. Peter Jakob, whom she married in 1944 in Kitzbühl

Security on location was ensured by armed guards in uniform.

In *Tiefland*, Leni used Gypsy extras from detention camps in Salzburg and Berlin. Here she inspects cast and costumes.

A beautiful young Gypsy extra, fate unknown

The Gypsy children were housed in stables before being once again put behind barbed wire or taken by train to Auschwitz.

Leni as the Gypsy dancer Martha
in *Tiefland* (not released until 1954)

A dramatic still of Pedro rescuing Martha in *Tiefland*, from
Leni's 1944 portfolio for Hitler, who had personally financed the film.
Note the similarity in style to *The Blue Light*, a decade earlier.

Lt. Col. Milton Medenbach (center) requisitioned Leni's Kitzbühl property for the U.S. Army, but befriended Leni, as well as Rolf Lantin (left), her personal photographer, and her husband Peter Jakob (right), known to the G.I.'s as "Jake the handyman."

Leni poses for Medenbach's camera while relaxing under house arrest in Kitzbühl, summer 1945.

Leni's postwar trials often featured weeping. Here she defends herself in Munich in 1949.

George Rodger's 1949 photograph of Nuba warriors
gave Leni new direction and a new career as
a photographer in Africa after the war.

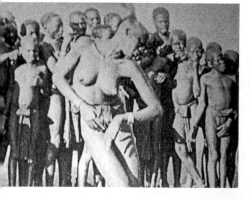

Another, earlier inspiration is suggested
by this frame blow-up from *Ways to
Strength and Beauty*, the film in which
Leni appeared in 1925.

Leni sent out thousands of postcards
of herself among "her" Nuba.
This one is inscribed to Peggy Wallace,
an American student of her work.

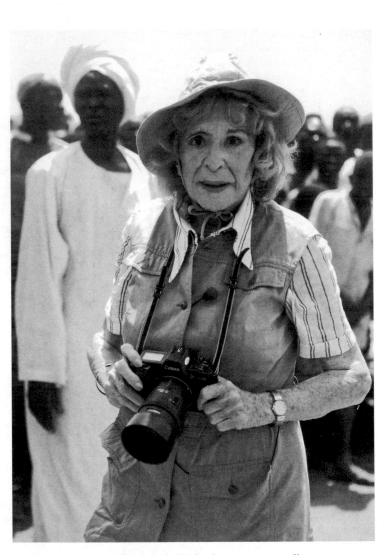

Her last safari and (almost) her last appearance on film:
Leni returns with a camera crew and director to civil war–torn Sudan
in 2000 in search of "her" Nuba. She was ninety-eight, camera at the ready.

eminently worth defending ten years ago, as a minority or adversary taste, no longer seems defensible today, because the ethical and cultural issues it raises have become serious, even dangerous, in a way they were not then." The new context included—in her essay—works as diverse as a slick paperback for the fetish and S&M audience called *SS Regalia* and films such as Liliana Cavani's *The Night Porter* and Luchino Visconti's *The Damned*. All, Sontag argued, were evidence of an "eroticization of fascism" that could be accounted for neither by the formal properties of art nor by a passing taste for cheap thrills. "Riefenstahl's films are still effective," she wrote, "because their content is a romantic ideal to which many continue to be attached," namely "the ideal of life as art, the cult of beauty, the fetishism of courage, the dissolution of the intellect; the family of man (under the parenthood of leaders)." Whether Leni premeditated these ideals was irrelevant. "She is no thinker at all," Sontag wrote, dismissing her as an "indomitable priestess of the beautiful"—a "beauty freak."

Sontag's critique inspired debate and dissent, most memorably from film critic Andrew Sarris in *The Village Voice*. He wrote that "the problem with either a prosecution or a defense of Riefenstahl is that so much of the evidence has disappeared in the rubble of the Third Reich that we can never be quite sure whether Leni was Little Eva (as she claims) or Lucrezia Borgia (as Sontag suggests) or (more likely) an opportunistic artist who has been both immortalized and imprisoned by the horror of history."

The view was indulgent and stroked Leni's sense of victimhood, but no rebuttal of Sontag's argument, however sympathetic, could remove the sting from what she felt was the most devastating attack she had suffered in half a century of often hostile public scrutiny. "In our many conversations," Kurt Kreuger remembered, "I do not recall Leni to have been hateful towards anyone, even Hitler, except Susan Sontag."

Her antipathy was so extreme, Kreuger said, that she misattributed to Sontag a charge made by others. The Nuba photographs were as inarguably erotic as the Olympic photographs had been, recalling her then assistant Heinz von Jaworsky's amusement that "she was absolutely fascinated by the black athletes." She had calculated rightly that her work in Africa would prove she was not racist when it came to beauty, but she inadvertently invited prurient speculation by attempting to preclude it. "I find the black skin more beautiful than the white," she told a French journalist, adding, "When a man is naked, the black skin makes him asexual. Among the Nubas, I never notice whether they are dressed or not."

A biting article in Germany's *Der Spiegel* titled *"Blood and Testicles"* (*"Blut und Hoden"* punned on the Nazi slogan *"Blut und Boden"*—blood and soil) was illustrated with suggestive photographs of Leni alongside nude African warriors. The writer Wilhelm Bittorf played on endowment fantasies of black sexuality and on the black uniforms for which the SS had been notorious in dissecting what he called the "Riefenstahl phenomenon." He saw the same fascist continuity in her work that Sontag had deplored: "The enthusiasm—even addiction—with which she once celebrated the cults of the Nazis and the bodies of the Olympians is now devoted to the cults and bodies of the Nuba. . . . For her, the Nuba are, finally, better Nazis, purer barbarians, the true Teutons."

Leni later conceded—and indignantly denied—reports that she (in her words) "occasionally withdrew to her tent with very big and 'strong' Nuba men," and her lasting fury with Sontag spilled over to include accusations Sontag hadn't made. Leni asked Kreuger, "How dare she write and assume my Nuba photography was the result of my being attracted by the male Nubian's oversize genitalia?" Especially, she added, when "I pride myself on my well-known almost virginal sexual history."

Neither the anthropologists' denunciations nor Sontag's critique slowed sales of the Nuba books or the admiration they inspired. Photography magazines in London, Paris, and New York vied with one another to devote covers to her work. A French critic hailed her as "the modern Plato and Michelangelo of the Leica." *People of Kau* won prestigious art awards for layout and design, and a third volume, *Vanishing Africa* (*Mein Afrika*), appeared in 1982. A boxed and oversized selection of her African photographs would be issued in 2002 in a numbered, autographed edition to celebrate her centenary titled *Africa* and priced at two thousand dollars.

The honors of her seventies were less ritually opulent than the state and royal banquets of her thirties, though her friend Ahmed Abu Bakr in Khartoum persuaded President Gaafar Mohamed el-Nimeiri to make her an honorary citizen of Sudan before he was overthrown. The tribute, which came with a Sudanese passport, followed mass shipments of her Nuba books by Sudan's ministry of tourism as public relations. The ceremony in the presidential palace honored her quickening of the local economy by attracting camera safaris that crisscrossed the interior by the busload, hastening eradication of the Nuba way of life she was credited with preserving.

Acclaim spun royalties and resulted in offers to photograph the ill-fated 1972 Munich Olympics for London's *Sunday Times* and the Montreal games in 1976. There were commissions to photograph rock 'n' roll royalty Mick and Bianca Jagger, of whom Leni had never heard, sessions enlivened, it was reported, by Rolling Stones guitarist Keith Richards's turning up in a rented SS uniform. Andy Warhol invited her to mingle among the bohemians and groupies at his Factory in downtown New York, and she signed autographs and books for new fans around the world who were not sure where Sudan was or were too young to know that Berlin and Germany had once been undivided.

Not least, she was able to build a sleek contemporary house of wood and glass in a village called Pöcking near Bavaria's Starnberger See as a getaway from her apartment and offices in Munich. The house boasted exterior balconies spilling over with geraniums, interiors with white marble floors, modern leather furniture, primitive African art, temperature-controlled archival storage vaults, fully equipped state-of-the-art cutting rooms, and was situated on a gated, bowered private lane. The press called it "the house the Nuba built."

EIGHTEEN

FORTUNE AND MEN'S EYES

*I have never done anything I didn't want to do, and
nothing I've ever been ashamed of.*
                                    —Leni Riefenstahl

EXCEPT FOR A BRIEF AND near-fatal return almost a quarter of a
century later, Leni left Sudan and her Nuba behind when she was seventy-
five. Her resounding commercial success there would have been a
gratifying last hurrah for any septuagenarian less restless and ambitious,
but even before leaving, she had propelled herself into another "new
life" and creative obsession, right next door.

In Kenya, she had signed an affidavit in 1972 swearing—as "Helene
Jacob"—that she was twenty years younger than her true age of seventy
to qualify for lessons at a German-run scuba-diving school outside
Mombasa. Her anonymity was preserved by her alias, but self-effacement
was less her goal than the weightlessness in water that eased pains for
which doctors could find neither cause nor cure.

If Sudan had provided respite from civilization with its "strange,
impalpable creatures" who asked no questions, the silent and nonjudg-
mental marine life and filigreed coral reefs of the Red Sea, the Caribbean,
and the Indian Ocean quickly became "addictive," she said, "sheltering
me from the outside world, removing all problems and worries." With an
oxygen tank strapped to her back, she became the oldest licensed diver in

the world and soon—with lamps and cameras clutched in her hands—the oldest functioning filmmaker in history.

She dove with her bulky, watertight still cameras (Horst manned the heavier movie and, later, video cameras) more than two thousand times into the oceans of the world to amass work that would fill sumptuous books of photography such as *Coral Gardens* in 1978 and *Wonders Under Water* in 1990. Her iridescent images vied in beauty with those of Jacques Cousteau and Douglas Faulkner, which had inspired her as George Rodger's Nuba wrestlers had once done. There would even be a valedictory film in 2002, released on the remarkable occasion of her hundredth birthday.

An ever-growing treasure of footage fed through the courtesy Steenbeck editing consoles installed for her in the house in Pöcking. She worked and reworked miles of marine and Nuba footage, reassuring herself and well-wishers that, as soon as a sponsor could be found, the long-promised African film would be released and then the underwater film. Meanwhile, Horst, enacting what a friend called "*Harold and Maude* in real life," saw to cooking and cleaning, eased her ailments, indulged her whims, suffered her demands and rages, and felt blessed and grateful that he could.

At almost eighty, she took a nasty spill on a skiing holiday in St. Moritz, and doctors nailed together bones that X rays said had mended and her body said had not. She had shrunken physically and walked with a limp following hip replacement surgery that aggravated the discomfort it was meant to cure. She cheerily concealed her ailments in public, but pain, except when she was in the water, was now as constant a companion as Horst. She fought off evidence of age with wigs, face-lifts, and live fresh cell injections at a Bavarian affiliate of the Niehans clinic, where Pope Pius XII, Winston Churchill, W. Somerset Maugham, and Charlie Chaplin had preceded her en route to the centenarians' club. She gamely subscribed to the fashion theory that you are only as old as you dress and took to wearing stiletto heels with spandex leggings and neon-patterned blouses and beachwear. When time blurred what it had not eroded, she dipped into cosmetic pots and painted on features from memory. Her old rival Dietrich had withdrawn into merciful shadow at seventy-five; Leni braved the world's beaches at high noon in a wet suit and flippers at ninety.

Though decades had passed since *Tiefland*'s failure and the collapse of *The Red Devils* and *Black Cargo,* a fresh generation of cinéastes viewed her old film work refracted through the prism of a new aesthetic theory whose influence had swept from postwar Paris to every capital of the world. Proposed by young critics fervent to become directors—François Truffaut and Jean-Luc Godard among them—the then-novel aesthetic held that a motion picture was, or could best be appreciated as, the product of an individual creator: an *auteur,* or author. The young French critics went on to establish careers of their own that spectacularly validated their thinking, but it was America's Andrew Sarris, the critic who thought Leni "imprisoned by the horror of history," who coined the term *auteur theory* and became its most eloquent advocate. Sarris viewed films as *films;* he appraised them as "personal art" and detected evidence of "personal signature" in unexpected places, asserting that "the worst film of a great director may be more interesting though less successful than the best film of a fair to middling director."

Many argued with a theory that seemed cultish or merely a revival (with a show business spin) of outworn romantic ideals of the solitary artist as a heroic figure. Most dubious were those invested in the realpolitik of day-to-day collaborative filmmaking, but no director likely to be enshrined in the auteurs' (or Sarris's) pantheon found such notions disagreeable. The pages of *Cahiers du Cinéma* and its English- and German-language counterparts and imitators literally rewrote great chunks of film history and rescued undervalued directors from obscurity or oblivion, resurrecting reputations in eclipse and rehabilitating controversial careers.

No filmmaker alive courted rehabilitation more or was as disposed to view herself an auteur as Leni. Almost alone among filmmakers of the world, she acted, directed, wrote, and produced; her commanding stance behind the cameras and months—even years—at the editing tables made her an auteurist's ideal, as did her affinity for the heroic, the spectacular, and her claims of intuition and dreams as inspiration. The new wave encouraged viewing her work for its style, for its formal qualities and technical innovations, as if her art were independent of subject and technique irrelevant to content. As for her sponsorship by Hitler, she minimized or dismissed it and told America's *Film Comment* that "I have never done anything I didn't want to do, and nothing I've ever been ashamed of," allowing questions of opportunism and morality to drift to the cutting room floor. "Art, creation, this is my life," she said, as if they were mutually mitigating and would justify forever her pursuit of the things she loved: beauty, and the image of self-created artist and genius she had cultivated since childhood.

Her advocates pointed out to her detractors that the same critics who castigated her as a pariah because of Hitler and the Nazis treated Eisenstein as a culture hero for films he made in service of Stalin and the Soviets. The analogy (a conservative Cold War argument in America) ignored that Eisenstein's films—such as *Strike*, *Battleship Potemkin*, *October*, and *Alexander Nevsky*—were re-creations of the near or distant past that, while mythically and propagandistically conceived, did not purport to be the unmediated versions of reality that Leni claimed for her Nazi films. That Eisenstein fell out of favor with the Kremlin and almost certainly turned against his masters with his never-finished *Ivan the Terrible* was muted, if not ignored.

Time softened some judgments and sharpened others. In America, the CBS television network broadcast a two-part *Camera Three* presentation on her life and work in 1973, with Leni on-camera demurely dressed in her armor of political naïveté and dedication to beauty. Critic Amos Vogel erupted angrily in the pages of the Sunday *New York Times* that, in the name of objectivity, CBS (underwritten by the New York State Education Department) had managed to whitewash *Triumph of the Will*, "the realization of a megalomaniac's outrageous fantasy," a film "only a fanatic Nazi could have created."

It was a familiar argument with familiar force, but controversy now drew more publicity than blood, and film festival bookers took notice. If the festivals lacked the glitter of Cannes, Venice, or Berlin (from which she had been disinvited in 1960 after public protests), they sparked with their organizers' needs to put themselves on the festival map. Headlines blazed in the Rocky Mountains in September 1974 when she was invited to Telluride, Colorado (population one thousand souls; altitude ten thousand feet), to receive tribute for her "exemplary contributions to the art of the film" in the village's first annual festival alongside old cinema's Gloria Swanson and new cinema's Francis Ford Coppola. She arrived with Horst by Jeep in the tiny mining-town-turned-ski-resort to be greeted by representatives of the American Jewish Congress and the Denver chapter of the Anti-Defamation League of B'nai B'rith whose homemade placards accused her of sharing guilt for the Holocaust. Telluride's thirty-four-year-old Jewish mayor assured protesters that "we are honoring the artist, not the individual" and volunteered after a midnight screening of *Triumph of the Will* (his first) that he couldn't see how the film had been considered propaganda in the first place. Leni dined and discussed *The Godfather* with Coppola and accepted Swanson's "I thought Hitler was dead" outburst as solidarity.

By the end of the festival, she was sufficiently unnerved by the parade of protesters and placards to cancel her press conference, though she noted graciously, "I have found the strength to come to terms with this fate without bitterness." On learning that demonstrators were already lining up outside her next stop at Chicago's Art Institute, she canceled her appearance there at the "Women in Film" festival.

A steady stream of appreciative Leni literature kept pace with the ascendant auteur theory and the gathering strength of the feminist movement as each sought to claim her as forerunner or exemplar (Sontag noted and dismissed both in "Fascinating Fascism"). Serious film journals around the globe devoted whole issues to her work, most of them drawing on personal interviews with their subject and indebted to the meticulously maintained archives she opened for their research and admiration.

She was the inexhaustible curator of her legend. She distributed copies of favorable articles about her work together with her denazification documents and diplomas of merit. She photocopied private correspondence from prominent admirers for ambitious young scholars, in one case duplicating a five-year span of intimate letters and handwritten diary entries from a particularly prestigious (and unsuspecting) champion as if they were press blurbs or celebrity endorsements.

Age had not withered her vitality or magnetism. Filmmaker Tony Palmer spent four days with her when she was almost ninety and recalled that "she came at me with a sexual energy that was real and quite undeniable. The aura of sexuality in the way she moved, talked, her gestures, her smile, her everything was forceful and authentic." Palmer was merely echoing reports of initial encounters with her in her sixties and seventies that were star turns of animation and allure. One of her sincerest admirers, filmmaker and writer Kevin Brownlow, met her in London in 1966 with fellow enthusiasts from the BBC. "She was always very beautiful," he wrote. "Now, nearing sixty [she was sixty-four], her appearance is even more impressive. . . . Her electric energy is transmitted unmistakably from the moment she steps into a room. This dynamism might be overpowering to those without interest in her work. To us it was inspiring; we sat enthralled from seven p.m. to two in the morning."

Brownlow's susceptibility to her charisma equaled his critical regard for her as "an artist of supreme sensitivity," a woman who was "among the most extraordinary people I ever met. Overwhelming. Brilliant. Exhausting." He wrote articles on her behalf denouncing "insidious propaganda" that kept her from working or blocked support. "Art transcends the artist," he pronounced in *Film*, adding sternly that "politics and art must never be confused," though few bodies of work so successfully commingled the two as Leni's. Brownlow's passionate defense of "the humanity, sensitivity and integrity of Leni Riefenstahl" prompted rebuttal from film historian Paul Rotha (who had had to pay her for using excerpts from *Triumph of the Will*) that Leni's "ardent fervour, her white-heat passion, her unqualified idolatry for Hitler and all Nazism stood for are indelible in her work. . . . [Her films] could not possibly be disassociated from a passionate belief in National Socialism; they reeked of it."

Leni's humanity, integrity, and sensitivity did not flinch from the preempting of potentially unfriendly testimony. When Peggy Ann Wallace, a Ph.D. candidate at the University of Southern California, traveled to Munich to tape interviews with her in the seventies, Leni flew into a rage on learning that Wallace had independently interviewed Arnold Fanck. "I have spoken with you about Dr. Fanck without any knowledge that you had already seen him," Leni blurted. "I told you a lot about him, private things too, and you say *not one word. Why?*"

Wallace defended her interviews with Fanck (and others) as objective dissertation research and denied any interest in "ugly, personal things. That is not my doctoral work."

"No, but it goes along with your work," Leni countered, dismissing Fanck as a bitter has-been bent on destroying her reputation. "Dr. Fanck will *never* tell you the truth even if he is speaking well about me. *Never.* He *lies, one hundred per cent!* You can't believe one word of what he says. He's a liar. *Very* bad!" Her voice rose in excoriation of Fanck's talent, his vanity, his politics, his finances, his romantic life, and his ingratitude, climaxing in outrage at his "telling people that my mother was Jewish!" Her agitation was strident enough to provoke Horst's alarm. "Is the [tape] machine still on?" he asked in panic, to which Leni shouted, "I don't care!"

From her point of view, she was merely (if definitively) spelling out terms for cooperation with a resourceful researcher. From Wallace's, she was exposing profound anxiety—even paranoia—that time was waning for the full rehabilitation she craved as a filmmaker and a woman. She was not wrong to worry. Fanck's goodwill had been exhausted years earlier, and the often-slavish lenience of her resurgent prominence fairly guaranteed rebuttal and challenge.

She had been resisting publishers' entreaties to write an autobiography at least since 1951. As one of the last high-profile survivors of the Third

Reich—and the only woman—she could, she knew, command a healthy advance for her life story. She had been tempted more than once, but found writing frustrating and confining and was unwilling to sacrifice precious time from her African and underwater expeditions. But globe-trotting was expensive, and so were the apartment in Munich (to which she had added an office), the house in Pöcking, the secretaries, the temperature-controlled archives, and the maintenance and reworking of the uncompleted Nuba film (which was shrinking and in danger of decomposing) and the ever-growing coils of underwater footage. As her eightieth birthday dawned, she signed a book contract that would enable her, as she put it, "to understand my life in all its strangeness" and "to tackle preconceived ideas and to clear up misunderstandings." Collaboration was no more realistic an option than it had ever been, and, after showing three ghostwriters and a research assistant the door, she undertook the arduous five-year task of setting down her life as she wanted it told.

Memoiren (*Memoirs*) was published in Germany in August 1987 to coincide with her eighty-fifth birthday. It was an immediate publishing event, the book's tone set by an epigraph borrowed from Albert Einstein: "So many things have been written about me, masses of insolent lies and inventions," it began. Her appropriation of Einstein—stripped of his citizenship by the Nazis because he was Jewish just as she was making *Day of Freedom*—struck many as ironic or outrageous and, together with the evasions, omissions, and half-truths that followed for almost a thousand pages, transformed what might have been a narrative of considerable historical interest into a referendum on its author.

The German press pounced. Headlines mocked her as "The Führer's Unconsummated Bride" who was purveying the "Idiotic Chatter of a Sycophant." Leni had calculated that her frank admission of naïveté and fascination for Hitler would seem candid, would strike sympathetic chords in an audience that had once justified its own gullibility on similar grounds. But that audience had in significant numbers pondered its past, known shame and guilt, and was not prepared to applaud alibis it had itself abandoned—however reluctantly—in the painful process of atonement. Nor had they ever been as close to center stage as the narrator who painted herself on virtually every page as Junta, the beautiful and misunderstood innocent seduced by idealism and victimized by fate.

English-language readers knew little of the negative reaction in Germany, and the book stimulated a variety of opinions when it was published—cut by almost three hundred pages—on Leni's ninetieth birthday as *The Sieve of Time* in England and a year later as *Leni Riefenstahl: A Memoir* in America. In London, Speer's biographer Gitta Sereny (who knew Leni and wrote that "when she is honest, she is very likeable") considered the book "devoid of any literary proficiency, style, or singularly, any suspicion of humour." In the end, "[it never] manages to evoke compassion, only embarrassment." Ian Buruma in the *Times Literary Supplement* found it "tiresome" and "ill-written," crippled by the author's "thirst for applause, her bottomless narcissism, [which] is worse than tedious; she is so dazzled by her own light that she notices nothing, but nothing, around her."

Reaction in America was more favorable, at least in the influential *New York Times Book Review,* where Leni and her memoir took the front cover. The appreciation by the usually acerbic John Simon was so effusive that it at first suggested Swiftian irony. Simon (whose first language was German) was widely feared for theater and film reviews that led, in rumor at least, to the death of careers. He began this review by declaring Leni "one of the supreme artists of the cinema, the greatest woman film maker ever," whose book "does not contain a single unspellbinding page. Some books," he clarified, "are merely so exciting that you can't put them down. This one is so exciting that you often must put it down, lest you overdose on thrills."

While catching his breath, Simon briefly considered the question of veracity. "Whether she lied to herself then and whether she is still doing so, one can't know," he decided, brushing doubts aside and judging it "a credible account of an extraordinary life" that "must, in the main, be true; it is far too weird for fiction." After swallowing long-discredited fabrications such as the Nazi Party's having had nothing to do with *Olympia*, he concluded that during Leni's glory years "she may have compromised her humanity. But her artistic integrity, never."

A less credulous view was articulated by Manohla Dargis in *The Village Voice* under the title "Queen of Denial." Dargis found the book "turgid" and deftly dismissed its "revisionist" fictions (she knew about *Olympia*). Building on exemplary awareness of the films and the Leni literature—from film journals to Sontag—she rejected apologists' "spurious formalist hedges," which seemed to suggest that the Third Reich was a rumor and only film technique was real. Politics aestheticized was still politics. Detaching *Triumph of the Will* or *Olympia* from their ideological identity, Dargis argued, was a "historical dodge," an attempt to "damn the subject while glorifying the artistry and artist" that led to the ultimate contention ("willfully stupid" she called it) that *Triumph* was "all form and no content," as a fawning glamour profile in *Vanity Fair* had phrased it.

Dargis challenged revisionists with "What does it mean to call a film like *Triumph of the Will* a masterpiece?" Without slighting Leni's technical achievements or innovations, she raised an issue that auteurists, feminists, apologists, academics—and contrarians such as Simon— avoided or declined to consider: "moral choice."

This was the issue Leni had sought to make irrelevant since her self-acquitting interview with the U.S. Army in 1945, which had suggested to interrogators her "lack of moral poise" in failing to grasp the consequences of her glorification of a criminally corrupt regime. Moral accountability was a theme without merit or traction among Leni's apologists, though she was never as naïve as they about the implications of her work. Her strident self-righteousness was a measure of her unease; she protested too much.

Moral choice in a specific instance came close to derailing her memoirs altogether just months after she began them. She interrupted her writing when, on December 6, 1982, one of Germany's national television networks aired an hour-long documentary about the making of *Tiefland* called *A Time of Silence and of Darkness* (*Zeit des Schweigens und der Dunkelheit*). Made independently on a shoestring by a thirty-five-year-old documentarian named Nina Gladitz, the film was in part a recycling of the *Revue* magazine charges about slave labor on *Tiefland* that Leni had taken to court in 1949, winning a settlement of six hundred marks that hinged on the technical definition of the term *concentration camp*. Gladitz's film reawakened the old charges with fresh evidence and with Leni's one-time Gypsy extras on-camera testifying that she had personally selected them at the Maxglan camp, had never paid them for their work, and had been aware that they were to be transported after filming to Auschwitz and other eastern camps where only a lucky few survived. The documentary and its charges not only had national television exposure but were also being marketed to the public on videocassette.

Leni sued. "I had to go to court for these lies were intolerable," she said. None of the film's charges had clear legal force, but litigation, she recognized and admitted, was vital "for the credibility of [my] memoirs."

Nina Gladitz cared deeply about moral issues and, like the young Leni, hoped to make dramatic films. While searching for a subject, she had come across letters written to Holocaust survivor agencies by the German Gypsy (he preferred the term *Sinto*) Josef Reinhardt. A Maxglan extra on *Tiefland* at thirteen, Reinhardt had been petitioning without success to be paid for his work on the picture since reading about the *Revue* trial in 1949 and *Tiefland*'s release five years later. The Reinhardt family, five of whom worked at the Krün location with him, had avoided almost certain extermination by their chance transport in April 1943 not to Auschwitz with the other Maxglan Gypsies, but to Lackenbach labor camp near the Austrian-Hungarian border, whose sanitary conditions were so dire that its first commandant succumbed to a camp typhus epidemic.

Reinhardt, now over fifty (he was born in 1927), had so admired Leni as a teenager that, as noted earlier, his father had challenged him, "If this woman is so nice and good, ask her if she can't do something for us."

Having failed to elicit Leni's intervention or help, he was willing, when Gladitz located him through survivor agencies, to work with her examining old production stills and snapshots so that names could be put to faces of Maxglan and Marzahn Gypsies for comparison to death lists from Auschwitz.

Gladitz discovered previously unknown documentation in the municipal archives of Salzburg, including the contracts between Leni's company and Maxglan's SS commandant Anton Böhmer, who had contributed the remarkable testimony in the *Revue* trial that no SS personnel were involved with *Tiefland*, having apparently forgotten that he himself supervised the Maxglan camp, drew up and signed the film contracts, and assigned armed guards to the location in Krün, to which he made personal oversight visits on three separate occasions.

A Time of Silence and of Darkness took four years to research and film. It could not begin to compare to Leni's filmmaking but generated sympathy and power in deposing its witness-survivors on-camera, especially Reinhardt. There was another personality on film lending ambiguous but unignorable impact: Leni herself, filmed while graciously presenting her Nuba photographs at bookseller-sponsored autograph parties.

Gladitz had falsely presented herself to Leni as a fan and filmmaker who wanted to make a film about "Leni Riefenstahl the artist" in order to get her signature on a release form for handheld shooting at a Nuba lecture and book signing in Freiburg. Gladitz planted the balding, mustached Reinhardt among the affluent crowd until he could timidly confront the unsuspecting Leni, who had not laid eyes on him for forty years. She was, with the cameras turning, at an uncharacteristic loss for words. While the "reunion" was a deceptive, even malicious prank, it created the impression that Leni had moved on to a new sphere of ease and renown and cared a good deal less about what had happened to her Gypsies—her "darlings"—than the film did. That Gladitz's deception had been carried out under the alias "Anna Madou" was a tactic that "Helene Jacob" might have recognized or even applauded for its enterprise, though Leni's reaction was a not entirely unjustified "Such treachery!"

Leni's trial against Gladitz ended after two appeals in 1987, five months before the publication of her memoirs. Though she would claim to the end of her life that she had won every lawsuit of the fifty or more she brought to defend her reputation, the final appeals court in Karlsruhe issued an irreversible ruling in March striking down three of the four counts on which she had sued. The court allowed, in effect, that she had personally selected Gypsies at Maxglan and Marzahn for *Tiefland;* she had not paid them for what was, by definition, forced labor; and she had led Gypsies she favored (such as Reinhardt's sister Antonie, whom she had urged to seek stage training) to believe she would or could alter their fates.

The fourth charge, asserted on-camera in a brief statement by Reinhardt, that she had acknowledged to him that he and the other Gypsies were destined "for Auschwitz," was the one charge the court disallowed, on the grounds that the place-names of death camps were unknown until after the war and the Reinhardt family had been transported, in the end, not to Auschwitz but to Lackenbach.

Gladitz's victory was partial and Pyrrhic. The court ordered removal of Reinhardt's five- or ten-second remark citing "Auschwitz," a stipulation that blocked existing prints and videocassettes and required reediting the film and remixing its sound track before distribution could be resumed. Gladitz was a freelance filmmaker without funds to undertake such minor but costly work, and German television had no incentive to finance alterations to a film that had already been broadcast and had triggered four years of litigation. Videocassettes were junked.

Leni claimed triumph. If she could not debate Sontag, she could enjoin Gladitz and her "outrageously mendacious film." Forbidding distribution of *A Time of Silence* in its original form effectively put an end to the film and to Gladitz's career. To the end of her life, Leni put film museums and other institutions on notice that if they showed the Gladitz film, they would be sued unless Reinhardt's remark about Auschwitz was deleted. Because no new copies were ever made, avoiding litigation required manually suppressing the sound track and masking the projector lens (to preclude lipreading) at the moment the remark occurred. Such a burden was rarely deemed worthwhile, and *A Time of Silence* was finally a little-known documentary about a failed film that few had seen or heard of anyway. That charges of forced labor and deaths in Auschwitz had been allowed to stand by the court went ignored in Leni's press statements mis-representing the case's outcome. "We saw nearly all of [the Gypsies] after the war," she said. "Nothing happened to a single one of them."

One intriguing question about *Tiefland* remained. As Gladitz pored over production stills and location photographs with Reinhardt to iden-tify extras from Maxglan and Marzahn, she realized that many depicted scenes that didn't appear in the finished film. Leni had long insisted that French authorities had stolen part of her negative after the war, charges the French firmly denied. Gladitz knew that *Tiefland*'s final editing had followed the *Revue* trial and speculated that Leni simply excised material that was morally incriminating or might recall the forced-labor charges. She learned that Leni at some point had quietly donated outtakes from *Tiefland* to the Bundesarchiv, though Gladitz was unable to confirm her theory that the mysterious "stolen" footage was deleted by Leni herself and deposited in the vaults for posterity. The outtakes remain sequestered.

NINETEEN

THE LAST PICTURE SHOW(S)

*The borderline between life and film is in constant flux
with Leni Riefenstahl.*

—Ray Müller

THE SCRUTINY OF THE Gladitz trial and reactions to her memoirs struck blows to Leni's carefully constructed public image, the persona that had for so long shielded her from self-doubt. There were economic concerns as well as the emotional. She had her book royalties and a Third Reich pension in the form of income from *Triumph of the Will* and *Olympia*, but, at nearly ninety, she had few prospects of future employment. On top of everything else, she was aggrieved to learn that she would have to share an inheritance from her mother that had unexpectedly materialized after the fall of the Berlin Wall in 1989 and the reunification of Germany.

The country house by the lake in Zernsdorf, where Alfred and Bertha Riefenstahl spent weekends outside Berlin, had been on the wrong side of the Iron Curtain since 1945, but reunification led to restitution of private property seized by East Germany after the end of the war. The country assets that had seemed lost forever now reverted to Bertha's estate as a windfall, but Bertha left no last will and testament when she died in January 1965. Under German law, her estate was therefore to be divided equally by her natural heirs, Leni and Heinz. Because Heinz had fallen in action in 1944, his 50 percent of the estate would be inherited equally by his legal heirs, the children Eckart and Uta, now in their fifties and living quietly in Stuttgart and Düsseldorf.

Leni petitioned the court to overturn the inheritance of her niece and nephew, her closest living relatives. She claimed her mother had hand-written a deathbed will leaving everything to her on October 23, 1964, shortly before her departure for Africa and her second Nuba expedition, during which Bertha died. No will was ever produced from Leni's legen-darily well-organized archives to substantiate the claim. The court in Munich administering inheritance issues wrote Eckart and Uta on December 28, 1992, that, in the absence of credible support for the "alleged testament," the court declined to pursue Leni's claim.

Maintenance was costly for a peripatetic, scuba-diving nonagenarian, even when expenses were paid for book tours or appearances at tribute events such as the "Leni Riefenstahl—Life" exhibit in Tokyo at the end of 1991 or the photographic exhibits or awards ceremonies that took place over the coming decade in Leipzig in 1995; Kuopio (Finland) and Milan in 1996; Rome, Hamburg, and Los Angeles in 1997; and Potsdam in 1998. All these events aroused the expected press controversy, and public outcry modulated only slightly as she edged closer to one hundred while maintaining the illusion of uncannily vigorous good health.

Her notoriety was her most viable asset. Film—not literature—was her medium, her natural habitat, and until the Nuba and underwater films were finished, might provide a forum for rehabilitation to counter the Sontags and Gladitzes of the world and provide income, too. Television had for some time been cannibalizing old films for nostalgic personality pieces, none more galling to her than a spate of recent Austrian docu-mentaries celebrating her old sparring partner Luis Trenker.

Trenker's greatest success had come, like Leni's, during the Third Reich, when he was the very embodiment of Aryan/Alpine masculinity, a sunshine-on-granite folk hero. He was able to defend himself against postwar charges of opportunism with mocking scorn of the Nazis (and of Leni) and by pointing out that he had spent most of the war in Rome making documentaries. To Leni, he typified the many friends and colleagues—such as Veit Harlan (director of *Jew Süss*, the most notoriously anti-Semitic film of the Nazi period), Arthur Maria Rabenalt, and countless others—whose former coziness with Goebbels and his ministry had merited barely a slap on the wrist before they resumed work in the postwar era, while she felt scourged and persecuted.

She had written cautiously about Trenker in her memoirs, but, when he died in 1990 at the age of ninety-seven, she approached his documentary producer, Hans-Jürgen Panitz, to suggest that she, too, would be a worthy television subject. The idea had been planted a year earlier by an inquiry from the BBC transmitted personally by David Irving, the controversial historian of the Third Reich who would be barred from Germany in 1993 and imprisoned by Austria in 2005 for Holocaust denial. Irving visited Leni in Pöcking on July 14, 1989, claiming to speak for a BBC producer who wanted her for just the sort of television exposure that had given Trenker such a sunset revival. Leni was noncommittal, but, after showing Irving her personal copy of *Triumph of the Will*, she dined and talked with him at home until midnight and allowed him to film her on 16 millimeter for a personal souvenir and, possibly, test footage.

Nothing came of the BBC inquiry, but, after Trenker died, Leni secured an expression of interest from Panitz and began searching for a director who could properly celebrate her in what would surely be her final starring venture. She pursued at least eighteen directors without success. Some were intrigued, such as British filmmaker Tony Palmer. Leni was a "film hero of mine," he explained. "*Triumph of the Will* is one of the few true manuals of the art of filmmaking, one that has influenced filmmakers from Orson Welles to George Lucas." He spent four days talking with her in Pöcking, growing cautiously enthusiastic before discovering he was unable to interest anyone in England in financing a Riefenstahl film. Other names on Leni's list, such as Marcel Ophüls, best known for his Holocaust-themed *The Sorrow and the Pity*, were not interested or found the idea repugnant. Still others were willing but were rejected by Leni as insufficiently gifted.

Finally an experienced but little-known documentary filmmaker named Ray Müller was intrigued by the many rejections she had received and "the difficulty of the project." He agreed to make a ninety-minute film for a consortium of European television companies put together by Panitz. Leni approved him, he believed, "because no one else would say yes."

Truer was that Leni thought she could dominate Müller. She had always been the least passive of movie actresses and was now, at ninety, on the threshold of the definitive version of the role she had been rehearsing all her life: Leni Riefenstahl, seeker and creator of beauty. If she lacked the stamina to direct a crew and herself, her drive to control Müller as her surrogate was no less steely than her determination to command legions had been in Nuremberg and Berlin.

The tension exacted by her willfulness never abated. "She always expected we were making an homage, and I always told her if we make an homage no one will show it. Until the very end she didn't understand that," Müller said, discovering that he had in hand a hot potato. "I wanted to begin the film with a montage of famous people responding to: what does the name Riefenstahl mean to you? But most of them didn't want to, Wim Wenders, for example. Basically no one wanted to be mentioned in connection with her name," he said. "Just being associated with the name of Riefenstahl is bad for your reputation. When rumors spread round that I was going to make the film, I was personally insulted by some people [who] called me 'Nazi Müller,' things like that."

Müller's producers had insisted contractually that Leni's cooperation be unconditional and without approval of the finished film. "The first fourteen days were horrible," Müller recalled. "She was obliged to answer everything and the producers were constantly afraid she might die before the end of shooting, so we confronted her with the unpleasant questions about her role in the Third Reich at the very beginning." These sessions would appear early in the film as Müller, in Pöcking, read passages aloud to her from Goebbels's diaries, some of them only recently recovered from Soviet archives. From the grave, Goebbels contradicted her version of bitter enmity and stressed instead his regard for her and their lively, even warm, social relationship. Leni leaped to her feet in imperious diva outrage—with cameras running—denying the existence of any such diary entries even as they lay open before her in Müller's hands.

She tried to call the project off and walked away from it at least twice before being persuaded by the producers to return. Quite apart from the financial sacrifice and liability she would incur if the film were not finished, "she found the thought unbearable," Müller believed, "that Leni Riefenstahl might be unable to bring yet another project to completion."

The film was designed as a more or less chronological review of her life, exploring "without preconceptions" whether she was, as the narration put it, "a feminist pioneer or a woman of evil." This nearly impossible task drew on copious film excerpts that alternated with Leni, wearing a bright pink raincoat and carrying a matronly handbag, explaining events in patient rhythms that suggested she had memorized her memoirs. To add a layer of spontaneity, Müller persuaded her to allow a "diary" of the film's making, shot with a video camera, to provide an "unofficial" record "for private use." The video results were cut into the final film and contributed startling vérité views of Leni's aggressive—even abusive—working personality that contrasted dramatically with the actress's gracious delivery of nostalgic reminiscences in the carefully lit and photographed set pieces.

The most memorable "diary" moments stemmed from her inability or unwillingness to take direction. She balked angrily at a shot Müller had planned on a sound stage at Ufa because it required her to walk and talk at the same time. "Talk? As I'm walking? No! I've never done that in my life!" she insisted. Müller later admitted that her outburst was the result of being so removed from studio technique that she had never worked with a moving camera and a microphone. She regularly complained about camera placement or light conditions ("Not in this shitty lighting!") and berated Müller for pursuing issues she wanted to ignore. Her anger so overwhelmed her when he tried to discuss *Victory of Faith* ("It has nothing to do with my *technique*!") that she grabbed him by the arms and physically shook him while the cameras turned. *Not* seen in the finished film were the medics who were then summoned to calm her or the two-hour break she required to regain her composure. "She tried to tell the cinematographers how to do the lighting and, at one point," Müller recalled, "became hysterical about a lens they were using. No one understood her complaint until she explained that the lens in question would reveal her wrinkles."

The ninety-minute film ballooned to three hours, a length its backers accepted without complaint. The excerpts from the Alpine films, *Tiefland, Olympia,* and, above all, *Triumph of the Will* (still banned in Germany), were too riveting and the unscripted glimpses into Leni's behavior too telling to cut, as were the samples of the never-seen Nuba and marine footage.

Müller pressed her when he could but was unable finally to shake her insistence on her political naïveté and ideological innocence. "Of what am I guilty?" she challenged him, adding (untruthfully), "No anti-Semitic word has ever passed my lips," and (truthfully), "I have thrown no atomic bombs." Perhaps the most suggestive moment in the film, the one that most hinted at unconscious self-revelation, showed Leni at her editing table in Pöcking raptly reviewing scenes from *Triumph of the Will* that she had doubtless seen a thousand times or more. Her eyes glittered, and it was not possible to know if she was lost in admiration for her superb editing skills, or for her film's chief actor as he surveyed the eager multitudes massed in submission to his will, or both.

"To say 'sorry' is too little," she told Müller when he challenged her apparent lack of remorse over the consequences of her work to anyone beyond herself. "But I can't tear myself apart or destroy myself. It's terrible. I've suffered for over half a century and it will never end, until I die." To his suggestion that she was viewed by many as "irredeemable," she replied, "It casts such a shadow over my life that death will be a blessed relief."

When Müller was criticized for allowing her to equivocate, he said, "I think I got to know her better than anyone. But no one can look into her depths. Why should someone at ninety step before the cameras to open that last interior window?" And anyway, "she had a creative life of seventy years, and to show only the eight years she worked under Hitler is not fair to the personality. Even if the other stuff may be less thrilling or less controversial, it's still what she did."

Predictably, when she saw the film, she hated it and told Müller it was an insult. Publicly she tried to distance herself. "The film contains some untruths and misunderstandings," she protested. "I also could have discussed more important things [in it] had the questions not been so provocative. But the director, in spite of having no contact with me whatever and bursting as he was with prejudice, did some good work. In any case," she added, "during the making of the film I suffered greatly."

When shown on European television as *Die Macht der Bilder* (*The Power of Images*) on October 7, 1993, the film was widely praised, even when commentators deplored Leni's regret for nothing about *Triumph of the Will* but the trouble it had caused her. The film was released theatrically at its full three-hour length in America as *The Wonderful, Horrible Life of Leni Riefenstahl* following its much-discussed première at the New York Film Festival in 1994. It stimulated thoughtful press attention to a ninety-plus phenomenon of energy and ego whose relationship to truth could never be taken for granted. "If you believe her, she's one kind of monster," wrote Terence Rafferty in *The New Yorker*, "if you don't, she's another."

Leni shed her distaste for the film as the world's spotlight grew, first sending Müller a grudging postcard, then a conciliatory letter, then calling to forge something like a wary friendship. Müller was—except for Horst—her last collaborator and one of her best. He was criticized for failing to subvert her narcissism, but his film came closer than any other to capturing the contradictory faces—flirtatious, arrogant, diffident, haughty, coy, tearful, dictatorial—that had alternately charmed and infuriated decades of admirers and adversaries. *The Wonderful, Horrible Life* became the ultimate Riefenstahl spectacle, a panoramic catalog of innovative techniques that concealed as they revealed without ever erasing what film critic Roger Ebert called "her unconvincing, elusive self-defense that continues to damn her."

In spite of "tremendous tension" while making the film, Müller emerged from it with the respect a battle-scarred veteran retains for a worthy opponent. After Leni died, he allowed that he thought her "a split personality," an aged woman in physical pain who was given to dramatic flights of self-pity but who also "would do anything for a good shot. In that respect, she's a model for every filmmaker."

Skeptics who derided the film as "Leni's Last Picture Show" underestimated her resourcefulness and ability to lure the spotlight even as her astonishing energy began to ebb. At a visibly infirm but still ambulatory ninety-eight, she called on Müller again in early 2000, consumed with the desire to embark on a sentimental return to Africa for a final reunion with her Nuba before she and they vanished altogether.

Civil war had raged in Sudan since her departure in 1977, killing thousands and brutally erasing the last vestiges of primitive tribalism. Rebel militias made any visit to Nuba regions perilous, logistically grueling even for a thirty-year-old. Still, a film could finance her return, she decided, a sequel—a coda—to round out her wonderful, horrible life. It could be titled *Leni Riefenstahl: A Dream of Africa* (*Leni Riefenstahl: Ein Traum von Afrika*).

The travel time was almost as daunting as the waiting. First came the twenty-hour journey from Pöcking to Khartoum. Then the week of waiting in the hundred-degree heat of the Khartoum Hilton for travel permits from a government with more on its mind than Leni; then the five-hour flight to the interior in a hastily requisitioned, obsolete Russian helicopter that was disabled by a flat tire hours short of its goal and was forced to land and off-load passengers for a final hours-long trek in vertebrae-jolting Land Rovers—all for a reunion that would not last a day.

Leni, Horst, Müller, and the film crew arrived at last in Kadugli to be greeted by a Nuba crowd in cotton housedresses and Bermuda shorts curious about the visitation of the strange European woman who had photographed them or their parents or their grandparents decades earlier.

She had brought along hundreds of photos, hoping this or that face would be recognized or even call to its original in the crowd. She handed them out in her safari suit and hat, feeding on the natives' enthusiasm, which momentarily conquered her frailty. When a few of the elders seemed at last to recognize her, Müller recalled, "she dove into a sea of sympathy."

The photos passed from hand to hand exciting chatter and, from the youngest, embarrassed laughter at the nudity long since banished by the Islamic regime. Finally, the crowd pushed a weathered woman forward, barely recognizable as the once-glistening young beauty in a portrait Leni had taken in another time and world.

Objectively speaking, the expedition was quite mad, even allowing for the follies of age. Leni sighed in the dusty clearing, "I'd like never again to leave," but admitted that the beauty of "her Nuba" was forever lost, degraded, like so much else, by this "terrible postwar world" into something "sad and dreadful."

Shortly after their arrival, as Müller took a break from filming and Leni was chatting up a cluster of aged Nuba, he heard an outcry. He looked up, alarmed to see Leni charging furiously toward him. She had just inquired after two of her oldest Nuba friends. Told they were dead, she had begun to weep when she suddenly realized Müller's cameras were idle. He had missed the dramatic moment, her emotion, and the proper angle to capture tears running down her face. Her fury mounted as she berated him and then stalked away, shaking with rage and frustration. Müller hurried to calm her, to explain he could not have known what she would hear, much less anticipate her reaction. She relented, giving him one last chance to rectify his inexcusable ineptitude with his cameras. She returned to the cluster of old men and, missing not a beat, repeated her inquiry, her shock, and her tears as if the moment were spontaneity itself. "I was fascinated," Müller recalled. "Even while grieving, this woman had already calculated the dramatic effect of her grief. The borderline between life and film is in constant flux with Leni Riefenstahl. And it *was* a key scene. She was right about that."

The reunion, in the end, lasted barely twenty hours. Early-morning gunfire threatened the filmmakers, and they were ordered to evacuate. Leni resisted until she was physically forced onto the Russian helicopter that had returned to fly them back to Khartoum. The outmoded aircraft, weighed down by ten passengers and flying low, attracted gunfire and crashed, overturning and rolling as it hit the ground.

Four passengers were seriously hurt, none fatally, but all endangered by fuel line breaks that threatened to ignite. Among them was Leni, who suffered broken ribs, a back injury, and cuts and abrasions to her face. Unconscious, she was transported by truck to a hospital in Khartoum and then back to Germany, where she regained consciousness several days later, having made headlines around the world. When she woke, she asked Müller if he had filmed her being dragged from the wreckage. He had not. Crestfallen, she wondered if they could fake the incident back in Munich, using blue-screen techniques. "Typical Leni," he thought.

Her physical courage had always been enormous, perhaps her greatest virtue, and it did not fail her now. She would never fully recover from the injuries she sustained in a crash that might have persuaded any other ninety-eight-year-old to give up the ghost. The pain in her back was so intense that she would require morphine injections every eight hours to get through the days remaining, and she still had miles to go.

Her centennial birthday was an event that would bring with it unprecedented public attention and—at last—the world première of her marine film, *Underwater Impressions*. She commissioned a score from pop composer Giorgio Moroder, who had recently fashioned a modern synthesizer score for Fritz Lang's *Metropolis*, the futuristic epic made at Ufa about the time Leni first stepped before cameras there in *Ways to Strength and Beauty*. Her forty-five-minute underwater film would be presented on television by the German-French arts channel Arte a week before her one hundredth birthday, when public interest would be at its zenith.

As her centennial approached, she seemed ubiquitous. Journalists around the world began running stories months in advance, perhaps afraid she might not make it to August 22. In America, she was interviewed at length on National Public Radio. In quick succession, the *New*

York Times, the *Los Angeles Times,* and *Time* profiled her, raising old questions and acknowledging old triumphs. European television ran interviews old and new beginning in early summer, airing clips from Alpine films most viewers were too young ever to have heard of. No nightly culture show was complete without coverage of her age, her past, her notoriety, and excerpts from *Olympia* and the still-banned *Triumph of the Will.*

Tabloid pages cackled with gossip about the lavish birthday party for almost two hundred guests to be held on a terrace overlooking Lake Starnberg from the Empress Elisabeth Hotel, named after the ill-fated "Sissi" of Austria, a onetime resident. Leni's guest list was tightly monitored, though mountain climber Reinhold Messner was sure to be there, alongside feminist publisher Alice Schwarzer, local politicians and television personalities, and—all the way from Las Vegas—Siegfried and Roy. The high-echelon turnout was minor on August 22, and most reporters left tactfully unstated the fact that no official congratulations arrived from the present occupant of the chancellor's office in Berlin.

When *Underwater Impressions* was broadcast a week earlier, it struck most viewers as undeniably beautiful in its lyrical revelations of coral reefs and creatures of the deep, but it was soporific. One reviewer called it "essentially trivial," another thought it "the world's most beautiful screen saver," and a wit wisecracked that Leni should have called it "Triumph of the Gill." It was preceded by a filmed introduction in which, meticulously coiffed and made up, Leni rhapsodized about beauty. Her remarks were unexceptional but jarring, for she pointedly underlined her membership in Greenpeace and her profound concern for the welfare of marine creatures destined for the aquariums of the world. They so often died in transport, she explained. It was impossible not to recall other transports and other deaths, for that same day, August 15, wire services buzzed with news that an injunction had been filed to spoil her birthday.

Her "darlings" were back with new and prominent champions. A Gypsy organization in Cologne called the Roma Union (Rom e. V.) had filed a complaint with the public prosecutor's office in Frankfurt accusing Leni of

Holocaust denial. Roma board members and well-known authors Ralph Giordano and Günther Wallraff acted as public spokesmen for the charge, brought in the name of a seventy-six-year-old Gypsy named Zäzilia Reinhardt, who had worked as an extra on *Tiefland* at fifteen and now called Leni "a filthy and shameless liar" for her widely reported claim that "we saw nearly all of [the *Tiefland* Gypsies] after the war. Nothing happened to a single one of them."

The evidence presented to the prosecutor's office that Leni's claim was reckless and untrue was overwhelming. It included dozens of names from Maxglan and Marzahn that matched death lists at Auschwitz or detailed prisoners' use as subjects in experiments there of Dr. Josef Mengele's, compiled from the Nazis' own records by survivors who scoured Leni's production stills and snapshots, much as Josef Reinhardt (who died in 1995 and was not related to Zäzilia) had done with Nina Gladitz in the eighties. Some of the photographs were entered as exhibits in the complaint, painstakingly identifying extras by name and Auschwitz prisoner number.

The Frankfurt court granted the injunction to halt Leni's claim that her Gypsy extras had uniformly survived the Holocaust. She signed an agreement to the judgment on August 9, thereby avoiding a civil trial and, with any luck, a press firestorm. But too many years had gone by with too many careless words and too little remorse. Roma press chief Job Tilmann had deftly timed announcement of the charges and Leni's compliance for the moment that press coverage of her film and birthday was most likely to gain attention from the international press.

Spokesmen Giordano and Wallraff minced no words about Leni. "I demand that she be honest," Giordano said, "that she rouse herself to a gesture that can prove she has learned something and has broken through her lifelong lies." Her birthday, he thought, "would be a good occasion for such a gesture." Wallraff was blunter, calling her "a terrible propagandist and beneficiary first class" of Hitler, of whom she remains "a glowing worshipper."

Just what a suitable gesture would be was unclear, though the Roma action was much more than symbolic. Holocaust denial is a serious crime in Germany, and if anyone knew the power of the courts, it was Leni. A possible solution, Roma announced, was that the credits of *Tiefland*, which acknowledged participation of anonymous "Farmers, Maidens, and Farmhands," would in future declare that they had been concentration camp inmates and unpaid forced labor. Nor was the gesture of reparations foreclosed, though no such costly demand was formally made.

Roma chairman Kurt Holl announced that Leni's recognition of her "moral duty" was the point. Her reckless, dishonest claims had reopened old "wounds" of a "still incredible trauma." In the end, a public statement would do and was, in fact, required by the court that had issued the injunction. "I regret," she said in response, "that Sinti and Roma had to suffer during the period of National Socialism." She added flatly, "It is known today that many of them were murdered in concentration camps."

As a statement, it was striking for its generic lack of conviction or even reflexive remorse. Perhaps it was futile to have hoped for more, for in Leni's memoirs, she had indignantly quoted an advertising blurb that accompanied videocassettes of the film Nina Gladitz made about her. "Is it legitimate," the blurb asked, "for the sake of art, to use the slaughter-house of a barbaric system for artistic aims? And is it legitimate to love the cinema so much that one violates human rights for the sake of art?"

Perhaps narcissism had blinded Leni to anything outside herself or self-righteousness had made her tone-deaf to any voice but her own, for she angrily mistook these questions as "slander."

TWENTY

AFTERLIFE

I am an artist through and through. That is Leni!
—Leni Riefenstahl

AS LENI LAY IMMOBILIZED in a hospital bed following the helicopter crash and before recovery was certain, Ray Müller asked if she regretted anything about her life. "My connection to the Third Reich," she said, nodding. "And," he continued, "if this were to be the last interview, what message would you want to leave behind?" "Say 'yes!' to life," she answered.

She had said "yes" to an extraordinary swath of it, full of striving and reward, daring and survival, fame and obloquy. But in the end, she admitted, repeating something she had told him a decade earlier, she could say yes to the "blessed relief" of death, too.

It came eighteen days after her one hundred and first birthday as Horst held her hand in Pöcking and her heart stopped beating at ten minutes before eleven on the evening of September 8, 2003. She had never fully recovered from the helicopter accident, though—physically courageous to the last—she had tried to ignore its aftereffects, announcing film projects she would complete if only she could find the money, such as the never-to-be-finished Nuba film or the old project about van Gogh and genius. She told reporters that she never went to bed before midnight and sometimes worked around the clock, but it was morphine and Horst that kept her going.

A few months before the end, she had experienced stomach pains, and doctors opened her up to find the cause of her complaint. They closed her up again and told her she was in amazingly good health for a woman of one hundred. Maybe she was, all things considered. The official cause of death was cancer, but it was finally the inevitable triumph of time.

International press reaction was avid and as mixed as ever. No major newspaper in the world failed to view her passing as page-one news, and none, now that litigation was safely foreclosed, shied from referring to her plainly as Hitler's propagandist.

Berlin, home to an official culture that by long tradition lavishly bestowed praise and honors on its artists, reacted coolly. The chancellor's office was silent, but Culture Minister Christina Weiss issued a carefully crafted statement confirming that the implications of Leni's life would live beyond her. "Leni Riefenstahl symbolizes a German artist's fate in the 20th century both in her revolutionary artistic vision and in her political blindness and infatuation. No one would deny that with her talent she developed cinematic methods that have since become part of an aesthetic canon. Her career also shows," the minister concluded, "that one cannot lead an honest life in service of the false, and that art is never apolitical."

Friends and acquaintances who had been largely silent during her lifetime spoke openly now that she was dead. Oscar-winning director of *The Tin Drum* Volker Schlöndorff thought it "a shame that she cannot now become an honorary member of the newly founded German Film Academy," and popular television actress Uschi Glas admitted that "for me she was a genius. I am very happy I was allowed to be her friend." Journalist and Hitler biographer Joachim Fest saw in her life and work a disturbing rebuttal to "the thesis that under National Socialism no art was possible, [although] her films portray a world of order and submission, of command and obedience, of rank and of file."

Other commentary in her homeland hinted at the links between life and art and artist and society. She was "an icon of the 20th century" who "conquered new ground in the cinema" as "the muse of the Nazis." If she was fascinated by Hitler, he was fascinated by her, and "their copulation took place in public—through the rape of the masses." She was "a vision-ary, a pioneer" whose "naïveté was an act" and whose "art always remained superficial" when it was not "beautiful and dangerous."

Hardly anyone failed to mention that an afterlife of sorts was in the offing. Two-time Academy Award winner Jodie Foster had earlier announced her intention to turn Leni's life into a film with herself in the lead. Controversy shook Foster's plans when the actress and the film-maker met in Munich and Leni insisted on her right—not Hollywood's—to dictate any depiction of her life story. She told the press that, in any case, Foster was not beautiful enough to play her on-screen. She saw Sharon Stone in the role.

Funeral services were held on the autumn afternoon of Friday, Sep-tember 12, at the crematorium of Munich's Ostfriedhof rather than at the Nordfriedhof, where Bertha had been laid to rest almost forty years ear-lier. The ceremonies were open to the public, who arrived by the hundreds to gawk or pay their respects and listen to musical selections from *Underwater Impressions* and *Tiefland*. They brought floral tributes to stand in for the official wreath from the government in Berlin that was conspicuous by its absence, and many laid old star photographs on the bier, where Horst, visibly shattered, laid his own farewell bouquet next to a fan's Leni scrapbook, open to an autographed portrait of Junta.

Invited guests and sightseers attended to a memorial speech delivered by Leni's friend and neighbor, the hostess of a popular television show on health and fitness named Dr. Antje-Katrin Kühnemann, who spoke with evident sincerity of Leni's genius and personal warmth. Then, after a few bars from *Tannhäuser* and a benediction, it was over. Nothing remained but an urn of ashes, some old star photographs, and the legacy of her work.

The films will survive. Susan Sontag, for all her perceptions, got one thing wrong. "Nobody making films today alludes to Riefenstahl," she had written. That was true, of course, if you discounted everything from George Lucas's *Star Wars* to the Disney company's *The Lion King* to every sports photographer alive to the ubiquitous, erotically charged billboards and slick magazine layouts to media politics that, everywhere in the world, remain both inspired and corrupted by work Leni perfected in Nuremberg and Berlin with a viewfinder that a film historian once warned suggested "the disembodied, ubiquitous eye of God."

The "horror of history" in which her apologists thought her "imprisoned" was a narrative of her own making about which she remained nostalgic and unrepentant. It was richly rewarded and free of any compulsion save personal ambition. She did not suffer from it but profited, and to suggest otherwise—as she often did—is an insult to the millions who died at the hands of a regime she took pride in glorifying, using, and enabling.

Thomas Mann once wrote that "art is moral in that it awakens," but Leni's art lulled and deceived. It will survive her not because of techniques that are already as often parodied as applauded but because it is the perfect expression of the machinery of manipulation it glorifies. Her films are, in the words of David Thomson, "the most honest and compelling fruit of fascist temperament [—] triumphant, certain, and dreadful." When future generations need to understand catastrophe in the twentieth century, they will look to Leni's work after she—"an artist through and through"—has been forgotten.

Simone Weil once noted, "The only people who can give the impression of having risen to a higher plane, who seem superior to ordinary human misery, are the people who resort to the aids of illusion, exaltation, fanaticism, to conceal the harshness of destiny from their own eyes. The man who does not wear the armor of the lie cannot experience force without being touched by it to the very soul."

Leni died as she had lived: unrepentant, self-enamoured, armor-clad.

ACKNOWLEDGMENTS

It is axiomatic that biographers are debtors—to the subjects who choose and compel them, and to those good Samaritans who help them keep an eye on the forest while thrashing through the trees. These generous souls furnish facts, anecdotes, and personal opinions, but, valuable as such offerings are, they are finally less vital, less of the essence than the moral imagination they sometimes bring to bear. When they do, the biographer's debt becomes limitless.

In the present case, I dutifully scoured the archives and found there secrets unrevealed and mysteries not yet unraveled. Libraries were valuable and the works of earlier researchers often illuminating, but nothing proved as indispensable as the generosity of Peggy Wallace, whom I sought out on a sunny California day in 2001 to discuss the doctoral dissertation she had written in 1975 at the University of Southern California titled *An Historical Study of the Career of Leni Riefenstahl from 1923 to 1933*.

After patiently answering my questions, Peggy (we quickly became first-name friends) revealed that she had originally planned to write a fuller and much more comprehensive work. As a result, she had taped lengthy interviews with a then-seventy-plus Leni Riefenstahl and some two dozen of her friends, collaborators, and critics, interviews that had gone unused and unheard following the decision to limit her thesis to the years before 1933.

All this material was, Peggy assured me, safely stored, waiting for a quarter century for the right moment and the right person. And so (miracles happen), I found myself loading cartons of meticulously preserved research treasures into a rental car, unconditionally entrusted with dozens of audiotapes in several languages, transcripts both raw and annotated, bundles of letters, piles of photographs, and hours of taped conversations with Leni Riefenstahl herself.

Thanks to this act of faith and generosity, I could consult people (many long gone) whose reminiscences and, often, moral imaginations clarified or suggested themes and issues as archives never can. Their taped voices include those of creative collaborators such as director Dr. Arnold Fanck; producer Harry Sokal; distributor Friedrich Mainz; art director Isabella Ploberger Schlichting; production manager Walter Traut; and cameramen Walter Frentz, Richard Angst, and Heinz (Henry) von Jaworsky, among many others.

Supplementing their accounts are the voices of Arthur Mayer and Peter Herald of the post–World War II American occupation authority, James Card of George Eastman House, and Robert Gardner of Harvard. Then there are those from inside the Third Reich, including Albert Speer, Fritz Hippler, Hans Weidemann, and more.

This was clearly an unparalleled windfall, but I am also indebted to those many who personally shared their time and insights with me. They include, in England, Kevin Brownlow, the late Hans Feld, David Meeker, Tony Palmer, Richard Westwood-Brookes, and the late Fred Zinnemann. In Europe I received guidance from Florian Beierl of Berchtesgaden; Oswald Iten of Zurich; the late Else Röhr of Nuremberg; and from Ray Müller, Florian Neubert, Mrs. Ernest Langendorf, Milan Pavlovic, Enno Patalas, and Gea Kalthegener, all of Munich. I declare an old debt to Hasso Felsing of Tenerife and a newer one to Karen Severns of Tokyo.

In America and Canada I owe Stephen Bates, Kate Buford, Linda Jäger D'Aprix, Tom Doherty, Scott Eyman, James C. Faris, Annette Insdorf, the late Kurt Kreuger, Richard Lamparski, Robert Lantz, Wayne Lawson, James May, Joseph McBride, Lt. Gen. Milton H. Medenbach (ret.), Col. Phillip C. Medenbach (ret.), the late George Pratt, Jan Rofekamp, Eric Rentschler, and Ruby Rich.

I am indebted to Dr. Elke Fröhlich of the Institut für Zeitgeschichte in Munich and the entire staff of that superlative institution; Stefan Drössler, Gerhard Ullmann, and Petra Maier-Schön of the Munich Film Museum; Gero Gändert and Werner Sudendorf of the Stiftung Deutsche Kinemathek in Berlin; Michael Stefan of the Staatsarchiv in Munich; Hans-Michael Bock of *Cinegraph* in Hamburg; Kay Hoffman of the Haus des Dokumentarfilms in Stuttgart; Jan-Christopher Horak at the Munich Film Museum and George Eastman House in Rochester; Rainer Rother of the Deutsches Historisches

Museum in Berlin; Timothy W. Ryback, director of the Salzburg Seminar in Austria; Charles Silver of the Museum of Modern Art in New York; Gerd Gmünden and Mary Desjardins of Dartmouth College; and Cooper C. Graham and Zoran Sinobad of the Library of Congress, Washington, D.C. My thanks as well to the staffs of the New York Public Library; Butler Library at Columbia University; the Staatsbibliothek in Munich; and Crossett Library at Bennington College in Vermont.

Sterling Lord deftly exercised his many skills in representation of this project, which also benefited from the legal eye and friendship of Stephen J. Sheppard. Both author and book enjoyed (again) the many privileges of being at Alfred A. Knopf, where Sonny Mehta's legend as publisher is daily justified and renewed. My editor, Jonathan Segal, proved once more that he is everything a writer could ask for in tact, taste, sophistication, and personal support.

I thank Ida Giragossian for her help and friendship, and Kyle McCarthy for being so reliable and so efficient so quickly. Art director Carol Carson was inspired in asking Gabriele Wilson to design the brilliant cover, and Peter Andersen happily assigned Kristen Bearse and her elegant visual style to the book's interior. I am again indebted to Kathleen Fridella for her meticulous production editing. Marci Lewis was an expert production manager; Kathryn Zuckerman guided public relations with rare enthusiasm and intelligence; Anke Steinecke read the manuscript with a lawyer's keen eye, and Sue Cohan saved me from embarrassment with her laserlike copyediting. Any remaining errors are, obviously, mine alone.

Finally, there are the intangible debts. First among my creditors is Werner Röhr of Munich and Vermont, followed closely by Dan Roth of Washington, James Kellerhals of New York, and Stephen Hollywood and Anke Heimann of Munich. In San Francisco (and wherever he happens to be) David Thomson is an unfailing source of witty, original, and morally imaginative thinking about movies and life, which is why—with my admiration—he shares the dedication in this book.

And—lastly—I hope these pages would have met the standards of Gea Kalthegener, Kay Rasco, and James Cresson, absent friends whose lights still shine.

NOTES

LIST OF ABBREVIATIONS

vii   Mann: *Magic Mountain,* p. 112. *"Die Kunst ist sittlich, sofern sie weckt."*

PROLOGUE

3   "broken record": From *Die Zeit,* August 19, 2002.
3   narrative that follows: See also Chapter 3 in these pages. This account is derived from several sources, notably Kreimeier, Kracauer, and Elsaesser, but is mostly based on the author's viewing of three 35-millimeter reels of *Ways to Strength and Beauty* at the Library of Congress in Washington, D.C., in June 2004 and July 2006. Though I have chosen 1925 because it

was the film's release date, it was filmed over the previous year and a half. Riefenstahl always denied being in the film, as, for example, to Rainer Rother (Rother, p. 186, n. 30). Many sources refer inexactly or tentatively to LR's participation in this film. Jürgen Trimborn, for example, claims she is identifiable in exterior exercise scenes (p. 59). She is not. A viewing copy is available through Transit Film in Munich, which administers its exhibition, but no video or DVD copies are available.

PART ONE: BERLIN

5 Gay: In *Weimar Culture*, p. 128.
5 Ratcliffe: Quoted in Everett, p. 9.

CHAPTER ONE: METROPOLIS

7 "I want to become": Gruel-Wemper.
7 "nowhere city" and "becoming": Ernst Bloch, quoted in Fritsche, p. 7.
7 Greater Berlin: Craig, *Germans*, p. 272.
8 "fastest city": Schutte and Sprengel, pp. 95–99.
8 dailies and weeklies: Fritzsche, pp. 12ff. Fritzsche cites 93 newspapers. Other sources count as many as 140. Peter Gay estimated 120 in *Weimar Culture*.
8 Kaiser Wilhelm: From his dedication speech for Berlin's Victory Column in 1901 (Everett, pp. 21–23).
8 more bridges than in Venice: Levy, p. 76.
8 "An art which": Everett, pp. 21–23.
9 "vanished Arcadia": Fest, *Hitler*, p. 96.
9 "apocalyptic landscapes": See Roters and Schulz, who borrowed the term from Meidner and used it generically for the 1987 "Ich und die Stadt" exhibition in Berlin.
9 "Tenement sickness": Korff and Rürup, p. 304; infant mortality: p. 42. The official date of this statistic is 1905.
9 one-reel movies being shot in Wedding: Berg-Ganschow and Jacobsen, p. 194. The small studio became known as the Komet-Film-Atelier in 1911 and from 1918 on was called Rex-Atelier. It was remodeled in the early 1920s and became home to actor-director Lupu Pick, who made well-known films there, including *Scherben* (1921) and *Sylvester* (1923).
9 crematorium: Korff and Rürup, p. 241.
10 Zille and Berlin-Wedding: Ibid., pp. 39–41.
10 "I hated": The friend was Gitta Sereny, *German Trauma*, p. 240.
10 Riefenstahl civil wedding and family dates, here and later: Reichsschrifttumskammer, "Abstammungs-Nachweis" ("Proof of

Descent"), Leni Riefenstahl file, Berlin Document Center (September 6, 1933). LR formally petitioned the film office for her identification card on October 2, 1933, and received card number 1352. LR file, BDC, as above.

10 father's firm and architects: Int. PW/IPS, July 2–3, 1971. Schlichting remembered meeting Alfred while she was working at an architectural firm in Berlin in the 1920s headed by Ernst Petersen, nephew of film director Dr. Arnold Fanck (see Chapter 3). This cannot be dated but raises the intriguing possibility that LR had an early contact to Fanck through her father that she never acknowledged.

10 born cross-eyed: LRM, p. 3. An odd editing error exists in the English translation of the memoirs, in which *Scherlach* is misspelled *Scherlack* throughout. The former is correct.

10 mother's mother and childbirth: LRMG, p. 15; in LRM, the same story is on p. 8.

11 Jewish rumors in the press: See, for instance, "La Disgrâce de Leni Riefenstahl," *Paris-Soir,* June 14, 1937, which seems to have been the primary source for subsequent reports published in Switzerland and elsewhere. In America, see "Is Hitler in Love with a Jewess?" in *Liberty,* July 16, 1938, or Padraic King's "The Woman Behind Hitler," *Detroit News,* February 21, 1937, both sensational in tone.

11 malicious campaign orchestrated by Goebbels: See LRM, pp. 206–7. For LR's anger on this subject, see int. PW/LR, August 8, 1971, tape 16a, transcript p. 12.

11 Fanck as Nazi: He joined the party on April 1, 1940, and carried membership number 7,617,249 (Horak, "Fanck: Träume," p. 59).

11 Isabella Ploberger: Int. PW/IPS, Alicante, Spain, July 2–3, 1971, tape 2, transcript pp. 17–18.

11 genealogical record of ancestry: The documents state that LR's grandfather Karl Scherlach was born in 1842 into a family that then spelled its surname "Schidlach." "Abstammungs-Nachweis," as above, from which family dates, names, and other details have been taken.

12 Ottilie was almost certainly: See LR, *Vogue,* August 2002, p. 228, plus LRM, pp. 22–23, and LRMG, p. 42.

12 confirmed as Protestant: LRM, p. 11.

12 "loved her": Sereny, *German Trauma,* p. 237.

12 Heinz, was born: LR gives his birth in Wedding and in 1905, but his marriage license certifies birthplace and date as Neukölln on March 5, 1906. Standesamt Berlin-Wilmersdorf, Nr. 1001, 1935–H.

13 Zeuthen was idyllic: LRM, pp. 7–10.

13 Berlin moves: LRMG, p. 24. LR mentions "Yorkstrasse." "Yorckstrasse" is the correct spelling.

13 "best friend": LRM, p. 38.
13 poetry and plays: Ibid., pp. 4, 7.
13 "driving force": Ibid., p. 4.
13 "Dear God": Ibid., p. 3.
14 "even insects": Ibid., p. 7. LR also cites poetry she wrote to the trees in *Vogue,* August 2002, p. 226, which began: *"Sie waren zwei Brüder"* (They were two brothers).
14 airline industry: LRM, pp. 10–11. Unlikely as this sounds, LR wrote a letter detailing these plans to a friend. The original letter, quoted in her memoirs, was displayed in a retrospective exhibition at the Potsdam Film Museum in 1998–99.
14 *Gymnasium* story: Int. PW/LR, August 6, 1971, tape 14, transcript 2. See also Wallace's dissertation, p. 59.
14 fairy tales: LRM, p. 4; LRMG, p. 17, where the magazine's title is given as *Es war einmal.* The English translation *Fairy Tale World* is approximate but incorrect.
15 "It was not": Sereny, *German Trauma,* p. 237. The acquaintance was, of course, Gitta Sereny.
15 "the good times": LRM, p. 14.
15 "a cloud" and "a dreamer": Ibid., pp. 13, 6.
15 The film was titled *Opium:* The film was press-screened in Berlin on February 6, 1919. LR dates her audition vaguely, but late 1918 is likely correct (Bier, p. 321).
16 motion picture debut: LRMG, p. 29. She dates this experience vaguely as well, but it may have occurred after the *Opium* tryouts rather than before.
16 went to someone else: The role went to an actress named Sigrid Hohenfels: Bier, p. 321.
16 "desire to rush": LRM, p. 12.
16 "I stood": LR, *Vogue,* August 2002, p. 228.
17 assassination estimate: Kessler, *Diaries of a Cosmopolitan,* p. 189.
17 "the faintest notion": LRM, p. 13.
18 Kessler quote: *Diaries,* pp. 59–60.
18 "a kind of insanity": Stefan Zweig, quoted in Gay, *Weimar Culture,* p. 130.
19 "No pain": LRM, p. 12.
19 "We had few": Ibid.
19 Anita Berber: Mostly from Fischer.
20 "national sewer": Fest, *Hitler,* p. 94.
20 "roaring like a rogue elephant": LRM, p. 14.
20 School of Arts and Crafts: Ibid., p. 17.
20 Hela Gruel: Gruel-Wemper.
21 "Siberia": Ibid.

21 "as long as I lived": LRM, p. 14.

21 "clever idea": Ibid., p. 19.

CHAPTER TWO: DEBUTS

22 Alfred Riefenstahl: LRM, p. 22.

22 "How I wish": Ibid., p. 19.

22 "Too bad": Ibid., p. 11.

22 LR as feminist role model: The New York Film Festival in 1973, for example, attempted to group LR with Agnès Varda and Shirley Clarke as feminist pioneers.

22 sexual preference: There are commentators eager to label her with lesbian adventures, but the claim seems unsupported. An example is the Russian George Rony, who worked with Eisenstein and called Riefenstahl "an alley cat" and worse. Int. PW/George Rony, February 2, 1971, tape 26.

23 Zweig: From *Die Welt von Gestern*, p. 287, quoted in Gay, *Weimar Culture*, p. 130.

23 "I was a very late": The friend was Gitta Sereny, who recounts the conversation in *The German Trauma*, p. 238.

23 son of the free-living poet: His name was Paul Walden. LR incorrectly calls him Paul Lasker-Schüler. The relationship is omitted in the English-language version (LRMG, pp. 29–30).

23 Kessler quote: Kessler, *Diaries*, p. 114.

23 slashed his wrists: Walter Lubovski receives more space in LRMG than in the English-language version (LRMG, pp. 23ff, 43ff). His brother Oskar later became LR's personal physician, and his sister Hilda married the sculptor Josef Thorak, about whom LR would produce a film during World War II (LRMG, p. 178). The family was Jewish. The quotation can be found in LRM, p. 24.

24 "silvery green silk gown": LRM, p. 28.

24 beauty contest and editor: Ibid., p. 29.

24 Vollmoeller: Ibid., p. 30. Vollmoeller was notorious for his attentions to young women, though he had a long-term alliance with the actress and journalist Ruth Landshoff.

24 jockey's wife: LRMG, p. 32.

25 "traumatic": LRM, p. 33; for "rape," see LR, *Vogue*, August 2002, p. 253.

25 "bondage": LRM, p. 38.

25 Haffner: Haffner, *Defying Hitler*, p. 45.

26 job on the stage: LR, *Vogue*, p. 228. She says she was trying to get a job as a dance extra at a theater on the Nollendorfplatz.

26 "You are as stubborn": LRM, p. 22.

26 "repugnance": Ibid., p. 33.

26 Wigman school: Ibid., p. 34.

27 postwar inflation: Haffner, *Defying Hitler,* pp. 5off; Friedrich, *Before the Deluge,* pp. 122–27.

27 sketches of her "dreadful": LRMG, p. 56. LR's friendship with the artist, who was named Willy Jaeckel, is almost entirely missing in the English translation.

27 Baltic Sea story: LRM, pp. 28, 35ff; LRMG, pp. 5off, 6off. Also, int. PW/HS, August 13, 1971. There are conflicts in the two versions of the story. LR says it was in Warnemünde, near Rostock on the Baltic, and Sokal cites Travemünde, near Lübeck. As Sokal was there to gamble and the latter town had a casino (Rostock had shipyards), it is likely that LR's version is faulty.

27 Heinrich Richard Sokal: Sokal was born February 20, 1898, in Craiova, Romania, and died·in Munich on March 7, 1979.

27 "And after ten seconds": Int. PW/HS, as cited, tape 12, transcript p. 1. Sokal later called himself Henry in exile from Nazi Germany.

28 "I realized": LRM, p. 28.

28 their affair: Sokal, in his PW interview, is frank about their love affair, here and later.

28 Bullock quote: Bullock, *Hitler: A Study in Tyranny,* pp. 90–91.

29 observer: It was William Shirer in *Rise and Fall,* p. 96.

29 Kershaw: *Hubris,* p. 201.

29 Malcolm Crowley: Quoted in Friedrich, *Deluge,* p. 125.

29 "Don't worry": Int. PW/HS, Munich, August 13, 1971, tape 12, transcript p. 3.

29 "I'm a gambler": Ibid., p. 1.

30 one American dollar: LRMG, p. 61. How LR's father financed her October debut in Berlin has not been determined. LR's writings give no clue. Harry Sokal might have been assumed the source of finance in his romantic campaign of LR, but he pointedly claims to have only financed the Munich appearance and a later one in Innsbruck.

30 house musicians: LR refers to the Klamt School's Herbert Klamt as her accompanist in all concerts, but the program for the evening in Munich credits the Paul Mueller-Melborn chamber trio (LRMG, p. 87).

30 dances and titles: Quoted from the original program, reproduced in LRMG, p. 61.

31 newsstand prices: Rother (German), p. 23.

31 critics: *Münchner Neuesten Nachrichten,* October 25, 1923, and *Münchner Zeitung,* October 25, 1923, both cited in Rother (German), pp. 23–24, and Rother (English), pp. 15–16. The translation here is partly from Dr. Anke Heimann.

31   "triumph": LRM, p. 26.

31   "Now, I believe": LRMG, p. 62.

31   Döblin anecdote: Willett, p. 75.

32   Vollmoeller tickets: LRM, pp. 36–37. Reinhardt was not personally involved in booking acts for his theaters, though Vollmoeller may have used influence in securing the bookings. LR's implication that Reinhardt was personally responsible is misleading.

32   earnings and clothes: LRM, p. 37.

32   Robison: LR misspells his name "Artur" (LRM, p. 38). It was Arthur: He was born in Chicago.

32   conflicting schedules: *Pietro* was shot from August to October 1924, according to Wolfgang Jacobsen, p. 276. LR was preparing dance bookings for the same period, though they were interrupted by injury.

32   "indescribable": LRMG, p. 64.

32   Sokal and bookings and furs: LRM, pp. 38–39.

33   "I had": LR, *Vogue*, p. 253.

33   "I wish with body and soul": Quoted in int. Hoffmann/LR, *Die Welt*, January 7, 2002.

33   press book: It was titled "Die Tänzerin Leni Riefenstahl, Auszüge aus Pressekritiken" (The Dancer Leni Riefenstahl, Excerpts from Critical Reviews).

33   "vaudeville": *National Zeitung*, December 17, 1923.

34   "charming wonder girl": *Kämpfer*, Zurich, February 24, 1924.

34   "marvelously gifted," etc.: As quoted and translated in LRM, p. 36.

34   no manager was likely to notice: Rainer Rother points out that the critic here published his review on December 12, 1923, in the *Münchner Neuesten Nachrichten* in reference to a return concert LR gave following her successful Berlin debut. LR consistently quotes this review in an edited version as if it referred to her maiden concert. See LRM, p. 36.

34   "hymn of praise": LRM, p. 36.

34   "When one sees": This is translated from the German version of LR's memoir. The English version omits the names of German dancers the reader presumably would not know and reads: "When one sees this girl move to the music, one has an awareness that here is a dancer who will appear perhaps once in a thousand years, an artiste of consummate grace and unparalleled beauty" (ellipses in original), which equally, if differently, distorts the critic's original meaning. See Fred Hildebrandt, *Berliner Tageblatt*, December 21, 1923, reprinted in *Fred Hildebrandt: Tageblätter, Erster Band 1923/24* (Berlin: Landsberg-Verlag, 1925), pp. 139ff. The English translation here is Dr. Anke Heimann's. LR misquoted this review as late as August 2002 in German *Vogue*, where she again cited the line "the

dancer who appears once every thousand years" as if it referred to her and not to an ideal that her performance failed to realize.

34 Hildebrandt had gone on: For the omitted portions of Hildebrandt's quote, see same as cited in preceding endnote.

35 arrival of a genius: Rother makes this point on p. 29 and throughout. His subtitle reflects the thesis: *The Seduction of Genius.*

35 Schikowski: *Vorwärts,* November 16, 1923, cited in Rother (German), p. 203.

CHAPTER THREE: CLIMBING

36 "A picture": Telegram from LR to Harry Sokal, circa 1925. Int. PW/HS, Munich, August 13, 1971, tape 12, transcript p. 4.

36 "unexpected": LRM, p. 41.

36 "regeneration": Quoted by Kracauer, p. 142.

37 hit of the day: Janssen, pp. 47ff.

37 "advocacy for restoring": Kreimeier, p. 177.

37 *Die Weltbühne:* Quoted in ibid.

37 publicity still: *Der Querschnitt,* April 1925, pp. 24–25; republished in *Der Querschnitt: Das Magazine der aktuellen Ewigkeitswerte, 1924–1933* (Berlin: Ullstein, 1981), pp. 30–31.

37 Wigman's ensemble dancers: Trimborn erroneously cites LR's appearance in outdoor exercise scenes (p. 59). Kreimeier cites Ufa documents confirming participation in the film (German version, p. 296) but does not claim to have seen it.

38 "comeback": Rother, p. 253. Rainer Rother located letters in the Bavarian State Archives (Akte Staatstheater, 12123) dating from August and September 1924 inquiring about possible future "comeback" dates between October 1924 and January 1925, though no such engagements took place (Rother, pp. 200–201).

38 "I sensed": LRM, p. 57.

38 poster description: Ibid., pp. 40–41.

38 "changed my life": Ibid., p. 40.

39 Heine on Novalis: *The Romantic School and Other Essays* (New York: Continuum, 1985), p. 76.

39 Critics routinely alluded: For example, re *Mountain of Destiny, Der Kinematograph*'s critic wrote: "These are images full of the Romantic, in their composition thoroughly stylized after the painting conventions of the 19th century" (quoted in Horak and Pickler, p. 29).

39 Rentschler: *Ministry,* p. 32.

40 as real and as dangerous as it looked: *The Holy Mountain,* for example, begins with titles announcing: "The well-known athletes who collaborated

on *'The Holy Mountain'* beg the public not to mistake their feats for photographic tricks, which they are not. The outdoor scenes were shot in the most beautiful regions of the Alps over the period of a full year. Actual German, Norwegian, and Austrian athletes ran the ski races. The screen story, timelessly in and of the mountains, derives from twenty years' life experiences in the high mountains."

40 "The very first": LRM, pp. 41–42.

40 "incomparable" and "ice-axes": Kracauer, *Caligari*, pp. 110–11.

40 He detected "a kind": Kracauer, pp. 111–12, introduction, and jacket. The classic complaint about Kracauer is that he is polemical, but that is his aim: His introduction, written in May 1946, a year after VE Day, cites the then-new United Nations and the difficulties it faced in dealing with a postwar Germany whose "deep psychological dispositions" (p. v) he believed "influenced the course of events during that time and which will have to be reckoned with in the post-Hitler era."

40 "Immaturity": Kracauer, *Caligari*, pp. 111–12.

41 Austrian Ski Association: Österreichische Skiverband's Aryan policy: The vote took place October 7, 1923. It inspired a counterorganization, the "Allgemeiner Skiverband," in anticipation of the 1924 Winter Olympic Games in Chamonix, to which Austria, though not Germany, was invited.

41 contemporary writer: T. Brandlmeier, "Arnold Fanck," in *Cinegraph*, 1984, quoted in Elsaesser, *Weimar Cinema*, p. 391.

42 distribution company acquired it: It was the German-American Film Distribution Company (Horak, "Dr. Arnold Fanck: Träume vom Wolkenmeer und einer guten Stube," p. 29).

42 "spellbound": LRM, p. 42.

42 Sokal on Heinz: Int. PW/HS, August 13, 1971, tape 12, transcript p. 3.

43 "long-forgotten fairy tales": LRM, p. 42.

43 "red cliffs": LR, *Kampf*, p. 11. A parallel and similar passage occurs in LRM. In neither version does LR allude to Sokal's presence.

43 Sokal and in following: Int. PW/HS, August 13, 1971, Munich, tapes 12 and 13. Here, tape 13, transcript pp. 21–23.

43 Trenker as architect: Trenker, *Kameraden*, p. 200.

44 "exalted": Georg Fruhstorfer, "So wurde ich Luis Trenker," *Die Neue Welt*, September 1971.

44 Trenker's "Ten Commandments": In Trenker, *Meine Berge*, p. 9.

44 "I'll learn how": LRM, p. 43.

44 Trenker and "I *must*": Int. PW/HS, tape 12, transcript 12, p. 4.

44 Trenker and Fanck's telephone number: LR, *Kampf*, p. 12. In this version, LR says she called Trenker in Bolzano from Berlin to get Fanck's number.

44 Rahn arranges meeting with Fanck: LRM, p. 43.

44 Pribram: LR, *Kampf*, p. 14.

45 Though no one knew (and following): LRM, pp. 43–45.

45 Fanck knew who she was: Riess, *Das gab's nur einmal*, vol. 1, pp. 252–62. Riess gives a breezy insider's account whose source appears to be LR. He maintains that Fanck knew who LR was when they met, as her well-publicized dance appearances in Berlin had occurred only months earlier. In his 1971 interview with Peggy Wallace cited here, Fanck claims to have seen her dance before writing his script. Riess does not mention Sokal.

45 Fanck to Trenker: Trenker, *Alles*, p. 209.

45 Sokal offers an intriguing variant: Int. PW/HS, as cited, tape 12, transcript 12, p. 4.

45 Sokal's deal and Leni: Horak, p. 39; also in Infield, pp. 163ff. Sokal's own version is on tape 12, transcript pp. 5ff.

46 "very much in love": Int. PW/HS, as cited, tape 12, transcript 12, p. 5.

46 "love affair with Fanck": Ibid., pp. 5ff.

46 "grew more": LRM, p. 47.

46 "painful decision": Ibid., p. 45.

46 "That was": Int. PW/LR, August 7, 1971, tape 15, transcript 2, p. 14.

47 "a death mask": Rentschler, *Ministry*, p. 36.

47 "A love story": Horak, p. 32.

49 "ugly and strange": LR, *Kampf*, p. 15.

49 "that film": Ibid.

49 "because he loved me": Int. PW/LR, August 8, 1971, tape 16a, transcript 16a, p. 15.

49 "the first time": LRM, p. 48.

49 "thunderstruck": Ibid.

49 "What would happen": Ibid., pp. 48–49.

49 "madman": Ibid., p. 49.

50 Fanck's recollection: Fanck memoir, translated by Leopold Zahn, pp. 153–54.

50 "sexual obsession": Horak, "Träume," p. 45.

50 Fanck interview: Int. PW/AF, July 23, 1971, tape 9, transcript 9, p. 1.

50 "What if": Fanck memoir, p. 153.

50 "Then Trenker came": Int. PW/AF, July 23, 1971, tape 9, transcript 9, p. 2.

50 "love things": Int. PW/LR, August 7, 1971, tape 15, transcript 2, p. 15.

50 bones in her foot: *Neue Rhein-Zeitung* (Düsseldorf), March 17, 1960. In another version, it was a broken ankle. See LRM, pp. 49–50. In LR, *Kampf* (p. 17), it is two bones.

51 Leni in the cabin: See LRM, pp. 52–53ff.

51 Fanck's version: Fanck memoir, p. 154.

51 Sokal's version: Int. PW/HS, tape 12, transcript 12, pp. 6ff.

51 "Ufa to take the whole picture": Ibid., p. 6. Two years later, Sokal told Glenn Infield a slightly different version. There he says: "She had told me herself one night when she left Trenker, who made her unhappy and crying, and was seeking consolation in the arms of Schneeberger" (Infield, pp. 163–64). In this account, Sokal suggests that LR's affair with Fanck continued at the same time. "The reason for my anxiety was threefold: three lovers!" (ibid., p. 163).

51 Leni directing: LR, *Kampf,* p. 24.

51 cable from Fanck: LRM, p. 55.

52 "very nice pictures": Fanck memoir, p. 160.

52 America: The picture was distributed in the United States in 1928 by Paramount, which retitled it *Peaks of Destiny,* inadvertently creating confusion with Fanck's earlier *Mountain of Destiny.*

52 Vienna review: Quoted in Trimborn, p. 74, though misdated September 24, 1926, three months before the film was actually released.

52 Berlin *Morgenpost:* Quoted in Trimborn, p. 74.

52 the reviewer who had earlier written: This was John Schikowski, cited in Rother (German), p. 203.

52 *New York Times:* Mordaunt Hall, November 29, 1927, p. 31.

CHAPTER FOUR: HIGHER

53 "so near": LR, *Kampf,* p. 37.

53 Trenker: *Meine Berge,* p. 9.

53 "The film is a masterpiece": Siegfried Kracauer, *Frankfurter Zeitung,* March 4, 1927, quoted in Rentschler, *Ministry,* p. 313.

53 "there is an outpouring": *Der Montag Morgan,* December 20, 1926.

54 "obtrusive propaganda": Alex Eggebrecht, *Die Weltbühne,* January 11, 1927.

54 review in caps: *Westfällischen Volkszeitung,* January 10, 1927, quoted in Horak, p. 33.

54 "He taught me": LRM, p. 51.

55 "already dedicated to me": LR, *Kampf,* p. 26, where she tells herself it is "your film."

55 *Film-Kurier: Film-Kurier,* June 24, 1926.

55 Schneider as lover: Fromm, *Blood and Banquets,* p. 130; bitter regret: Salkeld, p. 35. See also Walker.

56 Disney: LRMG, pp. 92–93.

56 "national cause": Kreimeier, p. 159.

56 Hugenberg's critics: Erich Schairer, quoted in Kaes, Jay, and Dimendberg, p. 72.

57 Fanck justified: Fanck, *Er führte*, p. 167.

57 "he was a child": Int. PW/HS, August 13, 1971, tape 12, transcript p. 6.

57 "He liked being led": LRM, p. 63.

58 "terrible grind": Ibid., p. 62.

58 "a marvelous feeling": Ibid.; also LR, *Kampf*, p. 37, for "stars."

58 Depressed: LRMG, p. 103.

58 "Prelude to the Olympics": Ibid. Compare to LR, *Kampf*, pp. 40–41.

59 "beautiful people": LR, *Kampf*, p. 40.

59 "gray hell": Ibid., p. 42.

59 Spiro: LRMG (p. 56) dates the portrait 1924 and ties it to her dance career. Other sources date it 1925, when LR was already acting. It would subsequently illustrate the dust jacket of the first German edition of LRMG.

59 filmed quickly in Vienna: LR told PW that the film was made while Fanck was in St. Moritz shooting the Winter Olympics, but that is clearly an error. The likely shooting date is January 1928. Int. SB/PW, 2001.

59 film is lost: There is, at the Film-Archiv in Vienna, a recent reconstruction of what remains of the film's Italian version. Fragments without LR exist in Berlin at the Bundesfilmarchiv.

59 Sokal unaware: Int. PW/HS, August 13, 1971, tape 13, transcript p. 20.

59 admitted only reluctantly: Peggy Wallace, interviewing LR in 1971, found her resistant to discussing the film at all.

60 Fromm: Fromm, *Blood and Banquets*, p. 130. Fromm misnames Sokal "Franz" and misspells his last name as "Sokall." Her book was written in American exile in the early 1940s. For her work as diplomatic correspondent of the *Vossische Zeitung*, see Gilbert, p. 833.

60 Betty Stern: LRM, p. 66. For Stern, also see Bach, *Marlene Dietrich: Life and Legend*.

60 "a love story": LRM, p. 63.

61 twenty-three: Ibid., pp. 152–53. She was more open about her ignorance in int. PW/LR, August 11, 1971, tape 17, side B, transcript 4, p. 7, where she says, "I didn't know exactly who this was" when the character was first mentioned to her. She had never heard of the play either. "So by this time I was curious to read the story. And then after I read it I was really fascinated."

61 *Penthesilea:* The work was a Reinhardt staple. Marlene Dietrich appeared in a minor role in the Reinhardt production at the Deutsches Theater in 1923 (Bach, *Marlene Dietrich*, p. 52).

62 "a single night": LR, *Kampf*, p. 42. In LR's memoirs, this is altered to read, "He wrote day and night" (LRM, p. 67).

62 "It was six or eight": Int. PW/HS, August 13, 1971, tape 12, transcript pp. 7–8. Sokal later told a similar version of the story to Frederick Ott (see Ott, p. 96).

62 "they *laughed*": Int. PW/HS, August 13, 1971, tape 12, transcript p. 8.

62 "tried to take": LRM, p. 67.

63 "a man who": Int. PW/HS, August 13, 1971, tape 12, transcript p. 10.

63 LR on Gustav Diessl: Sokal to Ott, in Ott, p. 96.

64 assistant director: Mark Sorkin, "Six Talks on G. W. Pabst," *Cinemontages 3* (New York: 1955).

65 "I passed the theater": Int. PW/HS, August 13, 1971, tape 12, transcript p. 8.

65 Mordaunt Hall: *New York Times,* September 27, 1930, p. 21.

65 *Variety* noticed: *Variety,* December 11, 1929. The reviewer ("Trask") misnamed both directors, calling Fanck "Frank" and Pabst "Papst."

66 "black magic": LRM, p. 74.

66 "mental anguish": Ibid., pp. 74–75.

66 "Every night": Ibid.; p. 71.

66 "At last": Ibid., pp. 72–73.

67 critical dismay: In addition to Kracauer, *Caligari,* see Herbert Ihering in Dahlke and Karl, p. 263.

67 "it was as if ": Trenker, *Kameraden,* p. 194.

67 Trenker's "Ten Commandments": In *Meine Berge,* p. 9. The first commandment goes in full: "Thou shalt undertake no ascent without being ready: thou must be superior to the mountain, not the mountain to thee. Thou shalt devote thyself to a goal suitable to thy abilities, but—if it must be—forsake the goal until the time is right. Thou shalt take thy time to reach thy maximum strengths, and not race the second hand of the stopwatch. Thou shalt not devour the peaks, but also not shrink from the manifold actions on the mountain climber's paths."

68 Trenker "would go through": Int. PW/HS August 13, 1971, tape 13, transcript p. 10.

68 Sokal on the completed film: Ibid., transcript p. 15.

CHAPTER FIVE: ABOVE THE CLOUDS

69 Balázs: Balázs, "Der Fall Dr. Fanck," p. vii.

70 Ufa, MGM, and Paramount: This connection was formalized as Parufamet and involved reciprocal distribution arrangements in America and Germany for all three companies. The American firms took shrewd advantage of Ufa's financial straits after *Metropolis* to profit at Ufa's expense. See Kreimeier, among others.

70 "I do not like civilization": Ott, p. 124.

70 Louise Brooks complained: Paris, pp. 321–22. The remarks are in letters to Brownlow from the 1960s.

71   "gabbing and laughing": Ibid., p. 323.

71   Female directors: There were exceptions, such as actress-producer Ellen Richter in Berlin, but the most famous European woman director from this period was Leontine Sagan, whose *Mädchen in Uniform* was released in 1931 to international success. Sagan was Viennese, raised in South Africa, to which she returned in the late 1930s. In America, there was Lois Smith, among the very few.

71   Fredersdorf: Int. PW/AF, July 23, 1971, tape 9, transcript p. 7.

71   "Fanck never forgave me": LRM, p. 79.

71   Sokal on Leni's relationships: Int. PW/HS, August 13, 1971, tape 12, transcript p. 5.

72   sexual energy: Documentarian Tony Palmer met with her in the 1990s and found that the sexual aura she gave off was palpable (int. SB/Tony Palmer, January 25, 2006).

73   Rist as "woodcut": Dr. Walter Bing, in Horak, p. 218.

73   Leni insisted: LRMG, p. 126. On Allgeier and LR, see Paris, p. 323.

73   "dramaturgical collaborator": In the book about the film—though not on-screen—Fanck credits Mayer, misspelling his name "Karl Maier" (*Stürme über dem Montblanc*, p. xv).

73   "greatest film portrayer": Balázs, "Der Fall Dr. Fanck," p. v.

73   "Dr. Fanck directs": Ibid., p. vii.

74   outgrossed even *Piz Palü: Storm* took in 2.3 million reichsmarks, compared to the earlier film's 2.2 million (Horak, pp. 39, 42).

74   Alpine publication: *Der Bergsteiger*, published by the German-Austrian Alpine Association. The writer was Dr. Walter Bing. Cited in Horak, pp. 214–19.

74   to alarm Siegfried Kracauer: Kracauer, *Caligari*, pp. 257–58.

74   "mountain-possessed": Ibid., p. 258.

74   reviewer from the *Times: New York Times*, B.W.N., March 26, 1932, p. 17.

75   sound in Berlin in the early 1920s: The process referred to here is sound-on-film, or optical sound, as opposed to sound-on-disk, which was less reliable and flexible. The first public exhibition of sound-on-film occurred in Sweden in 1921, though experiments had been under way in Europe at least since 1910 or even earlier.

75   bitter joke: Fest, *Hitler*, p. 314.

75   Ian Kershaw: *Hubris*, pp. 406–7.

77   re Hans Feld: Int. SB/Hans Feld, May 25, 1990. Re Karl Vollmoeller: Riess, in *Das gab's nur einmal*, vol. 2, p. 112. Vollmoeller knew Josef von Sternberg from America and was engaged by Pommer to work on the screenplay for *The Blue Angel* with Carl Zuckmayer and Robert Liebmann. Authorship of that script has long been debated, though Vollmoeller probably worked on

structuring it, rather than writing scenes or dialogue, and his main contribution may have been the prestige of his name.

77 "unfortunately one-sided": LRM, p. 77.

77 "Du-Du": Ibid.

78 Dietrich and Riefenstahl: A number of contemporary writers have paired the two in studies of stardom or in imaginary confrontations, as in Thea Dorn's *Marleni,* a witty radio play in German. In life, they had almost no direct contact, in spite of a famous photograph by Alfred Eisenstaedt of the two of them with Anna May Wong, who was something of a cult figure in Berlin, at the Berlin Press Ball of 1929 (not 1928, as is usually recorded). Riefenstahl clearly saw herself as Dietrich's rival, if only in the competition for most famous German woman of the twentieth century.

78 "Sternberg visited me" and "before Pommer": LRM, p. 77.

79 "talented admirer": Sternberg's student was the author.

CHAPTER SIX: *THE BLUE LIGHT*

80 "I used everything": LR quoted by Sokal, int. PW/HS, Munich, August 13, 1971, tape 13, transcript p. 13.

80 "it hadn't even": LRM, p. 90.

80 "I see everything": LR, *Kampf,* p. 67. This passage from 1933 is repeated with significant variation in the 1987 memoirs, in which Riefenstahl precedes the parallel text with the words "Almost against my will," although the earlier version makes clear that her determination was firm (LRM, p. 89).

80 "I am not gifted": Int. PW/LR, August 11, 1971, tape 17, side B, transcript 4, p. 4.

81 Fanck knew the novel: Fanck had introduced LR to Renker's novels when they were making *The Holy Mountain,* which was titled after an earlier Renker work called *Heilige Bergen* (*Holy Mountains*). For *The Blue Light,* Fanck stated she "took the story idea from one of the books of Renker" (Zsuffa, p. 454). He supplied Peggy Wallace a copy of the original Renker in 1973 to prove his point.

82 Renker's story: *Bergkristall,* p. 43.

82 "everything . . . came from my head": Wallace, p. 285.

82 "I began to dream": LRM, p. 89.

82 LR as Junta: This is a central theme of LR's at least since her 1965 interview in *Cahiers du Cinéma* with Michael Delahaye, reprinted in Sarris, *Interviews.*

83 "ladies' man": Zsuffa, p. 204.

83 "Balázs was not immune": Ibid.

83 "I find in Béla": LR, *Kampf,* p. 69.

83 with the aid of Carl Mayer: Mayer also worked on the editing of the picture (Zsuffa, pp. 215, 219).

84 slapstick comedy team: They were inspired by the Gebrüder Wolf, a Jewish brother team from Hamburg who enjoyed wide vaudeville popularity in the early years of the century.

84 "too boring": LRM, p. 89.

84 "I showed my *Blue Light*": Int. PW/LR, August 11, 1971, tape 17, side B, transcript p. 8.

84 "I wanted to make": Quoted in Rentschler, *Ministry,* p. 32.

84 "entirely my own": LR, *Kampf,* p. 15.

85 credit revision: A postwar release of the film in 1952 carried the still-misleading credit "a mountain legend by Leni Ricfcnstahl." The presently available restoration (with which LR was not involved) reinstated the original credits for television showings on Arte.

85 Wilder quote: Zsuffa, p. 209.

86 Balázs and infrared film: Loewy, p. 13, citing Ralmon, p. 18. The point about the Agfa film stock was of some importance to LR, who gave the impression that its designation as "R" was tribute to her, though Agfa confirms the stock preexisted *The Blue Light*. See LRM, p. 92.

86 "Film without": LR, *Kampf,* p. 15.

87 the artist who: LRMG, pp. 48, 142. He is identified only in the German version.

87 "redemption": Undated (circa 1932), unsourced clipping, German Film Institute, Riefenstahl file.

88 "mutilation": LRM, p. 99. For more positive versions, see especially Frederick Ott, p. 126, where he speaks of Fanck's "characteristic generosity" and LR's "happiness."

88 Fanck on rushes and editing: Int. PW/AF, July 23, 1971, tape 9, transcript pp. 5–7.

89 Leni told a more dramatic tale: Int. PW/LR, August 8, 1971, tape 16, transcript 16a (unauthorized by LR), pp. 14–15. LR refused to authorize a transcript of this tape about Fanck because he was still living and she felt her comments were "too personal." She also forbade quotation of her comments to him. Int. PW/SB, 2002.

89 Fanck and interviewers: Peggy Wallace was subjected to a tirade from LR in 1971 when it was revealed that she had spoken with Fanck (PW tape 16, transcript 16a, pp. 10–23).

89 "shattering," "boring," and following citations: Letter, LR to Béla Balázs, February 21, 1932. Cited from Balázs papers as MTA, Ms 5021/320, in Loewy, pp. 15–16.

89 "I learned cutting": Int. PW/LR, August 6, 1971, tape 14, side A, transcript 14, p. 19.

90 "an undreamt-of-success": LRM, p. 99.

90 "Berlin critics outdid": Ibid.

90 Sokal on Jewish critics: Int. PW/HS, August 13, 1971, tape 13, transcript 13, pp. 3–4. Sokal went on record in this regard several times with minor variations, most publicly in a letter in *Der Spiegel* that ran under the title "Über Nacht Antisemitin geworden?" ("Overnight an Anti-Semite?"). He wrote substantially the same account to LR biographer Glenn Infield on October 20, 1975 (Infield, p. 229). LR challenged his *Spiegel* letter with a letter of her own in the issue of November 15, 1976, as "Nie Antisemitin gewesen" ("Never an Anti-Semite").

90 "inwardly sick": Hermann Sinsheimer, "Zwei Legenden," *Berliner Tageblatt,* March 26, 1932. That her parents read the *Tageblatt:* Sereny, *German Trauma,* p. 239, where LR added in referring to the paper that it was "owned by a Jew until 1933."

90 *Film-Kurier:* March 26, 1932.

91 Rudolf Arnheim: Trimborn, pp. 363–64. The quotation is from a conversation with Arnheim conducted in Ann Arbor, Mich., October 10, 1999, by German journalist Tita Gaehme, for broadcast on German radio on January 1, 2000, under the title "I Always Trusted Reality: About Rudolf Arnheim."

91 1938 press releases: Quoted from press material prepared by Tobis, the distributor in 1938.

91 Paul Ickes: LR, *Kampf,* p. 6. Ickes wrote film reviews for *Deutsche Filmwoche.*

92 New York reviews: *Sun,* May 9, 1934; *Herald Tribune,* May 9, 1934.

92 suggesting that credits: Both reviews suggest that a revision of credits had already taken place by 1934, more than a year after the Nazi seizure of power.

92 The *Times: New York Times,* H.T.S. [Harry T. Smith], May 9, 1934, p. 23.

92 "only one wish": Letter to Béla Balázs, February 21, 1932, as cited above.

92 Sokal and exile: LR's memoirs deny that she and Sokal had an intimate relationship, and she trivializes his role in her career and life. She was writing, it should be noted, after Sokal's cooperation with Glenn Infield on the latter's hostile LR biography, after the *Der Spiegel* letter noted above, and after his death precluded rebuttal or litigation.

Her text is openly hostile. She barely acknowledges that he had to leave Germany because of Nazi racial policies and never mentions removal of his name from the credits of *The Blue Light*. She resents his having been able to transfer money from Germany to Switzerland when he went into exile and accuses him of gambling away "my fifty-percent share of the foreign receipts for my film" (LRM, p. 368). The charge is impossible to verify one way or the other, but it is likely that 50 percent of nothing was nothing. In any case, receipts would have gone first to repay distribution expenses, then outstanding production costs, which Sokal had borne or arranged for.

LR's version of Sokal's exile is inaccurate. She claims he left Germany for France and then America. In fact, he left Germany for England, where he produced a picture called *Dusty Ermine* in 1936. He then resettled in France, producing *Le Grand Élan*, before emigrating to America in 1941. There he was under contract to Monogram Pictures and associated with the Paul Kohner office after the war. He returned to Germany in 1950.

LR's charge that Sokal lied to her in claiming that the negative had been burned in Prague is impossible to verify. Such a claim could have been made as an evasive action to prevent discovery that it had been sold in America to Rony (see text).

LR further claims that Sokal, as the original producer, demanded a share of the proceeds from the 1952 revision of the picture. It is worth noting that at no time does LR ever refer to his sharing in or entitlement to proceeds from the 1938 rerelease.

92 Balázs had accepted: Zsuffa, pp. 229–30, 462–63.
93 LR to Streicher: The letter is in the Riefenstahl file of the BDC.
93 Leni was later to cite Balázs: LR claimed in *Five Lives* (p. 305) that she remained friendly (*"Freundschaftlich verbunden"*) with Balázs until his death in 1949, though there is no evidence for such a claim. Balázs's biographer writes, "She never tried to make amends for having failed to compensate 'the Jew Béla Balázs' for his labors on her film" (Zsuffa, p. 363).
93 George Rony: Here and hereafter: Int. PW/George Rony, February 2, 1971, interview 26. His reference to "an agent" is not clear. This may have been Sokal or possibly someone connected with Paul Kohner or his agency.
94 LR on Rony: LRM, pp. 367–68. LR says Kevin Brownlow told her about Rony.
94 Jaworsky on LR and *Mein Kampf:* Int. PW/HVJ, September 10, 1972, tape 30, transcript p. 7.
94 Sokal on *Mein Kampf:* Int. PW/HS, August 13, 1971, tape 13, transcript p. 2.
95 "I'll work for them": Int. PW/HVJ, September 19, 1972, tape 30, transcript p. 7.

PART TWO: ASCENT

97 Hitler: Quoted in Fest, *Face*, p. 147.
97 Streicher: Letter from Streicher to LR, July 27, 1937, Riefenstahl file, BDC. The letter is written in the familiar second-person form, *Du*.

CHAPTER SEVEN: LIGHTNING

99 "Once we come": LRM, p. 106.

99 "All I thought about": Sereny, *German Trauma*, p. 239.

99 voting statistics: As comparison, the steadily weakening Social Democrats attracted 21.6 percent of the vote, and the German Communist Party lagged with a mere 14.5 percent in the same election. The Social Democrats had gone steadily downward from 29.8 percent of the vote in 1928. The Communists were growing, but incrementally: Their 10.6 percent of the 1928 vote rose to 14.5 in July 1932 and peaked at 16.9 in November of the same year, an election that saw a falloff of the Nazis' vote from the high of 37.4 percent to 33.1 percent.

99 "All I thought about": Sereny, *German Trauma*, p. 239.

100 never heard radio: She made the claim to Sereny. Ibid. For 1932, see Chapter 6 and Rudolf Arnheim.

100 "did not know enough": West, *Train of Powder*, p. 34.

100 stimulated by *Mein Kampf:* LR admitted owning the book at a later date but sidestepped the issue of her first exposure to it, implying that all she knew of Hitler before hearing him speak was what she was told by strangers. See LRM, pp. 100–101.

100 "I read it on the train": John Beevers, "The Girl Hitler Likes," *Sunday Referee* (London), December 4, 1938.

100 German historian: Fest, *Face*, p. 71.

100 "to destroy the foul legends": *Mein Kampf*, unpaginated p. vii.

100 "I was so": LRM, p. 100.

101 Fanck adamantly opposed to LR: Fanck, *Er führte*, pp. 253–54.

101 LR on Universal: LRM, p. 102; the actual fee: Fanck, *Er führte*, pp. 253–54.

101 Kohner's name removed: Int. SB/Gero Gändert, SDK, August 8, 2003. Kohner discovered that his name was removed on the night of the première, August 30, 1933. In some accounts, he had a nervous breakdown because of LR's Hitler salute from the stage. See Horak, p. 49. Gändert of the SDK doubts the nervous breakdown but confirms that Kohner was outraged by LR's salute.

Kohner's tryst with LR: Andrew "Bandy" Marton was directing another picture for Kohner and Universal, a comedy called *North Pole, Ahoy!* and was the editor on the English-language version of *S.O.S. Iceberg*. Marton became a longtime Kohner client. Int. PW/Andrew Marton, December 14, 1970, tape 29, transcript p. 2.

101 "Leni came to me": Fanck, *Er führte*, p. 254.

102 "without a doubt": LRM, p. 113.

102 "Don't let that little tramp": Knopp, p. 102, though Knopp misattributes the remark to Ertl, who was quoting Riml.

102 "might help": LRM, p. 103.

103 dubbed in London: Garnett, p. 152.

103 Alfred Wegener: Wegener died in 1930; his remains were discovered the following year. Two members of his expedition served as consultants on *S.O.S. Iceberg*.

104 Hitler rally: Hitler spoke at only one rally in Berlin in late February, which was LR's dating of the event. Hitler's citizenship is a matter of public record on February 26, 1932.

104 Ernst Jäger: LR makes this claim in the Ray Müller film *Wonderful, Horrible Life*.

104 "It was like": Sereny, *German Trauma*, p. 240.

104 "I had an almost": LRM, p. 101.

104 Joachim Fest: Fest, *Hitler*, p. 324.

104 Nietzsche's sister and American journalist: Ibid., pp. 327–28; Fest is quoting Kessler's diary entry of August 7, 1932. The American, Fest notes, was H. N. Knickerbocker.

105 Ernst "Putzi" Hanfstaengl: Hanfstaengl, p. 34. "Putzi" Hanfstaengl (Harvard 1909) was half American. His mother was a Sedgwick from New England, and he was descended from two American Civil War generals. His Munich family was prominent in art publishing in Europe and New York, where Hanfstaengl sat out World War I as an enemy alien forbidden to leave the United States. It was his American dollars during the postwar inflation that enabled the then-obscure Nazi Party to buy its own newspaper, the *Völkischer Beobachter*. Hanfstaengl was important in attracting other socially prominent supporters in the early 1920s. He escaped from his former Nazi cohort to England and finally to America during World War II, where he furnished American intelligence with insights into Hitler's psychology.

105 "Sometimes he reminded me": Ibid., pp. 35–36.

105 Haffner quotes: Haffner, *Defying Hitler*, pp. 71–72. Though Haffner's memoir was not published until after his death, it was written in the midthirties.

105 Shirer: *Twentieth Century Journey*, p. 127.

105 "deeply affected" and "hail a cab": LRM, p. 101.

105 "unreservedly": Ibid., p. 102.

106 letter to Hitler: LR's memoir contains what she asserts is a remembered version of the letter on p. 103. It reads:

  "Dear Herr Hitler,

  "Recently I attended a political rally for the first time in my life. You were giving a speech at the Sportpalast and I must confess that I was so impressed by you and by the enthusiasm of the spectators that I would like to meet you personally. Unfortunately, I have to leave Germany in the next few days in order to make a film in Greenland so a meeting with you prior to my departure will scarcely be possible; nor indeed do I know whether this letter will ever reach you. I would be very glad to receive an answer from you.

"Cordially, Leni Riefenstahl"

106 "my curiosity": LRM, p. 105.
106 "The most beautiful": Ibid.
106 "Was this chance": Ibid.
106 LR on AH: Ibid., p. 106.
106 "Once we come": Ibid.
107 "prescribed films" and "I have to have": Ibid.
107 "racial prejudices": Ibid.
107 Hitler's advance: Ibid., p. 107.
107 Hanfstaengl quotes: Hanfstaengl, p. 203. Re Hitler's impotence and possible homosexuality: Hanfstaengl, pp. 22–23.
108 Walter Frentz quote: Int. PW/Walter Frentz, August 3, 1971, tape 11, transcript pp. 26–27.
108 what Fest calls: *Hitler*, p. 254.
108 "I suppose": The friend was Gitta Sereny. *German Trauma*, p. 243.
108 "I told no one": LRM, p. 107.
108 "private airplane": Int. PW/Andrew Marton, tape 29, transcript p. 5. The detail of the bouquet of flowers is from Salkeld, p. 80.
108 copy of *Mein Kampf:* Sorge, p. 203.
108 "photographs of Hitler": Marton, as above, transcript pp. 5–6.
109 with Hans Ertl: Ertl, quoted in Salkeld, p. 86.
109 Hitler's air campaign: Kershaw, *Hubris*, p. 363.
109 campaign technology: Fest, *Hitler*, p. 318.
109 "We must": Kershaw, *Hubris*, p. 364.
109 "The basis of ": Quoted by Fest, *Hitler*, p. 319.
110 "I did not": Ibid., pp. 342–43.
110 "The question": Kershaw, *Hubris*, p. 381.
110 "I've chosen my path": Ibid., p. 389.
111 "Only the weak": LRM, p. 127.
112 Hitler scene in the Kaiserhof: Ibid., pp. 128–29.
112 Sereny: *German Trauma*, p. 242.
112 historical records: Kershaw, *Hubris*, p. 401.
112 Goebbels re suicide: Quoted in Shirer, *Rise and Fall*, p. 177.
112 Goebbels on Strasser: Ibid.

112 "Without having uttered": LRM, p. 129.

113 "his special charm": Ibid., p. 133.

113 "not a tempestuous love": Ibid., p. 152.

113 "oddly enough": Ibid.

113 Ertl phone call anecdote: "Ich, Hans Ertl," German television, 1992.

CHAPTER EIGHT: THE TURNING POINT

115 Haffner: *Defying Hitler*, p. 144.

115 Goebbels: Diaries, June 12, 1933.

115 "chance, frivolity": Fest, *Hitler*, p. 367.

116 Erich Ludendorff: Quoted in Kershaw, *Hubris*, p. 427.

116 Goebbels told his diary: Diary entry for January 31, 1933, quoted in Kershaw, *Hubris*, p. 423.

116 "mass desertion" and "fog": Fest, *Hitler*, pp. 373, 391.

116 "to preserve": Ibid., p. 391.

117 "God-given signal": Quoted in Kershaw, *Hubris*, p. 458.

117 an emergency decree: Fest cites this decree as "the decisive legal basis for Nazi rule and undoubtedly the most important law ever laid down in the Third Reich" (Fest, *Hitler*, p. 398).

118 violence claimed the lives: Shirer, *Rise and Fall*, p. 190.

118 "glorious triumph": Quoted in Kershaw, *Hubris*, p. 461.

119 Dachau headlines: Gellately, p. 52.

119 Dachau restrictions: Werner Meyer, "KZ Dachau—davon hat jeder gewusst," *Abend-Zeitung* (Munich), January 31, 2003, p. 10. The Dachau KZ (concentration camp) is today an official historic site, whose exhibits attest to public awareness of the camp's establishment. For contemporary news stories, see Meyer, above, and Stackelberg and Winkle, p. 145. See also Distel and Jakusch, and Ryback, "Report from Dachau."

119 Streicher's boycott: In Stackelberg and Winkle, pp. 143–44.

119 "an imposing": Quoted in Gilbert, p. 35.

119 Ian Kershaw: *Hubris*, p. 475.

120 LR on parents: Sereny, *German Trauma*, p. 239.

120 Alfred Riefenstahl: Bundesarchiv: 3200/S0019 NSDAP-Mitgliedskartei (National Socialist Party Membership file).

120 Carl von Ossietzky: Ossietzky had always been a troublesome journalist. He had first fallen afoul of the Nazis before Hitler took office by revealing the pre-Nazi program for rearmament, a violation of the Versailles Treaty.

120 "loudmouthed": Ossietzky, "Ein Wintermärchen," in *Die Weltbühne*, January 1, 1933, p. 4.

121 "Hitler did not come": Fest, *Hitler*, p. 374.

121 Leni returned to Berlin: LR often is vague about dates. In *Five Lives* (p. 307), she states she returned to Berlin in June knowing nothing of events such as the book burnings or Jewish boycott. In fact, by May 16, she already figured in Goebbels's diary in Berlin.

121 LR on Ufa: LRM, p. 136.

121 Ufa's skittishness: Ufa minutes of September 5, 1933, reveal unreadiness to sign a contract with LR until "her artistic qualities have been subjected to careful scrutiny . . . undertaken in absolutely objective terms" (Rother [English], p. 190, n. 28). In any event, LR was already making her first Nazi Party rally film by the date these reservations were recorded.

121 Hamburg: Book burnings occurred there on May 15 and, because the turnout was disappointingly small, were repeated on May 30.

121 Goebbels spent much of the opera: Goebbels, *Tagebücher*, vol. 2, p. 421, May 17, 1933 (for May 16). LR's account of the visit to *Madame Butterfly* (specifically cited) is undated. JG's entry for May 16 reads, "Evening with Magda and L. Riefenstahl to *Butterfly*. Well sung and played. Afterwards, we chatted at the Traube." See LRM, pp. 167–68.

122 clubfoot: Reuth, p. 8.

122 "petit bourgeois": Fest, *Face*, p. 139.

122 recording in his diary: April 19, 1926.

122 anti-Semitism of JG: Fest, *Face*, pp. 130–51.

122 "He is a genius": Quoted in Fest, *Face*, p. 140 (diary entry for July 24, 1926).

123 Goebbels on propaganda: Quoted in ibid., pp. 142, 141.

123 Hitler on propaganda: *Mein Kampf*, p. 177.

124 Goebbels's order to film companies: *New York Times*, April 2, 1933, p. 1.

124 Thalberg and Kauffmann: Gabler, pp. 338–42.

124 David Stewart Hull: Hull, p. 24. The moment eerily prefigures the studios and television networks preparing blacklists without being asked during the McCarthy period in the United States.

125 Ufa figures: Mostly Kreimeier, p. 228.

125 stages statistics: Beyer, p. 21. He refers in German to "studios," but the term is too grand for what were mostly small companies with stages for hire.

125 Goebbels to Ufa: Beyer, p. 22, and Hull, p. 21.

125 Goebbels at the Kaiserhof: Kreimeier, pp. 208–9; Beyer, p. 21; and Riess, *Das gab's nur einmal*, pp. 205–10.

125 Jewish artists: Some witnesses to Goebbels's speech, such as Friedrich Mainz, later head of Tobis Film, believed that Goebbels didn't know he was lauding Jews. See int. PW/Friedrich Mainz, July 29, 1971, tape 10, transcript pp. 13–14.

126 civil service law: Quotations from Article 1, Article 3, and Article 4 of the

"Law for the Restoration of the Professional Civil Service" ("Gesetz zur Wiederherstellung des Berufsbeamtentums"), in Stackelberg and Winkle, pp. 150–51.

126 Peter Gay: *Weimar Culture*, p. xiv.

126 Coordination of the film industry: On April 8, the *New York Times* reported that production had "almost completely ceased at all studios pending the passage of expected film laws" (cited in Hull, p. 20).

126 June 30 rules: Hull, p. 26.

126 Goebbels retaliated against the Actors and Directors Association: Ibid., p. 22. The organization was known by its acronym DACHO, the umbrella trade union of filmmakers, Dach-Organisation der Filmschaffenden Deutschlands.

127 until June or July: See *Die Zeit-Magazin*, no. 36/1997, p. 13, where she claims, "In the first five months of the takeover of power I wasn't even in Germany, but shooting with the Americans on location in the Bernina Pass in Switzerland. We lived there in a mountain cabin, without television or even radio. I didn't experience the takeover at all and had no hint of the book burning. I came back to Germany only in July 1933."

It is worth noting that LR consistently uses the *"Machtübernahme,"* or "takeover of power," locution rather than *"Machtergreifung,"* or "seizure of power."

127 "a Hitler film": JG diaries, May 17, 1933.

127 meetings with JG: The JG diaries for 1933 cite meetings on the following dates, generally in diary entries made the following day: May 16, May 25, June 11, June 12 or 13, June 15, June 20, July 4, July 9, July 14, July 17, July 18, August 13, August 15, August 16 (pp. 421–58). The visit to Goebbels during his wife's absence (see Chapter 9) was on Sunday, August 13 (p. 457). (Hereafter, dates without page numbers refer to the date of entry rather the date of meeting. It should be noted that the indexes of the Goebbels *Tagebücher* are imperfect and omit some dates listed here.)

127 "her new film" and "She is": JG diaries, June 12, 1933.

127 "spoken with Hitler" and "is now starting": JG diaries, June 14, 1933, for June 12 or 13.

127 "Very nice": JG diaries, June 16, 1933.

127 publication in the 1930s: See JG, *My Part in Germany's Fight*, published in January 1935 as a translation of *Vom Kaiserhof zur Reichskanzlei, Eine historische Darstellung in Tagebuchblättern, vom 1 January 1932 bis zum 1 Mai 1933*, published in Germany in 1934.

128 suggested . . . tainted: See Gitta Sereny, who makes the point that their publication was a kind of "guarantee" in *Albert Speer: His Battle with Truth*, p. 133.

128   JG and *Piz Palü:* JG diaries, December 1, 1929.

128   "I, I alone": To Michel Delahaye in *Cahiers du Cinéma,* here from Sarris, *Interviews,* p. 459.

128   "you must make": LRM, p. 106.

CHAPTER NINE: TOTAL DEVOTION

129   Hitler epigraph: From *Tischgespräche,* dated July 26, 1942, quoted in Fest, *Face,* p. 498.

129   London review: *Observer,* December 3, 1933.

129   "most fervent wish": LRM, p. 136.

129   Josef von Sternberg: Ibid., p. 131.

130   "There is no greater": Ibid.

130   at the behest of Erich Pommer: Jacobsen, pp. 120–21. Pommer left for New York at the new year and did not return to Berlin until the *Machtergreifung* was complete and would stay only briefly.

130   He had traveled to Berlin: Bach, *Marlene Dietrich,* pp. 164–66. Also Sternberg, p. 229. LR attributes to Sternberg a degree of political awareness that he made a point of disclaiming.

130   "penniless": LRM, p. 135.

130   a full-time maid: Ibid., p. 129.

131   private screenings at Hitler's residence: JG diaries, July 14, 1933, for July 13. Location visit: JG diaries, July 9, 1933, for July 8, to Seckendorf and a film then titled *Blut und Scholle,* released as *Thou Shalt Not Envy.*

131   opera and theater: JG diaries, July 4, 1933. For "Auwi," JG diaries, July 18, 1933, for July 17. Altogether the Goebbels diary cites fourteen separate social occasions or professional meetings from May 16 through August 16.

131   late-May picnic excursion: JG diaries, May 26, 1933. Meetings with AH: LRM, p. 136. Mid-June at AH's private residence: JG was present as well. JG diaries, June 16, 1933.

131   another trip to the Baltic: LRM, p. 141; Viktoria von Dirksen: Fest, *Hitler,* p. 301.

132   "I wept": LRM, p. 135. Re Balázs: LR mentions letters from Balázs, but Zsuffa (p. 229) claims that Balázs wrote her in December 1933 to tell her he was suing.

132   Hitler offers filmmaking post: LRM, p. 137. Horst Wessel: The film about him was released, withdrawn, recut, and finally reissued as *Hans Westmar* late in 1933. LR had nothing to do with it, though Ernst "Putzi" Hanfstaengl composed the music.

132   Fichte: Int. SB/Timothy Ryback, July–August 2002. LR's dedication to Hitler read, *"Meinem lieben Führer in tiefster Verehrung."* The final word

translates as "devotion" or "worship" in German and has a note of submission not conveyed by the approximate "admiration."

132 "a veritable blizzard": Ryback, "Hitler's Forgotten Library."

132 Hitler re party rally film: LRM, pp. 143–44.

133 Hitler's rant and "such an honor": Ibid., p. 143.

133 "ordinary newsreel footage": Ibid., p. 144.

133 Ufa's reservations voiced after Nuremberg: See notes to Chapter 8 re Ufa's decision.

133 "the tasks I have set": LR, "Wie der Film vom Reichsparteitag entsteht," *Der Deutsche*, no. 14, January 17, 1935, here quoted after Rother (English), p. 98. The reference is to *Triumph of the Will*.

134 film division established: Loiperdinger, "*Sieg des Glaubens*," p. 36.

134 not reached until late July: Zelnhefer, p. 64. Stuttgart had been competing as a possible rally site, with Nuremberg dragging its municipal heels about the 1933 rally until Hitler delivered an ultimatum to city officials on July 22. The decision was announced on July 25. At issue was the financing of future rallies, which the city of Nuremberg was expected to underwrite.

134 Nuremberg as AH symbol city: Fest, *Speer*, p. 56.

134 "The masses need": Fest, *Face*, p. 498.

135 "glacial crevasse" nickname: This was ubiquitous. For one citation among many, see Zuckmayer, *Geheimreport*, pp. 93–94.

135 "cripple": Sereny, *Speer*, p. 134.

135 repelled by Goebbels's behavior: LRM, pp. 129–42; "his face" is on p. 142.

135 "hated me": Ibid., p. 146.

135 1936 Olympics: Int. PW/Friedrich Mainz, July 29, 1971, tape 10, transcript p. 9. Mainz was the eventual commercial distributor of the Olympics film(s).

136 perceptive acquaintance: This was Gitta Sereny, in *Speer*, p. 134. Sereny refers to "her shame."

136 "Hitler film": Loiperdinger, Moeller, and Rother never mention that the Nuremberg rally was not conclusively scheduled until late July and therefore speculate differently on the "Hitler film" issue. The July decision seems strongly to suggest that the rally film and the "Hitler film" were separate projects.

136 August dates LR and JG: JG diaries, pp. 457–59.

136 late-August itinerary for AH: JG diaries, August 1933 inclusive.

136 August 23: Loiperdinger, "*Sieg des Glaubens*," p. 37. The announcement was made by the film division of the propaganda administration—that is, Goebbels's office. An almost identically worded announcement also appeared two days later in *Film-Kurier*, August 25, 1933. The dating is significant, in that LR claimed that she was told of the commission only three

days before the beginning of the rally—that is, on August 27 or 28 (LRM, p. 144).

137 cost of admission and number of participants: Zelnhefer, pp. 66, 153.

137 Hitler and Goebbels conferred: JG diaries, August 23–25, 1933, pp. 460–61. The diary entries make clear that no comprehensive planning for the rally had been done before late August.

137 "nailed to a truss": Sereny, *Speer*, p. 100.

137 "shooting match": Ibid.

137 "huge, marvelous": Ibid.; also Fest, *Speer*, pp. 32–33.

137 Hitler "stood": Ibid., p. 32.

137 "big, that's all": Sereny, *Speer*, p. 100.

138 Speer on LR: Int. PW/AS, tape 1, transcript p. 1.

138 LR meets Speer: Sereny, *Speer*, p. 132.

138 She thought him: Ibid., p. 136.

138 "total devotion": Ibid.

138 "humiliation": LRM, p. 147.

138 "Nobody understands": Int. PW/AS, tape 1, transcript pp. 5–6. Speer is adamant on this point. "Goebbels was out."

139 gossip at Ufa: A letter dated August 28, 1933, reports that the Aryan wife of a Jewish screenwriter at Ufa named "Katscher" claimed to be LR's first cousin and that LR's mother was Jewish. Apparently no interview with Frau Katscher survives, but her husband was Leo Katscher, who emigrated from Germany and turned up in Hollywood in 1943 working for Samuel Goldwyn. He contributed to a number of screenplays in the 1950s, most notably *The Eddie Duchin Story* in 1956. See Horak, *Fluchtpunkt Hollywood*, p. 92. Riefenstahl file, BDC.

139 Arnold Raether and LR's racial descent: The report, dated September 6, 1933, is signed "v. Allwörden," who also wrote the letter referred to in the preceding note. A letter written by Raether on September 8, 1933, states, "I brought the matters . . . to Herr Hess's attention in Nuremberg. He decided to investigate the case [but] it has not been possible to discover anything detrimental to her regarding her descent." LR submitted a "Questionnaire" on October 4, 1933, where she merely filled in blanks with the word *Arisch* (Aryan). Riefenstahl file, BDC.

139 Speer on LR and Hess: Int. PW/AS, tape 1, transcript p. 5. LR's weeping is from this account. The investigation into LR's ancestry was still under way at the time of this interview, and if Speer was aware of it, he is mute on the subject. LR's version of the interrogation by Hess is in LRM, pp. 145–46, where she describes herself as "furious" and not, as Speer had it, weeping. It is highly unlikely that she knew an investigation into her racial descent was being conducted at the time.

139 "network of . . . bureaucracies": Speer, interview by Norden, p. 83.

140 "totally involved," "genius," and "hard work": Int. PW/AS, tape 1, transcript pp. 10–11.

140 task was "to glorify": Ibid., transcript p. 6.

140 cameramen added to the team: All of them would later work on *Triumph of the Will*. Frentz says he was interviewed and hired by LR at her apartment in Berlin, not Nuremberg (int. PW/Walter Frentz). If this is true, it would mean that LR was working on the film before her arrival in Nuremberg on August 27.

141 opening credits: They state: "All of the German newsreels made available their footage for this film." Though *Victory of Faith* was long thought lost, copies began to resurface in Germany and England in the 1980s, minus the opening credits and the opening Nuremberg sequence, though a complete copy was found in the 1990s in the former East Germany. In 2003, a small American company issued the full film, including credits and Allgeier's Nuremberg footage, on DVD. The author has relied on both the film version of the Munich Film Museum and the more complete (but photographically inferior) DVD version.

141 LR's reshooting: These staged scenes are obvious in the film, as are similar scenes in *Triumph of the Will*. Too-careful lighting and photographic effects not possible outside of a studio stand out even to the unpracticed eye.

141 Speer's account in his memoir: See Speer, *Inside the Third Reich*, pp. 61–62. There are several memory failings in Speer's account, including LR's producing a newspaper clipping bearing his image, an event that Gitta Sereny dates to later in the decade.

141 entire chapter: "A Mistake in Speer's Memoirs," LRM, pp. 572–75. The "figment" reference appears on p. 574.

142 "a sentence" from Streicher: Ibid., p. 575.

142 "a people that": This is from shot 114 of *Triumph of the Will*, as in Smith, p. 27.

142 "she wanted to have": Int. PW/AS, as above, tape 1, transcript p. 13.

142 Walter Frentz confirmation: Int. PW/Walter Frentz, Überlingen, August 3, 1971, tape 11, transcript 11, p. 22.

142 Reviews in the party-controlled press: Citations from *Film-Kurier* and *Licht-Bild-Bühne*, December 2, 1933, after Loiperdinger, "*Sieg des Glaubens*," p. 40.

142 *Angriff:* After Rother, p. 53.

143 London review: *Observer*, December 3, 1933.

143 intended audience: Twenty million is from Loiperdinger and Culbert, "Leni Riefenstahl, the SA," citing Curt Belling, p. 16.

143 James May: Telephone int. SB/James May, January 12, 2002; *New York Times,* "Leni Riefenstahl and Me, in 1934," January 9, 2002, letters. May believed it would have been impossible for LR to have been unaware of the propaganda uses to which her film was put.

143 "thankless task" through "picture": LRM, p. 150.

144 Discipline among the crowds: Zelnhefer, pp. 245–49.

CHAPTER TEN: TRIUMPH

145 "Whoever has seen": Goebbels, quoted in Knopp, p. 11.

145 "It doesn't contain": Michel Delahaye's interview in *Cahiers du Cinéma,* cited from Sarris, *Interviews,* p. 460.

145 "Leni Riefenstahl was not": Int. PW/Walter Traut, Munich-Harlaching, August 10, 1971, tapes 5 and 6, citation from transcript 5, p. 17.

145 Even Hitler took note: Dr. Koeppen, *Hitlers Tischgespräch Herbst 1941,* IfZ, Munich, Riefenstahl file Fa 514, November 7, 1941, p. 79082. LRM claims similar remarks by Hitler about overwork. See pp. 167 and 227.

146 defenselessness: See Lenssen, *Leben und Werk,* p. 30.

146 April 19, 1934: Rother (English) (p. 195, n. 9) cites Ufa minutes of August 28, 1934, quoting from a letter dated April 19, 1934: "Fräulein Riefenstahl has artistic and technical responsibility for the film, having been appointed by the Führer in the name of the NSDAP's [Nationalsozialistische Deutsche Arbeiterpartei, or National Socialist German Workers' Party] Reichsleitung [Administration]."

146 AH in October: LRM glides over Hitler's decision in her memoirs, where she is setting the scene for another denunciation of Goebbels, but *Five Lives* reprints the same passage drawn on here (LRM, pp. 146–47), clarifying that AH's statement that "the motion picture about the national Party rally is to be made by Fräulein Riefenstahl and not by the Party film people" referred specifically to *Triumph of the Will.* See *Five Lives,* p. 308. It is probably an accident of history, but at virtually the same time (October 5, 1933), Hitler decided the Reich should build a new sports stadium for the 1936 Olympics.

146 "if you weren't": LRM, p. 147. This is one of the rare dated exchanges in LR's memoirs. She puts it on October 13, 1933, the day Goebbels flew to Geneva to announce Germany's withdrawal from the League of Nations. There are no diary entries by JG for that date.

146 "Tell me one person": In Barsam, *Filmguide,* pp. 15–16.

147 Julius Streicher: LR's power of attorney letter, cited in the notes for Chapter 6, was dated December 11, 1933. The Gestapo later tracked LR's contacts to Streicher (see Chapter 14): IfZ, Munich, doc. MA 612/57, p. 60381.

147 Davos: Int. PW/LR, August 11, 1971, tape 17, side A, transcript 17, p. 1.

147 favorite of Hitler's: Hamann, p. 64.

147 gray Mercedes: LR mentions the car several times in LRM, dating it before the making of *Triumph of the Will*. According to her sister-in-law, it was a gift from Hitler (Collignon, p. 169).

148 copyright: There are multiple issues here. Most important is LR's false claim of independence from the party in the making of the film. The important late-life question for her was almost solely economic.

For purposes of making *Triumph of the Will*, the name L-R-Studio-Film was changed to Reich Party Rally Film (Reichsparteitag-Film GmbH). Following the collapse of the Reich, the ownership of LR's films for the party became the subject of intense legal maneuvering by LR (see Chapter 17). The Museum of Modern Art's Charles Silver told SB that its print of *Triumph of the Will* was frequently shown at the museum's film center and almost always elicited a demand from LR or her representatives for royalty payments.

On ownership: "Every serious investigation . . . has come to the conclusion that the NSDAP should be regarded as the producer of *Triumph des Willens*, as well as of *Sieg des Glaubens* and *Tag der Freiheit*" (Rother [English], pp. 72–73). For *Olympia*, see Chapters 11 and 12 below.

148 Ufa deal approved by Hitler: Rother (English) cites Ufa minutes: "The Führer has given his approval for the film to be distributed by Ufa" (p. 195, n. 9).

148 Reich Film Credit Bank: The Filmkreditbank was founded in June 1933 as a means of controlling what got made. Funds were provided for privately produced films that were deemed politically acceptable or desirable and withheld from those that were not. When the Reich officially took over Ufa and other film studios in 1937, the bank was no longer necessary as a control institution. Beyer, p. 22.

148 costs of *Triumph of the Will:* No final accounting is possible, but LR claimed to Michel Delahaye in 1965 that the picture "was a very cheap film. It cost only 280,000 marks," but this figure is almost certainly a fantasy or a mistranslation, cited here from Sarris, *Interviews,* p. 458. Elsewhere (see text) LR claimed that fully one-third of the three hundred thousand reichsmarks advanced by Ufa were spent before production ever began, but an advance is a form of down payment, not a budget.

148 bought the film rights to *Tiefland:* Int. PW/LR, as cited above, tape 17, side A, transcript 17, p. 2.

148 Walter Ruttmann: Kreimeier, p. 272.

149 "educated for war": Kreimeier, p. 272.

149 "revisit all the": *Film-Kurier,* September 3, 1934, cited in Rother (English), p. 196, n. 14.

149 traveled to England: LRM, p. 153. A German-language news article signed by G. L. von dem Knesebeck and bearing the title "Leni Riefenstahl with the Oxford Students" carries an Oxford dateline of April 30. It includes a photograph of LR with officers of the German Club and states that LR told them that no film she had made took less than a year to complete and that *The Blue Light* had taken a year and a half. The text quotes a student: "Leni Riefenstahl brought an atmosphere from Germany with her that inspired us all. Now we know quite exactly what the spirit of the New Germany must be."

150 forty to one: Shirer, *Rise and Fall*, p. 205. Alan Bullock estimates half as much (Bullock, *Hitler: A Study*, p. 285).

151 letter to Röhm: *Völkischer Beobachter*, January 2, 1934, here quoted from Shirer, *Rise and Fall*, p. 208.

151 just before the Nuremberg rally of 1933: JG diaries, August 25, 1933, p. 461. Here the issue is made explicit: "Chancellor and Reich President united in one office."

152 Ian Kershaw: *Hubris*, p. 516.

152 "The measures taken": Quoted from Fest, *Hitler*, p. 468.

152 "horror at the butchery": Kershaw, *Hubris*, p. 517.

152 two-hour oration: Quoted from Fest, *Hitler*, p. 469.

152 murder in the interest of the state: Kershaw, *Hubris*, p. 518.

153 Hindenburg's statement: Shirer, *Rise and Fall*, p. 312.

153 "We love him": Gen. Walther von Reichenau, quoted in Kershaw, *Hubris*, p. 497.

153 Hitler at mercy of military: Fest, *Hitler*, p. 457.

153 "if the army": Ibid., p. 471.

153 "national myth" and "greatness": Quoted by Fest, *Hitler*, p. 475.

154 oath "by God": *Reichsgesetzblatt* 1934, I, p. 785, quoted in Stackelberg and Winkle, p. 174. The words here are from the law of August 20, 1934.

154 "Up to then": Fest, *Hitler*, p. 469.

154 "power of forgetting": *Mein Kampf*, p. 180.

154 "The bond": LR, "Wie der Film vom Reichsparteitag entsteht," *Der Deutsche*, no. 14, January 17, 1935, quoted after Rother (English), p. 205.

154 "glorification": See Müller, *Wonderful, Horrible Life*, in which she uses the word matter-of-factly as challenge and achievement.

155 Walter Frentz: Int. PW/Walter Frentz, August 3, 1971, Weberlingen, tape 11, transcript 11, pp. 20–22.

155 Walter Traut: Int. PW/Walter Traut, as cited, tapes 5 and 6, citations from transcript 5, pp. 23 ("many days before"), 18 ("a conception"), and 17 ("Leni Riefenstahl was not ordered").

155 "since May": LR, *Hinter*, p. 16.

155   acknowledgments: Ibid., "Zum Geleit" (foreword), n.p. LR told Peggy Wallace she was particularly unhappy with the book's expression of gratitude to Goebbels for having "supported the completion of the film work in every way" (PW, tape 4, transcript pp. 10–12).

155   "I didn't write": Weigel, "Interview," p. 408.

156   Reich Culture Office: The document is part of the LR file, BDC, dated July 24, 1935. Richard Barsam and others cite LR's receipt from Jäger for one thousand marks for his services on the book, a copy of which is in LR's Berlin Document Center files. It would seem unlikely that LR would not have retained approval of the text.

156   autograph for Bormann: Bormann's personal copy of the book was autographed by LR on April 2, 1935, "with sincere gratitude" (*"mit herzlichem Dank"*).

156   Emil Schünemann: LR's letters to the film division of August 17, 1934, and August 29, 1934, are part of her BDC file. The translation here is based on Rother (English), pp. 195–96.

156   Nuremberg in August: An exact date is not certain, though Hitler traveled to Nuremberg on August 20 to approve plans for the rally and was photographed with Riefenstahl on his visit, placing her there at least two weeks before the rally began.

156   production staff: The numbers vary slightly from account to account. Those here are taken from the official listing in *Hinter den Kulissen* and from Barsam, p. 23. Brian Winston has noted discrepancies and cites one aerial cameraman rather than the nine in Barsam, though this seems an error, as nine is LR's own figure in *Hinter*.

157   *Newsweek:* LR appeared on the cover as "Hitler's Friend" on September 15, 1934. Flanner's *New Yorker* article, "Führer: A Document," is reprinted in Flanner, pp. 375–415. The citation here appears on p. 383.

158   uniforms of light gray: Int. PW/Walter Traut, as cited above, tape 5, transcript 5, p. 25. Traut boasted that the uniforms were designed by a Berlin couturier.

159   Gordon Craig: In *Germany, 1866–1945*, p. 545.

159   tea party and quotes: Rother (English), p. 59, quoting "Leni Riefenstahl's Abschied von Nürnberg," *Fränkische Tageszeitung*, September 13, 1934.

160   "something of the mysticism": Shirer, *Twentieth Century Journey*, p. 120.

160   Shirer "emperor" quote: Ibid., p. 119.

161   Ian Kershaw: Kershaw, *"Hitler Myth,"* p. 70.

162   according to Speer: Int. PW/AS, Heidelberg, August 14, 1971, tape 1, side A, transcript p. 3.

162   "a pure historical film": Michel Delahaye in Sarris, *Interviews*, p. 460.

162   "architecture": See, for instance, ibid., p. 461.

162 footage lengths: LRM, p. 162.

162 Speer recalled, "She was": Int. PW/AS, as cited, tape 1, side A, transcript p. 10.

162 Geyer: LRM, p. 184. The expansion of the facilities was completed for the editing of *Olympia*, but the construction began on *Triumph of the Will*.

163 Walter Ruttmann: *Film-Welt*, no. 7, February 17, 1935, *"Triumph des Willens,"* by Hans Erasmus Fischer, refers to LR's filming "together with Walter Ruttmann." Rother (English and German) maintains mistakenly that no press mentions of Ruttmann occurred after December.

163 Excerpts from his script: Rother (English), p. 62, n. 196, *Film-Kurier*, no. 235, October 6, 1934.

163 a visit to the set and news reports: For news reports, see *Licht-Bild-Bühne*, no. 247, October 23, 1934, and "Die letzte Szene für 'Sieg des Willens' wird gedreht," October 20, 1934, DZT, Deutsches Institut für Filmkunde files. The second article cites Babelsberg shooting "on Monday" as well as further scenes to be shot in November. The writer claims that "Sieg des Willens" was an early title, only recently changed to "Triumph des Willens," and refers to the original release date as December 1934.

Hitler's visit to LR's editing rooms on December 6, 1934, is cited by Rother, p. 63.

163 "the new god": Kershaw, *Hubris*, p. 484.

163 "These things": LR to Delahaye in Sarris, *Interviews*, p. 461.

164 As Speer observed: Int. PW/AS, as cited, tape 1, side A, transcript p. 11.

164 even lectured about it: Rother, p. 199, n. 49.

164 Press headlines: After Trimborn, p. 222.

164 "the greatest film": After Kinkel, p. 84.

165 "Whoever has seen": Knopp, p. 11.

165 "forged to the tempo": *Deutsche Allgemeine Zeitung*, May 2, 1935.

166 noted historian: Kershaw in *Hubris*, p. 484.

CHAPTER ELEVEN: THE OLYMPIC IDEA

167 LR epigraph: Quoted in LRO, p. 96.

167 Klemperer epigraph: Klemperer, *Diaries*, p. 175.

168 "the only thing": LRMG, pp. 245–46, and LRM, pp. 175–76.

168 *Film-Kurier:* After Culbert and Loiperdinger, p. 8.

168 "Nuremberg triptych": Susan Sontag refers to it as "the third in her triptych of fascist visuals" in "Fascinating Fascism," p. 87.

169 "the most murderous": Reitlinger, p. 7.

169 "most beautiful Führer speech": Enno Patalas to SB, Munich, January 17, 2002.

169 "joy" and "to forget": LRMG, p. 191.

169 "magic garden" and "freer" and "drove out": Ibid., p. 244.

170 Davos—"no air like it": LRM, p. 167. LR and the Lantschner family: Int. PW/LR, August 11, 1971, Munich, tape 17, transcript 4, p. 4. Guzzi and Otto Lantschner were well known for distributing National Socialist literature at sporting events. Their sister was on the German women's ski team.

170 Max Reinhardt: LRM, pp. 152–53.

170 "Germany needs": LRO, p. 3. The citation is from the "peace" speech of March 21, 1935.

171 "Who else but you": LRMG, p. 251. In LRM, p. 179, "could" is mistranslated as "should."

171 "If one has invited": LRO, p. 13; too small: Kershaw, *Nemesis*, p. 6; post-1940: Sereny, *Speer*, p. 154.

171 "Under the Heel": Cited in Mandell, p. 75.

172 Kessler: *Diaries*, pp. 467–68. Kessler emphasizes that the Olympic committees of France, England, and elsewhere had made plain that they would not send athletes to Berlin were Lewald to be removed from his position. "After the Games he becomes irrevocably non-Aryan," Kessler added.

172 he reassured the world: Quoted in LRO, p. 6.

172 Streicher: Ibid., p. 5.

172 Brundage and Jewish athletes: LRO, pp. 7–8.

172 Brundage quotes: "Politics" is from Tony Blankley, *Washington Times*, July 18, 2001. "Certain Jews" is from an official Olympics publication, cited by Furlong.

172 "Germans are not": The secretary was Frederick W. Rubien (Mandell, p. 84).

173 December 1935 vote: LRO, p. 7. See also Mandell, pp. 87–88. Many charges have been leveled at Brundage, who later became president of the International Olympic Committee and aroused controversy when he insisted the 1972 Munich games continue after the massacre of Jewish athletes. He died in Garmisch-Partenkirchen, site of the 1936 Winter Olympics.

173 Diem as "perfect miracle": Mandell, p. 94.

173 "the Olympic idea": LRM, p. 169.

173 Fanck's detailed analysis: "Was soll mit der Verfilmung der *Olympiade* bezweckt werden?" These pages are in the Fanck Collection of the Munich Film Museum.

174 "I do not like": Quoted in LRO, p. 96.

174 "I could see": LRM, p. 171.

174 Reich Sport Leader: Von Tschammer und Osten was one of the so-called old comrades of Hitler's early struggles. Frick was hanged following the Nuremberg trials.

174 Diem sidelined: Quoted in LRO, p. 13.

174 LR and Tobis: This version has had many outings by LR, though it is not supported by the evidence. See LRM or Hitchens, "An Interview," for examples. The most elaborate—and untrustworthy—is LR's legal description of 1958, Appendix C in LRO, pp. 270–79.

175 Tobis guarantee: LR consistently misstated the Tobis guarantee as 1.5 million. Friedrich Mainz confirmed in 1958 and again in 1971 that the amount he agreed to was 750,000 RM (int. PW/FM, July 29, 1971, tape 10, transcript 10, p. 19). The amount in the Tobis contract is 800,000 RM, but the discrepancy appears to be the result of Ufa's last-minute reconsideration of its rejection of August 1935. Ufa debated internally whether or not to buy Tobis out for 800,000 RM (it elected not to). It appears likely that Tobis had a deal but no signed contract until December 4, 1936, a date some have suggested is a mistake and should read 1935. The dating is almost certainly correct, however, as the contract refers to two pictures, the second to be guaranteed 200,000 RM. The decision to make two pictures came only in November 1936 after LR had reviewed her footage. See LR's letter to Paul Kohner (below), September 1936, at which point the German distribution question was still unresolved.

Barkhausen (p. 11) points out that Tobis's accounting was made both to Olympia-Film and to the propaganda ministry.

175 "She's a clever thing!": JG diaries, August 17, 1935, for August 15, vol. 2, p. 503.

175 By October 4: Ibid., October 5, 1935, for October 4, vol. 2, p. 523.

175 "Contract . . . approved": Ibid., October 13, 1935, for October 13, vol. 2, p. 526.

175 By November 7: Ibid., November 7, 1935, for November 6, vol. 2, p. 537.

175 Hitler's approval: August 21, 1935, LRO, p. 19.

175 "certain to bring revenue": Finance ministry memo of October 17, 1935, cited by Barkhausen, p. 9.

175 Olympia-Film GmbH: The document cited is from the propaganda ministry (Herr Ott) to the district court of Berlin, January 30, 1936, and quoted after Rother (English), pp. 82 and 201, n. 17. See also Barkhausen, p. 10. See LRM, pp. 176–77, for LR's quite different version; and LRO, pp. 16–24 and 30–37. Appendix C in LRO, pp. 270–79, reproduces LR's postwar legal positions, which rarely coincide with the documentation and which Barkhausen terms "products of Leni Riefenstahl's imagination."

Barkhausen cites a further letter from the Reich Film Chamber to the Berlin court on February 12, 1936, reaffirming that "we are not talking then about a private enterprise, or about an enterprise with ordinary commercial aims, but about a company founded exclusively for the purpose of external organization and production of the said film. It is inadvisable [*untunlich*] for the government itself to appear as the producer."

176 LR and Heinz as stockholders: The incorporation documents claim an investment of eighteen thousand reichsmarks by LR and two thousand by her brother, but neither sum had been paid ten months after the Berlin courts noted the company's establishment. Barkhausen (p. 10) cites a letter from the examination board of the propaganda ministry of October 16, 1936, to that effect. That the company was basically fictitious did not mean that it was free of bureaucratic rules and requirements.

176 front for the Reich: No current accounts dispute the point. See mainly Barkhausen and LRO.

176 Kohner letter: LR to Paul Kohner, September 16, 1936, Kohner Collection, Stiftung Deutsche Kinemathek, Berlin. It is worth noting that here the distribution question in Germany had not yet been settled, and LR refers twice to "film" in the singular. The plan for two films had not yet been proposed.

176 "sensational amount": LRM, p. 172.

176 *Angriff:* From Mandell (p. 156), who notes the *New York Times*, July 6, 1936, n.p.

176 "preventive custody": Mandell, p. 157, and Lewy, p. 25. Gypsies: Lewy, p. 22; Berlin-Marzahn as first racial camp: Gilsenbach, pp. 141–47, 167–69, and Rosenberg, p. 139, n. 1. See also Hoess, p. 92. The future commandant of Auschwitz was part of the "preventive custody" roundup in Berlin for the Olympics. The Gypsy to reenter LR's life was Charlotte Rosenberg (Rosenberg, p. 142, n. 8). Browning, in *Origins,* p. 180, cites an earlier camp in Cologne.

177 Shirer incident: Shirer, *Twentieth Century Journey,* pp. 230–32.

177 flags: Mandell, pp. 65, 159.

177 *Time* magazine cover: She was on the cover February 17, 1936, just as the Winter Olympics ended.

178 LR on training: Int. PW/LR, August 7, 1971, Munich, tape 15, transcript 15B, pp. 5–6.

178 Color was investigated: Ibid., pp. 13–14. Cameraman Heinz von Jaworsky confirmed testing with color.

179 "everything would have": LRM, p. 173.

179 "impossible": LRMG, p. 259.

179 "to shoot the Olympics": LRM, p. 186.

179 "actually, any camera": Ibid.

180 Goebbels and television: "Nazi TV," Spiegel TV, 2000.

181 "It was just" and "No": Willy Zielke, quoted in LRO, p. 45.

181 "The moment I had": Michel Delahaye, *Cahier du Cinéma,* reprinted in Sarris, *Interviews,* p. 467.

182 "struggle" and "poetics": Int. PW/LR, August 7, 1971, tape 15, transcript 15B, p. 22.

182 "You only see": Ibid., p. 11.

182 torch race: Mandell, pp. 145–54.

182 "Shoot more of him": Heinz von Jaworsky, quoted in LRO, p. 62.

182 Anatol Dobriansky: Mostly from LRM, pp. 188–89.

183 Zielke in love: Ertl made the claim in his memoirs (Ertl, p. 184).

183 "She didn't need": Int. PW/Robert Gardner, Cambridge, Mass., January 26, 1971.

183 LR's affair with Glenn Morris: LRM, p. 196.

183 "grabbed me": Ibid.

183 "Never before had I experienced": Ibid., p. 199.

183 Glenn Morris photographs: They appear in *Beauty of the Olympic Games*, the book of still photographs published under LR's name about the games. Almost all of the photographs are by her cameramen or are frame blowups, signed—though not made—by LR.

183 Castle Ruhwald: LRMG, p. 264.

184 *Film-Kurier* citation: August 4, 1936, quoted from Rother (English), pp. 78–79.

184 Bella Fromm: Reprinted in *Als Hitler mir die Hand küsste*, pp. 249–50, as cited in Rother (English), p. 200. A different, somewhat harsher translation appears in Fromm, *Blood and Banquets*, pp. 225–26.

184 Hans Ertl: Ertl, p. 221, here quoted from LRO, p. 101.

184 *New York Times:* August 14, 1936, quoted from ibid., p. 100.

185 Leni threatened: Jäger, cited in LRO, p. 93. LR's own version is that she called the referee "Schweinehund": LRMG, p. 269, or "bastard" in LRM, p. 194. She does not mention threatening a Hitler confrontation.

185 Goebbels demanded she apologize: JG diaries, August 6, 1936, vol. 2, p. 655.

185 "cried bitter tears": LRM, p. 194.

185 Her tears: Int. PW/LR, August 6, 1971, Munich, tape 14, transcript 14B, p. 10.

185 Robert Gardner: Int. PW/Robert Gardner, January 26, 1971, Cambridge, Mass., transcript 25, p. 2.

185 "I didn't have a talent": Int. PW/LR, August 6, 1971, Munich, tape 14, transcript 14B, p. 9.

186 disbursement and receipts: Barkhausen, p. 9.

186 would later claim credit: The Cathedral of Light had been introduced by Speer at the 1934 rally but became famous during the Olympics. LR told Gitta Sereny after Speer's death that it had been her idea. Sereny, *Speer*, p. 129.

187 Margot von Opel, Nuremberg: LRO, p. 144.

187 Goebbels's fury: JG diaries, September 18, 1936, vol. 2, p. 680.

187 "Let's not be petty": Barkhausen, p. 11.

187 "white-collar crime": LRO, p. 147.

187 LR and shortfall: LRM, p. 200.

188 shambles and audit: LRO, pp. 143–53.

188 "pig sty of a mess": JG diaries, October 25, 1936, p. 707.

188 Leni resisted: LRO, p. 149. The quotation is from postwar testimony of 1948 by Friedrich Mainz of Tobis.

188 two films instead of one: LRM claims that Tobis accepted the notion of two films before the fact, but all such claims appear to be of postwar origin. *Film-Kurier,* July 5, 1937, quotes LR as deciding she needed two films sometime between December 1936 and January 1937, though the Goebbels diaries mention that decision in November. The official change from one film to two would not come until seven months later, on May 18, 1937, in a memo from the Reich Film Chamber to Goebbels (LRO p. 159).

188 Jäger's wife and open marriage: Int. SB/Linda Jäger D'Aprix, February 24, 2006.

188 "insolence": LRM, p. 201.

188 described her fate as "tragic": LRO, Appendix C, p. 277. The term is found in LR's unpublished "Ein Bericht über die Herstellung der Olympia-Filme," an unreliable document from the 1950s prepared in part to advance her copyright claim in the film on which royalties depended.

188 "I began to weep": LRM, p. 201. LR's memoirs are very vague with dates here. She places the meeting with AH in November, though evidence suggests December. See LRO, p. 150.

189 Goebbels learned of it on November 6: JG diaries, vol. 2, p. 717.

189 footage review: LR cited the figures here in *Film-Kurier,* July 5, 1937, p. 2. By the time she wrote her memoirs, the length of time had dramatically increased to fourteen-hour days for four months (LRM, p. 204).

189 usable footage, 70 percent and 5 percent: Delahaye in Sarris, *Interviews,* p. 465.

189 ban by Goebbels on publicity: LR asserted this in court as part of her lawsuit to gain royalties from the film as well as in LRM, p. 200. See LRO, pp. 145–46.

189 Tabloid items: The most widely reprinted of these was *Paris-Soir*'s front-page story "La Disgrâce de Leni Riefenstahl," June 14, 1937.

190 Goebbels's "very sharp denial": JG diaries, June 16, 1937, vol. 3, p. 175.

190 luxurious new villa: The chapter "Dahlem, Heydenstrasse 30" in LRMG is deleted from LRM. In German, LR says Hans Ostler and Max Otto designed the house, though Rother cites sources naming Ernst Petersen.

Petersen had appeared alongside Trenker as LR's suitor in *The Holy Mountain*. Why LR would misstate this is unknown, but her father had business connections with Petersen's family firm as early as the 1920s. See Rother (English), p. 206, n. 35.

190 Leni carried proofs: LRM, p. 208.

190 his diary brims with: JG diaries, November 24, 1937, for November 23, vol. 4, p. 344.

190 dined with Hitler: JG diaries, November 26, 1937, for November 25, vol. 4, p. 347. He discusses Jews and the theater on p. 346.

191 Zielke's classical prologue: See LRO, pp. 156–58. LRM spends considerable time refuting Zielke's later charges against her, including, among other things, that she had him institutionalized and castrated. See LRM, pp. 203–4.

191 "It had no": LRO, p. 158; and "I made": Delahaye in Sarris, *Interviews,* p. 467.

191 diving sequence: Int. PW/LR, Munich, August 7, 1971, tape 15, side B, transcript 15, p. 11.

191 "I could have edited": Mannheim, cited by Graham, LRO, p. 158.

191 "As a composer": Delahaye in Sarris, *Interviews,* p. 467.

191 marathon conception: Int. PW/LR, Munich, August 7, 1971, tape 15, side B, transcript 15, p. 9.

192 "a nightmare": LRM, p. 220.

192 Hermann Storr: LRMG, pp. 302–3.

193 Windt and chorus: LRO, p. 177.

193 "waterfall": Downing, p. 48.

193 final première date: LRM claims that LR traveled to Innsbruck and convinced Hitler personally to move the première from April 19 to April 20 (pp. 220–23). This account has been refuted on evidence of Hitler's travel schedule. See Trimborn, p. 537.

193 LR in *Film-Kurier:* "Leni Riefenstahl zum 10. April," *Film-Kurier,* April 9, 1938, p. 3, quoted by LRO in a slightly different translation, p. 181.

194 *Triumph* on Vienna screens: Weyr, p. 71.

CHAPTER TWELVE: TOMORROW THE WORLD

195 LR epigraph: LRM, p. 237.

195 Winchell epigraph: *New York Daily Mirror,* November 9, 1938, p. 10.

196 The world's diplomats: LRO, pp. 186–87.

196 Heydrich: See Fest, *Face,* pp. 155ff.

197 "A masterly achievement": JG diaries, April 21, 1938, part 1, vol. 5, p. 267.

198 bonus: JG diaries, April 22 and April 23, 1938, part 1, vol. 5, pp. 267, 269.

198 the king of Belgium: LRM, p. 235.

199 "the unpolitical": Ibid., p. 231.

199 re Jesse Owens: Propaganda ministry directive, cited in LRO, p. 254.

199 Goebbels and point lists: LRO, p. 255.

200 Golden Lion: See LRM, p. 235.

200 "blatant": *Daily Film Renter*, cited in LRO, p. 208.

200 LR on Hitler: Quoted by Angus Quell in *Royal Screen Pictorial*, May 1935, cited in Fraser, p. 12.

200 Mussolini: See the "Mussolini" chapter in LRM, pp. 181–84. Specifically, she interpreted small talk to mean that Italy would not interfere with German plans to violate the Locarno Treaty by invading the Rhineland.

201 cameramen's photographs: The first edition of *Schönheit* credits Willy Zielke, among others, for photographs. The first edition (1937) includes this text: "Most of the pictures are enlargements from the *Olympia* film. The shots of the temples, sculptures and nudes are by Willy Zielke. Arthur Grimm took the stills. The photographs of work in progress are by Arthur Grimm and Rolf Lantin. Guzzi Lantschner selected the pictures from the film footage. Enlargements and preparation of the photographs: Gertrude Sieburg and Rolf Lantin" (p. 283).

The Olympic photographs are currently marketed and exhibited as LR's own work—with her approval and (often) her signature—though they are hers only in the sense that the photographers were in her employ. Int. SB/Cooper C. Graham, Library of Congress, Washington, D.C., June 7–10, 2004. LR's presentation copy of her similar Olympics portfolio, inscribed to Hitler, is in the rare-book collection of the LOC.

201 "Even the dishwashers": The witness was Jäger, "How Leni," part VI, June 2, 1939.

201 Klingeberg: LRO, p. 211.

201 Reich was fully financing the trip: An advance of eight thousand reichsmarks for the tour had been made by the economics ministry, though Goebbels's ministry would demand an accounting.

202 "non-Aryan sectors": *Film-Kurier*, September 24, 1938, cited by Rentschler, *Ministry*, p. 46. It is perhaps noteworthy that in LRM and LRMG, she places herself in Rome with *Olympia* at the time of the Munich conference, though the Rome première took place in August. She was, in fact, then in Munich for the rerelease of *The Blue Light*.

202 shipboard companions: LRO, p. 212. For the Whiteheads, see LRM, p. 242. LR claims there that she knew them well enough in Berlin that the couple had presented her with a puppy she kept and trained.

202 "giggled": Unsourced news article, author's collection.

202 Winchell: *New York Daily Mirror*, November 9, 1938, p. 10.

203 Mahoney statement: LRO, p. 213.

203 Heydrich's directive: Shirer, *Rise and Fall*, p. 431.

203 "night of horror" and "human misery": Kershaw, *Nemesis*, pp. 140, 141. Shirer also uses the phrase "night of horror" in *Rise and Fall*, p. 431.

203 murders in Buchenwald: Gilbert, p. 69.

203 confiscation of property: Ibid., p. 73; 267 synagogues: Friedländer, p. 276; Kershaw quote: *Nemesis*, p. 143.

204 "carefree": LRM, pp. 237ff. Re King Vidor: conversation SB/King Vidor, Malibu, December 31, 1970. Vidor said he sent "professional congratulations" through an intermediary after seeing *Olympia* in Europe but never personally met LR.

204 "It was only" and "had I": LRM, p. 237.

204 diplomats advise LR: LRO, p. 216. Graham cites Consul General Dr. Borchers and Heinz Bellers, the representative of the propaganda ministry in America, among others, as having urged her to cut short her trip and return home. "Hurricane": Ambassador Hans Dieckhoff, cited in LRO, p. 216.

204 Gestapo agents: Jäger, "How Leni," part VII, June 9, 1939, p. 14. The Gestapo reportedly advised LR not to accept an offer for *Olympia* from the manager of Sonia Henie.

204 "I have to wait": Ibid., p. 13. Jäger is problematic because his publishing about LR seems as opportunistic as he accused her of being. Still, he knew LR well, was present throughout the American tour, and, as LR later complained in a legal deposition, was constantly at her side taking notes.

205 "cheerful atmosphere": LRM, p. 237.

205 Aryanization: Kershaw, *Nemesis*, p. 131.

205 synagogues: Ibid., p. 132.

205 as Goebbels remarked: Ibid., p. 135.

206 Henry Ford: LRO, p. 218.

206 Hubert Stowitts: Here and following mostly from LRO, pp. 182, 225–26. Also, McDonagh, "Gay Bears: The Hidden History of the Berkeley Campus," University of California at Berkeley, http://sunsite.berkeley.edu/gaybears/Stowitts. See also Stowitts Museum. LR says in LRM that she had known Stowitts since 1934.

207 decorating and dieting: LRMG, pp. 325–26.

208 Kohner and MGM: Kohner had offered the picture to William Goetz, son-in-law of Louis B. Mayer. The Kohner Collection at the Stiftung Deutsche Kinemathek contains a letter to Goetz dated September 30, 1936, two weeks after LR's original request, and another to LR dated October 9 informing her of Goetz's lack of interest.

208 advertisements: *Hollywood Reporter*, November 29, 1938, p. 5; *Daily Variety*, same date, p. 5.

209 "the greatest sports film": Graham, "*Olympia* in America," p. 439.

209 Garland to Brundage: Ibid., p. 443. The letter is in the Avery Brundage Collection, (Applied Life Studies Library, University of Illinois, Champaign-Urbana, Illinois), dated December 2, 1938.

210 *Hollywood Citizen-News:* The reviewer was Henry McLemore, cited in Graham, "*Olympia,* "p. 444. Original is dated December 17, 1938.

210 *Los Angeles Times:* Cited from Graham, "*Olympia,* " p. 445, and from unsourced reprint of review, later used as advertising material for the film. Graham Collection, Library of Congress.

210 Budd Schulberg: Cited in Graham, "*Olympia,*" p. 444.

210 *Daily Variety:* December 7, 1938, cited in Graham, "*Olympia,*" p. 443. *Motion Picture Herald,* November 12, 1938, p. 19.

211 new lover: Jäger does not identify him, but LR was socially active in California. Following her return to Germany, her office notified the Reichsfilmkammer that an actor of German origin named Ferdinand Geigel, then living in La Crescenta, California, wanted to return to Germany if he would be allowed to work in the industry. Letter, LR to Reichsfilmkammer (Abteiling Fachschaft Film), July 22, 1939, BDC, Riefenstahl file.

211 "Hitler's girl friend": *Los Angeles Herald-Examiner,* December 27, 1938.

211 "It is all": *San Francisco News,* December 31, 1938.

211 "There are four walls": *San Francisco Chronicle,* December 31, 1938.

213 Jäger chose to remain in America: Int. SB/Linda Jäger D'Aprix, February 25, 2006, and int. SB/Robert Lantz, January 13 and July 27, 2006. There is an undocumented assumption that LR helped protect Charlotte Jäger and her son Frank, both of whom relocated to South America sometime before 1942. Jäger survived difficulties with American immigration authorities and eventually worked his way to Hollywood after menial jobs at (among other venues) the Jewish Children's Hospital in Denver. See also Lewinski, pp. 11–75.

213 Tobis in America: *Motion Picture Herald,* November 12, 1938, p. 19. The closure of the Tobis office alone indicates that Tobis had nothing to do with the hoped-for licensing of *Olympia* in America, which was solely an endeavor of LR and the Reich.

213 Jäger's articles: These articles (Jäger, "How Leni") are well known, and LRM refers to them as "mixtures of facts and infamous lies" (p. 247). LR notes, "These articles included passages that were true, sections that Jäger had copied from my letters" (ibid.). In spite of this seeming admission, the articles need to be approached with caution. Jäger remains, apart from LR, the principal source for private events during the American tour.

213 Paris lecture: Kinkel, p. 167.

213 Hamburg interview: *Hamburger Tageblatt,* January 30, 1939, here from Kinkel, pp. 170–71.

214 She told Goebbels: *Tagebücher,* vol. 3, p. 569.

214 retroactive reimbursement: After LRO, pp. 228–34, especially pp. 229–30.

214 fully nationalized film industry: See Hull, pp. 107–25.

214 request for percentage: After LRO, pp. 228–34, specifically p. 230.

215 "The Olympics films are Reich property": LRO, p. 233.

215 "20% of the remaining net proceeds": Ibid.

215 Hitler financing: JG diaries, June 21, 1939, part I, vol. 6, p. 387.

216 film studio for her personal use: Rother (English), pp. 99–103.

216 Italo Balbo: In Venice: LRM, p. 235; meeting in 1932: JG, *Tagebücher,* December 11, 1932. Balbo, an intimate of Mussolini's since 1922, was killed in 1940 at Tobruk in what may have been a "friendly fire" incident.

216 Germania project financed by the Reich: Horak, p. 58. Horak speculates that Fanck's joining the party was suggested to him by LR or one of her colleagues.

PART THREE: AFTERMATH

219 Hitler epigraph: *Mein Kampf,* p. 177.

219 Klemperer epigraph: Klemperer, p. 295.

CHAPTER THIRTEEN: LENI AT WAR

221 Hitler epigraph: See "Hitler speech" below.

221 LR epigraph: LRMG, p. 908.

221 Hitler speech: Stackelberg and Winkle, p. 246, from U.S. Department of State Publication 6462, *Documents on German Foreign Policy, 1918–1945,* series D, vol. VII, pp. 205–6.

221 "world collapsed": LRM, p. 254.

222 Berlin reception: Ibid., p. 253; "happy and filled": Ibid., p. 254.

222 Reichstag address: LRM's chronology here is especially slippery. LR claims she drove late in the afternoon or early evening from Bolzano to Berlin to arrive in time for Hitler's Reichstag address at 10:00 a.m. on September 1 (LRM, p. 254). The driving distance of hundreds of kilometers strains credulity. In LRM, she never mentions the Berghof and claims to have seen Hitler twice in late August in Berlin. She writes of a Berlin screening for Hitler of Soviet newsreels of Stalin that Speer and Goebbels also attended shortly before the announcement of the Nazi-Soviet Pact (ibid., p. 253). According to both men, the cited screening took place at Hitler's Berghof.

222 "This night": Bullock, *Hitler: Study*, p. 547. The hour was misstated; the attack had begun at 4:45 A.M.

222 William L. Shirer: *"This Is Berlin"*: "They listened" (p. 74); "Polish thing" (p. 75); FDR (p. 72); "not only" (p. 79). All are from the first week of September 1939.

223 "high-ranking": LRM, p. 257.

223 "Special Riefenstahl": The documents are found in BA-Militärarchiv: RW 4/185 and RW 4/261. These and other Bundesarchiv documents confirm the establishment of the unit as official, but operating independently, as *"sonder"* (special) would indicate.

223 Heinz Kluth: LR misnames him "Knuth" in LRMG, p. 352, and LRM, p. 259.

223 September 10: This is the correct date. LRMG cites it as September 8 on p. 350. In LRM, it appears as September 9, p. 257. A Bundesarchiv document (BA-Militärarchiv W 01-6/377) refers to the 7:00 a.m. departure on September 10. Details of the convoy are from Kinkel, p. 217.

223 Dessau execution: His name was Johann Heinen, according to Shirer, *"This Is Berlin,"* p. 81.

224 headlines: Ibid., pp. 79–80.

224 sixty thousand: Kershaw, *Nemesis*, p. 241.

224 LR to Manstein: Manstein, p. 43.

224 Manstein on LR: Ibid.

225 "I hadn't imagined": LRM, p. 258.

225 DNB and "We promise": Shirer, *"This Is Berlin,"* p. 82.

225 Leni heard rumors: LRM, p. 258; "terrified they were digging": Ibid.

225 She remembered a German police officer: Ibid.

225 Leni said she cried out: Ibid., p. 259.

225 Leni said she went to General von Reichenau: Ibid.

226 Konskie synagogue and rabbi: Rabbi Weingarten, according to Wirth, p. 246.

226 She later wrote: LRM, pp. 258–59; "I was so upset": Ibid., p. 259.

226 Kershaw "orgy": *Nemesis*, p. 240.

226 executions carried out and "the nobility": Ibid., p. 243.

226 Another was Wloclawek: Rhodes, pp. 6–7.

226 later actions: See Heer, *Vernichtungskrieg*, the catalog of the exhibition that occasioned public controversy in Germany in 1996.

227 Horst Maetzke: Riefenstahl file, Institut für Zeitgeschichte, Munich. Thanks to Frau Frölich for directing me to this source.

227 aide to General von Manstein: This was Rudolf Langhaeuser. His testimony is quoted here from Rother (English), p. 211, citing *Die Welt*'s coverage of the Manstein trial, November 4, 1949.

227 Manstein confirmed this: Manstein, p. 44.

228 "severe expiation": *Die Welt*, November 2, 1949, cited after Rother (English), p. 130. Reichenau's remark was quoted in the 1949 war crimes trial of von Manstein.

228 Hitler's amnesty decree: Kershaw, *Nemesis*, p. 246.

228 Two weeks later: Ibid., p. 247.

228 Rainer Rother quote: Rother (English), p. 133. Corpses quote: LRMG, p. 908; LRM, p. 653.

228 Hitler arrived in Danzig: LRM, pp. 259–60.

229 Siegfried Line: Ibid., p. 270.

229 Fritz Hippler: The film was called *Westwall*. Hull, p. 172; Moeller, *Filmminister*, p. 126.

229 Hippler confirmed that Leni: Int. PW/Fritz Hippler, Berchtesgaden, August 18, 1971, tape 8, transcript p. 7.

230 telegram: Riefenstahl file, BDC, June 14, 1940.

230 "artistic challenges": Riefenstahl, "Why I Am Filming *Penthesilea*," pp. 192–215.

231 "Penthesilea and I": LR to Michel Delahaye, in Sarris, *Interviews*, p. 470.

231 Her description limns: LR, "Why I Am Filming *Penthesilea*," p. 203.

231 Gottfried Benn: Letter to Frank Maraun, May 11, 1936, cited in Remak, p. 163.

231 King Leopold: Int. PW/Walter Traut, Munich, August 10, 1971, tape 5, transcript p. 14. LR had met Leopold during her *Olympia* tour. See LRM, pp. 231, 235.

232 no screenplay: LR's "Why I Am Filming *Penthesilea*" is a long series of production notes dated August 7, 9, and 11, 1939. In them, LR states several times that no screenplay had yet been written.

232 Kleist Society: Kleist Gesellschaft; int. PW/IPS, Alicante, Spain, July 2–3, 1971, tape 2, transcript p. 20.

232 She had envisioned action: From LR, "Why I Am Filming *Penthesilea*": "at a gallop" (p. 207); "the earth" (p. 209); "on poles" (p. 208); "rough" (p. 212); "silver armor" (ibid.); "mastiffs" (p. 206); "the shining sun" (p. 198).

232 "the harmonious": Ibid., p. 197.

232 "a fresco": Int. PW/LR, Munich, August 11, 1971, tape 17, side A, transcript p. 19; "film opera": LR, "Why I Am Filming *Penthesilea*," p. 202.

232 "not a single scene": LR, ibid., p. 201.

232 "demonical and the classical": Ibid.

232 "ecstasy of beauty": Ibid.

232 "Every thigh": Ibid.

233 A colleague remembered: Isabella Ploberger Schlichting, who was her art director on *Tiefland*. Int. PW/IPS, Alicante, Spain, July 2, 1971: "always working," tape 2, transcript p. 20; "She wasn't so," tape 2, transcript p. 18.

233 "no longer felt": LRM, p. 261.

233 film rights: See Chapter 10. Though LR had purchased them in the mid-1930s, she would have assigned them to Terra had the film been made. LR mentions, perhaps not irrelevantly, that Lloyd's of London covered Terra's losses when the picture was abandoned. In LRM (p. 156), her tone is grateful; in LRMG (p. 220), it seems grudging.

233 Goya and El Greco: LRMG, p. 355.

233 Vienna command performance: Hamann, p. 64.

233 Traut deal with Tobis: Int. PW/LR, Munich, August 11, 1971, tape 17, side A, transcript 4, p. 14.

233 Martin Bormann: The paper trail linking Bormann to *Tiefland* is broad and detailed. A representative example is Bormann's letter to the economics ministry of August 2, 1942, in which he writes: "Riefenstahl Film GmbH was founded with the special support of the Führer, and the Führer has instructed that the costs of the *Tiefland* film . . . be borne from the funds managed by me." Letter cited by Rother (English), p. 208, from BA R 43/II 810b, p. 81.

233 Tobis memorandum: The memorandum notes that payments will be *"schwartz,"* quoted from Enzensberger.

234 film right and percentages: Memo on "Acquisition of Film Rights" from propaganda ministry (Hinkle), March 9, 1944, LR file, BDC.

234 Alfred Riefenstahl firm: Lenssen, p. 86, citing BA R 3/1609, Bl. 33–35.

234 *Paradise:* The title in German is untranslatable ("The Greatest Happiness in the World on Horseback") but alludes to a quotation from Friedrich von Bodenstedt in which happiness is rendered by the German for "Paradise"; hence, "Paradise on Horseback."

235 Leni's complaints: Int. PW/LR, Munich, August 8, 1971, tape 16a, side A, transcript p. 12 (unsigned by LR). In late life, LR was vitriolic about Fanck. For the interview cited here, she refused to sign the transcript (though the tape exists). Fanck was still living at the time, and LR was furious that Peggy Wallace had interviewed him (transcript p. 11). (See Chapter 18.)

235 Fanck's villa and Speer: Trimborn, pp. 345–47. Trimborn asserts that LR urged Speer in this matter, though the evidence amounts only to Speer's letter informing her of his action.

235 planning for Leni's studio: Rother (English), p. 102.

235 the creation of Ufi: Moeller, *Filmminister,* pp. 93–96; Beyer, p. 25.

235 three private companies: Int. PW/Dr. Walter Müller-Goerne, Munich, August 14, 1971, tape 21, transcript p. 1. Müller-Goerne was a lawyer in the Reich Film Chamber and later legal consultant to Ufi. He was in charge of the liquidation of Olympia-Film GmbH in 1942.

235 "No one else": Int. PW/Fritz Hippler, Berchtesgaden, August 18, 1971, tape 8, transcript p. 7.

236 script of 1934: Who wrote that script is uncertain. In LRMG (p. 355; omitted from LRM), she mentions a script by Richard Billinger, but it is unclear if she is referring to 1934 or 1940. Her mention of director Frank Wisbar (Wysbar) in this connection suggests the earlier date, as Wisbar was by then in the United States.

236 Harald Reinl: Int. PW/Harald Reinl, Munich, August 10, 1971, tape 5, transcript p. 10. Reinl confirmed that the Kitzbühel meeting with LR was "accidental."

237 "This is Pedro" and Eichberger: LRM, pp. 262ff.

237 Troops in formation: *Berliner Illustrierte Zeitung*, no. 43, 1940, cited "mountain troopers," a charge reprinted in *Revue*, May 1, 1949, which occasioned the libel suit LR brought after the war (see Chapter 15); see *Prozessakte (Urteil) des Amtsgerichtes München*, November 30, 1949, p. 12.

237 "dusty": Int. PW/AF, Freiburg, July 23, 1971, tape 9, transcript p. 10.

237 "fairy tale": Int. PW/Harald Reinl, Munich, August 10, 1971, tape 5, transcript p. 14.

237 ordering from Agfa: Int. PW/LR, Munich, August 6, 1971, tape 14, side B, transcript p. 3

238 Albert Benitz as lover: Int. PW/Andrew Marton, Los Angeles, December 14, 1970, tape 29, transcript p. 11.

238 showed her script to Goebbels: "Difficulties" and "I won't" are from March 30, 1940, *Tagebücher*, part 1, vol. 7, p. 371; "first rate" is dated April 2, 1940, *Tagebücher*, part 1, vol. 8, p. 31.

238 "Leni Riefenstahl may not": JG, April 4, 1940, *Tagebücher*, part 1, vol. 8, p. 34.

239 cost of reconstruction: LRM, p. 265. On the same page, LR refers to "preliminary contracts for twelve billion dollars" at Tobis, which is a mistranslation of LRMG, p. 360, and should read "twelve million marks." The reference is to exhibition guarantees and is unverified.

239 Fanck on script: Int. PW/AF, Freiburg, July 23, 1971, tape 9, side A, transcript p. 9.

240 "except for" and "aghast": LRM, p. 267. Fanck's claim re the dog: int. PW/AF, Freiburg, July 23, 1971, tape 9, side A, transcript p. 10.

240 Fanck and lenses: Int. PW/IPS, Alicante, Spain, tape 2, transcript pp. 4–6.

240 Fanck remembered: "And Leni said": Int. PW/AF, Freiburg, July 23, 1971, tape 9, side A, transcript p. 11.

240 "Then the winter": Int. PW/IPS, Alicante, Spain, tape 2, transcript p. 6.

241 give Goebbels a preview: *Tagebücher*, part 1, vol. 9, p. 37.

241 Mathias Wieman: Kreimeier, p. 290. State actor was an honor bestowed by the Nazi Party.

241 "Spanish flavor": LRM, p. 266.

242 "asocial": Thurner, p. 9.

242 Himmler policy: Evans, *The Third Reich in Power*, p. 526.

242 arrest decree: Thurner, p. 13.

242 Sterilization: Ibid.

242 "The final solution": Evans, *Third Reich in Power*, p. 527, the wording is from the decree of December 1938.

242 "location hunting": LRM, p. 267. As noted, principal photography in the Dolomites had begun during reconstruction of the sets in Krün.

243 Gypsy testimony: Rosa Winter quoted in Knopp, p. 195. Reinhardt from Enzensberger, *Triumph des Vergessens,* cited in Kinkel, p. 230.

243 "primitive huts": Böhmer, "Ehemals 'Geheimes' Dokument, erstellt von Lagerleiter Böhmer, über die Umsiedlung der Zigeuner nach Polen," July 5, 1940. This and subsequent documents (hereafter "Gladitz Files") were made available to me by Eric Rentschler, together with other documents relating to the two postwar trials involving LR, the Gypsies of *Tiefland,* and the later suit LR brought against filmmaker Nina Gladitz.

243 description of camp: Ibid.

243 police commission report: Ibid.

243 contract terms: Gladitz Files.

244 housing provided in barns: LRM, p. 359. According to LR, local residents would not house the Gypsies elsewhere because of their reputation as thieves.

244 numbers of extras: An initial group of four was requisitioned but returned to Maxglan without explanation. An additional nineteen were subsequently requisitioned, including two of those originally selected and returned, for an apparent total of twenty-one. A final letter regarding the Gypsies' behavior in Krün, however, cites fifteen children and eight adults, for the total of twenty-three. Gladitz Files.

244 Marzahn requisition date: Rosenberg, p. 142; Gilsenbach, p. 167; also Enzensberger, *Tageszeitung,* March 5, 1985.

244 Charlotte Rosenberg: Rosenberg, p. 142.

244 payment of fees in Berlin: Gilsenbach, p. 167; Thurner, p. 18.

244 "welfare . . . camp": *Abend,* November 24, 1949 (clip, n.p.), asserting that LR made the claim during her trial against *Revue* in 1949.

244 "darlings": LRMG, p. 361.

244 LR pleased: Gladitz Files.

245 Antonie Reinhardt: From Böhmer's testimony in Gladitz Files; Enzensberger, p. 16.

245 Reinhardt family: Enzensberger, p. 14; Thurner, p. 148.

245 Camp regulations: Gladitz Files.

245 Josef Reinhardt on Gypsy fate: In Enzensberger, p. 16.

246 "We saw": LRM, p. 267; "nothing happened": *Der Spiegel,* August 16, 2002, p. 32.

246 "No doubts": LR in Enzensberger, p. 17.

246 generic statement of regret: *Der Spiegel,* August 16, 2002, p. 32.

CHAPTER FOURTEEN: GOODBYE TO ALL THAT

247 AH to LR epigraph: LRM, p. 271.

247 "White Rose" epigraph: From leaflet 2, Fall 1942.

247 "largest *finca*" and "soft spot": LRM, p. 291.

248 "Chinese wall": Hugh Trevor-Roper, in Sereny, "Children," p. 79.

248 a historian: Fest, *Face,* p. 194.

248 Bormann on LR Film GmbH: Bormann to Reichsminister Lammers, August 2, 1943, BA R 43/II 810b, p. 81. Citation is after Rother (English), pp. 112–13.

248 "This Bormann": U.S. Army Intelligence Report, p. 37. Full sourcing: "Ft. Meade documents, CIC Report, Ref. No. PWB/SAIC/3—PWB CPT HQ 7th Army, German Intelligence Section, Special Interrogation Series #3, dated May 30th, 1945," pp. 490Q–490T, IfZ, Munich (hereafter U.S. Army).

248 "direct access": Bernhard Minetti makes the claim in *Erinnerungen eines Schauspielers,* cited by Trimborn, p. 323.

248 Rabenalt: Letter to Deputy Parbel of the Reichsfilmkammer from Herr Teichs at Terra Film, June 23, 1944. The film was titled *Wir beide liebten Katharina* (*We Both Loved Katharina*), and Terra claimed that LR had been informed almost a year earlier of the signed Benitz commitment. Riefenstahl file, BDC. (Teichs's letter notes that Benitz and Rabenalt had made an entire picture together during one of Benitz's long periods of inactivity on *Tiefland*.)

248 Dr. Max Winkler: Letter LR to Winkler, June 18, 1944, BDC; also cited in Rother (English), p. 113, as BA R 109 III/16. Note that LR dealt directly with Winkler, who had already secured studio space in Prague for her use in August 1944, postponed until September.

249 "thrilling": LRM, p. 269.

249 "revenge": Ibid. For the Siegfried Line film, see Chapter 13.

249 two historical dramas: LR cites *Ohm Krüger* and *Der alte und der junge König* in LRMG, p. 364, but Rother ([English], p. 208, n. 20) notes that neither film was shot then or at Babelsberg.

249 Goebbels dismissed her: *Tagebücher,* March 1, 1941, part 1, vol. 4, p. 521.

249 "The difficulties": Int. PW/Fritz Hippler, Berchtesgaden, August 18, 1971, tape 8, transcript pp. 2–3, 9. "She had the protection of Hitler": p. 2.

249 "I was so upset": LRM, p. 270.

249 "I advised her urgently": JG, December 16, 1942, *Tagebücher*, part II (*Diktate*), vol. 6, p. 456.

250 "nothing to do with" and "already over five million": Ibid. No final cost figures are known. *Kolberg* was budgeted at 8.5 million reichsmarks, and *Tiefland* may have approached or even surpassed that.

250 Dr. Theodor Morell: Hitler's personal physician treated LR without success on several different occasions during the war (LRM, pp. 271, 293).

250 "The optimism": LRM, p. 271. AH was talking about film prints on metal so that the image would be permanent and nondegradable. He discussed the same idea with Goebbels, who mentioned it in his diaries.

251 fifty years later: LR gives a demonstration of *Tiefland*'s lighting to Ray Müller in his documentary *Wonderful, Horrible Life*.

251 She was dismayed that Pabst: LRM, p. 273.

251 Rabenalt: LRM, p. 274.

251 Ploberger told a more prosaic version: Int. PW/IPS, Alicante, Spain, July 3, 1971, tape 18, transcript pp. 1–2.

252 Peter Jacob, on the other hand: He was born Eugen Karl Jacob on December 30, 1909. Marriage certificate: Standesamt XIIIb, Berlin, Nr. 1331/1902.

252 he had acting ambitions: Collignon, p. 97. Ilse Riefenstahl Collignon mentions seeing him perform on the stage in Goethe's *Götz von Berlichingen*.

252 according to Ploberger: Int. PW/IPS, Alicante, Spain, July 3, 1971, tape 18, transcript pp. 2–3.

253 "emotional suffering": LRM, p. 281.

253 "I clung": Ibid., p. 286.

253 "a miracle" and "you've made": Ibid.

254 two hundred essential workers: The number is Ilse Riefenstahl's (Collignon, p. 126).

254 marriage of Heinz and Ilse: Ibid., pp. 68ff.

254 "*kaputt*": Ibid., p. 108.

254 Heinz received his notice: Ibid., p. 121.

254 Heinz's induction and assignment: Ibid., pp. 119–21. Also: letter to Michael Stephan, Staatsarchiv München, from Herr Kühmayer, Deutsche Dienststelle, V2-677/345, October 14, 2003, detailing Heinz Riefenstahl's military service. See LRM, p. 296, for LR's account of his punishment and "death commando" assignments.

254 "buying meat": LRM, p. 289.

254 "whom he adored": Ibid., p. 296.

255 "was friendly" and custody threat: Ibid., p. 296. LR names "SS General Wolff" here, but he was promoted to general only later (see below). The

point is important, for LR claims to have letters from him, which, if they exist, would be unlikely to claim a rank he would attain only in the future.

255 Karl Wolff: Wolff had been "Himmler's chief adjutant" (Kershaw, *Nemesis*, p. 149). He was an SS general and named military governor of Italy in 1943. He negotiated with Allen Dulles of the OSS for peace in Italy with the Allies though forbidden to do so by Hitler. Wheal and Shaw, p. 306; Kershaw, *Nemesis*, p. 834.

255 Wolff tried to have Heinz recalled: Collignon, pp. 119–21. On p. 125, Collignon claims Wolff tried to get Heinz recalled from duty in the summer of 1944, just before Heinz was killed.

255 custody agreement: Ibid., pp. 112–13. Alimony: Ibid., p. 117.

255 "on high": Ibid., pp. 114–15.

255 divorce and LR's use of influence: See Collignon, pp. 108–15; Speer on Bormann: p. 108; further to Speer: p. 115.

255 "like a lamb": Ibid., p. 116.

255 alimony payments: Ibid., p. 117.

255 Heinz and *Rassenschande:* Ibid., pp. 115–21. It is significant that these charges were published when LR was still living. They were not contested. The woman remains nameless but may be someone Collignon elsewhere refers to as "Minnie N." See p. 78.

256 Heinz's induction: LR's version of denunciation by a treacherous "best friend" may have substance, but Collignon believed his accuser was his chauffeur, a dedicated National Socialist disgruntled by his use of official vehicles for after-hours joyrides (fueled by Leni's personal gasoline rations) and offended by a lavish party Heinz gave on the national day of mourning following the German surrender at Stalingrad. See p. 120.

256 Speer and Fanck: Letter, Reichsfilmintendant Dr. Bauer to Frl. Scheibner, Abteilung Film, Berlin, April 18, 1945. Fanck's exemption from combat is specifically laid to Speer.

256 LR, Heinz, Speer: Lenssen, "Leben," p. 86, citing BA R 3/1609, Bl. 11.

256 Goebbels's speech: Stackelberg and Winkle, pp. 299–300.

256 "Is your trust": Cited here from Kershaw, *Nemesis*, p. 561; compare to Stackelberg and Winkle, pp. 299–300.

256 prescreened audience: Kershaw, *Nemesis*, p. 561.

257 " '*Ja*' ": Kershaw in *Nemesis*, p. 562, citing Willi Boelcke's *Wollt Ihr den Totalen Krieg?*, p. 25.

257 the Gestapo arrested: The crime was termed "preparation to commit treason" (Scholl, p. 148).

257 "life itself": Ibid., p. 37; "complicity," p. 79; "every people," p. 32.

257 "An end": From resistance leaflet 2, Fall 1942. After Stackelberg and Winkle, p. 304.

257 LR on Spain: LRM, p. 290.

257 "a caricature": Goldensohn, p. 252.

257 "blood ran cold": LRM, p. 146.

258 *Olympia* screening: Rother (English), pp. 59–60.

258 houseguest in Nuremberg: During the 1938 Nuremberg rally, she and mountain climber Anderl Heckmair stayed with Streicher (Heckmair, p. 78). Also cited in Salkeld, p. 191. Hans Ertl also noted Streicher's role as "Hausherr" during the making of *Day of Freedom* (Ertl, p. 200).

258 "You absolutely": The occasion was the Berlin première of *Triumph of the Will*, from *"Lieber Stürmer": Leserbriefe an das NS-Kampfblatt, 1924–1945*, cited by Trimborn, p. 368.

258 Streicher's letter: Streicher to LR, July 27, 1937, Riefenstahl file, BDC.

258 noted by the Gestapo: A surviving document stamped *"Geheim"* ("secret") reported, "On 29 October 1943, Frau Leni Riefenstahl and her fiancé, bearer of the Knight's Cross Major Jakob [*sic*], stayed in Nuremberg at the Hotel Deutscher Hof. She made immediate contact with the former gauleiter Julius Streicher [at his home] in Pleikershof and visited him there." Source: Institut für Zeitgeschichte, Munich, ref. Microfilm MA 612, Rosenberg file 105, doc. no. 60, p. 831.

258 Streicher at Nuremberg: Conot, pp. 381–87. Prosecution quotes, from the International Military Tribunal transcripts of the trial, cited in Conot, pp. 384–85.

258 Seebichl Haus: LRM, pp. 292–93. It is today a privately owned hotel.

259 no kitchen: Int. SB/Lt. Gen. Milton H. Medenbach (ret.), Wayne, Pa., May 7, 2005.

259 Ploberger and Bertha: Int. PW/IPS, Alicante, Spain, July 2–3, 1971, tape 2, transcript pp. 17–18. It was then that Ploberger came to accept Bertha as Jewish.

259 "negatives": LRM, p. 292.

259 "enormous" and "stylized": Ibid., p. 297.

260 Leni married Jacob: Ibid., p. 293.

260 marriage license: Standesamt XIIIb, Berlin, Nr. 1331/1902.

260 with Speer to Berchtesgaden: Sereny, *Speer*, p. 450. The date was "a few days before July 20, 1944."

260 "I noticed": LRM, p. 294.

261 "To my Führer on his birthday": [*"Meinem Führer zum Geburtstag in Treue und Verehrung"*]. This unique portfolio of forty-four images from Hitler's personal library is in the Library of Congress Prints and Photographs Division in Washington, D.C. Card #: 2005685824.

261 "officer clique": Kershaw, *"Hitler Myth,"* p. 215.

261 "I want": Fest, *Plotting*, p. 296.

261 *"für Führer"*: Letter to Alfred Riefenstahl from Squadron Leader Captain Riggers, July 28, 1944. Source: Deutsche Dienststelle. The letter was addressed to the senior Riefenstahl's residence in the Adolf-Hitler-Strasse.

261 "still cannot": LRM, p. 296.

262 "I held": Ibid., p. 294.

262 Bertha to Kitzbühel: Ibid., p. 301.

262 governess hired by Leni: Her name was Lilo Albin (Collignon, pp. 127–29). LR's version of this episode—in LRM, p. 297—is misleading. LR claims to have been given custody of the children under the terms of Heinz's will, which would not be certified until November in Berlin. She further claimed that both children (whose ages she misstates) were in her care (only Eckart was) and that she traveled from Prague to Kitzbühel immediately on learning of Ilse's visit there. This is not verifiable.

262 Leni was back in Berlin: LRM, pp. 298–99.

263 "absurd and inexplicable": Ibid., p. 299.

263 demands for continued draft deferments: The letters are part of the LR file, BDC.

263 "on a ship": LRM, p. 298.

263 LR to hospital in Merano: Ibid., p. 299.

264 "if you refuse": Collignon, pp. 168–69. Regarding the denunciation: Ilse was accused of defeatism on the grounds that she had remarked to Heinz at the time of the Russian invasion that this was "the beginning of the end." She was convinced that only LR could have known of the remark or seen to it that it turned up as evidence against her. Collignon, p. 108.

264 Spandau: Ibid., p. 170.

264 seventeen million refugees: Fest cites Goebbels's own estimate, *Speer*, p. 248.

264 gasoline and Brown House aid: LRM, pp. 302–3.

264 Schneeberger and Gisela: Ibid., p. 303.

265 "It is not necessary": In Fest, *Speer*, p. 250.

265 "like the end of the world": LRM, p. 290.

265 Ploberger and "some weeks": Int. PW/IPS, Alicante, Spain, July 3, 1971, tape 1, transcript pp. 9–10. LRM does not mention the Schneebergers' daughter, though Ploberger stressed her presence.

265 death of Hitler: LRM, pp. 304–5.

265 LR and the Schneebergers: Ibid., pp. 304–6.

CHAPTER FIFTEEN: PARIAH

266 Duras: *The War: A Memoir* (New York: Pantheon, 1986), p. 48.

266 "did all the talking": "Prozess gegen die *Revue*," *Revue*, December 11, 1949.

266 "A world had collapsed": LRM, p. 306.

266 "what could have changed": Ibid., p. 305.

266 "at the mercy" and "no legal protection": Ibid., p. 327.

266 "With the end of Hitler": Kershaw, *"Hitler Myth,"* p. 224.

267 "the Third Reich is": Klemperer, May 11, 1945, p. 904.

267 "my first escape": LRM, p. 307.

267 Lt. Col. Milton H. Medenbach: LR incorrectly refers to him in LRM (p. 308) as major. Int. SB/Lt. Gen. Milton H. Medenbach (ret.), Wayne, Pa., May 7, 2005.

268 "the Jewish element": Int. SB/Medenbach, as cited.

268 *"Mutti"* and "Jake": This and other details and quotations re Seebichl Haus and Medenbach are from int. SB/Medenbach unless otherwise indicated. Medenbach's photograph album contains photographs of some of LR's visits from old friends, including Gustav Diessl, her costar in *Piz Palü*.

268 "Herr Colonel": Letter, Medenbach to SB, June 25, 2005.

268 "I found myself": LRM, p. 309.

268 "I hid my face in my hands": LRM, p. 311. LR was, in this case, given something of a special dispensation. Ordinary local populations were required by American occupation forces to tour the camps in person and witness directly the horrors of which they claimed ignorance. Ration cards for foodstuffs and the like were issued only after completion of such tours, an experience LR was spared.

269 "gigantic eyes": Ibid., p. 313.

269 "incomprehensible" and Balázs: Ibid., p. 312.

269 "alibi Jews": Augstein, p. 75.

269 interrogation quotes: U.S. Army at IfZ, Munich.

269 "a certain admiration . . . shared the responsibility": Ibid.

270 Ernest Langendorf: Int. SB/Mrs. Ernest Langendorf, Munich, February 19, 2002.

271 Hitler's sexuality: LRM, pp. 314–15.

271 "Hitler, as I knew him": Ibid., p. 313. The untenable assumption that Hitler knew nothing of the Holocaust remains widespread.

271 "After all": Ibid., p. 314.

271 Privately, she continued: The citations here are from Friedrich Mainz (see below), but her use of *"der Führer"* was well known. Enno Patalas observed to SB that she referred to his speeches in her films as *"Führerrede"* (Führer speeches), a word she apparently coined.

271 Friedrich Mainz: Int. PW/Friedrich Mainz, July 29, 1971, tape 10, transcript pp. 11–12.

273 Bethouart affair: LRM, p. 328. Her former cameraman Richard Angst was among those who credited the affair (int. PW/Richard Angst, July 7, 1971, Berlin, tape 18, side B, transcript 18b, p. 5).

273 "done my bit": Schulberg, "Nazi Pin-Up Girl," p. 11.

273 Schulberg citations: Ibid., pp. 9, 11ff.

274 bank accounts: LRM, pp. 328, 333.

274 She would never see this money: Reichsmarks would be revalued on a ratio of ten to one as a result of the currency reform of June 21, 1948. According to this formula, the money would have amounted to thirty thousand deutsche marks, still a considerable sum.

275 trustees of her firm: LRM, p. 328. LR accused Gisela Schneeberger of testifying that "my film equipment at Seebichl House consisted of personal gifts from Hitler," which was, strictly speaking, true. All of the equipment had been financed by Hitler's funds through Bormann, something LR never admitted.

275 "undesirable": "*Tiefland* etwas verschollen," *Der Spiegel*, no. 40, August 29, 1949.

275 Arnold Fanck: LRM, p. 329.

275 "love-hate": Ibid., p. 330. Her staff included cutter Emmy Steffen, secretary Minna Lück, and bookkeeper Willi Hapke.

275 "intolerable" and "undignified": Ibid.

275 "mental torture": Ibid., p. 331. LR uses the word *torture* several times to describe her ordeal.

275 "chronic paranoia": Ibid., p. 327; "persecution mania": Rother (English), p. 209.

275 "a nymphomaniac": Sereny, *German Trauma*, p. 240.

276 "My life's work": LRM, p. 333.

276 "insane asylum": Ibid., pp. 333–34.

276 "at the orders": Ibid., p. 334.

276 a live-in patient: The alternate version referring to the clinic of Professor Beringer appears in an interview in the *Mannheimer Morgen* of January 16, 1954 (Rother [English], pp. 209–10, n. 3). As Rother notes, it is impossible to determine which version is true, though the extremely vague language ("I have retained very little about this black episode": LRM, p. 334) would suggest the 1954 version is more credible.

276 Jean-Pierre Desmarais: LRM, pp. 335–38; had been born a Jew: Kretzmer, p. 2.

276 "I would have signed" and "I don't care": Ibid., p. 337.

276 London journalist: See Kretzmer, p. 2. Here she acknowledges Desmarais was Jewish, though she could not recall his name. After prodding, she located his surname in an old address book but could not remember his first name. Kretzmer: "This may, of course, be the sign of weak memory. It is also, surely, a sign of a particularly weak capacity for human gratitude."

277 "by orders from above": LRM, p. 338.

277 diary generated headlines: Ibid.

277 Hitler's quoted remarks: Ibid., pp. 351–52.

277 "criminal" and "impossible for me": Ibid., p. 352.

277 "gross fabrication": Ibid., p. 339.

277 Desmarais beat a hasty retreat: He resettled in Montréal, where he was active in French-speaking commercial circles. In LRMG (pp. 486–88), he makes one more attempt to gain control of *Tiefland*.

278 Luis Trenker: LRM, p. 348.

278 Eva Braun's family: Ibid., p. 349. LR claimed, "I had never even seen Eva Braun," which seems unlikely considering LR's many visits to the Berghof, where Braun lived openly as its mistress. The point was legally irrelevant, in any case.

278 "professionally qualified": Gritschneder adopted the phrase as the title of his memoir.

278 Gritschneder citations: Gritschneder, *Forum*, transcript p. 3.

278 obtained an injunction: The date was September 10, 1948, and the publication enjoined was *Wochenend*, a magazine published in Nuremberg.

278 "over fifty" and "the lawyer": LRM, p. 349.

279 Villingen hearing: LRM (p. 352) misstates the date as December 1948. It was November 5, 1948. Riefenstahl file, BDC.

279 "so many of the successors": Polgar. He wrote: "*so viele von diesen Nachfolgern mit ihren Vorgängern identisch sind.*"

279 recent study: Edith Raim, lecture, Staatlichen Archive Bayerns, Munich, January 11, 2005.

279 "Not a single": LRM, pp. 353–54.

279 "political incrimination": Ibid., p. 352. This first verdict came on December 1, 1948. The hearing dated January 13, 1950, concluded with the extraordinary statement that, regarding evidence presented against LR, "It is not the business of this chamber to prove how much is true or false." BDC.

279 letter and editorial writers: Notable among the letters was one from cameraman Emil Schünemann regarding his contretemps with her at the time of *Triumph of the Will* (see Chapter 10) in *Die Welt* on January 25, 1949. He claimed that her villa in Dahlem was the gift of Hitler and that she would not have hesitated to report him to the Gestapo had he not had his own protectors.

280 the woman who had taken: Her name was Erika Schmachtenberger.

280 One news source: The *Süddeutsche-Zeitung:* "Ich bekam keine Reichsmittel," November 24, 1949.

281 "only a loan": Clip, *Sozialdemocrat*, November 29, 1949.

281 "glad to escape": "Prozess gegen die *Revue*," *Revue*, December 11, 1949.

281 Gypsy testimony: "Like dogs" is from the *Hamburger Abendblatt,* and "better cared for" is from the *Münchner Merkur,* both cited in *Revue,* "Prozess gegen die *Revue,*" December 11, 1949.

281 "fierce" and "duels": *Hamburger Abendblatt,* November 24, 1949, and *Sozialdemocrat,* November 29, 1949.

281 "devil's director": "Regisseurin des Teufels," *Hamburger Freie-Press,* November 24, 1949.

281 "carnival": Düsseldorf's *Mittag,* cited in "Prozess gegen die *Revue,*" *Revue,* December 11, 1949.

281 "laughter": Ibid.

281 "wildly": "Ich bekam . . . ," *Süddeutsche-Zeitung,* Munich, November 24, 1949.

281 "never allowed": *Die Welt,* cited in Rother (English), p. 211, n. 12.

281 "did all the talking": "Prozess gegen die *Revue,*" *Revue,* December 11, 1949.

281 "When she spoke": Polgar.

281 semantic technicality: The reasoning would resurface in the Nina Gladitz trial yet to come, but even LR cites this ruling, which depended on labeling (LRM, p. 338).

282 Alfred Polgar: "Die tragische Farce der Entnazifizierunq," *Der Weg,* July 28, 1950, cited in Rother (English), p. 126, as from *Aufbau,* December 30, 1949, p. 5 (sources identical). Polgar had recently returned to Vienna from wartime self-exile in the United States and was in Munich to attend the trial.

282 "fellow traveler": Riefenstahl file, BDC. The five possible classifications were: *Hauptschuldige* (major offender guilty of crimes), *Belastete* (directly involved as activist, militarist, war profiteer), *Minderbelastete* (lesser offender not known to have committed crimes), *Mitläufer* (fellow traveler through sympathies or opportunism), and *Entlastete* (innocent and anti-Nazi). Wheal and Shaw, p. 70.

282 Historians agree: Kershaw in *Nemesis,* p. 838.

282 Helmut Kindler and *Revue:* April 19, 1952, pp. 6–7, here cited from Rother (English), p. 127.

283 "gave up": LRM, p. 385.

283 Stubbening: The blackmailer LR referred to went by "Freitag." Whether he was named Stubbening and called himself Freitag or vice versa or whether there were two separate individuals is unknown. See "Ein Erpresser schoß sich daneben," *Stern,* May 11, 1952, p. 10. See also Julia Encke, "Amateurfotografen als Augenzeugen: Bilder aus der Dunkelkammer des Krieges," *Süddeutsche-Zeitung,* no. 289, December 14–15, 2002, p. 16, "Literatur."

283 document center in Hamburg: "Ein Erpresser schoß sich daneben," *Stern*, May 11, 1952. Leni produced eyewitnesses: "Ein Erpresser . . ." in *Stern*, May 11, 1952. LRM, p. 387.

283 East German State Security Police: The author obtained copies of these photographs pursuant to a request of the East German Riefenstahl file.

283 court's decision: LRM, p. 387.

284 "moral damage" and "millions": Ibid., p. 395.

284 settlement with Kindler: Ibid.

284 Kindler's exposé: Kindler had already demonstrated in the first *Revue* trial that Bormann had supplied funds for the picture. Further revelations of this sort threatened property judgments that would not have been to LR's advantage.

CHAPTER SIXTEEN: SURVIVOR

285 "No one needs to know": Letter, LR to KK, from Munich, November 18, 1958.

285 "She is, after all": Int. PW/FM, Munich, July 29, 1971, tape 10, transcript p. 25.

285 "Anyone like me": "Leni will wiederkommen," *Westfalenpost*, Hagen, March 16, 1951.

285 "to promote": Kreimeier, p. 370.

286 "pockets were full": Polgar. For unknown reasons, she specifically mentioned Argentina and Spain.

286 cameraman Richard Angst: Int. PW/Richard Angst, Provinz, July 7, 1971, tape 18, side B, transcript p. 5. Angst was offended by reports of LR's affair with General Bethouart.

286 Friedrich Mainz: Int. PW/FM, Munich, July 29, 1971, tape 10, transcript p. 24.

287 "She spent millions": Ibid., p. 1.

287 "*very* egocentric": Ibid., pp. 23–24.

287 "She always had": Ibid., p. 23. "She mixes": Ibid., p. 1. "If you need": Ibid., pp. 24–25.

287 Mainz on LR and AH: Ibid., p. 2. Mainz's interview conveys appreciative delight in stories of LR's love affairs.

287 "I asked my lawyer": Ibid., p. 23. Mainz did not detail LR's debt to him, but she refers to him in LRM (p. 451) as "my chief creditor."

288 Waldi Traut: Int. PW/Walter Traut, Munich, August 10, 1971, tape 6, transcript pp. 7–8.

288 Hans Albers and "that woman": LRM, p. 370. LR tars Albers here as one

of Hitler's favorite actors, which may have been true with pictures such as *Münchhausen*, though Albers was known to have distanced himself from the party during the Third Reich.

288 "she still mourned": Letter, HS to Glenn Infield, 1975. Infield, p. 234.

288 "I made pictures": Int. PW/HS, Munich, August 13, 1971, tape 12, transcript p. 12.

288 "unable to sacrifice": LRM, p. 368.

288 "my own destiny": Michel Delahaye in Sarris, *Interviews*, p. 456.

289 canisters of film: LRM, p. 371. There is a discrepancy here. In her memoirs, LR states at one point that the negative to *The Blue Light* was stored in Berlin, in another place that it was near Kitzbühel.

289 Lantschner brothers: Screenwriter Willy Clever was hired by LR to write the script. "Neuer Millionen-Sportfilm," *8 Uhr-Blatt*, Nuremberg, July 16, 1952.

289 *Red Devils* plotting: Hinton, 3rd ed., pp. 94–96.

289 "grotesque": Rother (English), p. 140.

289 Harald Reinl: Reinl later claimed that he had no part in the writing of the script, which was done entirely by Bartsch. Int. PW/Harald Reinl, Munich, August 10, 1971, tape 5, transcript p. 14. Bartsch had earlier worked for LR on a short equestrian film made from Olympics footage.

289 blond in Italy: "Leni Riefenstahl filmt Incognito," *Frankfurter Allgemeine Zeitung*, October 5, 1950.

290 "It was not made": Cited in Rother (English), p. 137.

290 "the redemption": See Chapter 6.

290 Press releases: Cited in Rentschler, *Ministry*, p. 31.

291 "dazzling gala": LRM, p. 384.

291 "no Party funds": LRM, p. 393; and LRMG, p. 518.

291 partial documentation: It consisted mainly of the articles of incorporation of her firm, which listed herself and Heinz as principals. It was, as indicated, a sham. There was, of course, no copyright on the film itself, as it was unfinished.

292 "dazzlingly" and "countless": LRM, p. 397.

292 "out of date": Ibid.

292 "quite sick": Ibid.

292 "objective": Ibid.

292 "When one sees": Ulrich Seelmann-Eggebert in *Mannheimer Morgen*, cited in Rother (English), p. 212.

292 serious film journal: *Der neue Film*, February 22, 1954, cited in Rother (English), p. 138.

292 "No lie": LRM, p. 397.

293 "inconsistent": Ibid., p. 398.

293 "roaring success": Ibid.

293 archival footage: Int. SB/Stefan Drössler, Munich, January 25, 2006.
     According to Drössler, sources at the Bundesarchiv acknowledge the exis-
     tence of this footage but claim there is nothing "of interest" in it.

294 *Tiefland* as "tyrannicide": This is the view of Helma Sanders-Brahms in
     "Tyrannenmord," pp. 173–76; and Robert von Dassanowsky in
     " 'Wherever You May Run, You Cannot Escape Him': Leni Riefenstahl's
     Self-Reflection and Romantic Transcendence of Nazism in *Tiefland*."

294 "intensity" and "poetry": LRM, p. 399.

294 "very serious reservations": Ibid.

294 Cocteau as collaborator: He wrote enthusiastically about Breker when the
     sculptor's works were exhibited in Nazi-occupied Paris in 1943. See Kaplan,
     p. 278, n. 196.

294 *From Here to Eternity* from the United States: Fred Zinnemann, who
     directed that picture, told SB that he first heard rumors about LR and
     Konskie during the 1954 Cannes festival, suggesting that LR's claims of
     political harassment were not unfounded.

294 Cocteau told Leni: LRM, p. 403.

295 "satirical": Ibid.

295 Cocteau on Marais: Ibid., p. 401.

295 "symphony of colors": Ibid., p. 393.

295 "bare-faced lie": Ibid., p. 402.

295 documentary about Spain: *Sol y Sombra* is in LRMG, p. 537. *Bullfights:*
     Feiden.

295 The Dark Continent: Udet: Int. SB/Hasso Felsing, April 1988; Morell
     had been a ship's doctor in Africa (Junge, p. 80); the cameraman was Kurt
     Neubert, in Culbert and Loiperdinger, *Tag*, p. 7.

296 Kurt Heuser: Heuser had written screenplays for G. W. Pabst and Detlef
     Sierck before the latter went to America and changed his name to Douglas
     Sirk.

296 plot line: Unpublished film treatment "Afrikanisches Tagebuch, eine
     Filmdichtung über Afrika gestaltet von Leni Riefenstahl." Kurt Kreuger,
     Beverly Hills, furnished a copy to SB, November 8, 2001.

296 big-game hunter: Hans Otto Meissner. His book was a popular hit of the
     period.

296 "I was obsessed": LRM, p. 409.

296 reawaken interest in *The Red Devils:* All the LR correspondence of this
     period refers to *Red Devils* as an ongoing project.

296 Traut investment: LRM (p. 418) cites the lower figure. However, in a
     handwritten letter from LR to KK from Rome on May 26, 1957, LR put
     Traut's direct investment at $75,000 plus a loan of a further $25,000

(expressed in U.S. dollars). Other friends of Traut later estimated his investment in the neighborhood of 500,000 marks, or around $125,000. See Hitchens, "Leni Riefenstahl Interviewed by Gordon Hitchens," p. 144, where Heinz von Jaworsky claims Traut told him he had lost half a million marks on the picture.

297 safari firm investment: LRM, p. 418.

297 "plague": LRVA, p. 20.

297 "intoxicated": Ibid., p. 14.

297 "They seemed": Ibid.

297 "vision of strangeness": LRM, p. 411. The drug image occurs also in LRVA, p. 14.

297 "new life": LRM, p. 411.

297 "I could uproot": Ibid., p. 416.

297 Ernst Jäger: LR's secretary noted Dr. Edwin Janss of the Investment Corporation and Jäger as Hollywood contacts. Letter, LR's office to Kurt Kreuger, April 3, 1956.

298 Paramount: Letter, LR to KK, July 16, 1956. LR claimed that Paramount's exhibitors had expressed strong interest in the picture.

298 "fully Jewish": Letter, KK to LR in Munich, n.d. (circa August 1956).

298 "you can imagine": Ibid.

298 Kreuger and "Helene Jacob": Int. SB/Kurt Kreuger, Beverly Hills, November 8, 2001. Also letter, LR to KK, July 16, 1956, and letter, KK to LR, August 1, 1956, in which KK protests that presenting the film as the work of "[Helene] Jacob" would violate his business practice of being "honest and direct." LR's lawyer for Stern Film reiterated in a letter to KK of August 8, 1956, that LR was prepared to use—outside Germany—the name "Helene Jacob" or no name at all in order to secure financing.

298 "No one needs": Letter, LR to KK, from Munich, November 18, 1958.

298 Universal figures: Letter from KK to Walter Traut in Munich, August 1, 1956. Hasso was Swedish, Lindfors was Swedish, and King was born in France.

299 Bergman and Hepburn: Letter, LR to KK, July 16, 1956.

299 Universal's conditions and LR's response: Letter, Dr. Bayer of Stern to KK, August 9, 1956. Bayer was the lawyer for Stern Film.

299 "Africa had": LRM, p. 411.

299 "unapproachable": Ibid., p. 416.

300 "nervous condition": Ibid., p. 432; tranquilizer injections: Ibid., p. 431; morphine: Ibid., p. 433.

300 Universal's remained: Letter, KK to Dr. Bayer and Traut, September 14, 1956, and letter, KK to LR, n.d. (circa same date).

300 "been wrong": LRM, p. 427.

301 "a Judas": Ibid., p. 432. This may have been a Herr Grunewald, who wrote an article critical of the production in Munich's *Abend-Zeitung* on July 10, 1957. LR answered in a letter to the editor on July 24 challenging his assertion that "the money gave out and we worked too little to get more." A letter from LR to KK from Munich on May 16, 1958, accuses the attorney Dr. Bayer, who was also involved with Gloria Film, of causing the film's collapse.

301 "financial death": Int. PW/Walter Traut, Munich, August 10, 1971, tape 6, transcript p. 14.

301 Traut on LR: Ibid.

301 "She had all": Ibid., transcript p. 7.

301 Universal revised its potential investment: Letter, KK to LR in Munich, February 2, 1957. Other consulted correspondence dates from mid-January, including four cables from LR to KK.

301 The firm was MGM: Int. SB/KK, Beverly Hills, November 8, 2001. Also: letter, KK to LR in Munich, November 14, 1958, and LR to KK from Munich, November 18, 1958.

302 "how a genius": Linder, p. 439.

302 German distributor: LRM, p. 402.

CHAPTER SEVENTEEN: COMEBACK

303 Grierson: LRM, p. 446; *TV Guide*, London, February 11, 1960.

303 Mekas: *Village Voice*, November 7, 1974, p. 88.

303 "There must be": Int. PW/LR, Munich, August 6, 1971, tape 14, transcript p. 6.

303 "When I am": Weigel, "Interview," p. 410

304 *Olympia* in New York: *New York Times*, H.T.S. [Harry T. Smith], March 9, 1940, p. 19, and March 30, 1940, p. 11, both parts at the 86th Street Garden Theatre.

304 cuts in *Olympia*: LRM, p. 434; "to make some money": Letter, LR to KK, Munich, May 16, 1958.

304 "history": Vernon Young in *Accent*, Spring 1955, cited in Salkeld, p. 237.

304 Montagu publicly denounced: Cited in Salkeld, p. 239.

305 "Satan himself": Ibid., p. 238.

305 John Grierson: LRM, pp. 446–47; *TV Guide*, London, February 11, 1960.

305 "did not care": LRM, p. 445.

305 "appropriate": Interoffice Memo, BFI, February 25, 1960, signed "EHL." The solicitors were H. A. Crowe & Co. in London. The copyright claim was inaccurate. See below.

305 rights to remake *The Blue Light:* LRM, p. 443.

306 "an influential": Ibid., p. 440.

306 ballet limitations: LR wrote her extensive thoughts about the ballet version in an unpublished document dated October 29, 1958. PW, document T78.

306 temporary injunction: LR routinely overstated the results of her lawsuits (see below). Here she attempted to have the book withdrawn, but Parisian courts settled for retraction of the claim: "Leni Riefenstahl gewinnt Prozeß," *Frankfurter Allgemeine Zeitung,* December 3, 1960. Also, "Entscheidung gegen Leni Riefenstahl," *Tagesspiegel* (Berlin), March 11, 1961.

306 British solicitor: LRM, p. 448.

307 "groundless": "Leni Riefenstahl zieht Klage gegen *Daily Mirror* zurück," *Deutsche Zeitung,* October 25, 1960; *Der Spiegel,* November 16, 1960.

307 *Evening Standard:* December 13, 1960, cited in Salkeld, pp. 239–40. Also, *Bild am Sontag,* December 25, 1960.

307 The *Standard* remarked: Cited in Salkeld, p. 240.

307 "Everywhere else": *London Sunday Dispatch,* December 18, 1960, cited in Salkeld, p. 240.

307 "this Ophelia": *Spectator,* February 10, 1961, cited in Salkeld, p. 242.

307 "The denials": Pem., "Leni Riefenstahl weinte nur," *Der Kurier* (West Berlin), December 12, 1960.

308 Rotha quote: *Film till Now,* p. 591.

308 paid her for footage: "Jedoch ihr Wille triumphierte nicht," *Der Kurier* (West Berlin), December 6, 1962. LR acknowledged receiving payment for footage used in the Rotha film via Walter Koppel, a German film distributor, though she claimed the footage was taken from *Olympia* (letter, LR to Kevin Brownlow, January 20, 1967).

308 charity donation: LRM, p. 451.

308 Leni in movie theater: "Ihr Kampf," *Der Spiegel,* no. 3, January 11, 1961. Length: In LRM, the claim of 2,000 feet is made on p. 567. The actual length was 337.31 meters, or a bit more than 1,100 feet, roughly ten or eleven minutes of screen time.

308 *"Mein Kampf* was": LRM, p. 451. Sum and profits: Rother (English), p. 149.

308 "my financial problems": LRM, p. 501.

308 Minerva: Rother (English), p. 149, citing *Düsseldorfer Nachrichten,* December 10, 1960. Interestingly, Leiser gave interviews in which he referred to "the spoils of war," implying he got his footage from the American and French governments, though LRM charged that the footage came from East Germany. See "Ihr Kampf," *Der Spiegel,* no. 3, January 11, 1961.

308 debt to Fanck: LRM, p. 451.

309 Headlines: "Reward" is in *Der Abend,* December 10, 1960; "Dirty Money"
     is in Berlin's *Morgenpost,* December 11, 1960; "Ihr Kampf" is from *Der
     Spiegel,* January 11, 1961.

309 A Berlin daily: *Berliner Morgenpost,* December 11, 1960.

309 Frankfurt editorial: *Frankfurter Rundschau,* December 13, 1960, cited by
     Rother (English), as 1969, p. 150.

309 a Swedish daily: *Dagens Nyheter,* cited in "Ihr Kampf," *Der Spiegel,*
     January 11, 1961.

309 copyright decision: December 29, 1966, verdict of the Federal Supreme
     Court in the matter of *Mainz v. Minerva.* An appeal resulted in a final con-
     firmation of the verdict on January 10, 1969 (Bundesgerichtshof file I ZR
     48/67). Mainz was ordered to pay court costs, which he estimated at eighty
     thousand marks. LR refused to share these costs with him.

309 "stunned" and "miscarriage": LRM, pp. 567–69. In LRM, the latter phrase
     is translated as "a judicial error," though LR uses the term *"Fehlurteil,"*
     better rendered as "miscarriage of justice" in English. LRMG, pp. 767ff.

309 Arnold Raether: LRM reproduces the affidavit on p. 569. It is clear that
     Raether misunderstood Ufa's role in the film (Ufa paid a distribution
     advance but did not finance the picture). See Chapter 10.

310 *Olympia* and Transit: The *Olympia* case came as a result of television pre-
     sentations of the picture in West Germany and was settled in 1964. The
     Mainz v. Minerva ruling was handed down in 1966.

310 Olympia Film Company and the Reich: See Chapter 11.

310 Transit finding: Rother (English), p. 154, and LRO, p. 242. The bracketed
     phrase replaces "LR and her brother" in the original; they were the only
     stockholders in Olympia-Film GmbH.

310 "What kind of people": LRM, p. 500.

310 When confronted with the paper trail: See LRO, p. 244. See also LRM, p.
     500, where LR claims that her lawyer "proved" that the tax dodge was real.
     No court accepted this argument.

310 "Both parties pledge": Agreement of January 16, 1964, between Transit-
     Film GmbH and LR. Cited here from LRO, pp. 242–44. The fullest
     documentation of these legal issues can be found in Loiperdinger, *Rituale,*
     and in LRO.

311 *"to describe herself"*: BA R 109 I/2163, agreement of January 16, 1964,
     between LR and Transit, cited here from Rother (English), p. 217, n. 32.

311 copyright to IOC: IOC newsletter, "Olympic Turn Around," July 15,
     2005, p. 2. The sale occurred in December 2003 after five years of negoti-
     ation. LR's death may have cleared the way for the sale.

311 U.S. copyright: LRM, pp. 620–21.

311 (FDP): Rother (English), p. 158.

311 dispatched emissaries: SB observed this at the Munich Film Museum with regard to *The Blue Light* in 2003.

312 "systematic": LRM, p. 458, LRMG, p. 619; "crawling about": LRM, p. 454.

312 "nobody knows": Letter, LR to Kevin Brownlow, from Davos, February 20, 1967.

312 Japanese entrepreneurs: LRM, pp. 455–58.

312 Quandt and Krupp: Ibid., pp. 460–61.

312 Emmy Whitehead: LRMG, pp. 624–26. The passages are cut from LRM.

312 German distributor: LRM, p. 461.

312 "Africa crazy": Ibid., p. 462.

312 "the dark": Ibid.

312 "like a sculpture": Ibid.

312 The photograph had been published: It was also published in London's *Weekly Illustrated* in 1949, though LR almost certainly saw it in the *Geographic*. For Rodger: details from Naggar and from Peter Hamilton in Rodger, *Village*.

313 "subconsciously arranging": Naggar, p. 139.

313 "so horrific": Ibid., p. 140.

313 "get rid of the stench": Ibid., p. 149.

313 "Dear Madam": Ibid., p. 190. See also p. 297, n. 17.

313 "there was no other": LRM, p. 462.

313 the book he published: Rodger's book was published in France in 1955 as *Le Village des Noubas*. The English edition dates from 1999. Re *National Geographic* in February 1951: "With the Nuba Hillmen of Kordofan," text by former colonial officer Robin Strachan. LR's locating Rodger to make a cash offer is evidence of a concerted research effort. For Cooper, see the bibliography.

313 Cooper thought them: Cooper, p. 467.

314 "You are ten years": LRVA, p. 22.

314 "not even a travel bureau": LRM, p. 462.

314 "to make a record": Luz, p. 677. S. F. Nadel worked among the Nuba in 1938–39 and published his book about them in 1947. (See the bibliography.) The universities for which the Nansen Society was gathering material included the Anthropological Institute of Tübingen and the Institute for Scientific Films at Göttingen. The Nansen group included, in addition to Oskar Luz and his son Horst, economist Rolf Engel of the Max-Planck Institute in Munich and educator Friedrich Rothe of the University of Tübingen.

314 "no notion": Mannheim, p. 94.

314 "a very good deal": Letter, LR in Munich to KK in Beverly Hills, September 26, 1962. In LRM, there is no mention of her plan as outlined to KK.

315 "usually grumpy": LRM, p. 464.

315 "he wouldn't work": Ibid., p. 465.

315 "what is beautiful": Michel Delahaye in Sarris, *Interviews*, p. 462.

315 "no different from": LRM, pp. 467–68. LR admits rejecting subjects who would not remove their clothing (LRM, pp. 558–59).

315 "A young girl": Ibid., p. 468.

315 "black nymph": Luz, p. 679.

315 "One or two": LRVA, pp. 22–23. Nearly identical passages occur in LRM and LRMG. See LRM, p. 468.

315 Luz's version: Luz, p. 679.

315 exploiting nudity: LRM, p. 457.

316 "what is average": Michel Delahaye in Sarris, *Interviews*, p. 462.

316 "tableau," "motif," and "an army": LRM, p. 487.

316 "angry argument": Ibid., p. 474.

316 "shattered": Ibid., p. 468.

316 Luz's account: See "Proud Primitives." Luz and his associates had produced a thousand color and black-and-white stills, fifteen films, and some eighty tape recordings of Nuba songs and speech (Luz, pp. 677, 698). None of this, of course, was LR's work.

316 Robert Gardner and Odyssey: Gardner, "Can the Will Triumph?"; int. PW/Gardner, Cambridge, January 26, 1971, transcript 25, p. 2.; and LRM, pp. 505, 521–23. "It was": LRM, p. 521.

317 "she couldn't collaborate": Int. PW/Robert Gardner, Cambridge, January 26, 1971, transcript 25, p. 1.

317 "charm . . . unemcumbered": Gardner, p. 28; "gullible" and "gentle": ibid., p. 30.

317 "She is an actress": Int. PW/Robert Gardner, Cambridge, January 26, 1971, transcript 25, p. 3.

317 "admiration for the technical": Gardner as quoted by Hussman, p. 15.

317 "Oh, she's tough": Int. PW/Robert Gardner, Cambridge, January 26, 1971, transcript 25, p. 3

317 "one of the worst": Cited in Salkeld, p. 250.

317 "I couldn't envision": LRMG, p. 693.

317 Horst Kettner: See LRM, especially "How I Found Horst," pp. 546ff.

318 cartons and tonnage: Walk, p. 163.

318 Schweitzer: LRM, p. 526 and elsewhere. "How well I understood Albert Schweitzer," she writes.

318 "paradise": LRVA, p. 21.

318 "Nowhere in the world": Letter, LR to KK, from Munich, November 18, 1958.

318 "come to me": LRVA, p. 28.

319 *National Geographic:* LRM (pp. 504–5) assigns this failure to a missed deadline. See int. PW/James Card, George Eastman House, Rochester, N.Y., tape 24, transcript pp. 4–5. James Card: *"National Geographic* were willing to buy the slides from her outright and use all of them. They promised to give her any amount of film she needed but they wanted all rights to whatever she would shoot over there, including all American rights to the film she would make. That was completely against anything she felt she could do."

319 L. Ron Hubbard and apartheid: LRMG, p. 613. The incident is deleted from the English-language version.

319 *Stern:* December 14, 1969.

320 *Newsweek:* December 16, 1974, p. 94.

320 Eudora Welty: *New York Times Book Review,* December 1, 1974, p. 405.

320 Jonas Mekas: *Village Voice,* November 7, 1974, p. 88.

320 Cartier-Bresson and "more humanity": Cited by Naggar, p. 275.

320 "real tragedy" and "The children": Mannheim, p. 94.

321 "a scientific text": Loney, p. 32.

321 prospective English publisher: This was Tom Stacey. The book was subsequently issued by Collins.

321 Speer and editing: LRM, p. 576.

321 "drivel" and "hopelessly racist": Letter, James Faris to SB, September 3, 2005, p. 2.

321 "I had a dream": LR, *People,* p. 8; LRM, pp. 588–89.

321 " 'my' Nuba": LRM, p. 469; LR, *Last of the Nuba,* p. 10; etc.

321 "her facts": Faris, in *Newsweek,* December 13, 1976, p. 44.

322 "permanent . . . importance": From the dust jacket of the 1995 edition from Havill, London.

322 LR on Faris: LRM, p. 636.

322 "ignorant": Faris, "Photographic Encounters," p. 7.

322 European cosmetics: Ibid., pp. 7–8; letter, Faris to SB, September 3, 2005.

322 "grotesque perversion," "profoundly," and "grossly": Faris, "Leni Riefenstahl and the Nuba Peoples," pp. 96, 97.

322 "a large compound": Letter, Oswald Iten to SB, August 29, 2005.

323 Iten wrote in the Swiss and German press: See Iten, "Bilder und Zerrbilder"; also letter, Oswald Iten to SB, August 29, 2005.

323 "There is something appalling": Cited by Kimmelman, p. 15.

323 "It is as if ": Faris, "Photographic Encounters," p. 9.

323 "Helene Jacob": LRM, p. 602.

323 "eaten up": Ibid., p. 638.

323   "slander" and "this young": Ibid., pp. 637–38.

323   Susan Sontag: "Fascinating Fascism," *New York Review of Books*, February
        6, 1975. Citations here are from *Under*, in which the essay is reprinted
        with corrections and is (mis)dated 1974.

323   "to call": Sontag, "On Style," in *Against Interpretation*, p. 25.

324   "certainly the most ravishing," *"Triumph,"* and "ever made": Sontag,
        "Fascinating Fascism," in *Under*, p. 95.

324   "mercilessly clever": Holthusen, p. 572.

324   "the third": Sontag, "Fascinating Fascism," in *Under*, p. 87; "aloof ": ibid.,
        p. 73; "continuous": ibid., p. 86.

324   "when people claim": Ibid., p. 97.

324   "primitivist ideal": Ibid., p. 86.

324   "sanctimonious promotion": Ibid., p. 97.

324   "to filter out": Ibid., p. 95.

324   "more than beauty": Ibid., p. 97.

324   "fascist art": Ibid., p. 91.

324   "Art that seemed": Ibid., p. 98.

325   "eroticization": Ibid., p. 100.

325   "Riefenstahl's films" and "the ideal of life as art": Ibid., p. 96.

325   "She is no thinker": Ibid.; "indomitable": ibid., p. 97; "beauty freak": ibid.,
        p. 85.

325   "the problem with": Sarris, "Notes on," p. 33.

325   "In our many conversations": Letter, KK to SB, September 9, 2005.

326   "absolutely fascinated": Int. PW/Heinz von Jaworsky, September 10,
        1972, transcript p. 5.

326   "I find the black skin": *Oui*, May 1973, p. 106.

326   "Riefenstahl phenomenon": Bittorf, p. 228; "the enthusiasm": ibid., pp.
        228–31. LR quotes this passage in LRM, p. 632, but the English translation
        misassigns Bittorf's comments to *Vanishing Africa* rather than to *People of
        Kau*, which LR refers to correctly in LRMG (p. 869).

326   "occasionally withdrew": LRM, p. 638.

326   "How dare she": Letter, KK to SB, September 9, 2005.

326   French critic: Cited in LRM, p. 651.

327   Keith Richards: Ray Müller, quoted in "Riefenstahl and Jagger," *Barista*,
        March 2, 2004, http://dox.media2.org/barista/archives/ 0436.html.

327   "the house": Schiff, p. 260. LR moved into the house in 1979.

CHAPTER EIGHTEEN: FORTUNE AND MEN'S EYES

328   LR epigraph: Hitchens, "Interview with a Legend," p. 7.

328   scuba-diving school: LRM, pp. 585–86.

328 "strange, impalpable": LRVA, p. 28.

328 "addictive": LR, *Wonders*, p. 7.

328 "sheltering me": Ibid.

329 *"Harold and Maude"*: Müller, "Besuch," p. 66. Horst grateful: int. Florian Neubert/Ray Müller, Munich, September 15, 2005.

329 skiing at almost eighty: Letter, LR to Kurt Kreuger, June 23, 1981.

329 Niehans treatments: LR may have also taken fresh cell treatments in Switzerland, but her clinic of choice was in the German town of Lenggries (*Frischzellen Journal*, Deutsches Zentrum für Frischzellen-Therapie, no. 2, 1984, reprinted in *Konkret*, issue 27, 1985, p. 17).

330 "personal art" and "personal signature": Sarris, *American Cinema*, pp. 15, 19; "the worst film": ibid., p. 17. Sarris's remains the standard work: witty, erudite, occasionally eccentric, but enduringly influential.

331 "I have": Hitchens, "Interview with a Legend," p. 7.

331 "Art, creation": Michel Delahaye in Sarris, *Interviews*, p. 468.

331 Eisenstein: See Berson and Keller for a particularly conservative (political) view. See also Sarris, "Films," where he compares LR to Eisenstein's "flagrant lying" in *Ten Days That Shook the World*. LR was careful to note that the Berson and Keller article in support of her work was written by an "American Jewish writer" (*sic*) (Brownlow, "Leni Riefenstahl," p. 18).

331 Amos Vogel: "Can We Now Forget the Evil That She Did?" *New York Times*, May 13, 1973, section 2, p. 19.

332 disinvited: LRM, p. 449.

332 Telluride and mayor: Andrews, p. 15.

332 "I have found the strength": LRM, p. 598.

332 Sontag noted both: "Riefenstahl's recent promotion to the status of a cultural monument surely owes to the fact that she is a woman," and "Riefenstahl's defenders . . . now include the most influential voices in the avant-garde film establishment" (both on p. 84 in *Under*).

333 photocopied private correspondence: Peggy Wallace received such papers from LR in Munich in 1971, and they are now part of the author's archive.

333 Tony Palmer: Int. SB/Tony Palmer, Munich, January 24, 2006. Palmer met with her in the early 1990s to discuss what became of Müller's documentary on her life.

333 "She was always": Brownlow, "Leni Riefenstahl," p. 15.

333 "an artist": Ibid., p. 16.

333 "among the most": Letter, Kevin Brownlow to SB, August 10, 2005.

333 "insidious propaganda": Brownlow, "Leni Riefenstahl," p. 15.

333 "Art transcends": Ibid.

333 "the humanity": Ibid., p. 19.

333 Paul Rotha: Rotha, "Leni Riefenstahl," *Film*, Spring 1967, pp. 13–14.

334 LR and Peggy Wallace: Citations are from int. PW/LR, August 8, 1971, Munich, tape 16, transcript 16a, pp. 9–12. The entire explosion regarding Fanck is twenty-four pages long, somewhat less than a half hour of audiotape time.

335 "to understand": LRM, p. 3; "to tackle": ibid., p. 656.

335 ghostwriters: Kinkel, p. 294.

335 Albert Einstein: The full epigraph reads: "So many things have been written about me, masses of insolent lies and inventions, that I would have perished long ago, had I paid any attention. One must take comfort in the fact that time has a sieve, through which most trivia run off into the sea of oblivion."

335 Headlines: These are virtually untranslatable. "Bride" ("Führerbraut ohne Geschlechtsverkehr"—literally "The Führer's Bride Without Sexual Intercourse") is from Rudolf Augstein in Der Spiegel, August 10, 1987; "Idiotic" ("Dumme Plaudereien einer Hofschranze") is from Fritz J. Raddatz in Die Zeit, October 9, 1987.

336 cutting: The English-language version is 656 pages plus index. Scores of deletions, including whole chapters, largely account for the difference. Most of the cuts consist of anecdotes involving personalities not known outside of Germany or center on mountain climbing and skiing.

336 "when she is honest": Sereny, German Trauma, p. 243; "devoid": ibid., pp. 241–42.

336 Ian Buruma: "A Lethal Thing of Beauty," pp. 3–4.

336 "one of the" and "does not contain": Simon, New York Times Book Review, September 26, 1993, p. 1.

336 "Whether" and "a credible account": Ibid., pp. 29, 1.

337 "she may have": Ibid., p. 29.

337 "turgid" and "revisionist": Dargis, p. 8.

337 "spurious": Ibid., p. 10.

337 "historical dodge": Ibid., p. 9; "damn the subject": ibid., p. 10.

337 "willfully stupid": Ibid., p. 10. The "all form" remark is from Stephen Schiff, p. 294.

337 "What does it mean": Dargis, p. 10.

337 "moral choice": Ibid.

337 "moral poise": See Chapter 15.

338 "I had" and "for the credibility": LRM, p. 360.

338 Nina Gladitz: She had been alerted to Reinhardt's letters by the Union of Persecutees of the Nazi Regime (Vereins der Verfolgten des Nazi-Regimes). Sources for Gladitz unless otherwise indicated include: Gladitz, "Über alles ist Gras gewachsen . . ."; Enzensberger; and the Gladitz Files, which underlie Chapter 13.

338 typhus in Lackenbach: Lewy, p. 110; and Thurner, p. 44.

339 Anton Böhmer and the SS: This testimony was never contradicted and may have stood unchallenged because the guards at Krün were officially drawn from the Salzburg Kripo (or criminal police). Böhmer's memos and directives are always signed with the SS lightning bolt symbol. On a visit the author made to Krün in summer 2005, the mayor of the town said he was disappointed that no reminders of the film remained for historians. At the filming sites, I was unable to find a single resident or innkeeper who would acknowledge having heard of the film or of Riefenstahl.

339 "Anna Madou" subterfuge and "Such treachery!": LRM, p. 362.

340 "outrageously": Ibid., p. 361.

340 threats to exhibition: Int. SB/Stefan Drössler, Munich Film Museum, January 25, 2006. The author was present at one such highly cumbersome screening in 2004.

341 "We saw": LRM, p. 267; "nothing happened": *Der Spiegel*, August 16, 2002, p. 32, citing *Frankfurter Rundschau*, April 27, 2002.

341 outtakes: Int. SB/Stefan Drössler, Munich Film Museum, January 25, 2006. Drössler discussed the issue with Gladitz, who told him the Bundesarchiv informed her it would only confirm the footage's existence at her 1987 trial under subpoena. Drössler himself recently applied to view the footage but was told, "There is nothing interesting there."

CHAPTER NINETEEN: THE LAST PICTURE SHOW(S)

342 Müller epigraph: Müller, "Besuch," *Stern*, p. 68.

343 court administering inheritance issues: Letter, Amtsgericht (Nachlaßgericht) München to Eckart Riefenstahl and Uta Riefenstahl Flamm, December 28, 1992. A handwritten page attached to the file copy notes the October 23, 1964, date of the "alleged testament." Eckart and Uta Riefenstahl were earlier confirmed as Heinz Riefenstahl's heirs in a letter to their mother, Ilse Collignon, October 15, 1959, from the Amtsgericht Charlottenburg in Berlin (file number: 24 VII R 5955). The death notice requesting Bertha Riefenstahl's death certificate and registry with the inheritance bureau was entered on January 19, 1965, by which time LR had returned from Africa to Munich. Though it asks for a complete list of survivors, only LR is indicated. Todesanzeige, Standesamt III, Munich, Bertha Riefenstahl, file no. 599/93.

344 David Irving: "A Radical's Diary," *David Irving's Action Report*, Focal Point,http://www.fpp.co.uk/online/99/12/Riefenstahl.html!#Riefenstahl. Irving has since been convicted of Holocaust denial in Austria and is serving a prison term there.

344 Tony Palmer: Int. SB/Tony Palmer, Munich, January 24, 2006. Palmer tried but failed to interest Channel 4 in England. Ironically, Channel 4 was one of the television networks underwriting production of the film that resulted.

345 "difficulty" and "because no one": Int. Florian Neubert/Ray Müller, Munich, September 15, 2005.

345 "She always": Cited in Lenssen, "Leben," p. 116, from *Frankfurter Rundschau*, March 26, 1994.

345 "I wanted": Ibid.

345 "Just being": Starkman, p. 22.

345 "The first . . . very beginning": Int. Florian Neubert/Ray Müller, Munich, September 15, 2005.

346 "she found": Ibid.

346 "unofficial" and "for private use": Ibid.

347 "She tried to tell": Ibid. Müller's version of the walking-talking argument comes from the same interview. A close viewing of the film suggests that it was a case of actress nerves rather than unfamiliarity with the technology.

347 "I think": Cited in Lenssen, *Potsdam*, p. 116, from *Frankfurter Rundschau*, March 26, 1994.

348 "she had": Sklar, p. 22.

348 LR on film: Lenssen, "Die fünf Karrieren der Leni Riefenstahl," *epd Film*, vol. 1, 1996, p. 29, cited in Trimborn, p. 497.

348 "If you believe her": Rafferty, *New Yorker*, March 28, 1994, p. 108.

349 Roger Ebert: *Chicago Sun-Times*, June 24, 1994.

349 "tremendous": Müller, cited by Starkman, p. 22.

349 "split personality": Int. Florian Neubert/Ray Müller, Munich, September 15, 2005.

349 "would do anything": Sklar, p. 24.

350 "she dove": Narration to *Ein Traum*.

350 "I'd like" and following citations: Ibid.

350 LR's tears and "I was fascinated": Müller, "Besuch," *Stern*, p. 68. The incident is preserved in *Ein Traum von Afrika*.

351 "Typical": Müller, "Besuch," p. 68.

351 morphine injections: *Abend-Zeitung*, September 10, 2003, p. 5.

352 "screen saver": Unsigned television review, ARD network, August 17, 2002; "Triumph of the Gill," Eric Rentschler, in conversation with the author.

353 "filthy": Cited by Erik Eggers, *Tagesspiegel Kultur*, August 16, 2002; "we saw": LRM, p. 267; "Nothing happened": *Der Spiegel*, August 16, 2002, p. 32, citing *Frankfurter Rundschau*, April 27, 2002.

353 evidence presented: Virtually every news organization in Germany covered this important story. The lists of names are fully documented in Reimar Gilsenbach and Otto Rosenberg's "Riefenstahl's Liste" in *Berliner Zeitung Magazin*, February 17, 2001, almost a year and a half before the complaint was officially registered. The complaint was triggered by LR's remarks of April 2002.

353 Spokesmen Giordano and Wallraff: *Frankfurter Allgemeine Zeitung*, August 16, 2002.

354 Kurt Holl: *Frankfurter Allgemeine Zeitung*, August 16, 2002, and *Freie Presse Politik*, August 17, 2002, p. 1.

354 "I regret": The statement was reprinted widely. Here it is quoted from *Frankfurter Neue Presse Kulture*, August 16, 2002, 22:59.

354 "Is it legitimate": LRM, p. 363.

354 "slander": Ibid.

CHAPTER TWENTY: AFTERLIFE

355 Riefenstahl epigraph: LR to Ray Müller in *Ein Traum von Afrika*.

355 LR to Ray Müller: In *Ein Traum von Afrika*.

355 "blessed relief": The phrase occurs in both *Wonderful, Horrible Life* and *Ein Traum*.

356 Culture Minister: Cited in *Der Tagesspiegel Kultur*, September 10, 2003, p. 23, and by Hannah Cleaver, "Admired and Hated—Hitler's Filmmaker Dies," *Telegraph* (London), September 14, 2003. The citation is an amalgam.

356 Schlöndorff, Glas, Fest: All cited in "Eine Meisterin aus Deutschland," *Der Tagesspiegel Kultur*, September 10, 2003, p. 23.

356 Other commentary: All citations from BBC News, September 10, 2003. They are, in order, from *Die Welt, Die Welt, Berliner Tagesspiegel, Das Bild, Berliner Tagesspiegel, Die Tageszeitung, Berliner Zeitung,* and *Das Bild*.

357 LR and Jodie Foster: Lewis Beale, "Jodie Foster's Nazi-Era Era 'Project,'" *New York Daily News*, December 2, 1999, p. 24.

357 "Nobody making films": Sontag, "Fascinating Fascism," p. 95.

358 film historian: Thomas Elsaesser, in Chu, p. 2.

358 Thomas Mann: *Magic Mountain*, p. 112.

358 David Thomson: *Biographical Dictionary*, pp. 633–34.

358 Simone Weil: *"The Iliad" or "The Poem of Force"* (pamphlet; Wallingford, Pa.: Pendle Hill Publications, 1993), p. 36.

BIBLIOGRAPHY

BOOKS

Allen, William Sheridan. *The Nazi Seizure of Power: The Experience of a Single German Town, 1930–1935*. New York: New Viewpoints, 1973.

Anonymous. *Film Photos wie noch nie*. Facsimile of 1929 edition (Giessen: Kindt & Bucher Verlag). Köln: Verlag der Buchhandlung, 1978.

Arendt, Hannah. *Eichmann in Jerusalem: A Report on the Banality of Evil*. New York: Viking, 1965.

Ascheid, Antje. *Hitler's Heroines: Stardom and Womanhood in Nazi Cinema*. Philadelphia: Temple University Press, 2003.

Bach, Steven. *Marlene Dietrich: Life and Legend*. New York: Morrow, 1992.

Balázs, Béla. *Theory of the Film*. London: Dover, 1952.

Barsam, Richard Meran. *Filmguide to* Triumph of the Will. Bloomington: Indiana University Press, 1975.

Belach, Helga. *Wir Tanzen um die Welt: Deutsche Revuefilme, 1933–1945*. Munich: Hanser Verlag, 1979.

Bell, Arthur George, [and Nancy Bell]. *Nuremberg*. London: Adam and Charles Black, 1905.

Benjamin, Walter. *Berliner Kindheit um Neunzehnhundert (Fassung letzter Hand)*. Frankfurt am Main: Suhrkamp, 1987.

Berg-Ganschow, Uta, and Wolfgang Jacobsen.... *Film ... Stadt ... Kino ... Berlin*. Berlin: Argon, 1987.

Berg-Pan, Renata. *Leni Riefenstahl*. Boston: Twayne, 1980.

Beyer, Friedemann. *Die UFA-Stars im Dritten Reich: Frauen für Deutschland*. Munich: Heyne, 1991.

Bezirksamt Tempelhof, Abteilung Volksbildung, ed. *Die Ufa: Auf den Spuren einer grossen Filmfabrik*. Berlin: Elefanten Press, 1987.

Bier, Marcus. *Schauspielerportraits: 24 Schauspieler um Max Reinhardt*. Berlin: Hentrich, 1989.

Brady, Frank. *Citizen Welles: A Biography of Orson Welles*. New York: Scribner's, 1989.

Browning, Christopher R. *Ordinary Men: Reserve Police Battalion 101 and the Final Solution in Poland*. New York: Harper Perennial, 1998.

Browning, Christopher R., with contributions by Jürgen Matthäus. *The Origins of the Final Solution*. Lincoln and Jerusalem: University of Nebraska Press and Yad Vashem, 2004.

Bullock, Alan. *Hitler and Stalin: Parallel Lives*. New York: Vintage, 1993.

————. *Hitler: A Study in Tyranny*. Rev. ed. New York: Harper & Row, 1964.

Burleigh, Michael. *The Third Reich: A New History*. New York: Hill & Wang, 2000.

Chéroux, Clément. *Mémoire des Camps: Photographies des Camps de Concentration et d'Extermination Nazis, 1933–1999*. Paris: Marval, 2001.

Collignon, Ilse. *"Liebe Leni . . .": Eine Riefenstahl erinnert sich*. Munich: Langen Müller, 2003.

Conot, Robert E. *Justice at Nuremberg*. New York: Harper & Row, 1983.

Craig, Gordon A. *The Germans*. New York: Plume, 1991.

————. *Germany, 1866–1945*. New York: Oxford, 1981.

Dahlke, Günther, and Günter Karl. *Deutsche Spielfilme von den Anfängen bis 1933*. Berlin: Henschelverlag Kunst und Gesellschaft, 1988.

Distel, Barbara, and Ruth Jakusch. *Concentration Camp Dachau, 1933–1945*. 10th ed. Comité International de Dachau. Munich: Lipp, 1978.

Doherty, Thomas. *Projections of War: Hollywood, American Culture, and World War II*. New York: Columbia University Press, 1993.

Dönhoff, Marion Countess. *Before the Storm: Memories of My Youth in Old Prussia*. New York: Knopf, 1990.

Downing, Taylor. *Olympia*. London: BFI, 1992.

Eisner, Lotte H. *Fritz Lang*. New York: Da Capo, 1976.

————. *Ich hatte einst ein schönes Vaterland: Memoiren*. Heidelberg: Wunderhorn, 1984.

Eksteins, Modris. *Rites of Spring: The Great War and the Birth of the Modern Age*. Boston: Houghton Mifflin, 1989.

Elsaesser, Thomas. *Weimar Cinema and After: Germany's Historical Imaginary*. New York: Routledge, 2000.

Ertl, Hans. *Meine wilden dreißiger Jahre*. Munich: Herbig, 1982.

Essner, Cornelia. *Die "Nürnberger Gesetze" oder Die Verwaltung des Rassenwahns, 1933–1945*. Paderborn: Schöning, 2002.

Evans, Richard J. *The Coming of the Third Reich*. New York: Penguin, 2003.

————. *Lying About Hitler: History, Holocaust, and the David Irving Trial*. New York: Basic Books, 2001.

————. *The Third Reich in Power*. New York: Penguin, 2005.

Everett, Susanne. *Lost Berlin*. New York: Gallery, 1979.

Fanck, Dr. Arnold. *Er führte Regie mit Gletschern, Stürmen und Lawinen.* Munich: Nymphenburger Verlag, 1973.

————. *Freiburger Berg-und Sportfilm-Gesellschaft.* 1956.

————. *Stürme über dem Montblanc.* With a foreword, "Der Fall Dr. Fanck," by Béla Balázs. Basel: Concordia, 1931.

Faris, James C. *Nuba Personal Art.* London: Duckworth, 1972.

Fest, Joachim. *The Face of the Third Reich.* Translated by Michael Bullock. London: Penguin, 1988.

————. *Hitler.* Translated by Richard and Clare Winston. New York: Vintage, 1975.

————. *Plotting Hitler's Death: The Story of German Resistance.* Translated by Bruce Little. New York: Metropolitan, 1996.

————. *Speer: The Final Verdict.* Translated by Ewald Osers and Alexandra Dring. New York: Harcourt, 2002.

Fischer, Lothar. *Anita Berber: Tanz zwischen Rausch und Tod, 1918–1928 in Berlin.* Berlin: Haude & Spener, 1988.

Flanner, Janet. *An American in Paris: Profile of an Interlude Between Two Wars.* London: Hamish Hamilton, 1940.

Friedländer, Saul. *Nazi Germany and the Jews: The Years of Persecution, 1933–39.* Vol. 1. London: Phoenix, 1997.

Friedrich, Otto. *Before the Deluge: A Portrait of Berlin in the 1920s.* New York: Fromm, 1986.

————. *Blood and Iron: From Bismarck to Hitler—the Von Moltke Family's Impact on German History.* New York: Harper Perennial, 1996.

Fritzsche, Peter. *Reading Berlin, 1900.* Cambridge, Mass.: Harvard, 1996.

Fromm, Bella. *Als Hitler mir die Hand küsste.* Reinbek: Rowolt, 1993.

————. *Blood and Banquets: A Berlin Social Diary.* New York: Carol / Birch Lane, 1990.

Gabler, Neal. *An Empire of Their Own.* New York: Crown, 1988.

Garnett, Tay, with Fredda Dudley Balling. *Light Up Your Torches and Pull Up Your Tights.* New Rochelle, N.Y.: Arlington House, 1973.

Gay, Peter. *Weimar Culture: The Outsider as Insider.* New York: Harper & Row, 1968.

Gellately, Robert. *Backing Hitler.* London: Oxford, 2001.

Gilbert, Martin. *The Holocaust: The Jewish Tragedy.* London: Fontana, 1987.

Gilsenbach, Reimar. *Oh Django, sing deinen Zorn: Sinti und Roma unter den Deutschen.* Berlin: BasisDruck, 1993.

Goebbels, Dr. Joseph. *Die Tagebücher von Joseph Goebbels: Sämtliche Fragmente, Aufzeichnungen, 1924–1941.* Vols. 1–4. Edited by Elke Fröhlich, Institut für Zeitgeschichte (Institute for Contemporary History), Munich. Munich: Saur, 1987.

————. *Final Entries, 1945: The Diaries of Joseph Goebbels.* Edited by Hugh Trevor-Roper. New York: Putnam's, 1978.

————. *My Part in Germany's Fight.* Translated by Dr. Kurt Fiedler. London: Hurst & Blackett / Paternoster Library, 1938.

Goldensohn, Leon. *The Nuremberg Interviews: An American Psychiatrist's Conversations with the Defendants and Witnesses.* Edited by Robert Gellately. New York: Knopf, 2004.

Goldhagen, Daniel Jonah. *Hitler's Willing Executioners: Ordinary Germans and the Holocaust.* New York: Vintage, 1997.

Graham, Cooper C. *Leni Riefensthal and "Olympia."* Lanham, Md.: Scarecrow Press, 2001.

Grimm, J. and W., et al. *German Fairy Tales.* New York: Continuum, 1985.

Gritschneder, Dr. Otto. *Fachlich geeignet, politisch unzuverlässig: Memoiren.* Munich: Beck, 1996.

Günther, Dr. Walther, ed. *Olympia: Staatspolitische Filme,* Heft 8/9. Reichspropagandaleitung der NSDAP. Berlin: n.d.

Haffner, Sebastian. *Defying Hitler: A Memoir.* London, Weidenfeld and Nicolson, 2002.

————. *The Meaning of Hitler.* London: Phoenix, 2000.

Hamann, Brigitte. *Hitler's Vienna: A Dictator's Apprenticeship.* New York: Oxford, 1999.

Hanfstaengl, Ernst. *Unheard Witness.* Philadelphia: Lippincott, 1957.

Harris, Robert. *Selling Hitler: The Story of the Hitler Diaries.* London: Faber & Faber, 1986.

Heckmair, Ander. *My Life as a Mountaineer.* London: Gollancz, 1975.

Heer, Hannes, and Birgit Otte, eds. *Vernichtungskrieg: Verbrechen der Wehrmacht 1941 bis 1944.* Hamburg: Hamburger Edition, 1996.

Hildenbrandt, Fred. . . . *ich soll dich grüßen von Berlin: 1922–1932.* Frankfurt/Main: Ullstein, 1986.

Hinton, David B. *The Films of Leni Riefenstahl.* 2nd ed. Metuchen, N.J.: Scarecrow Press, 1991.

————. *The Films of Leni Riefenstahl.* 3rd ed. Lanham, Md.: Scarecrow Press, 2000.

Hitler, Adolf. *Mein Kampf.* Translated by Ralph Manheim. Boston: Houghton Mifflin, 1971.

Hoess, Rudolf. *Commandant of Auschwitz: The Autobiography of Rudolf Hoess.* Translated by Constantine FitzGibbon. Introduction by Primo Levi. London: Phoenix, 2000.

Horak, Jan Christopher, with Gisela Pickler, eds. *Berge Licht und Traum: Dr. Arnold Fanck und der deutsche Bergfilm.* Munich: Bruckmann, 1997.

Hull, David Stewart. *Film in the Third Reich: Art and Propaganda in Nazi Germany.* New York: Touchstone, 1973.

Infield, Glenn B. *Leni Riefenstahl—Fallen Film Goddess*. New York: Crowell, 1976.

Ishioka, Eiko. *Leni Riefenstahl Life*. Tokyo: Kyuryudo Art, 1992.

Jacobsen, Wolfgang. *Erich Pommer: Ein Produzent macht Filmgeschichte*. Berlin: Argon, 1989.

James, Clive. *Even as We Speak: New Essays, 1993–2001*. London: Picador, 2001. (See James in "Articles.")

James, Harold. *A German Identity: 1770 to the Present Day*. London: Phoenix, 2000.

Janssen, Wolfgang. *Glanzrevuen der zwanziger Jahre*. Berlin: Hentrich, 1987.

Jaubert, Alain. *Fotos die Lügen*. Frankfurt am Main: Athenäum, 1989.

Judt, Tony. *Postwar: A History of Europe Since 1945*. New York: Penguin, 2005.

Junge, Traudl. *Until the Final Hour: Hitler's Last Secretary*. Edited by Melissa Müller. New York: Arcade, 2004.

Kaes, Anton, Martin Jay, and Edward Dimendberg, eds. *The Weimar Republic Sourcebook*. Berkley: University of California Press, 1994.

Kalbus, Dr. Oskar. *Vom Werden deutscher Filmkunst*. 2 vols. Bahrenfeld: Cigaretten-Bilderdienst Altona, 1935.

Kapfer, Reinhard, ed. *Rituale von Leben und Tod: Robert Gardner und seine Filme*. Munich: Trickster, 1989.

Kaplan, Alice. *The Collaborator: The Trial and Execution of Robert Brasillach*. Chicago: University of Chicago Press, 2000.

Keegan, John. *The First World War*. New York: Knopf, 1999.

Kershaw, Ian. *Hitler, 1889–1936: Hubris*. New York: Norton, 1998.

———. *Hitler, 1936–1945: Nemesis*. New York: Norton, 2000.

———. *The "Hitler Myth": Image and Reality in the Third Reich*. London: Oxford, 2001.

Kessler, Count Harry. *Diaries of a Cosmopolitan, 1918–1937*. Edited and translated by Charles Kessler. Introduction by Ian Buruma. London: Phoenix, 2000.

Kessler, Harry Graf. *Tagebücher, 1918–1937*. Edited by Wolfgang Pfeiffer-Belli. Frankfurt am Main: Insel [Taschenbuch 659], 1982.

Kimmelman, Michael. *The Accidental Masterpiece*. New York: Penguin, 2005.

Kinkel, Lutz. *Die Scheinwerferin: Leni Riefenstahl und das "Dritte Reich."* Hamburg: Europa Verlag, 2002.

Klemperer, Victor. *The Klemperer Diaries, 1933–1945*. Edited by Martin Chalmers. London: Phoenix Press, 2000.

Knopp, Guido. *Hitlers Frauen und Marlene*. Munich: Bertlesmann, 2001.

Korff, Gottfried, and Reinhard Rürup, eds. *Berlin, Berlin: Die Austellung zur Geschichte der Stadt*. Berlin: Nicolai, 1987.

Kracauer, Siegfried. *From Caligari to Hitler: A Psychological History of the German Film*. New York: Noonday, 1960.

————. *Theory of Film: The Redemption of Physical Reality.* New York: Oxford, 1960.

Kramer, Jane. *Europeans.* New York: Farrar, Straus & Giroux, 1988.

Kreimeier, Klaus. *The Ufa Story: A History of Germany's Greatest Film Company, 1918–1945.* New York: Hill & Wang, 1996.

Laqueur, Walter. *Weimar: A Cultural History, 1918–1933.* London: Phoenix, 2000.

Large, David Clay. *Where Ghosts Walked: Munich's Road to the Third Reich.* New York: Norton, 1997.

Lebert, Stephan. *My Father's Keeper.* London: Abacus, 2002.

Lebor, Adam, and Roger Boyes. *Surviving Hitler: Corruption and Compromise in the Third Reich.* London: Pocket Books, 2002.

Levy, Lucien. *Berlin um 1900.* Munich: Verlag Max Hueber, 1986.

Lewinski, Heinrich. *Ernst Jäger-Filmkritiker.* Munich: Edition Text + Kritik, Richard Boorberg Verlag, 2006.

Lewy, Guenter. *The Nazi Persecution of the Gypsies.* London: Oxford, 2000.

Lichtblau, Albert (Projektleiter). *"Arisierungen," beschlagnamte Vermögen, Rückstellungen und Entschädigungen: Bundesländervergleich Burgenland, Oberösterreich, Salzburg,* Band 4. Vienna: [Austrian] Historikerkommission, 2002.

Lifton, Robert Jay. *The Nazi Doctors: Medical Killing and the Psychology of Genocide.* New York: Basic, 1986.

Linder, Herbert, ed. *Filmkritik: Leni Riefenstahl.* No. 188, August 1972.

Loewy, Hanno. *"Das Menschenbild des fanatischen Fatalisten, Oder: Leni Riefenstahl, Béla Balázs und Das Blaue Licht"* in *Medium und Initiation. Béla Balázs: Märchen, Ästhetik, Kino.* Frankfurt am Main. (Dissertation, 1999.)

Loiperdinger, Martin. *Der Parteitagsfilm "Triumph des Willens" von Leni Riefenstahl: Rituale der Mobilmachung.* Opladen: Leske + Budrich, 1987.

Lucas, James. *Last Days of the Reich: The Collapse of Nazi Germany, May 1945.* London: Grafton, 1987.

Lukacs, John. *The Hitler of History.* New York: Knopf, 1997.

Machtan, Lothar. *The Hidden Hitler.* New York: Basic, 2001.

Mandell, Richard D. *The Nazi Olympics.* New York: Ballantine, 1972.

Mann, Thomas. *Joseph and His Brothers.* Translated by H. T. Lowe-Porter. London: Penguin, 1978.

————. *The Magic Mountain.* Translated by John E. Woods. New York: Knopf, 1995.

Manstein, Erich von. *Verlorene Siege.* Munich: Bernhard und Graefe, 1978.

Maser, Werner. *Heinrich George: Die politische Biographie.* Berlin: Quintessenz Verlag, 1998.

Miller, Judith. *One, by One, by One: Facing the Holocaust.* New York: Simon & Schuster, 1990.

Mitscherlich, Alexander, and Margarete Mitscherlich. *Die Unfähigkeit zu trauern: Grundlagen kollektiven Verhaltens.* Munich: Piper, 1967.

―――. *The Inability to Mourn: Principles of Collective Behavior.* New York: Grove, 1975.

Mitscherlich, Margarete. *Über die Mühsal der Empanzipation: Die Frau in der Gesellschaft.* Frankfurt am Main: Fischer, 1990.

Moeller, Felix. *Der Filmminister: Goebbels und der Film im Dritten Reich.* Berlin: Henschel, 1998.

Nadel, S. F. *The Nuba: An Anthropological Study of the Hill Tribes in Kordofan.* London: Oxford, 1947.

Naggar, Carole. *George Rodger: An Adventure in Photography, 1908–1995.* Syracuse, N.Y.: Syracuse University Press, 2003.

Nuremberg Municipal Museum. *Fascination and Terror: The Nazi Party Rally Grounds in Nuremberg.* Nuremberg Municipal Museum, 1996.

Ott, Frederick W. *The Great German Films: From Before World War I to the Present.* Secaucus, N.J.: Citadel, 1986.

Overy, Richard. *Interrogations: The Nazi Elite in Allied Hands, 1945.* New York: Viking, 2001.

Paris, Barry. *Louise Brooks.* New York: Knopf, 1989.

Petropoulos, Jonathan. *Art as Politics in the Third Reich.* Chapel Hill: University of North Carolina Press, 1996.

Potsdam Filmmuseum. *Leni Riefenstahl.* Berlin: Henschel, 1999.

Read, Anthony, and David Fisher. *The Fall of Berlin.* London: Pimlico, 2002.

Reitlinger, Gerald. *The Final Solution.* New York: Perpetua, 1961.

Remak, Joachim. *The Nazi Years: A Documentary History.* New York: Touchstone, 1969.

Renker, Gustav. *Bergkristall.* Basel/Gütersloh: Bertelsmann, [1930].

Rentschler, Eric, ed. *The Films of G. W. Pabst: An Extraterritorial Cinema.* New Brunswick, N.J.: Rutgers, 1990.

―――. *The Ministry of Illusion: Nazi Cinema and Its Afterlife.* Cambridge, Mass.: Harvard, 1996.

Reuth, Ralf Georg. *Goebbels.* Translated by Krishna Winston. New York: Harcourt, 1993.

Reuther, Hans. *Die Grosse Zerstörung Berlins: Zweihundert Jahre Stadtbaugeschichte.* Frankfurt: Propyläen, 1985.

Rhode, Eric. *A History of the Cinema: From Its Origins to 1970.* New York: Penguin, 1984.

Rhodes, Richard. *Masters of Death: The SS Einsatzgruppen and the Invention of the Holocaust.* New York: Knopf, 2002.

Riefenstahl, Leni. *Afrika.* With an introduction by Kevin Brownlow. Munich: Taschen, 2002.

————. *Five Lives*. Cologne: Taschen, 2000.

————. *Hinter den Kulissen des Reichsparteitag-Films*. München: Zentralverlag der NSDAP/Franz Eher, 1935.

————. *Kampf in Schnee und Eis*. Leipzig: Hesse & Becker, 1933.

————. *Korallengärten*. Munich: List, 1978.

————. *The Last of the Nuba*. London: Collins, 1976.

————. *Leni Riefenstahl: A Memoir*. New York: St. Martin's, 1993. Published in England as *The Sieve of Time*.

————. *Mein Afrika*. Munich: List, 1982.

————. *Memoiren*. Munich: Albrecht Knaus, 1987.

————. *Die Nuba: Menschen wie von einem anderen Stern*. Munich: List, 1973.

————. *Die Nuba von Kau*. Munich: List, 1976.

————. *Olympia*. New York: St. Martin's Press, 1994.

————. *People of Kau*. New York: Harper and Row, 1976.

————. *Schönheit im olympischen Kampf*. Berlin: Deutscher Verlag, 1937.

————. *Vanishing Africa*. New York: Harmony, 1982.

————. *Wonders Under Water*. London: Quartet, 1991.

————. *Wunder unter Wasser*. Munich: Herbig, 1990.

Riess, Curt. *Das gab's nur einmal: Die große Zeit des deutschen Films*. 3 vols. Frankfurt/Main: Ullstein, 1985.

————. *Joseph Goebbels: A Biography*. With an introduction by Louis Lochner. London: Hollis and Carter, 1949.

Rodger, George. *Village of the Nubas*. London: Phaidon Press, 1999.

Rosenberg, Otto (as told to Ulrich Enzenberger [*sic:* Enzensberger]). *A Gypsy in Auschwitz*. Translated by Helmut Bögler. London: London House, 1999.

Rosenfeld, Gavriel D. *Munich and Memory: Architecture, Monuments, and the Legacy of the Third Reich*. Berkeley: University of California Press, 2000.

Roters, Eberhard, and Bernhard Schulz, eds. *Ich und die Stadt: Mensch und Grossstadt in der deutschen Kunst des 20. Jahrhunderts*. Berlin: Martin-Gropius-Bau, 1987.

Rotha, Paul. *The Film till Now*. London: Vision, 1949.

Rother, Rainer. *Leni Riefenstahl: Die Verführung des Talents*. Berlin: Henschel, 2000.

————. *Leni Riefenstahl: The Seduction of Genius*. Translated by Martin H. Bott. London: Continuum, 2002. (English translation of above title.)

Salkeld, Audrey. *A Portrait of Leni Riefenstahl*. London: Jonathan Cape, 1996.

Sarris, Andrew. *The American Cinema: Directors and Directions, 1928–1968*. New York: Dutton, 1968.

————. *Interviews with Film Directors*. New York: Avon, 1969.

Sayler, Oliver M., ed. *Max Reinhardt and His Theater*. New York: Brentano's, 1924.

Schirach, Henriette von. *Frauen um Hitler*. München: Herbig, 1983.

Schmidt, Alexander. *Geländebegehung: Das Reichsparteitagsgelände in Nürnberg*. Nuremberg: Sandberg, 2002.

Scholl, Inge. *Students Against Tyranny: The Resistance of the White Rose, Munich, 1942–1943*. Middletown, Conn.: Wesleyan University Press, 1970.

Schrader, Bärbel, and Jürgen Schebera. *Kunst-Metropole Berlin, 1918–1933*. Berlin: Aufbau-Verlag, 1987.

Schulte-Sasse, Linda. *Entertaining the Third Reich: Illusions of Wholeness in Nazi Cinema*. Durham, N.C.: Duke University Press, 1996.

Schutte, Jürgen, and Peter Sprengel, eds. *Die Berliner Moderne, 1885–1914*. Stuttgart: Reclam, 1987.

Sebald, W. G. *On the Natural History of Destruction*. New York: Modern Library, 2004.

Seligman, C. G., and Brenda Z. Seligman. *Pagan Tribes of the Nilotic Sudan*. London: George Routledge & Sons, 1932.

Sereny, Gitta. *Albert Speer: His Battle with Truth*. New York: Knopf, 1995.

———. *The German Trauma: Experiences and Reflections, 1938–2000*. London: Allen Lane, Penguin, 2000.

———. *Into That Darkness*. London: Pimlico, 1995.

Shapiro, James. *Oberammergau*. New York: Vintage, 2000.

Shirer, William L. *Berlin Diary: The Journal of a Foreign Correspondent*. New York: Knopf, 1941.

———. *The Rise and Fall of the Third Reich*. New York: Fawcett, 1985.

———. *This Is Berlin: Reporting from Nazi Germany, 1938–40*. With an introduction by Sir John Keegan. London: Arrow, 2000.

———. *Twentieth Century Journey: The Nightmare Years, 1930–1940*. New York: Little, Brown, 1984.

Smith, David Calvert. *"Triumph of the Will": Document of the 1934 Reich Party Rally*. Richardson, Tex.: Celluloid Chronicles Press, 1990.

Sontag, Susan. *Against Interpretation*. London: Andre Deutsch, 1987.

———. *Under the Sign of Saturn*. New York: Anchor, 1980.

Sorge, Ernst. *With Plane, Boat, and Camera in Greenland: An Account of the Universal–Dr. Fanck Greenland Expedition*. New York: Appleton-Century, 1936.

Speer, Albert. *Erinnerungen*. Berlin: Propyläen, 1969.

———. *Inside the Third Reich: Memoirs*. New York: Macmillan, 1970.

Staatlichen Archive Bayerns. *Wege in die Vernichtung*. Edited by Albrecht Liess. München: Staatlichen Archive Bayerns, with Institut für Zeitgeschichte, 2003.

Stackelberg, Roderick, and Sally A. Winkle. *The Nazi Germany Sourcebook: An Anthology of Texts*. London: Routledge, 2002.

Stern, Fritz. *Dreams and Delusions: National Socialism in the Drama of the German Past*. New York: Vintage, 1989.

————. *Einstein's German World*. London: Penguin, 2000.

Sternberg, Josef von. *Fun in a Chinese Laundry*. New York: Macmillan, 1965.

Stürmer, Michael. *The German Empire, 1871–1919*. London: Phoenix, 2001.

Thomson, David. *A Biographical Dictionary of Film*. 3rd ed. New York: Knopf, 1994.

Thurner, Erika. *National Socialism and Gypsies in Austria*. Translated by Gilya Gerda Schmidt. Foreword by Michael Berenbaum. Tuscaloosa: University of Alabama Press, 1998.

Trenker, Luis. *Alles gut gegangen: Geschichten aus meinem Leben*. Hamburg: Bertlesmann, 1965.

————. *Kameraden der Berge*. Berlin: Rowohlt, 1932.

————. *Meine Berge*. Berlin: Knaur, 1936.

Trimborn, Jürgen. *Riefenstahl: Eine deutsche Karriere*. Berlin: Aufbau, 2002.

Tuchman, Barbara W. *The Proud Tower*. New York: Macmillan, 1966.

Von Cziffra, Géza. *Es war eine rauschende Ballnacht*. Frankfurt/Main: Ullstein, 1987.

Wallace, Peggy Ann. "An Historical Study of the Career of Leni Riefenstahl from 1923 to 1933." Ph.D. diss., Los Angeles, University of Southern California, 1975.

Warburg, Sidney. *The Financial Sources of National Socialism: Hitler's Secret Backers*. Translated by J. G. Schoup. Phoenix: Research Publications, 1983. Translation of *De Geldbronnen van het National-Socialisme, Drei Gesprekken met Hitler*, Door Sidney Warburg, vertaald door I. G. Shoup [*sic*]. Amsterdam: Vol Hardt En Waeckt, 1933.

Welch, David. *Propaganda and the German Cinema, 1933–1945*. New York: Oxford, 1989.

West, Rebecca. *1900*. London: Weidenfeld & Nicolson, 1982.

————. *A Train of Powder*. New York: Viking, 1955.

Weyr, Thomas. *The Setting of the Pearl: Vienna Under Hitler*. New York: Oxford, 2005.

Willett, John. *The Theater of the Weimar Republic*. New York: Holmes & Meier, 1988.

Wirth, Morris, project coordinator. *Pinkas Hakehillot: Encyclopedia of Jewish Communities, Poland*. Jerusalem: Yad Vashem, n.d.

Wulf, Joseph. *Theater und Film im Dritten Reich*. Gütersloh: Rowohlt, 1966.

Wyman, David S. *The Abandonment of the Jews: America and the Holocaust, 1941–1945*. New York: Pantheon, 1984.

Zelnhefer, Siegfried [Museen der Stadt Nürnberg]. *Die Reichsparteitage der NSDAP in Nürnberg*. Nürnberger Presse, 2002.

Zglinicki, Friedrich von. *Der Weg des Films*. Berlin: Rembrandt, 1956.

————. *Die Wege der Traumfabrik*. Berlin: Transit, 1986.

Zsuffa, Joseph. *Béla Balázs: The Man and the Artist.* Berkeley: University of California Press, 1987.

Zuckmayer, Carl. *Als wär's ein Stück von mir.* Salzburg: Deutscher Bücherbund, 1966.

————. *Geheimreport.* Göttingen: Wallstein, 2002.

ARTICLES

Alpert, Hollis. "The Lively Ghost of Leni." *Saturday Review,* March 25, 1972, pp. 65–67.

Andrews, Rena. "Hitler's Favorite Filmmaker Honored at Colorado Festival." *New York Times,* September 15, 1974.

Augstein, Rudolf. "Leni, die 'Führerbraut.' " *Der Spiegel,* no. 33, August 10, 1987, p. 75.

Balázs, Béla. "Der Fall Dr. Fanck." In Fanck, *Stürme über dem Montblanc.*

Barkhausen, Hans. "Footnote to the History of Riefenstahl's *Olympia.*" *Film Quarterly,* vol. 28, no. 1, Fall 1974, pp. 8–12.

Barsam, Richard Meran. "Leni Riefenstahl: Artifice and Truth in a World Apart." *Film Comment,* November 1973.

Berson, Arnold, and Joseph Keller. "Shame and Glory in the Movies." *National Review,* January 14, 1964.

Bittorf, Wilhelm. "Blut und Hoden." *Der Spiegel,* October 25, 1976, pp. 228–36.

Brown, Georgia. "The Empire Strikes Back." *Village Voice,* March 22, 1994.

Brownlow, Kevin. "Leni Riefenstahl." *Film* (London), no. 47, Winter 1966.

————. Introduction to Riefenstahl, *Afrika.*

Bulgakowa, Oksana. " 'Riefenstein': Demontage eines Klischees." In Potsdam Filmmuseum, *Leni Riefenstahl.*

Buruma, Ian. "Blood Libel." *New Yorker,* April 16, 2001.

————. "A Lethal Thing of Beauty." *Times Literary Supplement,* no. 4671, October 9, 1992, pp. 3–4.

Chu, Jeff. "In Her Own Image." *Time Europe,* August 1, 2003.

Cooper, Merian C., [and Ernst B. Schoedsack]. "Two Fighting Tribes of the Sudan." *National Geographic,* October 1929, pp. 464–86.

Culbert, David, and Martin Loiperdinger. "Leni Riefenstahl's *Tag der Freiheit:* The 1935 Nazi Party Rally Film." *Historical Journal of Film, Radio and Television,* vol. 12, no. 1, 1992, pp. 3–40. (See also Loiperdinger and Culbert.)

Dalichow, Bärbel. ". . . verweile doch, du bist so schön . . ." In Potsdam Filmmuseum, *Leni Riefenstahl.*

Dalichow, Bärbel, and Claudia Lenssen. "Focus Leni Riefenstahl." In Potsdam Filmmuseum, *Leni Riefenstahl.*

Dargis, Manohla. "Queen of Denial." *Village Voice Literary Supplement*, March 9, 1994.

Dassanowsky, Robert von. " 'Wherever You May Run, You Cannot Escape Him': Leni Riefenstahl's Self-Reflection and Romantic Transcendence of Nazism in *Tiefland.*" *Camera Obscura*, vol. 35, 1995–96.

Deford, Frank. "The Ghost of Berlin." *Sports Illustrated*, vol. 65, no. 5, August 4, 1986.

Delahaye, Michel. "Leni and the Wolf: Interview with Leni Riefenstahl." *Cahiers du Cinema in English*, no. 5, pp. 48–55. (Also see Sarris.)

Doherty, Thomas. "Leni Riefenstahl: Ethics of an Auteur." *Chronicle of Higher Education*, August 9, 2002.

Elsaesser, Thomas. "Portrait of the Artist as a Young Woman." *Sight and Sound*, February 1993, pp. 15–18.

Enzensberger, Ulrich. "KZ Zigeuner tanz mit mir." *Konkret*, vol. 2, 1985.

Faris, James C. "Leni Riefenstahl and the Nuba Peoples of Kordofan Province, Sudan." *Historical Journal of Film, Radio and Television*, vol. 13, no. 1, 1953, pp. 95–97.

————. "The Nazi Who Won't Die—Leni Riefenstahl at 100." *CounterPunch*, September 11, 2002. www.counterpunch.org.

————. "Photographic Encounters: Leni Riefenstahl in Africa." Lecture. "Encounters with Photography." Iziko Museums of Capetown, South Africa, 2002.

Feiden, Max Karl. "Leni Riefenstahl sucht 'come back' in Afrika." *Hamburger Anzeiger*, October 30, 1958.

Flanner, Janet [Genêt]. "Berlin Letter." *New Yorker*, August 1, 1936, p. 40.

Flint, Julie. "Hitler's Favorite Filmmaker in New Controversy." *Observer*, January 30, 2000, p. 26.

————. "The Past Is Another Country." *Independent Weekend Review*, February 5, 2000, p. 8.

Fraser, J. "An Ambassador for Nazi Germany." *Films and Filming*, vol. 2, no. 5, pp. 12–14.

Frei, Norbert. "Vom Alter der jüngsten Vergangenheit." *Süddeutsche-Zeitung*, no. 24, January 30, 2003, p. 17.

Furlong, William Barry. "A Bad Week for Mr. B[rundage]." *Sports Illustrated*, March 11, 1968.

Gardner, Robert. "Can the Will Triumph?" *Film Comment*, Winter 1965.

Gilsenbach, Reimar, and Otto Rosenberg. "Riefenstahls Liste: Zum Gedenken an die ermordeten Komparsen." *Berliner Zeitung Magazine*, February 17, 2001.

Gladitz, Nina. "Über alles ist Gras gewachsen . . ." *Der Funke*, October 29, 2003.

Graham, Cooper C. *"Olympia* in America, 1938: Leni Riefenstahl, Hollywood, and the Kristallnacht." *Historical Journal of Film, Radio and Television*, vol. 13, no. 4, 1993, pp. 433–30.

Green, Ralph. Letter. *Film Library Quarterly*, vol. 5, no. 4, Fall 1972. (See Riefenstahl letter for *FLQ*, vol. 5, no. 3, Summer 1972.)

Gregor, Ulrich. "A Comeback for Leni Riefenstahl?" *Film Comment*, Winter 1965.

Gruel-Wemper, Hela. "Erinnerungen an Leni Riefenstahls Pensionzeit." *Filmwelt*, May 19, 1935.

Gunston, David. "Leni Riefenstahl." *Film Quarterly*, Fall 1960.

Hinton, David B., [and Susan Sontag]. "An Exchange on Leni Riefenstahl." *New York Review of Books*, September 18, 1975.

Hitchens, Gordon. "Biographical Sketch of Leni Riefenstahl." *Film Comment*, Winter 1965.

———. "An Interview with a Legend." *Film Comment*, Winter 1965.

———. "Leni Riefenstahl Interviewed by Gordon Hitchens." *Film Culture*, Spring 1973.

———. "New Book on Leni Riefenstahl." Review of *Berg-Pan. Variety*, May 13, 1981.

———. "*The Sieve of Time* Book Review." *Variety*, May 17, 1993, p. 119.

Holthusen, Hans Egon. "Leni Riefenstahl in Amerika." *Merkur*, vol. 29, no. 325 (June 1975), pp. 569–578.

Horst, Ernst. "Zäher als die Zähesten." *Frankfurter Allgemeine Zeitung*, July 2, 2002, p. 44.

Iten, Oswald. "Bilder und Zerrbilder der Nuba." *Tagesanzeiger Magazin*, no. 50, December 17, 1977, pp. 6–45.

Jäger, Ernst. "How Leni Riefenstahl Became Hitler's Girlfriend." Parts I–XI, serialized in *Hollywood Tribune*, April 28–July 17, 1939. In *Historical Journal of Film, Radio and Television*, vol. 13, no. 4, microfiche supplement 2.

James, Clive. "Hitler's Unwitting Exculpator" and "Postscript to Goldhagen." Both in *Even as We Speak*. Longer version and afterthoughts of James's "Blaming the Germans," as published in *The New Yorker*, April 22, 1996, pp. 44ff.

———. "Postscript to Goldhagen." See preceding entry.

Kanfer, Stefan. "Leni Riefenstahl Sees No Evil." *Civilization*, November–December 1994, pp. 47–51.

Kelmann, K. "Propaganda—A Vision—*Triumph of the Will*." *Film Culture*, Spring 1973.

Kramer, Hilton. "The Evolution of Susan Sontag." *New York Times*, February 9, 1975, sec. 2, pp. 1ff.

Kramer, Jane. "The Politics of Memory." *New Yorker*, August 14, 1995, pp. 48–65.

Kretzmer, Herbert. "The Woman in the Shadows." *Sunday Dispatch* (London), December 18, 1960, p. 2.

Kusztrich, Imre. "Leni Riefenstahl: Ein Leben wie im Rausch." *Bunte,* August 18, 1977, pp. 38–81.

"Leni Riefenstahl 'nicht betroffen.' " *Die Welt,* no. 5, January 13, 1949, p. 3.

Lenssen, Claudia. "Die fünf Karrieren der Leni Riefenstahl." *Edp Film,* January 1996.

————. "Leben und Werk." In Potsdam Filmmuseum, *Leni Riefenstahl.*

Loiperdinger, Martin. "*Sieg des Glaubens:* Ein gelungenes Experiment national-sozialistischer Filmpropaganda." *Zeitschrift für Pädagogik,* no. 31, 1993.

Loiperdinger, Martin, and David Culbert. "Leni Riefenstahl, the SA, and the Nazi Party Rally Films, Nuremberg 1933–34: *Sieg des Glaubens* and *Triumph des Willens.*" *Historical Journal of Film, Radio and Television,* vol. 8, no. 1, 1988, pp. 3–38.

————. "Leni Riefenstahl's *Tag der Freiheit:* The 1935 Nazi Party Rally Film." *Historical Journal of Film, Radio and Television,* vol. 12, no. 1, 1992, pp. 3–40.

Loney, Glenn. "Leni Riefenstahl: The Will Triumphant." *After Dark,* March 1976, pp. 28–32.

Luz, Oskar (text), and Horst Luz (photographs). "Proud Primitives: The Nuba People." *National Geographic,* November 1966, vol. 130, no. 5, pp. 672–99.

Maetzke, Horst. Unpublished eyewitness report re Konskie massacre and LR: 1992. Riefenstahl catalog file, Institut für Zeitgeschichte, Munich.

Mannheim, L. Andrew. "Leni." *Modern Photography,* vol. 38, no. 2, February 1974.

Maslin, Janet. "Just What Did Leni Riefenstahl's Lens See?" *New York Times,* Arts and Leisure, March 13, 1994.

McDonagh, Don. "Hubert Stowitts: The Painter Who Partnered Pavlova." *Dance,* March 2000.

Mitscherlich, Margarethe. "Triumph der Verdrängung." *Stern,* no. 42, October 8, 1987.

Moeller, Felix. "Die einzige von all den Stars, die uns versteht." In Potsdam Filmmuseum, *Leni Riefenstahl.*

Müller, Ray. "Der Besuch der alten Dame." *Stern,* no. 14/2000.

Museum of Modern Art [Riefenstahl, Leni]. "Outline of *Triumph of the Will.*" *Film Comment,* Winter 1965.

Patalas, Enno. "Die schönste Frrrede von allen." *Frankfurter Allgemeine Zeitung,* February 19, 2004.

Platthaus, Andreas. "Leni Riefenstahl blickt zurück im Zorn." *Frankfurter Allgemeine Zeitung,* October 21, 2000.

Polgar, Alfred. "Die tragische Farce der Entnazifizierung." *Der Weg,* July 28, 1950.

Richardi, Hans-Günther. "Untilgbare Spuren der Vernichtung." *Süddeutsche Zeitung*, no. 186, August 13–15, 1994, p. 9.

Richards, Jeffrey. "Leni Riefenstahl—Style and Structure." *Film Library Quarterly*, vol. 5, no. 3, Summer 1972.

Riefenstahl, Leni. "Bilder die noch keiner sah." *Stern*, December 14, 1969, pp. 86–99.

———. "The Games That Survived." *Sunday Times Magazine* (London), October 1, 1972, pp. 41ff.

———. Letter. *Film Library Quarterly*, vol. 5, no. 3, Summer 1972, p. 5.

———. "Notizen zu *Penthesilea*." *Filmkritik*, August 1972.

———. "Requiem für eine Nuba." *Kristall*, no. 22, 1964.

———. "Why I Am Filming *Penthesilea*." *Film Culture*, Spring 1973, pp. 192–215.

———, [and Mathias Forster, Ingeborg Harms, and Bernd Skupin]. "Der Wille zur Schönheit." *Vogue*, August 2002.

———, [and Wolfgang Höbel]. "Ich war fast getötet vor Entsetzen." *Süddeutsche Zeitung*, no. 187, August 14–16, 1992, p. 16.

———, and Hilmar Hoffman. "Zum 100. mein neuer Film." 3 parts. *Die Welt* (online), January 7, 2002.

———, [and Alexandra Lautenbacher]. "Jüngstes Gericht: Über ihr Dasein auf Erden wird befragt." *SZ Magazin*, no. 35, August 30, 1996, p. 46.

Rodek, Hanns-Georg. "Unsere Leni." *Die Welt*, January 7, 2002.

Rodger, George. "Die wilden Spiele der nachten Riesen." *Quick*, September 8, 1971, pp. 46–48.

Rosenberg, Tina. "In the Shadow of Goebbels." *New York Times Book Review*, June 2, 1996, pp. 26–27.

Rühle, Alex. "Grosse Menschen an der Kante des Möglichen." *Süddeutsche Zeitung*, no. 145, "Feuilleton," June 27, 2002, p. 17

Ryback, Timothy W. "Evidence of Evil." *New Yorker*, November 15, 1993, pp. 68–81.

———. "Hitler's Forgotten Library." *Atlantic Monthly*, May 2003.

———. Letters. *New Yorker*, December 20, 1993, pp. 8, 13.

———. "Report from Dachau." *New Yorker*, August 3, 1992, pp. 43–61.

Sanders-Brahms, H. "Tyrannenmord." In *Das Jahr 1945: Filme aus fünfzehn Ländern*, edited by H. H. Prinzler. Berlin: Stiftung Deutsche Kinemathek, 1990.

Sarris, Andrew. "Films." *Village Voice*, May 4, 1967.

———. "Notes on the Fascination of Fascism." *Village Voice*, January 30, 1978, pp. 1ff.

Schiff, Stephen. "Leni's *Olympia*." *Vanity Fair*, September 1992, pp. 118ff.

Schulberg, Budd. "Budd Schulberg re Riefenstahl." *Variety*, May 23, 1973.

―――. "Nazi Pin-Up Girl." *Saturday Evening Post,* March 30, 1946.

Schwartzer, Alice. "Leni Riefenstahl. Propagandistin oder Künsterlin?" *Emma,* no. 1, pp. 39–47.

Seesslen, Georg. "Blut und Glamour." In Potsdam Filmmuseum, *Leni Riefenstahl.*

Sereny, Gitta. "Children of the Reich." *Vanity Fair,* July 1990, pp. 76ff.

―――. "A Life in Black and White." *Observer,* July 7, 1996, Review Section, p. 13.

―――. "The Tales of a Blind Eyewitness." *Independent on Sunday,* September 13, 1992, pp. 3–7.

Simon, John. "The Führer's Movie Maker." Review of memoirs. *New York Times Book Review,* September 26, 1993, pp. 1ff.

Sklar, Robert. "Her Talent Was Her Tragedy: An Interview with Ray Müller." *Cineaste,* vol. 20, no. 3, Summer 1993.

Sontag, Susan. "Fascinating Fascism." *New York Review of Books,* February 6, 1975.

―――. "On Style." In Sontag, *Against Interpretation.*

―――, [and David B. Hinton]. "An Exchange on Leni Riefenstahl." *New York Review of Books,* September 18, 1975.

Speer, Albert. Interview by Eric Norden. "The *Playboy* Interview." *Playboy,* vol. 18, no. 6, June 1971.

Spiess-Hohnholz, Marieke. "Verlorener Kampf um die Erinnerung." *Der Spiegel,* no. 33, August 10, 1987, pp. 64ff.

Starkman, Ruth. "Mother of All Spectacles." *Film Quarterly,* vol. 51, no. 2, Winter 1997–98.

Stern, Fritz. Interview by Jordan Mejias. "Die Leni-Riefenstahlisierung: Zukunft unter Bush." *Frankfurter-Allgemeine-Zeitung,* January 20, 2005.

Strachan, Robin. [Photographs by George Rodger.] "With the Nuba Hillmen of Kordofan." *National Geographic,* February 1951, pp. 249–78.

Süss, Conny. "Riefenstahl erholt sich von Operation." *Münchner Merkur,* no. 162, July 17, 2003, p. 32.

Tremper, Celia, and André Groenewoud, ints. "Mit 99 ist noch lange nicht Schluss." *Bunte,* no. 35, August 23, 2001.

Tyler, Christian. "How Beauty Was Defiled by the Nazi Beast." *Financial Times,* September 27, 1992.

U.S. Army Intelligence (reference #PWB/SAIC/3, May 30, 1945). *Film Comment,* Winter 1965.

Vogel, Amos. "Can We Now Forget the Evil That She Did?" *New York Times,* May 13, 1973.

Walk, Ines. "Bildproduktion und Weltmodell." In Potsdam Filmmuseum, *Leni Riefenstahl.*

Walker, C. Lester. "A Way of Life." *New Yorker,* February 28, 1942.

Watts, Janet. "Triumph and Misery with Hitler." *London Observer,* September 27, 1992, p. 43.

Weigel, Herman. "Interview mit Leni Riefenstahl." *Filmkritik,* August 1972.

————. "Randbemerkungen zum Thema." *Filmkritik,* August 1972.

Weis, Kurt. "Die Priester der Muskelkraft." *Die Zeit,* no. 30, July 19, 1996, pp. 49ff.

Wieland, Karin. "Die Letzte: Leni Riefenstahl und das 20. Jahrhundert." *Merkur,* 2000, pp. 1193–1202.

Winkler, Willi. "Die arme Künstlerin." *SZ Magazin,* no. 298, December 29, 2000, p. 21.

————. "Die Schmierfilmerin." *SZ Magazin,* no. 32, August 9, 2002.

Winston, Brian. "Was Hitler There? Reconsidering *Triumph of the Will.*" *Sight and Sound,* vol. 50, no. 2, Spring 1981.

Zimmerman, Paul D. "Leni's Triumph of the Will." *Newsweek,* November 29, 1976, p. 72.

Zuckmayer, Carl. "In Führers Armen: Die Regisseurin Leni Riefenstahl." *Frankfurter Allgemeine Zeitunq,* no. 17, January 21, 2002, p. 41. See Zuckmayer, *Geheimreport.*

OTHER

Chodorov, Stephan, and John Musilli. *Camera Three.* CBS-TV, April 1–8, 1973.

Gritschneder, Dr. Otto. Interview by Isabella Schmid. *Forum.* Bayerischer Rundfunk Alpha, Munich, January 12, 2004. www.br-online.de/alpha/forum/voro401/20040112–i.shtml.

Husmann, Rolf. "Leni Riefenstahl and Robert Gardner: A Brief Encounter." A Session in Honor of Robert Gardner's Eightieth Birthday, AAA Annual Meeting, Washington, D.C., December 1, 2005. IWF Knowledge and Media. Göttingen, Germany, 2005.

Knopp, Guido. "Hitlers Frauen: Leni Riefenstahl die Regisseurin." ZDF Chronik. TV documentary, 2001.

Müller, Ray. *Ein Traum von Afrika.* Film, 2000.

————. *Macht der Bilder* [*The Wonderful, Horrible Life of Leni Riefenstahl*]. Film, 1992.

Panitz, Hans-Jürgen. *In Eis und Schnee: Dr. Arnold Fanck, Regisseur.* Munich: Bayerischer-Rundfunk, 1997. TV film.

Sünner, Rüdiger. *Schwarze Sonne: Kultorte und Esoterik des III. Reichs.* Elisabeth Müller Filmproduktion. Absolut Medien. DVD.

INDEX